Assessing the Benefits and Costs of ITS

Making the Business Case for ITS Investments

Transportation Research, Economics and Policy

VOLUME 10

The titles published in this series are listed at the end of this volume.

Assessing the Benefits and Costs of ITS

Making the Business Case for ITS Investments

edited by

David Gillen

David Levinson

KLUWER ACADEMIC PUBLISHERS
Boston / Dordrecht / New York / London

Distributors for North, Central and South America:
Kluwer Academic Publishers
101 Philip Drive
Assinippi Park
Norwell, Massachusetts 02061 USA
Telephone (781) 871-6600
Fax (781) 871-6528
E-Mail <kluwer@wkap.com>

Distributors for all other countries:
Kluwer Academic Publishers Group
Post Office Box 322
3300 AH Dordrecht, THE NETHERLANDS
Telephone 31 78 6576 000
Fax 31 78 6576 474
E-Mail <orderdept@wkap.nl>

Electronic Services <http://www.wkap.nl>

Library of Congress Cataloging-in-Publication

Assessing the Benefits and Costs of ITS:
Making the Business Case for ITS Investments/
David Gillen and David Levinson (eds.)
ISBN: 1-4020-7677-0

Printed on acid-free paper.

Printed in the United States of America

To Andraya and Andrew (David Gillen)

To Trinh Ann Carpenter (David Levinson)

CONTENTS

ACKNOWLEDGEMENTS

A number of people and institutions have contributed in a significant way to this book. First and foremost are the authors who produced papers for the original conference held in Sacramento in February of 2002. They have also been through two edits and have produced their work in a timely fashion. We also owe a considerable debt to Jay Riley and Caltrans Division of New Technology. Jay has been a source of inspiration, support and constructive criticism of our research in this area over the last several years. Other members of the Division of New Technology and Research have also contributed over the years including Mohamed Alkadri, Katie Benouar and Tori Kanzler.

The Institute of Transportation Studies at University of California Berkeley has been our home for all of this research. The Directors, Professor Adib Kanafani and Professor Martin Wachs have provided continual support and encouragement. We are also indebted to our numerous research assistants who have labored for us these last several years and have assisted in the numerous research projects. These include Elva Chang, Doug Cooper, Matt Haynes, Doug Johnson, Seungmin Kang, Madhav Pal and Julie Raffaillac. We also thank our colleagues Jianling Li and Joy Dahlgren with whom we have shared ITS projects.

We are indebted to the University of Minnesota Department of Civil Engineering and the Center for Transportation Studies for providing assistance. The School of Business & Economics at Wilfrid Laurier University in Waterloo provided financial support through the CMA Canada in editing the manuscript. Melodee Martin's editing skills turned a rough set of papers into a finished and polished product. We have also enjoyed the professional and cheerful working relationship with our editor at Kluwer, Marilea Polk Fried; she constantly encouraged and challenged us to turn out a better product. It was a pleasure working with her.

Chapter 1

ASSESSING THE INVESTMENT IN ITS: AN INTRODUCTION

David Gillen
University of California-Berkeley and Wilfrid Laurier University

David Levinson
University of Minnesota

This chapter provides an overview of the evolution of ITS in the United States and the policy background to the role of ITS in California. It serves as a context in which the remaining chapters can be placed. Our contribution is to examine ITS in an economics and business policy context where we provide an understanding of the costs and benefits associated with different ITS projects and how they might be measured. The chapter also provides an overview of the chapters in the book and how they are linked.

1. INTRODUCTION

This volume evolves from a conference on *Measuring the Contribution of ITS to Transportation Services* held in Sacramento in February 2002. The conference, sponsored by the California Department of Transportation (Caltrans), summarized the state of developing methods and information on evaluating Intelligent Transportation Systems (ITS) investments and applications. The term *Intelligent Transportation Systems* refers to the multimodal package of transportation innovations that use advanced technologies in electronics and information to improve the performance of vehicles, highways, and transit systems. Our research, supported through the PATH program at University of California-Berkeley, has initiated the move away from the engineering of ITS to an economic assessment. Policy-makers have long looked at ITS as a potential technological fix for problems of congestion and dwindling productivity of the state's transportation system. However, the bulk of the literature was highly technical and focused on the engineering and examining whether the features that were being supplied were issues rather than providing information on the benefits (and costs) of ITS implementation actually wanted and valued by the market.

The introduction of ITS projects into the surface transportation system raised some concern and confusion among transportation planners, policy-makers, and professionals about evaluation. Unlike other types of transportation investments, there were relatively few examples of the application of ITS technology upon which to draw some experience. ITS represents a technological change, and cannot be assessed solely as a capacity addition. While ITS allows us to do old things better (squeeze a few more vehicles onto a roadway, tend to highway incidents), it also allows us to do new things (know when a bus is coming so that transit becomes a reliable mode with minimal uncertainty, or use variable pricing to manage peak demand). Without new tools to allow the evaluation of these new things, transportation agencies were rightly concerned that good projects would not be implemented and bad ones not rejected. Because of a lack of information to provide direction for evaluation, there is a risk that significant investments will be made with little economic payoff. How then should one proceed? What are the important considerations and what should be ignored? Finally, how should these projects be evaluated?

2. ITS: A BRIEF HISTORY

The Intelligent-Vehicle Act of 1991, part of the Intermodal Surface Transportation Efficiency Act (ISTEA), established a national ITS program. ISTEA represented the first major transportation bill in the post-interstate era. The interstate of course reshaped the American landscape; yet it failed to match the growth in travel it, along with rising incomes, spurred. Congestion, safety, the environment, and energy emerged as concerns that could not be fully addressed with road construction. Sussman (1996) notes that consideration of the growing problems revealed two major points: (1) that national productivity and international competitiveness were closely tied to the efficiency of our transportation system and (2) the social and political costs could not be addressed by simply building additional conventional highways.

The forerunners of ITS date from the early days of the mass-produced automobile. Mechanical guides, that could be said to be the progenitors of modern electronic route guidance systems, provided detailed route instructions to drivers. One example, the *Live-Map*, consisted of a turntable connected by gears to one of the vehicle's wheels. After placing one of about 600 paper disks describing specific routes on the turntable, and setting the stylus to the beginning of the route, landmarks and course corrections would be announced.[1]

The first actuated traffic signal controller was installed in Baltimore in 1928. Unlike today's actuators which use magnetic loops embedded in the roadway or video cameras, this actuator was acoustical. A vehicle approaching on a side street could activate the green signal by sounding its horn (Kraft, 1998). One can imagine the neighbors were not overly pleased.

The 1960s saw the installation of computer-controlled traffic lights in Wichita Falls, Texas. Also, Chicago received automated freeway surveillance and ramp metering. The first ramp meters, like early intersection control, employed a police officer letting one vehicle at a time onto the freeway. Later traffic lights were installed (Piotrowicz and Robinson, 1995).

The Bureau of Public Roads (BPR) (the predecessor of today's Federal Highway Administration), then housed in the Department of Commerce, began research into application of communication and control technologies for surface transportation. One program, the Electronic Route Guidance System, was an early conception of today's in-vehicle navigation systems, but was based on real-time traffic information, something we still have difficulties implementing today. (Saxton, 1992).

In the 1970s, the Urban Traffic Control System (UTCS) aimed to interconnect individual signalized intersections to a central control center. At the control center, a computer would control the entire network by selecting the most appropriate timing pattern from a family of pre-computed timing plans which had been optimized for different sets of traffic conditions.

Other initiatives included the Passing Aid System (PAS) intended to let drivers on rural two-lane roads know whether or not it was safe to pull out and pass another vehicle; FLASH, a system for motorists to signal when they observed a disabled motorist; a roadside radio motorist information system; and a project to develop a fully automated highway system (Saxton, 1992). These projects all underwent field operational tests (FOT).

As an alternative to the proliferation of conventional highways, a 1971 USDOT report to Congress recommended additional funding for research and development of automated highway concepts as well as legislation for a Post-Interstate Highway Plan that would enable highways to accommodate automated operation. But necessary major policy and funding support for a full national program did not develop and most projects did not proceed beyond the early concept evaluation phase.

During rest of the decade, the FHWA continued research in traffic operations, motorist information and communications, and automated highway systems. The research program was also instrumental in working with the Department of Interior and the FCC to establish the Traveler's Information Service (Highway Advisory Radio).

During this same time period, the Department of Defense developed its satellite-based Global Positioning System (GPS) allowing such applications as vehicle navigation and location monitoring. The Bureau of Census developed maps and Geographic Information System (GIS) databases now employed automobile navigation and guidance systems, traffic management centers, and fleet dispatch offices.

Despite lack of federal research funding in the early 1980s in the United States, in Europe, advanced transportation projects were continuing. Globally, technological advances were occurring rapidly in semiconductors, electronics, computers, and cellular telephones. Congestion problems continued to grow.

In 1986, several events took place launching the modern efforts into ITS. The FHWA proposed an *R&D Program in Traffic Operations to Combat Urban Traffic Congestion* emphasizing seven major initiatives including navigation and vehicle control. In March, the Transportation Research Board of the National Academies hosted a workshop in Baltimore leading to a large research effort funded by the National Cooperative Highway Research Program (Saxton, 1993). It was suggested that ITS and a research effort into roadway powered electric vehicle (RPEV) technologies (the Santa Barbara Electric Bus Project) could be combined under a larger program to be run by the University of California. The Institute of Transportation Studies at U.C. Berkeley proposed that they assume the lead role in the broader program. In August, the PATH (Program on Advanced Technology for the Highway) Program began with the first contract from Caltrans to the University of California at Berkeley's Institute of Transportation Studies (Shladover, 1992). In October, Caltrans organized a conference to examine ITS as an alternative to road-building to relieve congestion. The program continues with a growing emphasis on evaluation methods, implementation issues, and economic analysis.

3. BACKGROUND

California's Transportation Plan (CTP) was designed to set the course for the future of transportation in California.[2] At the heart of the plan are three comprehensive policies:

1. Promoting the economic vitality of California by assuring mobility and access for people, goods, services, and information,
2. Providing safe, convenient, and reliable transportation, and
3. Providing environmental protection and energy efficiency.

The Caltrans Strategic Plan, in keeping with the CTP, envisions a balanced, integrated multimodal transportation network to move people, goods, services, and information freely, safely, and economically. In order to realize this vision, Caltrans has invested in the Advanced Transportation Systems Program. This multimodal research and development program provides a foundation for the application of advanced technologies to transportation in California. The objective of the program is to accelerate implementation of advanced transportation technology applications.

ITS projects are designed primarily to enhance the productivity of the existing highway system. Only on rare occasions does the ITS project result in physical expansion of the system. For example, the information system may suggest an alternate less congested route for a trip, wherein the traveler completes her trip at a lower cost than otherwise. The information system is ancillary to the roadway system yet certainly contributes to an increase in productivity of the roadway system. An electronic toll collection investment replacing a set of tollbooths reduces the travel time of most if not all travelers using a facility so they complete their trips using less time as well. This is another example of how additions to, or modifications of, the existing network allow it to be more efficient.

Among the various categories of ITS applications will be projects dealing with traveler information systems, traffic management systems, vehicle safety systems, public transportation systems, and commercial vehicle operations to name a few. In some cases these projects will require significant capital [hardware] investments and continuing operations and management expenses while other projects will represent relatively small capital investments. Some projects will cover a metropolitan urban area while others may be specific to a particular road segment or corridor. Simply put the projects will vary across a number of dimensions from size, capital intensity, and geographic coverage, to the people and agencies affected. This variety and coverage creates a challenge for project analysis.

Investments in infrastructure and their related management strategies under the new technology program will generate different types, magnitudes, and longevity of costs and benefits. Both costs and benefits will have different degrees of risks associated with them. Certainly in the case of infrastructure development the loss of resources from making a bad decision are not easily recovered or reversed. Hence, the risks are perceived to be higher. The variability of both benefits and costs will also create a degree of uncertainty both regarding the evaluation of projects as well as concerning the development of accurate values for benefits and costs. These features create an important challenge since California's transportation needs are met through private initiatives, public investment, and public/private partnerships. In each case the investment dollars will be available from the private sector only if it can be shown that these projects will meet California's transportation needs now and into the future in an efficient or cost effective way.

Funds are available from earmarked government sources such as gasoline taxes and federal transfers. Nonetheless not all projects can be undertaken and they need to be ranked in terms of economic returns. If these projects do not meet financial and economic tests in a transparent manner, including compensation for greater risk and uncertainty, the private sector is unlikely to undertake the development of new ITS products. This does not mean all projects must generate at least a market rate of return, indeed there may be some argument for subsidy. What it does mean is that significant policy issues can only be addressed if the benefits, costs, and risks can be identified for each project. Indeed, the lack of, or failure to use, aids that help guide the public use of scarce resources will threaten the quality of decisions.

Therefore, there appear to be two major reasons for undertaking a careful analysis of proposed ITS projects. First, the projects represent an expenditure of scarce public funds and planners and policy-makers should ensure they are obtaining the greatest benefits from their investments. Those who have to make decisions about whether to undertake a project or to decide among competing projects need to understand the differences in the benefits that the projects generate. Second, projects will have positive impacts as well as negative consequences. The decision-maker would like to select the appropriate design to maximize the positive impacts and minimize the negative.

4. OUR TAKE

We emphasize that this book differs from many previous efforts in that it focuses on deployed systems and the use of observed data. While simulation is an important technique, especially for speculative technologies, simulations calibrated with data, and the data itself, provide a much stronger basis to draw conclusions about the worthiness of ITS projects. For those reasons, this book does not comment on technologies such as Adaptive Cruise Control, Automated Highway Systems, and other high-profile, yet nascent ITS technologies.

We have discovered from our analyses that ITS technologies are most effective at *the edge of congestion* and for dealing with the unexpected. When traffic is uncongested, or very congested, there is little ITS can do but tell you, but at the margins, when traffic is about to become congested, ITS can provide relief through effective traffic management. While this may be little relief for those sitting on saturated streets, we note that there is at least one time at the margins each peak period, as traffic is transitioning from uncongested to congested. If this transition can be extended through management, there are measurable gains to be had, and congestion to be reduced.

By informing and managing users (with technologies such as ramp meters or electronic toll collection such as described by Burris in Chapter 10 and Liu, Recker, and Chen in Chapter 13), the transportation system becomes less variable and more reliable. This reliability has value, a point made by Lewis in Chapter 2, Hickman in Chapter 5, and Liu, Recker, and Chen in Chapter 13.

We further note that the question of "synergies" is raised in several chapters in this text. Bertini and El-Geneidy in Chapter 15 note that many technologies require the same data, and there are cost savings to be had. (The use of this common data is employed in a number of chapters, especially Chapter 14 by Levinson and Chen). In economic jargon, there are economies of scope resulting from the simultaneous production of multiple transportation services. But the more controversial notion, suggested by Brand in Chapter 3, is that there are benefits that are superadditive, having two technologies provides more benefits than the sum of having either. This is the claim that there are intertechnology economies (or economies of scope in consumption) which expand benefits when multiple ITS services are consumed together. While of course it would be nice if such demand-side synergies exist, we believe that the existence of synergies is not necessary to find benefits that exceed costs in ITS.

We need to think of ITS like other technologies, that goes through a cycle from birth through growth to maturity, the class S-curve. While many transportation technologies (such as highways) have reached the maturity phase, and some ITS technologies have in certain places (such as ramp meters in the Twin Cities), most that we consider here are still in the growth stage. As noted above, those still in the birthing stage are not considered here. Thus it may be premature to conclude the final state, and the more conservative tact, as suggested by Lee in Chapter 4, is to use more conventional cost-benefit analysis and find if the technology is warranted in that way. If it is, we will at least avoid the mistake of overinvesting. Deakin makes a similar point in Chapter 17 where she notes many decision-makers believe that ITS has been hyped. But Brand notes we still may make the mistake of underinvesting. However, it is our location in the maturity phase in the S-curve of conventional technologies that has prompted the search for new alternatives over the past few decades, as agencies shift from being builder to managers. Due to uncertainty, many technologies will be empty rabbit holes before the one technology that is meritorious is discovered. Inevitably, there will be overinvestment in research into a number of false leads before a true lead can be followed. Such is the nature of research.

Institutional issues also matter in the implementation of ITS. Deakin makes this point in Chapter 17; Giuliano and O'Brien discuss institutions in the context of transit in Chapter 7. Institutional issues have been raised regarding ramp metering in the Twin Cities, where the legislature had to force the engineers at the Traffic Management Center to objectively evaluate their system (see Chapter 9 by Levinson and Zhang). Similarly, freeway service patrol operations (such as described by Parthasarathi, Levinson, and Gillen in Chapter 11) are perceived to compete with private tow truck operators and auto clubs, and raise the question about the proper roles of the public and private sectors. The proper roles of value added services also confront advanced traveler information systems (see Khattak, Targa, and Yim, Chapter 12).

Most of the analyses here (and elsewhere) evaluate transportation within the confines of the transportation system. The time is approaching when it would be more appropriate to place the evaluation of ITS in the context of an economy. Transportation uses networks, and an analysis of the effects of an important project on a single link without considering its upstream and downstream effects would be flawed. Yet we know that transportation is used because it adds value to people and firms, and transportation decisions affect the individual's activity patterns and the firm's decisions within the supply chain. Investments in transportation thus change non-transportation markets. In Chapter 2, Lewis makes this point. ITS, if it changes travel patterns, will have effects beyond the transportation sector, not only the negative externalities such as pollution and noise, but restructuring effects in other markets. An economy is an integration of markets with all participants interacting. Understanding economic business decisions requires business and economic data. Economic methods such as Computable General Equilibrium (CGE) used in trade theory, begin to get at these impacts. But despite obvious applications, especially in freight, in transportation, these methods are still in their birthing stage, and have yet to be widely accepted.

5. OVERVIEW OF CHAPTERS

The chapters in this volume are divided into four sections. The next section provides information on the integration of ITS into the transportation system and into the economy. The following two sections provide case studies of ITS applications in transit and highways, respectively. The final section has a group of chapters that examine the integration of ITS into transportation practice.

Section 1 contains three chapters that have a broad theme of how and what does ITS contribute to the economy and how does one make the business case for ITS.

In Chapter 2, David Lewis argues that ITS serves as a basis for *Public-Private Partnering* in highway investment. He suggests that ITS offers benefits to private industry that public agencies need to recognize in order to leverage significant private financial participation in highway investment. The economics of a just-in-time economy turn on the effectiveness of the transportation system, central to which is the highway network. Reliability and predictability are the keys, without which there would be no business case for investing in the technology needed to facilitate just-in-time operations. The principal focus of analysts and planners in the ITS domain has thus far been in personal transportation, not the manufacturing and freight sectors. The conclusions warn that to ignore the manufacturing and freight nexus is potentially to miss the lion's share of what ITS has to offer.

In Chapter 3, Dan Brand considers *Benefit Measures, Values, and Future Impacts of ITS*. He argues that recognizing how ITS differs from conventional transportation improvements allows us to avoid seriously underestimating of the benefits of ITS, collecting expensive data, and making mistakes in our planning and investment policies. Even when it is without tangible benefit, Advanced Traveler Information Systems (ATIS) are valued by travel consumers for giving them a sense of control over their lives, as shown in surveys and focus groups which revealed that knowing what was going on was more important to consumers than saving time. Additionally, ATIS can act like added capacity in the transportation network in the sense that it can show where there is "available" capacity in real time. If we measure just aggregate changes in VMT and VHT on the network, we will grossly underestimate the benefits of ATIS.

In Chapter 4, *Making the Case for ITS Investment*, Doug Lee asserts the case for investing in ITS needs to be made on objective grounds that are credible to the decision-maker who is seeking balanced information. Benefit-cost analyses (BCA) evaluate actions by comparing the results of taking the action against a base case in which the action is not taken. Although BCA evaluation of ITS projects is feasible at a modest level of effort, few studies have been done, and, for most contexts, key data are not available. While BCA will never "prove" beyond a shadow of a doubt that ITS spending is either worthwhile or wasteful, it is readily possible to generate information that would be useful for guiding investment into productive projects and ensuring that their performance is as intended and expected.

Section 2 considers ITS applications in transit.

The section opens with Chapter 5, wherein Mark Hickman evaluates *Bus Automatic Vehicle Location* (AVL) *Systems*. A combination of on-board electronics, communications with a control center, and software are currently being used to achieve five broad categories of AVL applications: passenger information, transit operations monitoring and control, service planning, air quality improvements, and safety and security enhancements. He finds that at present there appear to be quantitative economic benefits of bus AVL systems. If the AVL data are used to create estimates of bus arrival times at bus stops, there is strong evidence that passengers perceive real increases in travel utility, reflected in reduced "costs" of waiting time and, possibly, some slight increases in ridership and revenue for the transit agency although there has been relatively little direct empirical evidence of these benefits to date. In the area of operations management, the improvements in schedule adherence and headway regularity are well documented. However, the evidence does not yet exist to connect these directly to waiting time or utility gains on the part of passengers. The evidence on AVL-based operations control measures is largely based on simulation results, but improvements in passenger waiting times are clearly possible. The waiting time improvements must be balanced by the effects on total passenger travel times, on bus running times, and on the resulting bus operating costs. At this time, a reasonably well-developed methodology does exist to evaluate the impacts of control actions using bus AVL data, but additional empirical evidence of these benefits is needed. Finally, in the area of service planning, AVL data can be used to analyze schedule performance, improve schedule efficiency, and even reduce bus and operator requirements. The challenge remains to have sufficient resources to exploit these data effectively among the many data-rich applications in service planning

Ed Sullivan and Jeffrey Gerfen undertook a *Case Study: Impacts of Advanced Technology on a Small City Bus System,* presented in Chapter 6. As part of a demonstration of low-cost Advanced Public Transportation System (APTS) technologies designed specifically for small transit systems, mobile data terminals with GPS locators were installed on all San Luis Obispo (SLO) Transit vehicles, with real-time bus location and emergency alarm data transmitted via radio modems using previously existing voice radios. Besides providing useful data for system planning, the real-time bus location data are used to advise drivers regarding schedule adherence and to generate messages regarding impending bus arrivals employing Smart Transit Signs at principal bus stops throughout town. The project has demonstrated the feasibility and positive impacts of applying APTS technologies to enhance small transit operations with indications to date that both the operators and bus customers perceive significant benefits from the deployment of this new technology.

In Chapter 7, Genevieve Giuliano and Thomas O'Brien seek to go *Beyond Benefits and Costs* to understand *Outcomes In Public Transit*. The purpose of Field Operational Tests (FOTs) is to determine whether the given technology application is appropriate for adoption on a larger scale. Six case studies of public transit technology tests were studied to identify determinants of successful deployment of ITS technology. The studies involve electronic payment and fare integration (San Francisco Bay Area TransLink, Washington DC SmarTrip, Chicago SmartCard), automated trip scheduling (Santa Clara SMART), and more ambitious service integration that may or may not include fare integration (San Gabriel Valley Smart Shuttle, Ventura Smart Card). Single agency FOTs were characterized by clear goals and objectives, an incremental approach to the technology, and effective management. These helped the agencies to make modifications to the technology as needed and appear to be requirements for all successful FOTs. Multi-agency tests, however, have had more mixed outcomes. While technical performance is essential, it does not guarantee FOT success. It is possible to deploy all the technological elements of a test and still not meet a given set of objectives. This is particularly the case with service integration. The tests also suggest that it is possible to only partially meet a test's technological objectives and still show some progress toward overarching service objectives. Operational tests in general can be valuable without being entirely successful because of the lessons they offer.

Part 3 explores ITS applications in the Automobile/Highway System.

Chapter 8, by Alex Skabardonis, details *Traffic Signal Control Systems*. Signal timing optimization, signal coordination, and advanced traffic control have all been proposed as components of ITS measures. This chapter presents the findings from the analysis of the impacts of these three signal control improvements based on a large number of real-world implemented projects. The results from over 163 implemented projects showed that signal timing optimization of coordinated signal systems produced an average of 8 percent drop in travel time and fuel use, 14 percent reduction in delays, and 13 percent reduction in stops for a typical weekday. Signal timing optimization is a highly cost/effective strategy because of its low cost. The estimated average benefit-cost ratio in the Fuel Efficient Traffic Signal Management (FETSIM) project areas is 17:1. Annual fuel savings alone outweigh the total program costs by more than 5:1. Signal coordination produces significant reductions in delay, stops, and fuel consumption. The average improvements include 11 percent reduction in travel time, 25 percent reduction in delay, and 27 percent reduction in the number of stops. Signal coordination worsens the performance on entry (uncoordinated) movements in the system, typically side streets, and the trade-offs should be carefully assessed.

In Chapter 9, David Levinson and Lei Zhang evaluate the effectiveness of *Ramp Meters*. For eight weeks in October, November, and December 2000, ramp meters in the Twin Cities of Minneapolis and St. Paul, Minnesota, were turned off allowing the collection of data, with and without ramp meters, from several representative freeways. The data were then analysed using a variety of measures of effectiveness (MOE) to determine the effect of ramp meters on freeway traffic in the Twin Cities area. The study shows that Route 169 performs better in the presence of operating ramp meters than in their absence, judged by a majority of the MOEs. In contrast, however, I-94 shows that improvements to the operations of freeway mainline do not always offset the additional ramp delay. Looking at the consistency of various performance measures developed in this chapter, it is found that mobility, consumers' surplus, productivity, and accessibility tend to provide the same conclusions on the effectiveness of ramp meters. However, when ramp metering is present, long trips benefit while short trips are hurt, suggesting a less equitable situation than without metering. If a ramp metering objective only pays attention to mobility (efficiency), its poor equity indications will inevitably lead to an important public policy debate

Mark Burris considers *Electronic Toll Collection And Variable Pricing* in Chapter 10. This research analyzed the incremental costs and benefits of ETC at a retrofitted toll plaza, open road toll collecting (ORT), and variable pricing at an ETC configured plaza. Benefits were found to include reduced delay, reduced fuel consumption, and reduced emissions while costs included the purchase price, installation, and operation and maintenance costs. Under both low and medium traffic congestion scenarios a positive net present value was found for retrofitted ETC. For ORT, benefits were found to be significantly larger than those associated with a standard ETC system. However, due to the large operation and maintenance costs of ORT, the benefit cost ratios were actually smaller, with the costs outweighing the benefits in the low volume scenario. Finally, the incremental costs and benefits of incorporating a variable toll rate with ETC showed a positive, incremental net present value. However, under uncongested conditions, benefits were minimal and a negative net present value was found. The cost and benefit values used in this analysis were obtained from empirical evidence collected at toll roads and variable pricing projects around the country. Using these values yielded average transaction costs that appeared reasonable when compared to results from around the country that might be used as a framework for cost-benefit analysis. A toll agency interested in evaluating the potential costs and benefits of implementing ETC (with or without variable tolls) would need to apply the specifications of its toll facilities to this framework to obtain an estimate of their potential costs and benefits.

Chapter 11, by Pavithra Parthasarathi, David Levinson, and David Gillen, estimates the insurance value of *Freeway Service Patrols*. The main goals of freeway service patrols (FSP), often called highway helpers, are to identify incident locations, reduce incident duration time, restore full freeway capacity, and reduce the risks of secondary accidents. Studies conducted so far have focused on the effectiveness or economic efficiency of such patrols. This chapter seeks to determine the value that people place on the benefits offered by freeway service patrols in comparison to private assistance services (PAS) by estimating how much they would be willing to pay to avoid being stranded when their vehicles break down on the freeway. A stated preference survey of over 1,000 individuals regarding choice of FSP or PAS showed that the variables Waiting Time, Cost, Gender, Age, Income, Auto Age, Maintenance Expense, Commute Length, Cell Phone Ownership, Towing Coverage, and Time-Of-Day were all significant. While freeway service patrols have value in improving traffic flow and safety by clearing incidents quickly, they also have value for the individuals who are helped by the patrols, who otherwise would have to wait for a private assistance service through their auto club or by calling a tow truck. The results indicate that freeway service patrols provide insurance benefits for their customers when they save time and money over private assistance services.

Asad J. Khattak, Felipe Targa, and Youngbin Yim observe *Advanced Traveler Information Systems* and relate it to traveler behavior in Chapter 12. The challenge for Advanced Traveler Information Systems (ATIS) is to provide dynamic information that meets traveler needs for making more informed decisions, is accessed and used, and contributes to improved travel experience for individuals and society. In congested networks, such systems can support several traveler choices including the selection of destinations, modes, routes, departure times, intermediate stops, and parking. Real-time information can also help with readjustments, e.g., diversions from the selected route to avoid unexpected traffic congestion. A growing body of empirical evidence from federally sponsored field operational testing suggests that such information is used by individuals to choose routes and set departure times. TravInfo, a regional traveler information system in the San Francisco Bay Area, began its field operational testing in September 1993 and has now moved to full deployment. A behavioral evaluation of the field test found that saved travel time and help with travel planning were the key perceived benefits of dynamic information. Many respondents also cited a reduction in anxiety as a benefit. Almost all people in the surveys had access to or ownership of at least one device (on average about four devices) that could be used to obtain dynamic travel information with radio being the most widely used. Two-thirds of all respondents received travel information either regularly or occasionally, and one-third changed their travel decisions in response to that information. The preferred types of information in order of desirability are: frequent updated traffic conditions on radio or television, detailed information about alternate routes around congestion, in-car navigational computer showing highways and roads, estimation of the time of delay and directions to get from the point of departure to the point of arrival, information about traffic conditions at specific locations, information about mass transit alternatives, and automatic notification of unexpected traffic congestion. Additionally, there seems to be significant (latent) demand for personalized information services that would allow users to retrieve information when needed, to the point where a significant number of Bay Area travelers stated they would be willing to pay either on a per-call basis or a monthly subscription fee for a customizable service provided that the new information must be superior to that obtained for free through radio or television or other Internet outlets and services.

In Chapter 13, Henry Liu, Will Recker, and Anthony Chen use real-time loop data to estimate the contribution of *Travel Time Reliability* in a mixed logit route choice model. A wide range of factors influences the route choice of individual travelers including perceived travel time, monetary cost, comfort, and safety. This model was applied to newly collected data concerning route choice in the California State Route 91 value-pricing project that gives travelers a choice of whether or not to pay a congestion-based toll in order to use the express lanes. It was found that the estimated median value of travel time reliability is substantially greater than that of travel time, and the median value of degree of risk aversion is greater than 1, indicating that travelers value more highly a reduction in variability than in the mean travel time saving for that journey.

Part 4 considers integrative issues.

Chapter 14, by David Levinson and Wei Chen, assesses the performance of *Traffic Management Systems.* Three important traffic management systems in the Twin Cities metro area—Ramp Metering, Variable Message Signs (VMS), and Freeway Service Patrol (FSP)—were evaluated using multiple regression models to predict link speed and incident rate based on two case studies. In the first, a database of about 40,000 observations covering three years' data was used to estimate the long run and systemwide performance of the traffic management systems for both the incident-free case and incident case. In general, ramp meters were found to increase freeway link speed and reduce the incident rate while Freeway Service Patrols increased link speed when incidents are present. The results for variable message signs are ambiguous.

In Chapter 15, Robert Bertini and Ahmed El-Geneidy use *Advanced Traffic Management System Data* to evaluate ITS investments. The quantification of ITS benefits and costs has been difficult using traditional transportation planning and analysis methods because such models lack the necessary sensitivity to many benefits derived from ITS technologies, and because information on the impacts and costs of many ITS technologies is not yet well-understood. Ten ITS program areas are introduced with examples of how Advanced Traffic Management System (ATMS) data are being used to evaluate their benefits. It is clear from these programs that each system cannot be deployed to stand alone in the overall transportation system.

Reinaldo Garcia reports on *ITS In Europe* in Chapter 16. With major infrastructure investment reaching its limits, Intelligent Transport Systems (ITS) are a viable solution to make the movement of people and goods more efficient, economical, safer, and environmentally sound for all transport modes and are vital for the development of a European transport policy requiring better use of its existing transport infrastructure. To date, ITS has been successfully employed in Europe in the areas of urban road traffic management, rail transport, air transport, and the shipping industry, including both maritime and inland navigation systems. Among future projects, a European Global Navigation Satellite project, Galileo, will play a central role as an ITS technology for all transport sectors.

In Chapter 17, Betty Deakin explores *Mainstreaming ITS*. The chapter employs results from interviews with over 50 leaders in California, noting that though leaders are aware of ITS, they think it is hyped. In particular they desire better information on the benefits and costs of ITS, particular benefits for users rather than system operators. However, it is unclear what direction future ITS investments should take, as ITS becomes a standard part of transportation projects.

Tom Horan summarizes the findings in the book and places them in context in Chapter 18, *Information Systems to Improve Surface Transportation*. Horan suggests ITS should be assessed for its contribution to the productivity of transportation systems, ITS should be tested against the demands of stakeholders, and ITS should be considered as an element of the broad information and communications technologies which have revolutionized daily activities.

NOTES

[1] See DOT Web site at http://www.its.dot.gov/tcomm/history.app.htm.

[2] See, California Department of Transportation, New Technology and Research Program, *Advanced Transportation Systems Program Plan: 1996 Update*, December 1996.

REFERENCES

Kraft, W. H. *Transportation Management Center Functions*, National Cooperative Highway Research Program, Transportation Research Board, National Research Council, Washington, D.C. National Academy Press, 1998, 69.

Saxton, L. Federal IVHS Program Initiatives Resulting From ISTEA of 1991 / Lyle Saxton and George Schoene (Federal Highway Administration), International Congress on Transportation Electronics, Detroit, Mich., 1992. Vehicle Electronics Meeting Society's Needs. Warrendale, PA: Society of Automotive Engineers.

Shladover, S. "The California PATH Program: A State Approach to IVHS Research," International Congress on Transportation Electronics, Detroit, Mich., 1992. Vehicle Electronics Meeting Society's Needs. Warrendale, PA: Society of Automotive Engineers.

Chapter 2

PUBLIC-PRIVATE PARTNERING

ITS in Highway Investment

David Lewis
HLB Decision Economics Inc.

This chapter argues that Intelligent Transportation Systems (ITS) offer benefits to private industry that public agencies need to recognize in order to leverage material private financial participation in highway investment. Technology investments that prompt more reliable and predictable highway travel times are disproportionately more valuable to movers of freight (shippers and carriers) than to auto users. This is because more reliable and predictable highway performance improves the business case for investing in just-in-time logistical systems of production, distribution, inventory management, and customer service. When the expected rate of return on private investment in advanced logistics is sufficiently high, firms will be willing to share in the investment costs of realizing such returns, including the costs of ITS. Yet signalling mechanisms are not in place through which highway agencies can identify the impact of prospective ITS investments on the private business case for advanced logistics; neither are the communications mechanisms in place through which agencies can convey such information to firms within reach of such benefits. If such mechanisms were in place, agencies could seek to negotiate ITS cost-sharing partnerships with private firms, including multi-national companies whose logistics-oriented investment decisions are made at the network level. The effect would be greater overall investment in ITS than justified by savings in auto user costs. A collateral effect would be a reduction in the free-rider effect of ITS when it fosters profitable investment opportunities for private firms.

1. TECHNOLOGY AND PRODUCTIVITY

In 1995, economist Robert Solow was quoted thus: "We see computers everywhere but in the productivity statistics." By the late 1990s, however, the massive levels of investment in computer technology were indeed evident in U.S. economic performance. Whereas growth in total factor productivity puttered along at a sluggish annual rate of 1.6 percent between 1991 and 1995, it revved to 2.7 percent a year between 1996 and 1999. The unprecedented advance in real GDP witnessed in the late 1990s is widely acknowledged to be the reward of this productivity growth. The biggest winners were households, for whom take-home pay grew faster than at any time since the early 1960s. Corporate shareholders also did well, of course.

Econometric research by Kevin Stiroh of the Federal Reserve Bank of New York published in the early 2000s attributes fully two-thirds of the late 1990s surge in productivity growth to investment in computer-related technology.[1] While a portion of this attribution is due to efficiency gains from automated processing in the semi-conductor and computer hardware and software manufacturing sectors themselves, the lion's share is ascribed to the so-called "embedded technology effect" in manufacturing. In short, manufacturers purchased machinery and equipment with embedded chip and digital components that gave labor greater leverage over its hourly output.

Stiroh's work makes its case with a number of econometric tests that show a robust link between information technology and productivity gains. The tests demonstrate that IT-intensive industries experienced a productivity acceleration that is about two percentage points greater than other industries, a result that holds when IT-producing industries are excluded from the analysis. Stiroh's findings also link productivity growth to IT intensity: The size of the productivity acceleration for 1995–2000 rises with the 1995 share of IT capital services. These types of relationships are noticeably absent in the post-1982 surge in U.S. productivity growth and suggest real productivity benefits from IT use after 1995. Stiroh points out that if recent productivity gains were primarily cyclical, one would expect them to be independent of IT intensity.

Perhaps the most striking finding of Stiroh's analysis is that IT-producing and IT-using industries accounted for literally all the direct industry contributions to the U.S. productivity revival of 1990s. In comparing 1995–2000 to 1987–1995, he shows that 26 IT-using industries contributed 0.83 percentage point to the aggregate productivity acceleration and the two IT-producing industries (semi-conductors and computer hardware) contributed 0.17. The remaining 33 industries made a negative contribution of 0.21 percentage point, on net, suggesting IT-related industries are driving the productivity revival.

The IT-inspired increase in productivity reported above spurred profit growth and liberated more funds for capital investment. The demand for capital spurred competition in the manufacture of yet more advanced plant and equipment, fostering a "virtuous circle" of labor productivity growth, more profit-led demand for advanced capital equipment, further advances in embedded technology, additional improvements in labor productivity, and so on.

In a speech at Boston College in 2001, Allan Greenspan said the following:

> *"Until the mid-1990s, the billions of dollars that businesses had poured into information technology seemed to leave little imprint on the overall economy. The full value of computing power could be realized only after ways had been devised to link computers into large networks. And we all know that day has arrived."*

2. INVESTMENT IN ADVANCED LOGISTICS

Nowhere have the advantages of networked computer technologies been exploited more effectively than in the mobilization of advanced logistics. Triggering a just-in-time revolution in the manufacturing sector, the availability of Internet-based "e-procurement purchasing systems," digitised assembly lines, advanced robotics, networked stock replenishment systems, and the like, have enabled manufacturers to substitute the transportation network for costly inventories and, accordingly, to shed millions of square feet in storage and customer service infrastructure.

The effects of the just-in-time revolution are palpable. Research for the U.S. federal government conducted by Professor Joseph Stiglitz and his colleagues[2] indicates that the average lead-time for ordering materials and supplies in advance of production has declined from 72 days in 1961 to less than 50 days by 1999. Inventories have fallen from roughly 1.6 times monthly sales in the 1970s to some 1.2 times monthly sales today. Whereas logistics costs (excluding transportation) represented 19.1 percent of U.S. GDP in 1990, these costs had fallen to less than 11 percent of GDP by the turn of the century.

Investment in advanced logistics is self-perpetuating due to the networked interrelatedness of firms in inter-industry supply chains. The Wall Street Journal reported recently that Ford Motor Company in Detroit now requires all its major suppliers to participate in e-purchasing arrangements, automated inventory management, and just-in-time delivery under stiff late penalties. Suppliers are thus compelled to make the capital investments needed at their end to assure Ford a decent return on investment in the logistics investments made at its end. While all firms might not share the resulting productivity gains proportionately, large and small, in such a supply chain—there are probably some absolute losers—the overall gain is no doubt positive for the regional economy.

It is dynamics like those illustrated by the Ford example that underpin the modern theory of strategic alliances and which spring from the economics of co-specialization and sequencing. Under the economics of specialization in the world of traditional logistics, plants enjoy economies by holding inventories of finished products, which are mixed to fill customer orders. Savings from longer productions runs and savings in transportation costs more than offset the costs of additional handling and storage. With *advanced logistics* grounded in Internet-based commerce, firms translate the economies specialization into the economies of *co-specialization* by extending the theory of specialization to multiple agents in the supply chain. Gillen states it well:

> *"An example of co-specialization could be the way that a trio of musicians create a stronger effect than they would playing as individuals. Co-sequencing refers to the extra value that is added when elements are combined in the most advantageous order. Both of them reflect the fact that the total value created by successive additions is more than the linear sum of the individual parts. The challenge is to sort out the benefits from each contribution."*[3]

3. THE TRANSPORTATION CONNECTION

The economics of a just-in-time economy turn on the effectiveness of the transportation system, central to which is the highway network. Reliability and predictability are the keys. Without reliable and predictable transit times, manufacturers could not hold smaller inventories without also holding significant "shock stocks;" they could not reduce storage and customer service overheads without holding costly spare capacity; and they could not transfer risk to transportation carriers through the imposition of late delivery and pick-up penalties. In short, without reliable and predictable highway transit times, there would be no business case for investing in the technology needed to facilitate just-in-time operations.

The significant role of reliability and predictability is evident in recent research findings on the value of time. A 1999 study conducted at the University of California at Irvine and HLB Decision Economics Inc. for the National Cooperative Highway Research Program employed a contingent valuation methodology to quantify and compare the value of reductions in average travel time versus the value of reductions in the variability of travel times. Based on a sample of 60 firms in six manufacturing sub-sectors, the study reports that whereas a one-hour time saving is valued at $195, a one-hour reduction in travel time variability is valued at $395 (each in constant

2000 dollars), more than twice as much. Not only are firms willing to pay large sums for improved reliability, they actually prefer improved reliability and predictability in *existing* average transit times over reductions in the average, absent improved reliability.[4]

The same study compared the way individuals (as distinct from firms) value travel time versus travel time reliability, finding that, not unlike firms, travelers value improved reliability more than twice as much as overall travel time improvements.[5]

4. ITS AND THE CASE FOR PARTNERSHIPS IN HIGHWAY INVESTMENT

The high measured rate at which firms are willing to pay for improved reliability in highway transit times is evidence of the enormous profitability of investment in advanced logistics. Yet mounting congestion and unreliable transit times in most major American centers are bound to be diminishing the business case for firms to continue investing in advanced logistics at the pace witnessed over the 1990s.

Continued investment in advanced logistics is important to both the public and private sectors. The private sector interest is obvious; greater productivity brings with it greater profitability and stronger shareholder returns. Equally important however is the impact of improved private sector productivity on the national economy and the standard of living. With growth in the working age population unlikely to exceed one percent per annum over the next quarter century, a sustained rate of growth in total factor productivity of at least two percent a year is needed just to maintain real disposable incomes at their current level.

Highway infrastructure investment that yields more reliable and predictable transit times is thus something in which both the public and private sectors should be motivated to participate. ITS is veritably unique among the various types of highway infrastructure in promoting more reliable and predictable highway performance. Of equal if not greater significance, ITS, by virtue of the flexibility it affords highway users to optimize their use of the network in both space and time, has the effect of extending the number of years during which a fixed amount of highway capacity can offer a constant level of service. The last point is of special significance to private firms. For them, any capital investment must generate benefits over a long enough period of time to earn sufficient returns. Logistics managers know well enough that nothing erodes the effectiveness of just-in-time dependent investments faster than highway congestion. By sustaining the level of highway performance over a longer period of time, ITS represents a significant hedge against the dilemma of "induced demand," namely the erosion of benefits from advanced logistics when highway improvements create new demand which dilutes investment benefits before sufficient time has elapsed from them to repay the investment.

Ironically, the principal focus of analysts and planners in the ITS domain has thus far been in the auto mode, not the manufacturing and freight sectors. As indicated in other chapters of this volume, the cost-benefit analysis jury remains in something of a deadlock regarding the economic merit of ITS in relation to the benefits it affords commuters and other motorists. Failure to address the potential of ITS from the freight perspective, on the other hand, presents a serious risk of inhibiting U.S. industry's shift to the post-modern model of industrial organization, the JIT model that distinguishes winners and losers in the 21st century global economy. Evidence that this risk is material is to be found in a recent study for the Federal Highway Administration.[6] Based on surveys of logistics managers in a wide range of industries, the study finds that firms sub-optimise their logistical operations in response to congested conditions without signalling infrastructure providers (namely, governments) that more or better capacity (including ITS-led improvements) would precipitate business investment in advanced logistics. This lack of a signaling mechanism places the onus on government proactively to reach out to industry in order to guard against persistent and structural under-investment in industrial modernization.

Why is this not happening now? Why is the freight side getting short shrift?

The answer most probably lies in the fact that freight transportation represents only about 10–15 percent of traffic volume in any given congested corridor. What deserves emphasis of course is that the ITS benefits I am addressing here are only incidentally borne by trucks. It is the massive manufacturing sector that fuels the trucking industry to which my argument is directed; and it is the massive influence that manufacturing productivity has on the economic well-being of the United States that represents the object of the argument, not the transit times of trucks per se.

5. CONCLUSION

I conclude that the relationship between ITS and the nation's manufacturing sector needs to be explored by the transportation policy and planning community. Three requirements represent the most immediate needs:

1. Develop an understanding of the role of ITS in the private business case for private investment in advanced logistics;
2. Develop methodological and communications strategies for transportation planners in public agencies and logistics managers in private firms. Establish ways of tying private firms into the ITS

planning and evaluation process at the corridor, regional, and national levels; and

3. Develop public-private partnering modalities through which public agencies and private firms can evolve win-win cost, risk, and benefit sharing arrangements that increase the volume of ITS investment while channelling such investment in the most economically beneficial directions.

The conclusions drawn here are not an argument against the case for ITS in relation to auto users. I do believe, however, that to ignore the manufacturing and freight nexus is potentially to miss the lion's share of what ITS has to offer.[7]

To the above conclusions one more, of a research nature, may be added: cost-benefit analysis of highway projects is almost universally conducted in a partial equilibrium, comparative statistics framework. While this approach makes sense in the consideration of traveler markets, freight-related benefits (beyond simple time savings) arising from industrial reorganization can only be measured in a dynamic, general equilibrium-modeling framework. The time to extend the scope of transportation modeling and project appraisal to the general equilibrium domain has, it would seem, arrived.

NOTES

1 Kevin Stiroh. "Information Technology and the U.S. Productivity Revival: What Do the Industry Data Say?," Federal Reserve Bank of New York, January 12, 2001 (reprinted in, *American Economic Review*, December 2002, 1,559). See also, Dale W. Jorgenson, "Information Technology and the U.S. Economy," The *American Economic Review*, March 2001.

2 Joseph E. Stiglitz, Peter R. Orszag, Jonathan M. Orszag. *The Role of Government in a Digital Age,* Commissioned by the Computer and Communications Industry Association, October 2000.

3 David Gillen. "Program-Wide Research Conference of California PATH (Partners for Advanced Transit and Highways)," October 24, 2002, (as cited in) *Institute of Transportation Studies Review*, Vol. 1, No. 2, December 2002.

4 Kenneth A. Small, Robert Noland, Xuehao Chu and David Lewis. "Valuation of Travel-Time Savings and Predictability in Congested Conditions for Highway User-Cost Estimation," National Cooperative Highway Research Program, Report 431, National Academy Press, 1999, page 4.

5 Ibid, page 3.

6 Federal Highway Administration. "Economic Effects of Transportation: The Freight Story, HLB Decision Economics Inc. and ICF Consulting, Eno Foundation," January 2002.

7 The U.S. Federal Highway Administration has developed a microeconomic framework for assessing the way in which improvements in highway system reliability influence the industrial reorganization decisions of private firms, with special reference to just-in-time logistics. The framework is presented in a White Paper entitled "*Benefit-Cost Analysis of Highway Improvements in Relation to Freight Transportation: Microeconomic Framework*" (prepared by HLB Decision Economics Inc. and ICF Consulting). The paper is available at the FHWA Web site, http://www.ops.fhwa.dot.gov/freight/.

Chapter 3

BENEFIT MEASURES, VALUES, AND FUTURE IMPACTS OF ITS

David Brand
Charles River Associates

This chapter examines how ITS provides user-centered benefits that differ from conventional system-centered transportation projects. Therefore, use of conventional methods to assess those benefits will result in an underestimate. For instance, Advanced Traveler Information Systems (ATIS) provide intangible benefits that do not show up in time savings or cost reductions, by improving the quality of the trip. Consumers value the control ATIS provides. Further, because of non-linear delay effects, ATIS can save time by showing in real time the location of excess capacity. Integrated information and management systems will provide additional benefits.

1. INTRODUCTION

This chapter is divided into three related sections. The first section discusses certain mistakes in prevailing assumptions about appropriate benefit measures for evaluating ITS improvements. Proper recognition of how ITS differs from conventional transportation improvements can avoid seriously underestimating of the benefits of ITS, expensive data collection, and mistakes in our planning and investment policies.

The second section describes how to value ITS mobility benefits using customer satisfaction methods. Direct measurement and valuation of ITS mobility benefits using (stated preference) survey methods avoids the problems of (a) how exactly to measure the utility-generating features of ITS information, and (b) observing the behavioral responses to ITS information, which involve expensive data collection.

The final section of the chapter describes the likely future benefits of ITS in transportation networks. These are closely tied to the impact of the information technology (IT) "revolution" on travel and regional development.

ITS can perform, and may already be performing, important functions associated with the future use and functionality of information technology. Transportation planners need to anticipate and plan for the likely far-reaching consequences of IT as much as is possible at this time.

2. ITS BENEFIT MEASURES

Substantial agreement exists now in transportation planning that our first priority is serving the needs of consumers—our customers—instead of the more narrow needs of the producers of new transportation capacity. A user-friendly infrastructure must provide not only transportation capacity but also information on how to use that capacity to lower travel costs and thus increase mobility. A user-friendly system will require different ways of measuring the costs and opportunities of travel for individuals and for the system as a whole[1].

When the pre-ITS concern was to improve the physical transportation infrastructure, improvements were evaluated based on the use of the network. It was a producer-side mentality. Investments produced VMT and VHT. Aggregate observable VMT on the network, and the congestion and travel times on links were the measures of interest. ATIS is different. Investments in ATIS produce more benefits than can be measured using the old aggregate measures of transportation system performance.

Measuring benefits has been an Achilles Heel for the ITS program. This is understandable because we haven't focused on the real benefits of ITS. These benefits, now and in the future, are and will be hard to observe and measure. But we can expect these benefits to be significant, even if they are more difficult to observe and measure than we'd prefer.

3. AN ITS BENEFITS FRAMEWORK

Figure 1 shows an ITS benefits framework that helps us identify appropriate ITS benefit measures, and understand how the goals and benefits of ITS are linked in a cause-and-effect framework. The figure includes linkages between the five traditional ITS goals (efficiency, mobility, productivity, safety, and energy/environment).[2] As in any transportation system, we have supply-side and demand-side goals and interactions. However, with ITS the supply/demand interaction is not straightforward, and the proper way to measure and predict ITS impacts is different than for conventional transportation improvements.

On the left side of Figure 1, ITS actions or improvements impact the supply-side operational efficiency goal. This is the engineering efficiency goal of more output per unit of input. Measures of achievement of this goal, namely throughput, vehicle occupancy, lane volumes, etc. can be directly observed in the aggregate after the deployment of an ITS improvement.

However, by themselves, these engineering efficiency measures have no inherent value to society. Affected consumers cannot internalize these network-level impacts. People are willing to pay more for something measured in higher throughput or higher lane volumes, so they don't actually enter into the benefits side of a benefit/cost analysis. But as shown on the left-

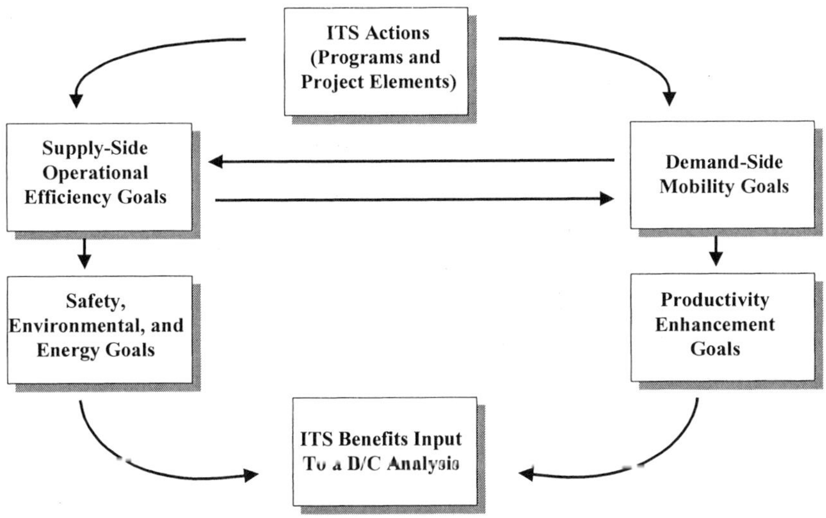

Figure 1. An ITS Benefits Framework

hand side of Figure 1, these measures do directly impact the safety, environmental, and energy goals. Measures of achievement of these goals include crashes, fatalities, fuel consumption, and emissions. We can directly observe these measures in the aggregate, and each of these measures provides value to the affected individuals, and therefore to society.

On the right side of Figure 1, ITS improvements impact the demand-side mobility goal. We want to increase the net benefits from travel, but the demand curve is hard to observe. This is because ITS travel information—Advanced Traveler Information Systems (ATIS) in this case—can increase greatly the rate at which people make travel substitutions. They travel smarter. They know in advance and control the level of service and congestion at which they will individually travel or ship their goods. ITS promotes demand adjustments in the short term and in the long term. These demand adjustments result in mobility benefits for individual travelers and productivity benefits for firms shipping goods. And these demand adjustments can be considerable!

4. MOBILITY BENEFITS

Mobility is defined as the net benefit from travel—the benefit from the activity at the destination minus the perceived cost of getting there. There's a lot of misplaced emphasis on time savings as the appropriate measure of the mobility benefit of ATIS systems. Delays on highway links measure congestion—an impediment to mobility. Mobility, which is what travelers seek, is measured by the net benefits from travel. We should plan to maximize these benefits from travel, not to produce an elusive level-of-service performance standard. Measures of mobility differ from measures of congestion.

ATIS information enables travel consumers to gain more satisfaction from travel. ATIS mobility benefits include better-informed travelers and a sense of control over one's life. It is knowing reliably where one is going to be. It is the freedom to plan around expected outcomes; the freedom of choice to plan one's time; to know whether one should, or wants to, get into that congestion. For example, the results of surveys and focus groups for TravInfo in the Bay Area told us what information people valued that was provided to them about four major highway incidents that resulted in large delays. The findings were that knowing what was going on was more important to people than saving time[3].

Another example is transit users in London who have variable message signs at bus stops that say the next bus comes in say one minute, the bus after that in say five minutes. London bus users (arriving randomly) were surveyed for the benefits of this new information. The respondents felt the change was valuable—worth something to them—and they thought that their waiting time had decreased, even though the frequency of bus service hadn't changed. ATIS had changed their perception of the cost of travel (waiting time) rather than an actual measurable changed in their travel time.

Understanding that users value improving their sense of control and travel time reliability, rather than saving travel time, enables us to design these systems with achievable benefits in mind. We shouldn't think we can design to provide unachievable benefits like delivering free-flow routes within a congested network with ATIS. Some years ago we may have thought that ATIS and ITS could magically deliver all sorts of travel time savings and free-flowing routes in a currently congested network. Now that we are smarter, it is likely to be more important to design ATIS to give drivers a sense of control and information on what the situation is, rather than trying to achieve the goal of delivering time savings.

In fact, using time savings as the main quantitative measure of ATIS mobility benefits greatly underestimates its benefits. Travel decisions involve all kinds of trade-offs. Without adding capacity, the information provided by ATIS increases the informed nature of these trade-offs and of all the adjustments people make to minimize their costs of travel. With good travel time information, provided in advance, people will forego, shorten, or delay low-value trips if congestion is greater than anticipated. Conversely, they will make additional or longer trips if congestion is less than expected. The result will be a lot of induced and foregone travel. Aggregate VMT and VHT, including travel times on the network, may stay the same or even *increase*, but the aggregate benefits may be very substantial to all the individuals who have been able to make these trade-offs in their own interest to manage the levels of congestion at which they choose to travel. But if we measure just aggregate changes in VMT and VHT on the network, we will grossly underestimate these benefits from ATIS. In fact, measured in this manner, we either may not be able to detect benefits at all, or the benefits may appear to be "negative."

Indeed, when congestion levels are high, reliance on travel time savings as the measure of benefit is *likely* to produce a negative result, even when measured at the individual traveler level. We used to say travel time budgets were constant. Now we're more sophisticated and we say that travel disutility budgets are constant. We understand now that the disutility of travel includes not only travel time but also other utility measures, such as reliability and the sense of control described above. We now understand that ATIS can reduce the *non*-travel time components of the travel utility function—the worry, the stress, the anxiety, and so on. So to keep the total travel disutility budget constant, travel time itself may *increase* in proportion to the decrease in all the other components. A homeostasis is likely to be operating, in which a longer trip time may be acceptably exchanged to gain ATIS' other benefits. And so, ironically, increases in travel time, equivalent to the increased value of activities from more or longer trips, could possibly be our most easily observable measure of ITS benefit, equal to the reduction in the other components of the disutility of travel to keep the travel disutility budget constant. At a minimum, as the stress and uncertainty of travel decreases with better information, people will be more willing to travel, resulting in more and/or longer trips, while at the same time, increasing overall utility and thus mobility.

The value from ITS determines system use and user benefits. The use of the transportation system determines loadings, throughput, and operational efficiency. Eighty percent or more of benefits from transportation improvements are usually mobility or user benefits, so estimating (valuing) user benefits is key to ITS planning and evaluation. And valuing the user benefits of ATIS is different from measuring and valuing the benefits from other transportation improvements.

In summary, travel time *savings* is an inadequate measure of the benefits of ATIS. Indeed, we don't even know the sign of the change. With ATIS, travel times may increase—along with the benefits of ATIS. The emphasis on time savings in "Operation Time Saver" is misplaced. We need to unhook user benefit measures from the aggregate observable measures of VMT and VHT in a network that are needed to calculate the remaining safety and environmental impacts of ITS (Figure 1). Measuring changes in VMT and

VHT will dramatically underestimate the potential mobility benefits of ATIS—and thus most of the benefits of ATIS.

5. VALUING ITS BENEFITS

A mixed data collection strategy is required to measure and value ITS benefits for input to a benefit/cost analysis:[4]

1. Direct observation for safety, environmental, and energy benefits, and
2. Individual disaggregate observation for mobility benefits.

ITS can generate a great deal of data for evaluation. Unfortunately it's use data—volumes and speeds. But use is not related to most of the benefits—the mobility benefits, as noted above[5].

5.1 Valuing the Mobility Benefits from ITS

With ITS, we seek to increase the mobility of consumers—our customers. Depending on the situation, the mobility benefits of transportation improvements can be valued in two ways:

1. We can measure them from actual changes in behavior. This requires observing or recording changes in behavior, together with potential causal factors.
2. We can measure satisfaction from survey research using quantitative and/or qualitative methods.

Unfortunately, for ATIS, we can't use the first method, observed travel behavior to value benefits. The value of ATIS improvements is derived from more than the utility generated by observable changes in travel. Observable travel time changes—the revealed preferences—even of individual travelers, do not reflect the value of ATIS improvements. They may even have the "wrong sign," as discussed above.

We also can't use purchase behavior changes—also revealed preferences—to value ITS user benefits. This is because, as yet, consumer purchases of ITS products and services do not take place in a marketplace or choice situation that is representative of future full-scale ITS deployments. The actual participation and behavior of ITS customers is experimental and based on limited information on the benefits and costs of participation. Until some or most of the risk elements are reduced or eliminated, ITS will not be a real marketplace where observable purchase behavior will be determined by readily available, reliable information on benefits and costs. Therefore, inferring the value of the benefits by observing and modeling changes in customer purchase behavior will also not provide valid estimates of ITS user benefits.

The alternative to revealed preference methods of valuing ITS products and services is to use survey methods (stated preference), the second method identified above. ITS "raises the bar" much higher than valuing conventional transportation improvements for which observable time savings and direct costs are the primary determinants of user decision-making and benefit.

6. STATED PREFERENCE "CUSTOMER SATISFACTION" METHODS

Customer satisfaction methods can directly measure and value the changes in user benefits from ITS products and services. These are survey methods that involve questions in which the user trades off cost with use or preference for the ITS product or service. We can use focus groups to identify the important descriptors of ITS and the important influences being traded off (e.g., information type, accuracy, coverage, and content).[6] We then ask people to trade off their satisfaction or preference for the ITS improvement with various levels of dollar expenditures. The trade-off surveys are administered to respondents experiencing the measured levels of ITS deployment and the survey data are analyzed using discrete choice models to quantify the dollar values or willingness to pay for the ITS benefits.[7] These dollar values can then be input to a benefit/cost analysis (BCA) and the results scaled up to forecast national commercial and economic benefits[8].

Since the basic premise of BCA is to *maximize economic efficiency*, which means the happy state of maximizing total net benefits from an investment or policy, the values assigned to the effects of a ITS project for input to a BCA—favorable or unfavorable—should be those of the affected individuals, not the values placed on them by economists, bureaucrats, evaluators, moral philosophers, or others. These values include more than the savings in the direct outlays needed to make and operate the new ITS investment since individuals and firms will make adjustments in their behavior in response to the new situation which are often very difficult to track and evaluate (e.g., substitutions in consumption or production processes toward inputs whose "prices" are decreased by the new policy). Direct measurement of these benefits using customer satisfaction methods avoids the need to collect data and fully understand or model all these behavioral changes.[9] Proper measurement of the mobility benefit can lead not only to economies in planning, but also to avoiding mistakes in monetizing the benefits of ITS for input to a BCA. We need to avoid traditional transportation modeling to infer the user (or customer) benefits from ITS information, lest we seriously underestimate ITS benefits and make serious mistakes in carrying out a BCA.

Of course, there are a large number of ITS actions that improve the operation of the surface transportation system (e.g., Advanced Traffic Management Systems/ATMS), without the user receiving information, or being *immediately* aware of a benefit at any given time. In these cases, lowering the "supply curve" of the surface transportation system (i.e., the travel time versus volume relationship) results in mobility benefits measured in the usual manner by travel time and cost savings. These time savings can be valued using revealed or stated preference methods. Therefore, in the case of a *pure* ATMS application of ITS, the use of time and cost savings in a BCA *is* valid and straightforward.

In summary, direct valuation of the benefits by the affected individuals using customer satisfaction (trade-off) surveys avoids the problems of how exactly to measure (1) the utility-generating features of the user benefit function, and (2) observing the behavioral responses which are very hard to observe, and not well linked to the utility-generating features of ITS.

7. FUTURE BENEFITS OF ITS IN TRANSPORTATION NETWORKS

ITS systems will likely result in higher value uses of time for work and leisure activities and more productive use of commercial and industrial resources. As travelers come to rely on more dependable information, they value it more highly. This has already happened in logistics and with overnight package delivery. The fax machine and email are other excellent examples of how *new technology* has escalated concern for service quality. New transportation technology can *make time more valuable*. As time becomes more valuable the result may be that people may indeed avoid congestion more than they do now. Mel Webber at U.C. Berkeley coined a wonderful aphorism many years ago: "Congestion is the price we pay for free movement." If time becomes much more valuable with our improved sense of control with ATIS, we may see congestion decrease—aggregate VHT decrease. But the mobility benefit, properly measured, will be greater still.

ATIS can act like added capacity in the transportation network in the sense that it tells you where there is "available" capacity in real time. So ATIS information can lead to more efficient use of the capacity that we have, and *substitute* for added capacity in this *limited* sense. In this sense, people may live and work at higher densities near our existing highways and beltways and make better use of existing transit services. But there are likely to be other more profound changes in travel and land use patterns in the future, particularly as living and work activities adapt to the information age.

Elting Morrison at MIT wrote a book, *Man, Machine and Modern Times*, back in the 1940s in which he described three stages of innovation. The first is when an innovation performs an existing function better than it is currently performed. Bill Garrison at U.C. Berkeley may have been the first to cite the early development of the automobile as the classic example of this first stage innovation. The automobile went faster than horses.

The second stage of innovation is when new uses are found for the innovation. New uses were found for the "horseless carriage," such as those performed by trucks and buses.

In the third stage of the innovation, the *structure* of the surrounding system, in this case the city, has adapted to the car so it can perform at still lower costs and increasing gain to individuals, at least in terms of the costs they currently confront and perceive when making their travel decisions. Urban regions have been changing rapidly to meet the motor car's needs. The structure of cities has changed to allow the automobile to operate more effectively, and the earlier transportation mode, fixed-route and scheduled public transit services, less effectively. The U.S. transportation system leads the world in the scale and extent to which one mode of travel, the motor car, has become so integrated into the daily lives and activities of Americans, influencing where and how people reside, work, shop, and socialize. And the rest of the world appears to be following the U.S. lead.

An entrenched third stage of innovation can't coexist with another third stage innovation performing the same function. The structure of our urban regions has adapted to the automobile. There must be a return to a first stage innovation—to perform an existing function better than before. Information Technology (IT) is, of course, our candidate innovation.

I would assert that we are already at the first and second stages of innovation with IT as it affects the transportation system and our cities and regions. The first stage—performing an existing function better—is ATIS (by itself). Information is provided to travelers on travel conditions and routing and destination options in real time so travelers can maximize their mobility—their individual benefits from travel.

The second stage of innovation occurs when new uses are found for the innovation. An example is integrated (coordinated) ATIS and ATMS systems. The ATIS information on system performance is used by public and private transportation providers to manage available system capacity in real time (ATMS). Transit operators now maintain headways using AVL systems. Advanced traffic control systems can make more efficient use of available highway network capacity. We look forward to integrated ATIS and ATMS systems that route traffic in real time to those parts of our highway networks that have available capacity, or which have signal systems that can be adjusted to favor directional traffic. Even more important, we can route traffic away from routes on the verge of breakdown flow volumes (V critical). We can even change the modes of transportation options offered, for example, by setting up high-occupancy vehicle and transit options as conditions warrant (e.g., major accidents and other incidents that cause the majority of traffic delays, in any event).

The promise of integrated ITS operation in a network is synergy, which means that the sum of the benefits of integrated ITS actions is greater than their benefits taken singly. Networks are generally needed to achieve this synergy. There is very little chance of synergy from ITS actions on a single link or route. For example, if ramp metering, variable message signs (VMS), and incident management are all applied on a single freeway, each action can reduce delays by itself, but introducing ("integrating") the second and third actions will reduce delay less than introducing each action singly. That is, since there is less delay to reduce as you introduce each additional action on the single link—the marginal benefit is less. But in a *network*, ATIS information integrated with ATMS can change the flows on links to take advantage of the operating characteristics of each link in real time. If the route guidance system doesn't change flows directly, people will, in response to the travel time information. Each traveler assesses the travel conditions—the travel choice environment, and manages and controls—with good information—the congestion levels at which she or he chooses to travel. Networks are needed to provide this synergy, and we are already at the beginnings of providing the benefits from this second stage of innovation with IT as it affects the operation of our urban transportation system.

This synergy is what characterizes (or will characterize) the second stage of ITS as an innovation. We can learn from the mistakes made in the first commercialization efforts of artificial intelligence (AI) in the 1980s. The advocates of AI thought then that it would replace people. What was discovered was that AI's successes were in making things possible that weren't possible with people alone. There are many examples of new uses for IT which enhance our vision and reach (e.g., telemedicine, Web meeting, etc.). However, transportation and urban systems are very complicated, so the adoption of new technology on a wide scale to provide benefits is taking a long time. I was designing computer controlled traffic signal systems (ATMS) 40 years ago, and electronic route guidance (ERGS) systems (ATIS), 30 years ago.[10]

The most interesting question, of course, is when and in what form IT will reach its third stage of innovation as regards our cities and the demand for travel. Cities exist to overcome the cost of distance, we learned in our first course in transportation planning. Transportation improvements reduce the cost of distance, so cities have spread out. Physical access now limits our physical interactions, but not virtual access. The IT revolution has caused distance to no longer be a determinant of the cost of communication. There's even a book called *Death of Distance*, by Frances Cairncross.

We're a long way from the death of distance in transportation. Travel costs increase with distance, whereas communications costs, with the Internet, effectively don't. There will be a substitution of communications for transportation to the extent that we can accomplish the same activities—at much less cost—that currently require travel. We know that the world is full of dot.com-ers hell-bent on creating Internet sites that are destinations—that provide every product and service that those dot.com-ers can imagine, and then some. Some of these are providing, or will provide, services and activities that we normally travel for, although the jury is out in the short term as, for example, shopping services like Peapod struggle or go bankrupt.

Up to now, improvements in communication were *complements* to transportation; they were accompanied by, or caused, increases in travel. The telephone was first thought to replace travel, but since it makes the benefits from travel more achievable, we make more trips to be able to receive those benefits. The Internet is also connecting us to many more people and places, that we might benefit from being there, which can lead to more travel. The Internet can also provide some of the benefits from travel.

So what *will* be the impact of the IT revolution on travel? We know that work activities are adapting to the information age. There is a revolution in logistics on the freight or goods movement side. Productivity is finally increasing in the U.S. due to the growth of information technology. Are we approaching the third stage of innovation in transportation with IT, as regards how the need for transportation is currently satisfied, as it affects personal transportation and the structure of our regions? Will the structure of our regions adapt to make transportation less effective (or necessary) and communication (IT) more effective? Is increasing bandwidth becoming a substitute for travel? How necessary is face-to-face interaction when telecommunications provides so much information?

Just as conventional transportation improvements (e.g., the interstate highway system) permitted specialization of functions; now, with the "death of distance," IT can promote this still further. There are so many examples. Let me just cite the example of my wife, who used to commute to work at a publishing company, writing and editing K–12 textbooks and tests. She now sits at her computer at home doing the same work. Her work product is transported at the same time as it is produced. She herself doesn't commute every day—the Internet substitutes for her daily travel—but she does fly around the country to her clients a few times a year for a few days at a time. She can plan her air trips so she doesn't look like a business traveler. This, multiplied many times, may be why the airlines thought there was a decline in business travel even before 9/11/01.

This kind of outsourcing is occurring in a variety of industries with obvious consequences for transportation and settlement patterns. The most quoted example worldwide is computer programmers working in south India, working for software companies in the U.S. Globalization even brings with it the advantage of 24-hour work on the same project, using shifts of personnel at various locations worldwide.

For activities requiring both communication and transportation, which means most work activities outside the home these days, transportation costs will increase as a percentage of the cost of both. Remember—the third stage of innovation is when the system adapts to make the benefits of the innovation more valuable, and the old way of accomplishing the function less valuable. As people—travelers—come to rely more on dependable ways of accomplishing their work and play, they value them more highly. New technology can make time more valuable.

One would imagine that the demand and transportation system performance impacts of such an important transportation program as ITS would be well known by now. The truth is that we may be as ignorant now of the consequences of ITS as we were of the impacts of the interstate highway program at its inception in the 1950s. That program had many unanticipated far-reaching consequences, including its impact on the shapes of regions in America. ITS can be seen as the information analogue of the interstate highway system.

Thus, as we approach the third stage of innovation, transportation planners need to think in terms of new regional structures and boundaries. More and more, we are living in regional cities—in regional places—and it is the region, transcending old urban area boundaries, that functions in the global economic landscape. Our new economies are regional, and regional boundaries don't necessarily conform to state or national boundaries. The reasons are legion, like access to specialized labor through the Internet, both highly skilled and unskilled (e.g., data entry and other back office functions). That's why there can be parts of a state or nation that are succeeding economically, and others that are failing economically. There can also be huge economic disparities between parts of a state that lead to severe housing and transportation disparities and inequities, of which California's Silicon Valley is, or has been, the national poster child.

With the advent of the third stage of the IT innovation, we need to recognize that it's not *only* our transportation networks that provide access and determine land value. The networks—the new infrastructure—include fiberglass and wireless. Public sector controls through highway construction are lessening. Development is leapfrogging auto travel times. This will enlarge regions still further. Our new regions will be defined by both physical travel as well as virtual travel. Virtual travel will increase the pressure for regional expansion, while infrastructure constraints on physical travel—read congestion and limited capacity—will increase the already considerable burden on people we currently call "interregional commuters."

8. SUMMARY

There are many different forces at work that affect the impact of ITS on travel in both the long and short run. In metropolitan areas, I would suggest that there is going to be some in-fill, some higher density development as ATIS systems increase our ability to utilize whatever capacity is available in our metropolitan areas. Conversely, ATIS will facilitate market-driven solutions to increasing mobility, and like the telephone before it, will significantly increase net benefits from travel. The result will likely be more travel in larger regions. Thus, ATIS like the telephone is more likely to be a complement rather than a substitute for travel.

In the private sector, market forces help guard against routinely poor investment decisions. In evaluating the benefits from ATIS, we have found so far that market forces are weak. We must make a deliberate effort to ensure that our ITS improvements make a positive contribution to the many diverse areas of our economy, and groups in our society. However, we can insure that ITS improvements result in net social benefits *only* if we focus on the right benefit measures, and *only* if the right tools are used to value these benefits as ITS is increasingly applied in our existing and future transportation networks.

The prevailing wisdom, not true to date, is that the private sector will do most of the investing in the information gathering and dissemination functions of ITS. We also know that those who profit the most in the information industry are those whose business is selling the *benefits* of the technology, not the technology itself. This is as true now as it was for 19th-century railroad investors who made their money from the land value benefits of the railroad, not from the railroad itself. Personal computers are now a low-margin commodity. The national ITS architecture with its emphasis on open architecture and open interface standards will allow ITS technology to become a commodity. Selling the customer benefits from ITS will likely be the profitable part of the ITS business. Progress in applying ITS may have been slowed to date by a lack of understanding of these consumer benefits of ITS. As discussed in this chapter, we *can* value these benefits, properly defined, using customer satisfaction measurement methods.

NOTES

1. See Daniel Brand, Conference Summary, "Moving Urban America," Proceedings of the TRB post ISTEA Conference, Charlotte, NC, TRB Special Report 237, 1993, page 4.
2. E.g., see IVHS Strategic Plan, Report to Congress from the US Department of Transportation, December 18, 1992, pp.17-18.
3. Y.-B. Yim, R. Hall, R. Koo, M. Miller. "*TravInfo*™, 817-1717 Caller Study," paper presented to the 78th Annual Meeting of the Transportation Research Board, Washington, DC, 1999. Also, Kenneth Small, et al., "Valuation of Travel-Time Savings and Predictability in Congested Conditions for Highway User-Cost Estimation," NCHRP Report 421, 1997.
4. As noted earlier, efficiency benefits don't have value by themselves.
5. Of course, safety, environmental, and energy benefits are related to use (VMT and VHT), but use (and possibly disbenefits) may increase with ITS as discussed above. In any event, measuring these benefits (or disbenefits) as a function of use, and valuing them using well accepted unit values is relatively straight forward.
6. Charles River Associates, "User Acceptance of ATIS Products and Services: A Report of Qualitative Research," prepared for the USDOT ITS Joint Program Office and the Volpe National Transportation Systems Center, January 1997.
7. Shomik Mehndiratta, Michael Kemp, Jane Lappin, and Daniel Brand, "What Advanced Traveler Information System Information Do Users Want? Evidence from In-Vehicle Navigation Device Users," *Transportation Research Record* 1679 (1999).
8. Daniel Brand, "Applying Benefit/Cost Analysis to Identify and Measure the Benefits of ITS," *Transportation Research Record* 1651 (1998)
9. The same trade-off survey methods can be used to value the increased output of organizations whose productivity has increased, but in ways that are difficult to measure (e.g., state government's increased inspections of trucks).
10. August 1972; and Daniel Brand, et al., "Real Time Information and Control Systems for Urban Transportation," Proceedings, American Institute of Aeronautics and Astronautics, 1971.

Chapter 4

MAKING THE CASE FOR ITS INVESTMENT

Douglass B. Lee, Jr.
USDOT Volpe Transportation Systems Center

The case for investing in ITS needs to be made on objective grounds that are credible to the decision-maker who is seeking balanced information. A basis for making such evaluations in the public sector is benefit-cost analysis (BCA). The BCA framework is applicable to ITS projects as well as to traditional physical improvements to highways or transit. The practice of BCA for evaluating ITS has not, however, been exemplary: although BCA evaluation of ITS projects is feasible at a modest level of effort, few studies have been done, and, for most contexts, key data are not available. These assertions can best be argued by describing examples of how BCA can be applied to ITS, and showing the difficulties in estimating performance parameters, especially effectiveness measures of the impacts of ITS deployment on benefits (e.g., the reduction in incident duration resulting from traffic surveillance). The application of BCA to ITS can yield valuable insights regarding which projects are likely to be worthwhile, but the robustness of the conclusions could be greatly strengthened with properly focused data collection.

1. INTRODUCTION

The substantive case for investing in ITS should be made using a framework that is consistent framework applied to conventional highway improvements and other transportation with other kinds of investment analysis, and should be the same as the investments.[1] The recommended framework is benefit-cost analysis (BCA).

The conclusions argued in what follows are:

1. Benefit-cost evaluation of ITS deployments (retrospective or prospective) is technically and analytically feasible, at a reasonable level of effort.

2. Conducting such evaluation is hampered by the dearth of empirical measures of the effectiveness of ITS (e.g., on saving time), leaving a large range of uncertainty in the evaluation results that can only be reduced by suitable data collection.
3. The low level of effort currently devoted to benefit-cost analysis of ITS investment should be increased substantially, both to provide better information to decision-makers about likely benefits and to identify the critical missing data.

The examples described below attempt to show where the missing information occurs, and why it is important for useful evaluation. Relatively simple formats, such as spreadsheet models, are generally adequate for computational purposes.

1.1 Objectives

A framework or methodology for estimating which ITS investments are socially worthwhile and under what circumstances should be able to answer a series of related questions:

1. What kinds of ITS work best (e.g., freeway surveillance, traffic signal coordination, ramp metering) or have the greatest potential?
2. What preconditions (e.g., traffic volumes, incident rates) can be used to identify settings where ITS applications might be valuable?
3. What performance requirements (e.g., response time, average speed improvement, share of trips diverted) must be achieved for a deployment to be successful?
4. How do ITS investments compare with physical highway improvements (e.g., additional lanes), and how can the best mix of projects be selected to generate the highest net benefits?
5. What synergies occur among ITS investments, and between ITS and non-ITS investments, at both individual project and network levels?

Methods for addressing these questions are illustrated below by means of a series of examples.[2] Questions [1] and [2] help locate problems in need of solutions rather than the other way around. Question [3] helps screen out weak projects before deployment, and Question [4] allows ITS projects to be compared to physical infrastructure improvements in the same capital program.

1.2 Benefit-Cost Analysis

The fundamental strategy of BCA is to evaluate an action by comparing the results of taking the action against a base case in which the action is not taken. The comparison is between a world "with" the project and another world "without" the project. An action, in the present instance, is a deployment of ITS. More precisely, a "project" is a package of mutually supporting actions, such as purchasing and installing hardware, developing and testing software, and marketing a service, that together have an impact on the transportation system. Deploying video cameras and loop detectors, building a traffic operations center, installing communications, and developing incident detection algorithms might be considered a project, for evaluation purposes.

An evaluation done prior to deployment, or prior to field testing, is a prospective evaluation and is useful for planning and deployment decision-making. An evaluation done after deployment is completed and the system has been in operation for a period of time is a retrospective evaluation, and serves the purpose of determining whether the assumptions used in the planning evaluation were borne out and whether the project should be extended or replicated. For a retrospective evaluation, the "without" case cannot be observed and must be estimated; for a prospective evaluation, the "with" case must be estimated. Evaluation can also be done at any point along the life cycle from planning to termination, for purposes of monitoring the deployment to see if it is meeting performance targets. The same BCA framework serves all of these purposes.

The intent of the following examples is to illustrate the information requirements for BCA and to show how the data and performance parameters are used in the analysis. None of the examples offer a complete analysis of a project, but together they seek to highlight steps in the evaluation where critical information typically is missing.

2. FREEWAY MANAGEMENT

Most large urban areas have deployed a combination of surveillance cameras, vehicle detectors, and communications on their expressway system. Often a traffic operations center (TOC) is added for purposes of coordinating activities of police, traffic management, emergency services, and other agencies. The example here uses the San Antonio freeway network.

2.1 Description of the Project

Statistics on what has been deployed in San Antonio are summarized in Table 1. Vehicle detectors are placed about half a mile apart in each lane. Closed-circuit television surveillance cameras can pan, tilt, and zoom, with a range of view of about one mile in clear weather. The main purpose of expanding traffic surveillance in San Antonio is to detect incidents on freeways faster and to collect traffic information more efficiently than can be done without the surveillance. The components of the system for gathering traffic data and providing information to drivers are shown in Figure 1. Loop detector information gathered from freeways becomes part of the San Antonio travel speed database, which can be used by in-vehicle navigation units and traveler information sources.

Table 1. Deployment Components and Quantities

Inductive loop detectors	1,251
Sonic detectors	63
Variable message signs	137
Lane control signs	359
Video surveillance cameras	96
Centerline mileage covered	55

Source: Carter et al. (1999)

Variable message signs (VMS) are the primary means for sending real time traffic information to the drivers on freeways. VMS are installed on approaches to major interchanges and upper/lower freeway splits to give drivers the option of exiting the freeway and using an alternate route before being committed to a closed or congested section of freeway. VMS can also be used to warn drivers of congestion or closures on an intersecting freeway, allowing them to use an alternate route. On the alternative routes, VMS can be used to guide drivers back to their original route.[3]

Lane Control Signs (LCS) provide a means for control of individual freeway traffic lanes, by diverting traffic to/from individual traffic lanes in a smooth and controlled fashion. This capability reduces last-minute lane changing and the resultant traffic congestion that occurs when a freeway lane is blocked unexpectedly. LCS provide limited communications with drivers in the form of one signal for each lane of the freeway. Signs are located at approximately one-mile intervals, or one-quarter mile at points of diversion in the freeway lane configuration, so as to draw more attention from drivers approaching a point of diversion.

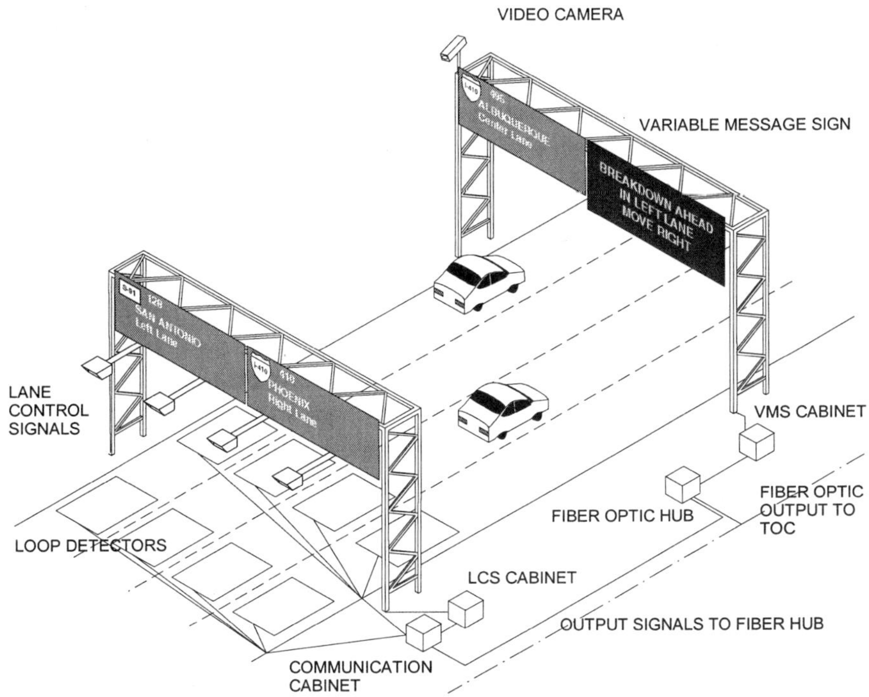

Figure 1. Freeway Management System

The overall strategy of freeway management is to monitor traffic conditions on urban freeways, and take actions to ameliorate adverse conditions. Actions range from dispatching personnel and equipment to treat incidents, to actuating traffic controls, to providing information to highway users.

2.2 Baseline

Without ITS deployment, freeway management consists of the following.

Incidents on the freeway systems are detected as a result of cellular and other phone calls, the presence of police or other emergency service vehicles, verbal communications between incident observers and police, aerial observers, and freeway service patrols (FSPs).[4] Traveler information about current conditions is obtained from broadcast radio and TV. Drivers on freeways observe traffic conditions, compare them with their normal expectations for congestion, and make route diversion, timing, and lane choices accordingly, both prior to and during travel.

The evaluation question, then, is how much can ITS improve upon these baseline conditions?

2.3 Actions

Under ITS deployment, information can also be received from other sources as a result of the deployment:

- Inductive loops, magnetic and sonic detectors, and other automatic vehicle detection devices are installed on the freeway, along with computers and communications.
- Video cameras are installed at one-half to one mile spacing.
- Radio frequency transponders are placed in vehicles used for electronic tolling or for other identification purposes.
- Surveillance data are transmitted to a control center, sometimes called a traffic operations center or a traffic systems management center.

With this information, the following actions are possible:

- The TOC may dispatch equipment and personnel to deal with incidents.
- The TOC may post messages on variable message signs (VMS).
- The TOC may broadcast messages via highway advisory radio (HAR).
- Freeway access control may be exercised in the form of ramp metering or police block.[5]
- The TOC may activate lane control signals that indicate clear, slow, or blocked lanes (LCS).

The above actions are intended to produce information and stimulate benefits via the impact linkages—from actions taken to benefits created—shown in Figure 2. The benefits include:

- Reduce incident detection and response time.
- Divert travelers away from blocked or constricted sections to alternate routes with more capacity.
- Smooth the flow of traffic.
- Reassure highway users that they will be informed of problems on their route if such exist.
- Induce additional traffic.

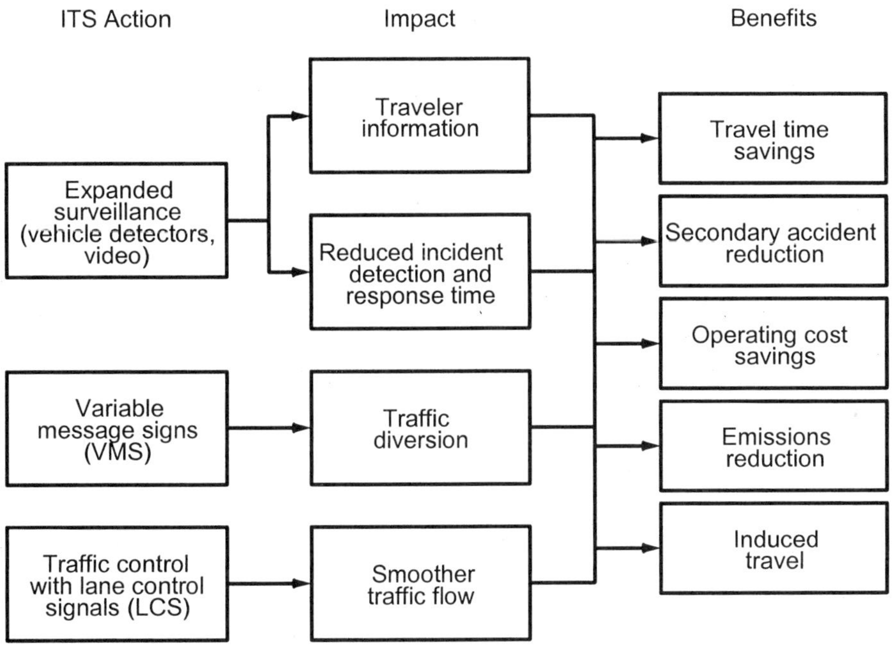

Figure 2. Impact Linkages for San Antonio Freeway Management

These impacts translate into benefits in the form of delay savings, reduced operating costs, reduced emissions, reduced agency costs, and consumer surplus from induced travel.

2.4 Modeling Incident Delay

The sequence of events during an incident, and the traffic consequences, can be represented by a non-steady state deterministic queuing model (a deterministic simulation). A graphic representation of the model is shown in Figure 3. Time is shown along the horizontal axis, with the phases of the incident (occurrence, detection, clearance, etc.) marked by vertical dotted lines. The vertical axis shows the cumulative number of vehicles passing over the facility. The higher straight dashed line through the origin represents vehicle capacity. Actual arrivals are shown by the gradually curving dashed line, indicating that arrivals during this period never exceed the normal capacity of the facility. The incident starts at time = 15 minutes, causing the capacity to be reduced, initially to zero, as shown by the lower solid line. The area between the arrival and departure curves represents the total vehicle-hours of delay caused by the incident.

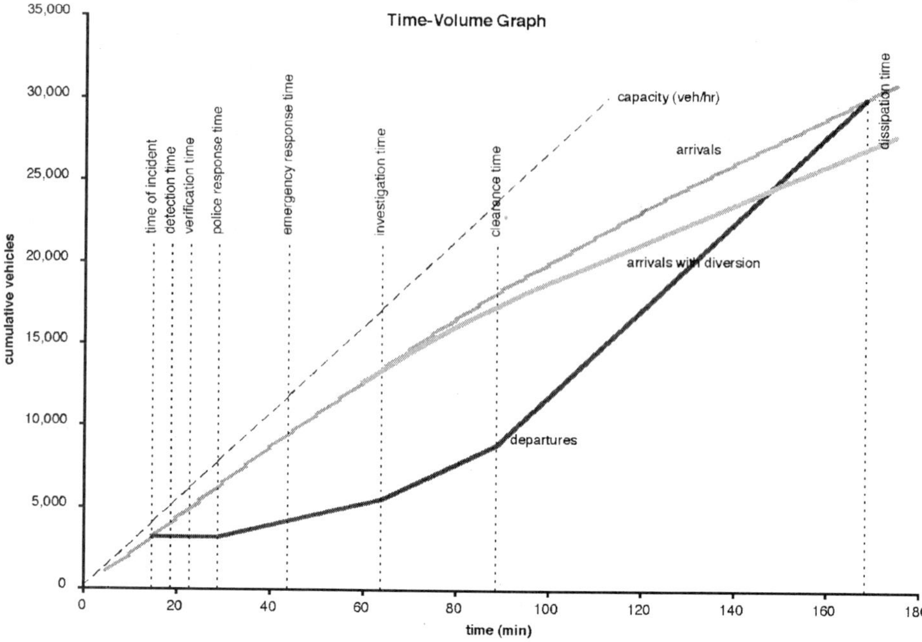

Figure 3. Phases in the Duration of an Incident

Although this model has several limitations, they do not present a handicap in using it for the analysis of incident treatments. Attributes such as queue length and location of the tail of the queue can be readily derived. The above example represents only one incident.

2.5 Incident Causes

Not all incidents are accidents; some are the result of breakdowns or debris on the road. More detailed distributions, however, require correspondingly rich data, which are currently lacking. One of the few sources for types of incidents by cause is shown in Table 2. Data are taken from several cities, showing accidents as only a small cause of incidents, and breakdowns as by far the predominant cause. The same data showed that the rate of incidents (per million VMT) on heavily used freeways, for all causes, is over three times higher during the peak period than off-peak, suggesting that the exposure measure might need to reflect vehicle hours and traffic density as well as vehicle miles.

Minor incidents (breakdowns, debris, and abandonment) probably don't cause much delay, and may not require extensive local data for estimating their impacts. For major incidents, some kind of grouping is needed of what is in reality a continuous distribution, using local data that permit reasonable estimates of average incident duration (by type) and how such incidents might be mitigated by service patrols and surveillance.

Table 2. Distributions of Incidents by Type, by Usage Level

	Peak		
	ADT/C<7	7<ADT/C<10	10<ADT/C
Abandoned	25%	25%	12%
Accidents	7%	6%	10%
Debris	2%	3%	2%
Mech/Elec	21%	24%	26%
Stalled	19%	21%	17%
Tire	15%	18%	17%
Other	11%	4%	15%
	100%	100%	100%
	Off-Peak		
Abandoned	25%	28%	35%
Accidents	7%	6%	8%
Debris	2%	3%	3%
Mech/Elec	21%	20%	20%
Stalled	19%	18%	13%
Tire	15%	19%	14%
Other	11%	6%	8%
	100%	100%	100%

Source: Calculated from Sullivan, Taff, and Daly (1995)

2.6 Incidents and Accidents

The negative consequences of incidents arise from different sources: delay is from the incident and its duration, property damage is from crashes, and injury costs arise from the number of persons injured and injury severity. The relationships among these factors are shown in Figure 4. Several factors have distributions that probably require at least some level of disaggregation: incidents by type (accident and other) and severity (measured as capacity reduction), and injury by severity (abbreviated injury scale). Other factors are important but of unknown magnitudes: crashes per incident and injuries per crash. Although accidents may be a minority of incidents, they are the source of a major share of costs.

2.7 Accident Frequency

Although traffic accidents are individually unpredictable, the probability of an accident varies systematically with traffic volume, weather and light conditions, vehicle mix, driver maturity and experience, and other factors. Starting with a highly simplified model, the number of accidents per year is

$$\text{number of accidents}_i = AADT \times FM \times AR_i \times 365$$

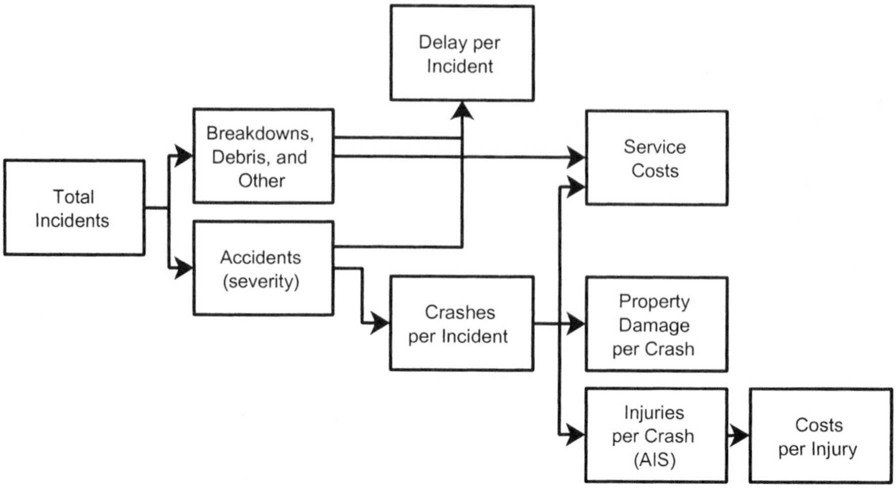

Figure 4. Relationships among Incidents, Accidents, and Injuries

where $AADT$ = annual average daily traffic on managed freeways, FM = freeway miles under management, AR_i = accident rate for accident type i, and the result is the annual system-wide number of each type of accident. The first two terms generate daily exposure in VMT.

"True" average values exist that will make this equation correct, but the averages cannot be measured directly as averages; they must be built up from sampling or comprehensive data collection. AADT, for example, varies among freeway sections, from day to day. Because the simple model above treats all VMT the same, using average VMT statistics to estimate a daily total is perhaps not a big source of error.

Accident rates are another matter. Because the severity of accident—both in terms of damage and of capacity reduction—follows a distribution that shows an order of magnitude more minor than major incidents, some level of disaggregation is warranted. One compromise is to average by two severity classes, major and minor. The next problem is to obtain averages for both costs and frequencies that classify incidents in the same way. The 1997 *Highway Statistics* report tabulates accident rates for urban interstates by state, for fatal, nonfatal, and "most serious injuries" (defined as incapacitating).[6] Fatal and serious are considered "major," for the San Antonio evaluation, and everything else is minor. The crash rates are shown in Table 4.[7] Minor incidents are estimated by inflating the nonfatal injury crash rate (158.8) by the ratio of non-accident incidents to total accidents, in Table 2. The rates differ by over two orders of magnitude. Of critical importance, then, is how the accident and incident data are classified.

2.8 Unit Crash Costs

Incident rates, no matter how precise, are of no use without matching unit costs. FHWA offers costs per injury for police-reported highway crashes on two categorizations, one known as "KABC" and the other being the Abbreviated Injury Scale (AIS), both shown in Table 3. Note that the major/minor categorization used above seems to match better with the KABC scale, although "Fatal" plus "Incapacitating" appears to include all four of the most severe categories on the AIS scale. Also, these unit costs are per injury. If crashes are estimated from exposure data, then injuries (by severity) need to be generated per crash.

Table 3. Accident Unit Costs

	Descriptor	$/Injury 1994	AIS	Descriptor	$/Injury 1994
K	Possible	19,000	1	Minor	5,000
A	Evident	36,000	2	Moderate	40,000
B	Incapacitating	180,000	3	Serious	150,000
C	Fatal	2,600,000	4	Severe	490,000
			5	Critical	1,980,000
			6	Fatal	2,600,000

Source: FHWA (1994)

FHWA claims that these numbers are "comprehensive," meaning that they include property damage, travel delay, and nine other components; implicit, then, are assumptions about the distribution of circumstances (e.g., number of injuries, traffic volume, capacity reduction, injuries per crash, crashes per incident) under which the accidents occur. For purposes of estimating ITS impacts, some of these cost items need to be removed.

2.9 Impacts of Surveillance on Incidents

The above discussion pertains only to construction of the base case; the impacts of ITS deployment still need to be incorporated. Traffic surveillance enables automatic detection of traffic incidents that cause sluggish or stopped traffic on freeway systems. Incident detection information is sent to the TOC for verification and location of the incident, and dispatching of appropriate emergency services. The average amount of time by which the duration of an incident is reduced, for each type of incident (i.e., the effectiveness of freeway surveillance), is not known in general or for San Antonio in particular. A reduction in incident duration can be translated into time savings, operating cost reduction, and secondary accident reduction, per incident of each type. Computational steps are shown in Table 4, with *assumed* impacts of ITS in terms of minutes of reduced incident duration.[8]

Table 4. Benefits from Surveillance

INCIDENTS	Major	Minor
Number of incidents per 100 million VMT	6.8	1,753
Average AADT (vehicles/day)	160,000	
Annual number of incidents under surveillance	103	26,625
Reduction in detection, response, or clearance time per incident (min)	10	1
Delay, operating cost, and accident savings per incident ($)	20,000	80
Annual incident mitigation benefits ($ million)	2.1	2.1

The relationship between deployment and incident mitigation needs to be more than just statistical. Establishing causality depends upon showing that the information from the surveillance was actually used in some way that resulted in shorter incident durations or other impacts. This evidence is not readily available.

2.10 Variable Message Signs

Variable message signs (VMS) allow the motorist to consider diversion before entering an incident or congestion queue. The benefit of this information depends upon such conditions as the volume of traffic, the length of delay, the location of the sign, the share of vehicles that divert, and the circuity and speed of alternative routes.

Average volume per incident, as shown in Table 5, can be derived from an incident model as previously described. Each VMS is assumed to have a range of effect: if the queue has built up too close to the sign for drivers to find an exit, or the incident is too far away and doesn't affect much of the traffic, there will be little response. Since warnings can be provided for major incidents well in advance, coverage can be widespread; for minor incidents, only a nearby warning is of much value. Of those incidents within range of a VMS, some share of traffic diverts, less so for a minor incident. The diversion may, on average, save the diverted traveler time, especially if diverting from a major incident.

Table 5. Benefits from Variable Message Signs

DIVERSION	Major Incidents	Minor Incidents
Average traffic volume per incident	20,000	2,000
Downstream range of VMS (miles, one direction)	1.5	0.5
Expressway miles covered	37	12
Annual incidents within range of a VMS	103	12,544
Share of traffic diverted per VMS	30%	10%
Annual volume diverted	619,507	2,508,851
Travel time savings, per vehicle per incident	10	1
Annual savings from diversion ($million)	1.0	0.42

Although some research has been done regarding optimal diversion shares, there are few empirical data on the share of traffic that actually diverts, or on whether these or other impacted travelers benefit from the diversion. The value of VMS cannot be evaluated without this information.

3. TRAVELER INFORMATION

Information on traffic conditions can be disseminated to travelers in general, as well as used to manage the freeways directly. ATIS (advanced traveler information systems) take numerous forms, but utilize real-time traffic data that are distilled into average travel speeds by link, and made available through Web sites and in-vehicle devices. For freeway incidents, benefits arise from traffic that would have gotten on the freeway affected by an incident but chooses not to because of information about specific delay locations, and from traffic on the freeway that learns of delay-causing incidents through in-vehicle devices rather than VMS.

Having traveler information available—whether or not the traveler uses it to change behavior—has some value in reassuring travelers that at least they won't stumble upon major incidents that are already affecting traffic flow on their route. This "serenity" value might be, say, $1 per vehicle hour, the difference between the cost of travel time under normal uncertainty, and the cost of informed or serene travel time. This adjustment to the value of travel time could be obtained through properly designed stated preference experiments, but so far this survey research has not been undertaken.

ATIS can also provide information about destinations, routes, and modes. The primary missing information regarding ATIS is how often travelers receive information about problems that might affect their travel, what behavior changes users make in response to the information, and to what extent these changes result in benefits to the traveler or the transportation system.[9]

4. COMPUTER-AIDED ACCIDENT INVESTIGATION

Normally, incident investigators use manual surveying methods to gather information—skid marks, locations of vehicles and occupants, road geometry—for reconstructing an incident. Use of electronic survey instruments, electronic data storage, and computer analysis can substantially reduce the amount of time needed to conduct an investigation, gather more information, and reduce errors and inaccuracies. Accident investigation time can be a major factor affecting incident duration, because police must take measurements and completely document an accident scene before any of the disabled vehicles can be removed. Police in the Phoenix area have acquired seven electronic survey stations, and some 25 officers received two days of training. The manufacturer calls the electronic surveying system a "Total Station."

4.1 Workload

The first factor in evaluating the electronic accident investigation hardware is the number of cases in which it might be used, over the course of some period of time such as a year. Types of traffic accidents that are investigated are fatalities, serious injury, damage to public property, truck involvement, and multiple vehicle collisions.

Not every incident in these categories is investigated, but these are the categories that generate investigations. No data on the number and types of investigations in Phoenix were available.

Using national statistical sources, some of these categories can be estimated, as shown in Table 6. Accident rates for fatalities and non-fatal injuries are tabulated by state and urban or rural; these rates are then applied to Phoenix travel to obtain estimated annual accidents in these two categories.[10] The shares that could be investigated using the electronic survey equipment, marked as "%TS," are simply trial numbers; they provide an annual total that is perhaps plausible for the Phoenix context.

Table 6. Fatal and Injury Accidents

Traffic and Accidents		**% TS**
Phoenix daily VMT (millions)	58	
AZ fatality rate (urban)	1.53	
AZ nonfatality injury rate (urban)	121.24	
Annual fatalities	324	50%
Annual nonfatal injury accidents	25,667	1%
Total investigated accidents by TS		419
Investigations per station per week		1.15

Note: rates are per million VMT

4.2 Getting Equipment to the Scene

If accident investigators or "reconstructionists" are specialists who perform only investigations, then seven stations could be kept with the investigators and ready for deployment wherever the investigators happened to be. If investigators also do other duties when not needed for investigation, and the number of officers trained in investigation is significantly larger than the number of stations, then the stations may frequently be traveling to and from scenes that do not require investigation. The unknown parameter is the time required to bring a station and crew to the scene of an accident that needs investigating. If the time it takes for the nearest investigation team to reach the scene is regarded as a baseline, then the question is how much longer does it take to get a team equipped with the electronic station?[11]

If the station-equipped team is already engaged in something it can't interrupt or pass off, or is located some distance removed, then the benefits in speed, labor saving, and higher quality of having the station must be weighed against the delay in getting started, compared to a manual investigation team.

The cost of the hardware is around $10–15,000, so acquisition of units is not heavily cost-constrained; the question is whether the units and trained officers can be efficiently utilized.

4.3 Benefits of Using the Station

With the surveying and data capture equipment, a trained crew can record the essential information describing an accident scene, in less time, with fewer people, and more accurately.[12] The benefits apply to the gathering and recording of data, the drawing of the accident diagram, and the transfer of data to analytic packages at the office.

Table 7 shows hypothetical labor savings from using the electronic station for various types of accidents. The time savings allow for some delay between when a "manual" team would arrive versus a station-equipped team. The average times and distributions across accident types is currently unknown, but might be obtained from police-reported accident logs.[13]

Table 7. Labor Savings from Use of Electronic Accident Investigation Equipment

Incident Categories	Fatality	Injury	3 or + Veh.	Public Property	Truck
Distribution of Incident Categories (%)	39%	40%	15%	3%	3%
Number of Incidents	162	167	63	13	13
Average Investigation Time Savings					
On Scene Data Collection (min.)	40	30	40	30	30
Accident Diagram (min.)	360	180	200	160	240
Paperwork (min.)	10	10	10	10	10
Average Time Savings/Incident (min.)	410	220	250	200	280
Average Cost Savings/Incident					
No. Staff for On-Scene Investigation	2	2	2	2	2
On-Scene Investigation Cost Savings	32	24	32	24	24
No. Staff for Accident Diagram	1	1	1	1	1
Accident Diagram Cost Savings	144	72	80	64	96
No. Staff for Paperwork	1	1	1	1	1
Paperwork Cost Savings	3	3	3	3	3
Avg. Cost Savings/Investigation ($)	$179	$99	$115	$91	$123
Total Annual Benefits ($)					**55,266**
Average Hourly Wage (Officers)	$24.00				
Average Hourly Wage (Clerical)	$15.00				

Sources: Agent, et al. (1994); Jacobson, et al. (1992); Nee, et al. (1995); Volpe spreadsheet

5. OTHER COMPONENTS AND BENEFITS

5.1 Other ITS Components

The above examples have been chosen to demonstrate the feasibility of conducting benefit-cost evaluations of ITS projects, at whatever stage they are in from concept to deployment. The examples also demonstrate the difficulties of obtaining many of the most critical data for measuring beneficial performance or effectiveness. Primary attention was given to a single ITS component—freeway management—both because it is representative of the problems and opportunities, and also because it has been widely deployed with, as yet, little documentation of its effectiveness.[14]

Many other ITS components, including those applied to public transit, can be evaluated in ways similar to the above examples.[15] Each component—e.g., transit service management—has characteristics that require different evaluation models, but the BCA methods are common to all components.

5.2 Network Benefits

Various impacts may interact synergistically, augmenting total benefits beyond the sum of each ITS component on its own. Alternatively, the impact of one component may reduce the benefits from another, such as diverting traffic from a queue whose length is shortened by another ITS action. The latter occurs in freeway management, in that the delay savings assuming that drivers have no prior information is larger than if it is recognized that some drivers will receive VMS or ATIS information that removes them from the delay queue.

Some examples of scale or network *dis*economies:

1. The more resources (e.g., police, travelers with cell phones, service patrols, surveillance cameras) are directed at detecting incidents, the higher the probability of detection in any time period, or the shorter the time between incident and detection. As the detection time gets shorter, however, the cost of an incremental reduction goes up, i.e., the remaining undetected incidents are harder to find.
2. The more traffic is diverted from an incident queue, the less the benefits from reducing incident duration. In the limit, if everyone is diverted there is no hurry clearing the incident. The effect of diverting travelers from the incident is shown in Figure 3 as "arrivals with diversion."

Some possible positive synergies, on the other hand:

1. Benefits of diversion from freeways during incidents can be enhanced if the diversion is coordinated with signal timing adjustments on parallel arterials.
2. Signal timing across jurisdictional boundaries may make the benefits from the treatment of a long arterial much larger than the sum of

benefits that can be achieved within each jurisdiction. Where such arterials are straight and evenly spaced (e.g., Phoenix), the potential is clear; it is less clear where arterials have many curves and signals are unevenly spaced (e.g., Seattle).

Some analysts assert that ITS cannot be evaluated at the project level because of "network effects," but there seems to be no basis for this claim. Scale economies and interactions among components, whether positive or negative, can be modeled using the same sorts of methods described above for doing project level analysis, without obviating the need for doing the project analysis.

6. SUMMARY OF NEEDED EVALUATION DATA

The examples described above illustrate some typical steps in evaluation of a few types of ITS applications. The analysis is not difficult, but data gaps are revealed when attempts are made to quantify the linkages between the ITS action taken and the benefits that might ensue.

In trying to estimate the benefits from ITS projects, some approximation is inevitable, but currently available empirical evidence leaves a wide range of uncertainty. This uncertainty could be greatly reduced by improvements in data collection:

1. The impact of deploying surveillance technology and traffic operations centers is largely unknown. Few efforts have been made to measure the frequency with which incidents are detected via surveillance before police or travelers report them, or whether such ITS efforts reduce incident duration, or what activities actually take place in a TOC.
2. Impacts of deployments need to be specific to a homogeneous ITS type (or "component"), such as "surveillance," "service patrols," or "ramp metering," not grouped together as "freeway management" or "incident management."
3. Accident reports need to be standardized on a common categorization of incident and injury severity, matched to unit cost rates, and should include information on times (detection, response, clearance, etc.) and location.[16]
4. The occurrence of secondary accidents is poorly understood, and pertinent data are sparse. Are accidents occurring in the opposing lanes on the opposite side of the median considered secondary, and do they increase with incident duration?
5. Estimates of injury costs need to be decomposed so that factors such as associated delay, crashes per incident, and lost earnings can be removed or adjusted.
6. When ITS devices such as electronic survey stations are deployed, data should be collected on how intensively and for what purposes the equipment is used.

7. Traveler information systems—in-vehicle, Web-based, call-in, transit stop, or other—cannot be evaluated until something is known about how often they provide information that causes the traveler to change behavior, and how much value (willingness to pay) travelers place on that information.
8. Valuations of travel time under a variety of circumstances—anxious, reassured, uncomfortable, meeting an appointment, going home, emergency—is needed.

These are only a few examples of the kinds of data that are needed in order to produce convincing benefit-cost evaluations of ITS applications. BCA will never "prove" beyond a shadow of a doubt that ITS spending is either worthwhile or wasteful, but it is readily possible to generate information that would be useful for guiding investment into productive projects and ensuring that their performance is as intended and expected.

ACKNOWLEDGEMENTS

Valuable and thorough comments were received from Barbara Staples and Rob Maccubbin of Mitretek Systems.

NOTES

1 Using a common evaluation framework reduces the need for a precise definition of what falls under ITS, since what matters is how well a deployment performs in creating benefits.

2 The case studies are extracted from Lee, Schimek, and Farver (2000).

3 VMS may also be used to provide non-traffic information, such as weather and recent news, descriptions of kidnappers, etc., but these purposes are not considered in this evaluation.

4 FSPs, or roving tow trucks or highway assistance services, are an established and relatively low-technology strategy for mitigating incidents, whose effectiveness has been confirmed under at least some conditions (Skabardonis et al., 1998). FSPs might be included in the base alternative, or treated as a separate project with its own performance parameters.

5 San Antonio does not use ramp metering or HAR, but did deploy electronic transponders in "probe" vehicles for purposes of data collection. Ramp metering should probably be evaluated as a separate project from surveillance.

6 1997 was the last year for which crash rates are published by FHWA (1998). Pedestrians are included and are 23% of fatalities. Because one crash may produce more than one injury, the fatality rate and the serious injuries rates are not strictly additive.

7 The estimated number of minor incidents averages about 23 per day, plus a few major incidents (not all of which are on the freeways), based on the TransGuide Web site (http://www.transguide.dot.state.tx.us/index.php).

8 A USDOT report (Proper, 1999) claims that the San Antonio freeway management system reduced accidents by 35%, and reduced secondary accidents by 30%. The single study cited as a source, however, did not apply data or methods that were adequate to draw these conclusions; no data were obtained, for example, on secondary accidents, and no attempt was made to distinguish secondary from primary accidents. Some of the problems in

obtaining or constructing data on secondary accidents are described in Raub (1997). The FHWA/FTA "Benefits Database" (www.benefitcost.its.dot.gov/ITS/benecost.nsf/ByLink/BenefitsHome) lists very few studies on freeway surveillance, and the limited results appear to be based on simulation, not observation of a TOC. Relationships in the ITS Deployment Analysis System (IDAS) assume that computer incident detection algorithms using vehicle detector data reduce incident duration by 4.5%, and that surveillance cameras separately reduce incident duration by 4.5%, yet there appear to be no studies measuring either factor let alone the independent effect of each one. When the effects of FSPs are added in for another 33% reduction, the sum of all three (via synergy) is claimed to be a 55% reduction in incident duration. When multiplied out, the combined effect is 39%, and since multiple systems have some redundancy in detecting the same incidents, the combined effect could be expected to be less than 39%, not more. IDAS is ostensibly based on studies in the ITS benefits database, and claims to "predict relative costs and benefits for more than 60 types of ITS investments" (IDAS Information Brochure, April 2000) including "incident detection/verification" (http://idas.camsys.com).

9 A spreadsheet model and application to the Seattle WSDOT Web site is reported in Lee (2000).

10 The VMT number is from the Maricopa Association of Governments Transportation Plan; *Highway Statistics* shows 51 million daily VMT for 1997.

11 Much of this information could be easily gathered and some of it must already exist; none was available for this study. Nee et al. (1995) report that two important factors for not using the Total Stations were (1) the equipment was slow to arrive at the scene, and (2) trained personnel were not available at the scene. Some jurisdictions store the stations in vehicles, some at an office.

12 The process of collecting and recording accident data using traditional surveying (triangulation) and the electronic surveying station are described in Nee, Koehne, and Legg (1995).

13 Respondents to the Nee et al. (1995) survey claimed that use of the stations did not require fewer people, and may not save time, but definitely provided higher accuracy and reliability; when asked about benefits, they were very positive about all forms, including improved safety and congestion reduction, but few had done any quantitative analysis and none submitted any quantitative evidence. The Washington study (Jacobson et al., 1992) used three accidents to compare times for coordinate and Total Station methods using both at the same scene, and measured 130 and 60 minutes respectively; the Kentucky study (Agent, et al., 1994) used a statistical database and estimated 198 and 115 minutes respectively.

14 One of the more detailed of the many "Lessons Learned" reports (Pearce, 2000) states "CCTV [closed-circuit television] is widely recognized as the key component that not only allows detailed determination of incident location, but also dispatch of the correct set of response resources....CCTV has also proven to be of great value in observing and resolving basic flow problems .... cellular telephones...will replace stationary vehicle detectors and incident detection algorithms [which] have never been highly effective because of the need to balance false positive readings and slow incident detection." Whether these conclusions are correct is less important here than the fact that they are based on, at best, undocumented anecdotal data. See Pearce and Subramaniam (1998) for a review of several incident management field operational tests, the report by Chang et al. (2000) evaluating an incident management program, and ITS JPO (2000) for incident management accomplishments.

15 See, for example, Casey et al. (1998).

16 Sullivan et al. (1995) offer several pages of recommendations for improving incident data.

REFERENCES

Agent, K. R., Deacon, J. A., Pigman, J. G., Stamatiadis, N., "Evaluation of Advanced Surveying Technology for Accident Investigation," Lexington, KY: University of Kentucky Transportation Center, College of Engineering, August 1994.

Carter, M., St-Onge, C., Luttrell, T., Dion, F., Riley, J., Novak, D., Cluett, C., Lappin, J., DeBlasio, A. "Metropolitan Model Deployment Initiative San Antonio Evaluation Report," prepared for USDOT FHWA/FTA Joint Program Office, draft, McClean, VA: SAIC, June 1999.

Casey, R. F., et al., "Advanced Public Transportation Systems: The State of the Art," Washington, DC: USDOT/FTA, 1998.

Chang, G., Deepak, S., Point-Du-Jour, J. Y. "Performance Evaluation of CHART in 1997: An Incident Management Program," College Park, MD: University of Maryland, May 2000.

Federal Highway Administration. *Highway Statistics 1997*, Washington, DC: USDOT/FHWA, November 1998.

Federal Highway Administration. "Motor Vehicle Accident Costs," *Technical Advisory* T7570.2, Washington, DC: USDOT/FHWA, October 31, 1994.

ITS Joint Program Office. "Incident Management Successful Practices: A Cross-Cutting Study," Washington, DC: USDOT/FHWA, April 2000.

Jacobson, L. N., Legg, B. B, O'Brien, A. "Incident Management Using Total Stations," Seattle, WA: University of Washington, Washington State Transportation Center, August 1992.

Lee, Jr., D. B., Schimek, P., Farver, J. "Benefit Cost Evaluation of ITS Projects (Draft)," prepared for USDOT FHWA/FTA Joint Program Office, Cambridge, MA: USDOT/VNTSC, October 2000.

Lee, Jr., D. B. "Benefit-Cost Evaluation of Traveler Information: Seattle's WSDOT Web site," *Transportation Research Record*, 1739, 2000, 25–34.

Nee, J., Koehne, J. L., Legg, B. B. "The Use of Total Station Surveying Equipment for Accident Reconstruction: A National Perspective," Seattle, WA: University of Washington, Washington State Transportation Center, June 1995.

Pearce, V. "What Have We Learned About Freeway, Incident, and Emergency Management and Electronic Toll Collection?," in Federal Highway Administration (ed.), *What Have We Learned About Intelligent Transportation Systems?*, 23–44, Washington, DC: USDOT/FHWA, December 2000.

Pearce, V., Subramaniam, S. "Intelligent Transportation Systems Field Operational Test Cross-Cutting Study: Detection, Verification, and Traffic Management," prepared for USDOT/FHWA ITS Joint Program Office, Washington, DC: Booz-Allen & Hamilton, September 1998.

Proper, A. T., "Intelligent Transportation Systems Benefits: 1999 Update," prepared for USDOT/FHWA, Washington, DC: Mitretek, May 1999.

Raub, R. A., "Secondary Crashes: An Important Component of Roadway Incident Management," *Transportation Quarterly*, 1997; 51, 3: 93–104.

Skabardonis, A., Petty, K., Varaiya, P. Bertini, R. "Evaluation of the Freeway Service Patrol (FSP) in Los Angeles," Berkeley, CA: Institute of Transportation Studies, University of California, September 1998.

Chapter 5

BUS AUTOMATIC VEHICLE LOCATION (AVL) SYSTEMS

Mark Hickman
Department of Civil Engineering and Engineering Mechanics, University of Arizona

This chapter provides a summary of the benefits of bus automatic vehicle location (AVL) systems. Some transit agencies have been able to exploit AVL data to improve service planning, to improve operations management, and to provide real-time bus information to passengers. These improvements have direct quantitative benefits and travel time savings that may be realized by the individual transit agency and by its passengers. In this chapter, methods for evaluating these benefits are presented. Also, recent empirical evidence from transit agencies in the United States and Europe is used to illustrate these benefits. Finally, some of the challenges to evaluating the benefits of AVL systems are highlighted.

1. INTRODUCTION

Over the past 30 years, transit agencies have been using software, hardware, and communications technology to improve service. These service improvements have included improved service reliability for passengers, better supervision of bus operations, improved scheduling, and timely passenger information about bus locations and travel times. One of the most common applications of this technology is in the area of advanced vehicle monitoring and control systems (commonly, AVM, or AVM/C). Vehicle monitoring and control systems generally use a combination of on-board electronics for vehicle diagnostics and location determination, communications with a control center, and software at the control center to monitor vehicle and system performance and to assist control center personnel to manage system operations.

This set of technologies has been called by various names over the years, but more recently has been referred to as automatic vehicle location (AVL) systems. While determining vehicle locations is a critical element, the term

AVL is used more commonly to refer to the full set of on-board, communications, and control center technology. Moreover, the primary benefits of the AVL system are in the communication and processing of that data for service monitoring, fleet management, and traveler information.

1.1 What is AVL?

The location of a bus can be known through a number of different technologies. Several recent reports document well the existing state of the practice for transit agencies in the U.S., including Okunieff (1997), Khattak and Hickman (1999), and Casey et al. (2000). The most common technology now is the Global Positioning System (GPS), a constellation of 24 satellites around the Earth that are constantly transmitting their position. Based on the triangulation of the signals from three or more satellites, an object on Earth can know its location, to a small error. The GPS signals are degraded slightly for commercial applications, but generally achieve errors that are small (within ± 50 m). Position accuracy can be improved by "differentially" correcting the GPS signals (so-called DGPS). This correction is achieved by observing the degradation pattern at a known fixed location and then applying this pattern to correct the signal received on the vehicle. This results in much greater accuracy (± 10 m).

Another technology in use primarily on older systems is a signpost system. Electronic beacons are set up at particular locations along a fixed route. In its most common mode, the beacon has a unique identifier, and transmits radio signals to a bus in its vicinity. Hence, a bus near the beacon will receive this signal and know its location within an acceptable level of accuracy. A second mode also exists in which the bus transmits a signal that is received by the local beacon, again allowing identification of the approximate location of the bus.

A third system, usually used in conjunction with a GPS or signpost system, is dead reckoning. In this case, the vehicle odometer, and in most cases compass headings, are used to identify the bus location with respect to an initial reference point (e.g., a route terminal, a depot, or a signpost).

Virtually all AVL systems include the capability of communicating the location using existing radio from the bus (or by wire from the signpost) back to a central management location during normal operations. This can be done at regular intervals ("polling") or on an exception basis. Polling is done every 60 to 120 seconds, meaning that the bus location is only updated at the control center once in this period of time. One common additional application is a "silent alarm" that allows the driver to inform the control center of the location of the bus and of an emergency on board the bus that requires assistance.

AVL systems can also be connected with small computer systems on board, called "Mobile Data Terminals" (or MDTs). These can display the current location of the bus, whether it is on schedule, and any other important messages that may be communicated between the driver and the control center.

1.2 What Can AVL be Used For?

Data on bus locations can be used for a wide variety of applications. The underlying applications of AVL information seen so far cover five broad categories (Turnbull, 1993):

- Passenger information
- Transit operations monitoring and control
- Service planning
- Air quality improvements
- Safety and security enhancement

The advantages of AVL for each of the first three bullets will be discussed in more detail in this chapter. It is useful to note that these applications have been addressed in a number of existing studies, including Morlok et al. (1993), Ball (1994), Okunieff (1997), Khattak and Hickman (1999), Goeddel (1996, 2000), and the chapter by Sullivan and Gerfen in this volume.

There are other possible social benefits that have received only modest attention, and are beyond the scope of this chapter. Most notable among these are the possible air quality improvements and the safety and security enhancements made possible by AVL. In the area of air quality, AVL may result in *direct* air quality impacts based on changes in pollutant emissions from buses, as a direct result of changes in bus operating cycles and of scheduling improvements. In addition, indirect air quality benefits may also result from changes in ridership that AVL may make possible. Perhaps without saying, these indirect effects are difficult to capture, and their overall magnitude is unknown. In terms of safety and security enhancements, there has been only very limited study and anecdotal evidence to date. This is surprising, in that often safety and security features ("silent alarms") are often one of the primary motivations for investing in AVL. Both of these possible social benefits of AVL are addressed later in this chapter in the discussion of research needs.

Perhaps given the advances in GPS technology and the large number of potential applications, the past decade has seen considerable planning and investment in AVL systems for bus transit. The motives behind this investment are largely specific to each transit agency. However, recent reviews by a number of authors suggest that there are some common themes to AVL investment (Turnbull, 1993; Hansen et al., 1994; Okunieff, 1997; Khattak and Hickman, 1999):

- *Special opportunities for funding and implementation of an AVL system.* As examples, AVL may be installed in combination with the replacement or upgrade of a mobile radio system, or in response to unique public or private funding opportunities;

- The connection of AVL as a solution to a perceived problem at the agency. Such problems could include challenges in maintaining schedule adherence, in managing operations, or in collecting service planning and performance data;
- A local champion within the organization;
- Commitment of agency management. Local agency management must be willing to commit resources to the investigation, adoption, and long-term operation of the AVL system; and,
- Organizational commitment to technological innovation.

These factors have in the past provided sufficient political and institutional justification to support investments in AVL.

1.3 Is There a Way to Value AVL Investments?

Overall, there is very strong interest in AVL investment in the United States (Casey et al., 2000), and there appear to be a wide variety of motivations for, and desired applications of, AVL. The challenge given in this chapter is to consider whether there is a way to value the possible improvements in transit service that are possible through an AVL system. This chapter provides a framework for assessing the benefits of bus AVL systems, and interprets the growing body of empirical evidence in this light.

This chapter presents this framework in the context of the three areas described previously. The next section provides a general framework for understanding the possible benefits of AVL for improved passenger information. In the area of operations monitoring and control, the third section provides an overview of the benefits of AVL data for bus operations management. The fourth section describes the benefits of AVL data within off-line applications to improve service planning. A fifth section provides some general conclusions and recommendations for additional research and evaluation.

2. PASSENGER INFORMATION

Transit agencies have been pursuing numerous strategies to provide useful service information to passengers. When pondering the use of AVL systems, it becomes possible to give passengers information on how service is *actually* delivered, not just based on the printed schedule. This means that real-time information on bus locations can be used to predict bus arrivals, to forecast travel times, and, in general, to help passengers better plan their trips.

Real-time bus arrival information is now being disseminated in a variety of cities in the U.S. and in Europe. This information is often available from a variety of media, including telephone, over the World Wide Web, through portable wireless devices, and message displays at stops and terminals. The studies by Casey et al. (2000) and Charles River Associates (2000) provide a now-dated list of agencies that are providing such information; a more comprehensive survey is beyond the scope of this report. Nonetheless, applications such as MyBus (Maclean and Dailey, 2002) and NextBus (NextBus, 2003) in the U.S., and a wide variety of European projects such as *COUNTDOWN*, *PHOEBUS*, *STOPWATCH*, and *PROMISE* (Charles River Associates, 2000) have all demonstrated the capability of providing real-time bus information to passengers.

While the technology is gradually being implemented in a variety of places, the *value* of such information, as a rationale for investment, is not well studied. The challenge in evaluating AVL systems is in determining how much this real-time passenger information makes the passenger better off. While one might generally agree that real-time bus arrival information has utility to passengers ("Is my bus running late?"), the means of determining the value of this information, in both a pre-trip and en-route context, is a continuing area of research. Also, as another application, archived AVL data can also be used to inform passengers about bus service more generally, to improve pre-trip decision-making. The value of AVL data for real-time information, and for passenger itinerary planning, is described below.

2.1 Passenger Valuation of Real-time Bus Information

The general principle in evaluating passenger information services is that travelers derive both intrinsic benefit from information, and that they may use that information in ways that allows them to make better travel choices. The benefits of information can be characterized in a number of different ways. From a purely prescriptive approach, Hickman and Wilson (1995) present an evaluation of real-time information for path choices and travel time savings in a transit corridor. This model used a mathematical approach to model passenger decision-making with real-time bus arrival and travel time information. This evaluation showed that the potential changes in passenger path choices from real-time information were substantial. However, the net travel time savings were likely to be small, on the order of one to two percent of the total travel time. While this result was based on a prescriptive path choice model, it provided a preliminary assessment of the potential travel time savings from real-time passenger information.

Most of the remaining work has been more behavioral (or descriptive) in nature. The most common framework for valuing information is in determining how that information affects a passenger's utility of travel. More specifically, the utility of different travel alternatives may be affected by information. Also, the simple availability of information itself may improve travelers' utilities.

In the traditional economic notion of utility, traveler information is seen as a commodity that provides additional value to the traveler. The utility of a travel alternative is modeled as a function of the traveler's attributes, given as a vector Z_n for a traveler n, and of the attributes of the selected travel alternative, given as a vector X_{in} for alternative i for traveler n (Ben-Akiva and Lerman, 1985). For a linear specification of utility, and assuming random error in measuring utility (i.e., a random utility model), one obtains:

$$U_{in} = \alpha_i + \beta_1 Z_n + \beta_2 X_{in} + \varepsilon_{in}$$

where
U_{in} = utility of alternative i to traveler n
α_i = constant for alternative i
Z_n = attributes of traveler n
X_{in} = attributes of alternative i to traveler n
β_1, β_2 = vectors of coefficients
ε_{in} = random component of utility for alternative i to traveler n

In this context, utility can be shown to be improved by information if the information results in:

- An increased awareness of travel choices, bringing additional alternatives into the traveler's choice set;
- A change in the value of particular trip variables (the X_{in}), such as travel times, service reliability, information availability for the trip, or other quantitative values in the utility function (including any choice-specific constants); or,
- A change in the perception or valuation of particular trip variables (the β's).

AVL data, translated into real-time bus arrival information, may affect the values of particular trip variables (the X's) or the valuation of those variables (the β's). Each of these two possibilities, which illustrate the main value of real-time bus information over traditional static information, is discussed here.

2.1.1 Change in Trip-Related Variables

In a random utility model, the attributes of the given travel alternative (the X_{in}) could include either or both of (1) travel times and service reliability variables, or (2) some variable capturing attributes of the real-time information directly. In the case of (1), having more accurate information on the *actual* travel time, or on the reliability of the service, may lead a traveler to value transit service or a transit route more highly. Changes in travel time and service reliability, if explicitly included among the alternative-specific variables (the X_{in}), can lead to changes in the traveler's utility. If variables such as service reliability are not included explicitly in the utility function for specific routes or modes, this attribute may be reflected in the alternative-specific constant α_i. In the case of (2), if attributes of the real-time information are explicitly included in the X_{in}, then the provision of real-time information to a traveler will directly affect their utility of a transit alternative.

As with other variables in the utility specification, the utility may change directly as information is provided.

The utility-related benefits can be explicitly valued in a number of ways, but the most common measures are: (1) an equivalent monetary value of the real-time information; and/or, (2) an associated increase in ridership. Consistent with utility theory, the equivalent monetary value of the change in utility can be found using the ratio of coefficients in the utility function. If β_c is the coefficient of a cost term, and β_i is the coefficient of any variable describing real-time information, the monetary value of information is determined by the ratio of the coefficients, or:

$$\text{Value of information} = \frac{\beta_i}{\beta_c} \quad \text{in \$/unit of information}$$

The most compelling evidence to date of this value of information has been shown in a number of European tests. The London Bus *COUNTDOWN* system provides real-time information on bus arrival times at bus stops on several bus routes in London, and is being deployed citywide. From various stated preference surveys conducted with *COUNTDOWN*, valuation of passenger's willingness-to-pay, the real-time information was valued at between 20 to 26 pence per trip (approximately \$0.30 to \$0.40 U.S.). In a related survey with stated preferences trading off higher fares for real-time information, a comparable value of information of 20 pence was found. This put the value of information at about 53 percent of the average fare (Smith et al., 1994). Similar user valuations of real-time information were 50 cents (EU) for the *PROMISE* program in Helsinki (cited in Charles River Associates, 2000). Both of these experiments give credibility to this method of passenger valuation of information.

Alternately, if the value of a particular variable is changed by real-time information, e.g., an estimate of travel time or waiting time is changed from X_0 to X_1 by the information, then the net value of the information to the passenger is given by:

$$\text{Value of information} = \frac{\beta_x (X_1 - X_0)}{\beta_c} \quad \text{in \$}$$

In the initial Route 18 demonstration of the *COUNTDOWN* system, passengers believed that their average waiting time had dropped from 11.9 to 8.6 minutes. A significant majority (65 percent) of passengers on Route 18 believed that their waiting time had decreased as a result of the *COUNTDOWN* system. Smaller percentages (21 percent–24 percent) were observed on other bus routes. These perceptions had changed, even though the actual waiting times had not changed (Smith et al., 1994). These findings illustrate that information has utility value to passengers, through the amount of time spent waiting.

If the random utility model is used to describe travel choices (e.g., in mode or route choice), the increase in utility from real-time information may also increase travelers' propensity to use transit. This could be observed empirically as higher bus ridership, or estimated using sample enumeration (Ben-Akiva and Lerman, 1985). Once ridership impacts are known, this can be quantified using a social benefit calculation. The net social benefit of a transit rider can be calculated by a number of techniques; see the extensive and recent summaries on the valuation of net benefits of transit provided by Small (1993) and ECONorthwest (2002). The net social benefit per rider is calculated and then multiplied by the number of new riders attributed to the real-time information system.

To date, there appears to be mixed evidence on the effect of real-time passenger information systems on system ridership. The *PHOEBUS* project in Brussels and Angoulème showed a 5.8 percent increase in ridership on routes equipped with real-time information about passenger waiting times (cited in Charles River Associates, 2000). On the other hand, the preliminary assessment of the *COUNTDOWN* project in London (Atkins, 1994; Smith et al, 1994), the *STOPWATCH* project in Southampton (cited in Sheikh, 1998), and the TravLink project in the U.S. (Cambridge Systematics, 1996) suggest that little to no noticeable changes in ridership are observed. This somewhat spotty evidence to date suggests that an important area of future research is the evaluation of ridership changes due to real-time information.

Indirectly, it could be there is no change in transportation mode or in the number trips made, but there is better planning of non-transport uses of time, or it could be that an alternative route choice may provide increased value to the passenger. The problem is AVL can affect non-transport choices and add value, but we generally monitor transport variables and see no perceptible change and therefore conclude that no value was added. This may indicate that we are not using an appropriate metric.

2.1.2 Changes in Perception or Valuation of Trip Attributes

A second way in which real-time transit information can affect passenger utility is through passenger valuation of travel attributes. As an example, it is well known that transit waiting time is typically valued by passengers two to three times higher than comparable in-vehicle (riding) time. This difference in valuation appears in the utility function in the coefficients (the elements of the β_2 vector). That is, the coefficient on waiting time is typically two to three times larger in magnitude than the coefficient on in-vehicle time.

The relative magnitude of coefficient of waiting time has generally been attributed to the level of discomfort and uncertainty experienced by the passenger during waiting. If some of the onerous nature of waiting time can be reduced, then travelers would not value the time as highly, relative to other travel time attributes. This is reflected in a smaller magnitude of the coefficient on waiting time, though it would still be expected to be negative.

The provision of real-time information, in this case, is a direct benefit to travelers. That is, passengers would experience economic benefits due to increased utility experienced in waiting time. This increase in utility would be reflected in two possible ways: (1) an explicit monetary gain to travelers, determined in the same manner as before; or, (2) in explicit increases in transit ridership. The former option (1) appears in the following valuation, as the coefficient on X changes from β_0 to β_1:

$$\text{Value of information} = \frac{(\beta_1 - \beta_0)X}{\beta_c} \quad \text{in \$}$$

In the evidence to date, it is not possible *directly* to separate this effect from the change in perception of waiting time described previously. Instead, it is possible that *both* the perceived waiting time *and* the valuation of that waiting time, are changing. For example, the evidence from the *COUNTDOWN* system shows a change in passengers' *perceived* waiting time, which directly affects their utility. At the same time, the passengers also considered waiting time less onerous: "... 83 percent of respondents agreed that if you know when the bus is coming the time seems to pass more quickly and 89 percent agreed that the display made the waiting time more acceptable." (Smith et al., 1994, p. 3053). Similar observations about changes in passenger valuation of waiting time have been observed in a number of U.S. operational tests, particularly in Seattle (cited in Charles River Associates, 2000) and in the TravLink operational test (Cambridge Systematics, 1996).

One might expect that changed valuation of waiting time would also result in a higher probability of choosing a transit mode or a transit route, and hence would be revealed as higher ridership. Again, this can be determined using the net social benefit of transit ridership, multiplied by the observed or estimated change in ridership. The lack of conclusive evidence to date on ridership changes due to real-time information suggests that more research in this area is needed.

2.2 AVL Data for Improved Itinerary Planning

AVL data may also be used by travelers to improve itinerary planning. A recent method using archived AVL data for itinerary planning has been developed by Hickman (2002), following on related work (although not explicitly tied to AVL data) by Hall (1982, 1983, and 1986) and Wellman et al. (1995). In Hickman's method, the AVL data can be used to examine the variability of travel times between the passenger's origin and destination. This variability in travel times is caused by the natural variation in bus travel times during normal operation. With this information, though, the passenger may make a more informed decision about the value of different paths for her trip: e.g., when to arrive at the stop, the likely timing of any transfers, and the variability of the arrival time at the destination. This is especially important if the passenger values service or travel time reliability. Hickman (2002) has used the AVL data to identify the "shortest" paths, and gives some examples of how this information can be presented to passengers to provide useful pre-trip itinerary planning information. While there has been no formal evaluation of the utility benefits of this information, this is an application of AVL data that is currently under investigation.

3. OPERATIONS MANAGEMENT

The concept of operations management and control is founded on the principle of improving service by enhancing service reliability. In general, service reliability implies that one is trying to keep fixed-route service on a given schedule (i.e., improving schedule adherence), or alternately, to maintain regular headways on the route. Bus AVL systems have been shown to have two major influences on operations: (1) the service tends to run closer to schedule, due to better monitoring of service by drivers and dispatchers; and, (2) more advanced operations control strategies can be employed to maintain service reliability.

3.1 Framework of Passenger Benefits from Service Reliability

The general objective of operations management is to improve the level of service to the passenger. Passenger waiting time is affected by schedule adherence and passenger waiting time. As a result, the most common passenger-related measure of benefit from service reliability is the passenger waiting time. Welding (1957) showed that the expected waiting time for a randomly arriving passenger is a function of both the expected headway of the service and the coefficient of variation of the headway. This is given in the following formula:

$$E[W] = \frac{E[H]}{2} \cdot \left(1 + \frac{Var[H]}{E^2[H]}\right) = \frac{E[H]}{2} \cdot \left(1 + COV^2[H]\right)$$

where:
$E[W]$ = Expected waiting time
$E[H]$ = Expected (average) headway
$Var[H]$ = Variance of the headway
$COV[H]$ = Coefficient of variation of the headway

When passengers do not arrive randomly, the expected waiting time is based on the ability of the route to maintain a regular schedule. Bus departures, for headways over 15 minutes, may be expected to occur at the scheduled departure time. In many cases, an "on-time" departure is defined as a bus departure within 0–5 minutes of its scheduled time. Early departures (before the scheduled time) have obvious waiting time penalties for passengers who arrive after the bus departs but before the schedule time: they must then wait an additional headway until the next bus arrives. Lateness greater than some threshold (five minutes, for example) also results in excess passenger waiting time, if the passenger coordinates her arrival at the stop with the bus schedule.

A method for estimating the waiting times for this passenger arrival pattern was given by Turnquist (1978) and revisited by Bowman and Turnquist (1981). In a combination of analytic and empirical results, this research estimated the expected waiting time as a function of the passenger arrival behavior at the stop and of the variability of schedule departure times at the stop. Significant changes in behavior were noted for longer-headway service (20-minute headways), since passengers coordinated their arrivals with the schedule. Passenger arrival times at the stop and the resulting waiting time were strongly correlated with the standard deviation of the bus departure times from the stop. In their example, average passenger waiting times for the 20-minute service were observed to decrease by 0.7 to 1 minute for each 0.5 minute decrease in the standard deviation of the bus arrival times (Bowman and Turnquist, 1981).

In both cases, of random and non-random arrivals, reductions in passenger waiting time are possible through reductions in the variability of bus arrival and departure times, or through reductions in the variability of headways. In turn, there are obvious economic benefits from a reduction in average waiting time: a reduction in time spent waiting results in a clear economic gain for the passenger. These savings can be assessed by multiplying the passengers' value of waiting time by the reduction in waiting time.

A second method of evaluating the benefits of improved schedule adherence is through explicit valuation in passengers' utility, or in passenger ridership. In the passenger utility framework presented previously, service reliability would take the form of an additional trip-related variable (or set of variables, the X_{in}), to reflect the impact of reliability on mode and route choices. One might obviously expect service reliability to affect traveler behavior. However, to date, there has been very limited direct evaluation of passengers' economic valuation of service reliability. The framework developed by Abkowitz (1980) provides some insight for future research in this area, in a random utility (mode choice) context.

Kimpel et al. (2000), using data from Portland TriMet's AVL system, introduced an alternate framework for ridership impacts of schedule reliability. This model estimates stop-level boardings as a function of the variance of delay at the stop. The variability of bus arrivals at time points on each route were generated using weekday bus operations data from TriMet's AVL system. A set of simultaneous equations were estimated, with equations for: (1) boardings as a function of the variance of departure delay or headway delay, among other variables; (2) mean scheduled headway as a function of load, to account for bus capacity effects; and, (3) headway variability or departure delay variability as a function of the scheduled headway, the boarding variability, the number of stops, and other related variables. In estimating stop-level boardings, a significant negative coefficient was observed for the headway variability and departure time variability. The value of the coefficient implied that a 10 percent reduction in the variability measure would result in an increase of 0.17 boardings per stop (Kimpel et al., 2000). While this value is unique to the Portland case study, it nonetheless suggests that ridership gains can be estimated using AVL data and through clear improvements in service reliability.

3.2 Benefits from Improved Schedule Adherence from AVL

In examining improvements in schedule adherence, many agencies in the United States have reported that service reliability, in the form of schedule adherence, has improved considerably simply from the implementation of AVL. That is, even without enhanced decision-making or operations control, drivers and supervisors are simply more effective at maintaining the schedule with the AVL system in place. This has the effect of reducing the variability of headways and/or of increasing the percentage of buses that are adhering to schedule. One would then assume that this would result in lower passenger waiting time.

The empirical evidence on improved schedule adherence is considerable. Table 1 lists a number of agencies that have documented the improvements in schedule adherence and headway maintenance simply from having an AVL system in place. Note that the phrase "on-time" may have a number of different meanings; a common interpretation is that the bus is 0–5 minutes late, although this is not a standard. From the table, substantial improvements (5–10 percent) in on-time performance can be attributed simply to the use of an AVL system.

Table 1. Schedule Adherence and Headway Maintenance Improvements from AVL

Transit Agency	Improvements Attributed to AVL Implementation
Baltimore, MD	On-time percentage grew by 23% on three routes in a system test
Denver, CO	On-time percentage grew from 88.0% to 89.6%
Hamilton, ON	On-time percentage grew from 82% to 89%
Kansas City, MO	On-time percentage grew from 80% to 90%, with 21% reduction in late buses and 12% reduction in early buses
Milwaukee, WI	On-time percentage grew from 90% to 94%, with a 28% drop in buses more than one minute late
Portland, OR	On-time percentage grew from 69% to 78% after installation in 1997. Further schedule changes using AVL data improved on-time percentage to 83%
	Bus bunching (headways under 70% of desired value) dropped by 15% on eight routes
	Average bus running times declined by 3.15%, or 1.45 minutes on average, for eight routes

Source: Transit ITS Impacts Matrix, Mitretek Systems, 2002. Some Portland results are also mirrored in the work of Strathman et al. (1999, 2000).

A more thorough assessment of the value of AVL for improved operations has been conducted by researchers at Portland State University in conjunction with Portland's TriMet (Strathman et al., 1999, 2000, 2002). The research reported in Strathman et al. (1999, 2000) reflects an analysis of headway variability, running time variability, and waiting time for passengers on eight routes at TriMet. The study examined these statistics for each of the routes, and also looked at different time periods (a.m. peak, p.m. peak, mid-day, and evening hours).

Interestingly, across the set of routes, the on-time performance increased substantially during the a.m. peak and p.m. peak periods, with more modest improvements in mid-day and no improvement for evening service. Waiting time improvements, however, were only noticed for the p.m.[1] peak period, with a 28 percent reduction in "excess" waiting time (i.e., waiting time due to headway variance). In the other periods, no reductions in waiting time were observed. What was found was that the headway distribution had shifted to the right: there was a significant reduction in "early" departures (before the scheduled time), and an increase in late departures. This explains in part why on-time performance was improved, but waiting time was not improved, in some cases (Strathman et al., 1999, 2000). This phenomenon deserves further analysis, but suggests that the intuition that on-time percentages translate directly into reductions in waiting time may not always be true.

Across all routes, the average waiting time reduction was observed to be 0.11 minutes per passenger, or about seven percent of the "excess" waiting time. Passenger in-vehicle time and bus running times were estimated to decrease by slightly over three percent (Table 1). Using these estimates of time savings, these were translated into monetary benefits, using corresponding values of time. This technique suggests that the capitalized savings from AVL can be significant, on the order of millions of dollars (Strathman et al., 1999, 2000).

3.3 Benefits of Operations Control Actions Using AVL Data

Whether in the form of improving schedule adherence or headway regularity, there are some common operations control strategies that are used (Levinson, 1991):[1]

- Hold an early vehicle at a stop
- Reduce layover times at terminals
- Provide a standby (or relief) vehicle, or divert a vehicle from another route
- Re-route the vehicle in any of the following ways:
  a) Let a following vehicle overtake
  b) Have the vehicle skip stops
  c) Send the vehicle empty to another part of the route

The particular set of strategies employed at an agency depends on the level of complexity and uncertainty in operating conditions. In most cases, any control actions taken at an agency are applied using only the driver or supervisor's best judgment or general ad-hoc rules. However, AVL data can be used to improve operations control actions.

The challenge in evaluating the benefits of operations control involves the measurement of passenger waiting times when control actions are implemented. Of the few research efforts to address this directly, Abkowitz and Lepofsky (1990) measured the benefits of holding control actions along several bus routes in Boston. Reductions in the standard deviation of headways were observed at several locations along each route, with resulting reductions of approximately eight percent in the passenger waiting time on route. The study also showed the challenges of collecting operations control data at time points along a bus route, in the absence of AVL data.

The research of Strathman et al. (2001) documented improvements in transit service during operations control actions at TriMet. In the experiment, holding actions for a set of six routes were coordinated at a common dispatch terminal. Both "with holding" and "without holding" cases were evaluated; in the "with holding" case, field supervisors were asked to record their holding decisions. In both cases, the AVL system was used to record headways and headway variability at downstream timepoints on each route. The results indicated that there were some reductions in headway variation near the control point, but these benefits deteriorated as buses moved further away from the control point. However, the net improvements in passenger waiting times were not statistically significant, so that no explicit benefits were identified. Nonetheless, the researchers provided a useful method for the empirical evaluation of bus control strategies.[2]

In part due to the challenges of field data collection, the most common evaluation technique for operations control strategies is through simple analytic methods and through Monte Carlo simulation. The predominant transit control policy that has been evaluated is the strategy of holding vehicles at certain stops to maintain headway or schedule regularity. The particular holding strategy (or strategies) employed depends on a route's operating conditions, including the volume and distribution of passengers along the route, the frequency of service, the variability of route running times and passenger loads, and other factors. Common holding techniques include threshold-based and schedule-based holding. The threshold technique involves holding a vehicle only if the preceding headway is below a certain amount of time (e.g., the desired headway); in this case, the vehicle is held only until the threshold time and then dispatched. On the other hand, schedule-based holding involves holding a vehicle only until its scheduled departure time and dispatching it immediately if it arrives later than this scheduled time. Typically, the objective of threshold- or schedule-based holding strategies is to minimize either the downstream passenger waiting time or some combination of downstream waiting time and the delay to passengers already on board.

Barnett (1974) developed a simple analytic model to show the benefits of a threshold policy on passenger waiting times. The work of Turnquist and Blume (1980) and Turnquist (1981) examines more specifically the conditions under which a threshold model is likely to produce benefits by reducing passenger waiting and travel time. Using an analytic model, the research found that the benefits of holding are highest when the headway coefficient of variation (COV) is high and/or when the ratio of on-board passengers to expected downstream passengers is small. They note that this is somewhat conflicting: headway COV tends to increase along the route, while the ratio of on-board to downstream waiting passengers tends to decrease. Hence, the choice of a holding station is not entirely obvious. The research concludes that control should be enacted at a stop where there is already substantial variation in headways, the vehicle load is light, and the number of downstream passengers is significant. These results on the selection of control sites were echoed in a number of subsequent simulation studies cited below.

A large literature on transit vehicle holding has developed using heuristics and Monte Carlo simulation. This approach is appealing because bus operations on a transit route are inherently stochastic and hence difficult to describe analytically. Examples of route-level simulations that examine threshold- and schedule-based holding strategies are shown in Table 2. More recent models by Zhao et al. (2001), Hickman (2001), and Fu and Wang (2002) have employed analytic methods to determine optimal holding times, but have used Monte Carlo simulation models to illustrate the potential benefits.[3]

Table 2. Selected Simulation Studies of Bus Operations Control

Simulation Study	Findings	Comments
Koffman (1978)	Reductions in waiting time for on-route holding (3-13%) Waiting time reductions from control of dispatch times at terminals was about 7% Skipping stops produces higher wait times (up 38% over base case), which exceeds the benefit to line-haul time	Investigated holding control, dispatching control, skip stop service, and bus signal priority Headway-based control for holding Illustrated using a bus route in Cambridge, MA
Andersson et al. (1979)	Average 8% reduction in passenger waiting time with simple holding action	Headway-based control for holding Scenario based on a bus route in Stockholm
Abkowitz and Engelstein (1984)	Average percent reduction in waiting time depended on route, ranging from 0% on one route, 3% on another, and 11–15% on the third Results dependent on the downstream boarding pattern	Headway-based control for holding Calibration data from bus routes in Cincinnati and applied with validation to 3 routes in Los Angeles Used a weighted combination of waiting time and in-vehicle time for determining the optimal threshold
Abkowitz, Eiger and Engelstein (1986)	Effect of holding control in reducing waiting time diminishes as bus moves downstream of control point 3–10% reduction in waiting times, depending on passenger loading profile	Headway-based control for holding Hypothetical bus route using a validated operations model from AVM system data from Los Angeles Used waiting time to determine optimal threshold and control stop
Abkowitz and Tozzi (1986)	1–3% reduction in waiting times for higher relative weights on waiting time than for in-vehicle time Waiting time benefits depend on passenger loading profile, from 1%–8% for heavier downstream loading Greater waiting time benefits (up to 11%) when dispatch headways have higher variability	Headway-based control for holding Scenario based on a bus route in Los Angeles Used a weighted combination of waiting time and in-vehicle time to determine optimal threshold
Vandebona and Richardson (1986)	Examined different thresholds for holding Waiting time minimized by using higher thresholds for dispatch Generalized time measure minimized when keeping scheduled time as threshold	Headway-based control for holding Scenario used a branching bus route in Melbourne, Australia Used a weighted combination of waiting time and in-vehicle time to evaluate thresholds
Senevirante (1990)	Illustrated methods to select bus control points using a threshold standard deviation of headways	Schedule-based control for holding Scenario based on a bus route in Halifax, Nova Scotia

Simulation Study	Findings	Comments
Lin et al. (1995)	Headway-based control more effective at reducing waiting time than schedule-based control, at 5 min. headways Higher headway thresholds reduce waiting time, increase bus running time and passenger in-vehicle travel time Stop skipping greatly increases passenger waiting time with only modest gains in in-vehicle travel time	Both headway-based and schedule-based control or holding Scenario used hypothetical bus route Used a weighted combination of waiting time, in-vehicle time, and bus operating cost to evaluate control strategies
Rossetti and Turitto (1998)	Threshold strategy works well in reducing passenger waiting times, with potentially large penalties to on-board passengers Optimal holding times tend to out-perform threshold strategy in reducing delay to on-board passengers, although overall system time may increase	Headway-based and optimal holding times determined using a weighted combination of waiting time and in-vehicle time Scenario used hypothetical bus route
Hickman (2001)	3.5% reduction in waiting times with holding control, falls to 2.3% in considering delay to on-board passengers 20% reduction in "excess" waiting times, above minimum waiting times with no variability of headways (drops to 13.4% in considering delay to on-board passengers) Waiting time reductions depend on weight on in-vehicle time	Optimal holding strategy determined using a weighted combination of waiting time and in-vehicle time Scenario used hypothetical bus route
Zhao et al. (2001)	Generalized time reduced by up to 10% for 5 min. headway service, 8% for 10 min. headways, 4% for 15 to 20 min. headways, and dropping to 2–3% for 30 min. headways	Used multi-agent systems (agent negotiation), as a combination of waiting time and in-vehicle time, to determine best holding strategy Scenario used hypothetical bus route
Fu and Yang (2002)	Generalized travel time improvements of 10%, with greater percentage reductions in passenger waiting time (up to 24%) Stronger headway control results in slower bus travel times on the route	Headway-based control for holding Investigated both a simple threshold model and an optimal holding value Scenario used a bus route in Waterloo, Ontario Used a weighted combination of waiting time and in-vehicle time

Generally, these simulation and analytical studies have concluded that threshold-based holding is more effective than schedule-based holding, at least for services with short headways where passenger arrivals are random. Nonetheless, both methods offer substantial improvements over no holding at all. As can be seen in Table 2, typical reductions in passenger waiting times for these holding strategies are on the order of 3–10 percent of the total passenger waiting time. These represent direct benefits to transit passengers.

At the same time, the results from the simulations suggest that there are also costs that are not explicitly included in most control strategies. Specifically, it is important to include the following items in the accounting of net benefits:

- Benefits due to reductions in waiting time
- Losses due to additional in-vehicle time for passengers on board during control actions
- Increases in bus running time, which ultimately affect the number of vehicles and operators required to serve a bus route

Recent simulation studies of bus operations control do not to consider bus operating costs explicitly. Some of the existing simulation results suggest that substantial increases in bus running times are possible with more aggressive holding control strategies. This is most likely to be true with the headway-based holding strategies, as the threshold values can result in more substantial increases in bus travel times. The more recent optimization methods, given in Hickman (2001), Zhao et al. (2001), and Fu and Yang (2002), generally do not share these significant increases in bus running times with the optimal holding strategies.

4. SERVICE PLANNING

A number of studies have explored the benefits of AVL for enhancing long-term service planning and performance. At a macroscopic level, Gillen, Chang, and Johnson (2000) have investigated transit agencies in the U.S. that implemented AVL systems between 1988 and 1997. Using federal transit statistics collected in the National Transit Database, they examined total factor productivity of transit agencies that implemented AVL, relative to a peer control group of agencies that had not. Using measures of service production and consumption, the authors noted that AVL had a positive impact on ridership, as measured by both passenger trips and passenger miles. Improvements in productivity were also noted in service outputs such as increases in vehicle revenue miles and reductions in fleet size requirements. Also, the operating cost per vehicle mile, and the annual maintenance hours, were reduced for agencies that had implemented AVL. The observations of this study were largely statistical, and no causal factors could be inferred as to how AVL was able to provide these productivity improvements.

In addition, recent reports by Morlok, Bruun, and Blackman (1993), Ball (1994), and Goeddel (1996, 2000) have examined the economic feasibility of

AVL. These studies have generally cited the likely benefits of AVL for service planning activities: reductions in fleet size, savings in operating costs, and ridership and ensuing revenue gains due to improvements in the level of service. These studies did not specifically investigate the causal factors behind these AVL benefits. Rather, they used a combination of empirical results and engineering judgment to estimate the potential benefits of AVL for service planning. These benefits, in turn, were used to estimate the economic feasibility of AVL using breakeven analysis. Various financing methods were also investigated by Morlok et al. (1993) and Ball (1994).

This section reviews some of the observations made by these previous authors, but with the intent to look more closely at causality and specific economic gains attributed to AVL. For this, the service planning and performance monitoring tasks may be decomposed into the following two areas: (1) monitoring and improving service reliability; and (2) scheduling and fleet sizing effects. In this section, the potential benefits in each of these areas are detailed, and recent evidence from AVL system deployments are described.

4.1 Monitoring and Improving Service Reliability

Surprisingly, the capabilities for transit agencies to archive AVL data, and subsequently to use the data for service evaluation, is not widely practiced in the United States (Furth, 2000). However, several agencies have been successful at overcoming the data management challenges to exploit historical AVL data. In these cases, use of the archived AVL data may reduce the cost of data collection for service planning. Most commonly, AVL data are used to analyze bus travel times and schedule adherence (Furth, 2000). The argument is made that the use of the AVL data in this way can result in cost savings when compared to more traditional, manual data collection methods. The summary by Mitretek Systems (2002) includes reported savings of $40,000 (Atlanta) to $50,000 (London, Ontario) per travel time survey. There are clear cost reductions to this form of automated data collection, when there is institutional and technical support for the archiving and analysis of AVL data.

The benefits of AVL realized for improving service reliability are described earlier in this chapter. Generally, AVL-related improvements in service reliability may result in direct reductions in passenger waiting time, and resulting improvements in passenger utility and increases in transit ridership. These are the most obvious long-term benefits for passengers of the AVL system. General ridership and revenue gains that have been attributed to service improvements from AVL are listed in Table 3. While the exact causes of these ridership improvements from AVL is not known, it is generally held that these improvements are due to improved service reliability resulting from AVL and improved dispatching at each transit agency. When combined with the results presented previously, there appears to be some general consensus that small increases in ridership, on the order of one to five percent, are possible with more concerted use of AVL data to improve service reliability.

Table 3. Ridership Gains Attributed to AVL

Transit Agency	Ridership Gains Attributed to AVL
Denver, CO	5.1% increase in ridership systemwide from 1995 to 1996
Milwaukee, WI	4.8% increase in system revenues between 1993 and 1997
Toronto, Ontario	0.5% to 1% estimated systemwide increase in ridership due to AVL

Source: Transit ITS Impacts Matrix, Mitretek Systems, 2002

4.2 Scheduling and Fleet Size Impacts of AVL

4.2.1 Scheduling

With AVL, the improvements in schedule adherence noted previously could also be combined with improvements in the longer-term scheduling process. Data from the AVL system can be used to collect travel time and schedule adherence data, and subsequent analysis can indicate where the schedules can be adjusted to improve operating efficiency (Furth, 2000). Moreover, reductions in bus running times and bus layover times can result in a reduction in the number of buses serving the route, or in improved scheduling to provide more frequent service.

An important principle in service reliability is the use of slack time in a given route schedule. This can take two different forms. First, transit agencies may insert some slack time in the schedule at selected time points along the route. This allows the bus to make up any time if it is running late while traveling along the route. Second, this slack time may also be inserted at the route terminal, resulting in layover time, before the bus continues on its next trip. This layover time at the terminal includes two elements. First, there must be sufficient time for vehicle and crew recovery: any break for the operator, time to prepare the bus for its next trip, and time for passengers to alight and board. Second, time may be added to the schedule to allow some additional time in case the bus arrives late from its previous trip.

Generally, the total slack time on route is determined by local policy, but often involves adding considerable time to a run, particularly if the route is long and prone to run late over particular segments of the route. The layover time at the terminal, on the other hand, typically involves more formal procedures, where the layover time is determined using some common rules of thumb, such as: (1) using the median bus arrival time at the terminal plus allowances for bus and crew change (Levinson, 1991); (2) adding 10 percent to the average running time (Transportation Management and Design, 1998); or, (3) using a 95 percent confidence interval on the bus arrival time at the terminal (Strathman et al., 2002). In total, the combination of on-route and layover time at the route terminals results in a considerable amount of time added to the vehicle schedule.

In the recent work by Strathman et al. (2002), a methodology is described to analyze AVL data to improve vehicle scheduling. Data on actual bus running times and running time variance from Portland TriMet were used to analyze the effectiveness of existing schedule running times and layover times. The scheduling standards at TriMet are such that the scheduled running time should be equal to the median observed running time, and that the total layover time should be equal to the difference between the 95th percentile and the median values from the running time distribution. This analysis of AVL data suggested that adjustments could be made to the running and layover times on a number of routes to bring them in line with these service standards. In some cases, excess running and layover time could be cut sufficiently (explained below) to allow the savings of a bus from the schedule without a reduction in the passenger level of service (Strathman et al., 2002). Such scheduling improvements can result in substantial cost savings, either through reductions in bus operating hours or through reductions in the number of buses serving a route.

4.2.2 Bus Fleet Size Improvements

The number of vehicles required to operate a headway of h on a route, for a given travel time T on the route, is given by:[4]

$$N = \left\lceil \frac{T}{h} \right\rceil = \left\lceil \frac{T_{run} + T_{slack}}{h} \right\rceil$$

where:
N = number of buses
T = total travel time, including running time T_{run} and slack time T_{slack}
h = headway

$\lceil\ \rceil$ = integer ceiling function; i.e. rounded to the next higher integer

Hence, if slack time is reduced, it is possible that the total number of buses can be reduced. The total time savings necessary to reduce the number of buses could be anywhere in the range from 0 to h, depending on how much rounding is involved. However, it can be observed that saving a time of h from the slack time and the running time would result in a decrease of one bus on the route.

If the AVL system is capable of improving schedule reliability and/or reducing bus running time to the point of reducing the number of buses on a route, two benefits may result. First, from the perspective of operations, both vehicle and crew costs can be reduced. Second, it is also possible that the vehicle and crew savings can be capitalized, meaning that fewer operators and/or fewer buses are needed in the long term. Capital cost savings may thus be realized. Alternately, the transit agency may choose to simply re-allocate vehicles and crews to other routes, resulting in no capital cost savings but a realization of benefits in the form of service improvements on other routes. In either case, the capital and operating costs represent benefits to the agency.

The most commonly cited empirical evidence on fleet size savings is from the Kansas City (MO) Area Transportation Authority (KCATA). Through improvements in on-time performance and resulting schedule adjustments, KCATA was able to reduce running times by 10 percent, and, as a result, realized a reduction in operations requirements by seven buses out of a fleet of 200. This amounted to a reduction in capital costs of $225,000 per bus (total of $1.575 million), with ongoing annual maintenance cost savings of $27,000 per bus per year (total of $189,000 per year) and associated labor cost savings of $215,000 per year (cited in Mitretek Systems, 2002). While these results may not be typical, reductions in fleet requirements due to improved scheduling and service monitoring with AVL data can be considerable.

5. CONCLUSIONS AND RESEARCH DIRECTIONS

This chapter has given a broad overview of the benefits of AVL systems. In addition to reviewing the primary benefits that have been observed, some of the more direct factors leading to these benefits have also been described. At this time, there is still much left to be learned about the uses of AVL data and the way in which these data can be exploited to enhance transit operations, planning, and passenger information. In many respects, this is still very much a growing field of study and application. A brief summary of the main findings to date is given below, followed by a discussion of some of the major research directions.

5.1 What Do We Know?

Table 4 gives a brief taxonomy and summary of the results presented in this chapter. The general state of the art seems to be that there are quantitative economic benefits of bus AVL systems. If the AVL data are used to create estimates of bus arrival times at bus stops, there is strong evidence that passengers perceive real increases in travel utility, reflected in reduced "costs" of waiting time and, possibly, some slight increases in ridership and revenue for the transit agency. However, there has been relatively little direct empirical evidence of these benefits to date.

Table 4. Taxonomy and Summary of Findings

Area of Benefits	Measures of Benefits	Findings
Passenger Information: Value of information	Utility or equivalent monetary value of information	Limited empirical evaluation Real-time information may reduce perceived waiting times, value of waiting time Net perceived passenger value of \$0.40 to \$0.50 per trip
Passenger Information: Ridership	Ridership changes	Limited empirical evaluation of direct effects of information on ridership
Operations Management: Monitoring	Schedule adherence Headway regularity Passenger waiting times Passenger in-vehicle times Bus running times	5–10% improvements in bus on-time performance are commonly observed Little empirical evidence on waiting time reductions from monitoring Limited empirical evidence on the effect of AVL on bus running times
Operations Management: Control strategies	Schedule adherence Headway regularity Passenger waiting times Passenger in-vehicle times Bus running times	Little empirical evidence on waiting time reductions from operations control Simulation results suggest: 1–5% reductions in waiting times from AVL-based holding control actions Small increases in passenger on-board delays and bus running times
Service Planning: Service monitoring	Data collection costs Ridership Same measures as Operations Management	Limited evidence suggests \$40,000 to \$50,000 reduction in travel time data collection costs, per survey wave Limited empirical evidence on ridership gains that can be attributed to AVL capabilities
Service Planning: Scheduling	Schedule efficiencies with bus and operator hours Fleet size requirements	Limited published evidence to date on AVL-based analysis of schedule efficiency Methods exist that use AVL data to improve running and layover times, fleet requirements Fleet size reductions from improved scheduling have been observed, with substantial capital and operating cost savings

In the area of operations management, the improvements in schedule adherence and headway regularity are well documented. However, the evidence does not yet exist to connect these directly to waiting time or utility gains on the part of passengers. The evidence on AVL-based operations control measures is largely based on simulation results, but improvements in passenger waiting times are clearly possible. The waiting time improvements must be balanced by the effects on total passenger travel times, on bus running times, and on the resulting bus operating costs. At this time, a reasonably well-developed methodology does exist to evaluate the impacts of control actions using bus AVL data, but additional empirical evidence of these benefits is needed.

Finally, in the area of service planning, the uses of AVL data are many. They can be used to analyze schedule performance, improve schedule efficiency, and even reduce bus and operator requirements. The challenge remains to have sufficient resources to exploit these data effectively among the many data-rich applications in service planning (Furth, 2000).

5.2 What Are the Research Needs?

Based on this review, there are a number of important areas for future research. These are itemized below, based on the three major areas investigated in this chapter. Additional topics related to the benefits of AVL deserve more attention, and these are also noted.

5.2.1 Passenger Behavior with Real-time Information

The European operational tests over the past 10–15 years have provided some preliminary evidence on the value of en-route information. One could hope that similar results could also be observed from other systems deployed in the United States. Continued investigation of the benefits of en-route information is warranted, and more empirical evidence is needed. In addition, there is no evidence to date that real-time information has a significant value to passengers in a *pre-trip* context. In part, this is because many transit agencies have struggled to determine cost-effective ways of delivering real-time information in a pre-trip context. Nonetheless, it remains to be seen whether having real-time information prior to the trip has value to travelers, in a manner that can be quantified.

In terms of travel behavior, a number of researchers have developed frameworks for the evaluation of traveler information systems (see, for example, Brand, 1994; Ben-Akiva, Bowman, and Gopinath, 1996). To date, however, there has been relatively little direct application of these methods. Stated preference experiments have been used in a number of contexts to evaluate traveler's mode choice for transit under different information scenarios (see, for example, Abdel-Aty et al., 1996a, 1996b; Abdel-Aty, 2001; Reed, 1994; and Reed and Levine, 1997). The work of Reed (1994) and Reed and Levine (1997), in particular, gives some evidence that real-time information has considerable value to transit passengers in at bus stops (en-route). However, Reed and Levine (1997) also found that real-time information has little to no value in affecting long-term choices of transit as a travel mode. These results are obviously preliminary, and there is still the need for more comprehensive investigation of information effects on behavior, both using stated preference and using revealed preference data.

At the same time, one must acknowledge the obvious: capturing the benefits of real-time information on travel behavior is very hard. The challenge is remains to come up with behavioral data collection and modeling techniques to capture travelers' activity patterns, information-seeking behavior, and the cognitive processes (immediate decision-making and longer-term learning behavior) that lead to changes in travel behavior (Ben-Akiva, Bowman, and Gopinath, 1996). This is a daunting task, but clearly this is a needed area of long-term research.

5.2.2 Operations Management

In the area of operations management, much of the general framework for evaluating bus system performance is well known. At the same time, the application of AVL data for this evaluation, and for support of real-time operations control, is an important area of research. The preliminary work of Strathman et al. (2001, 2002) gives a useful framework for field evaluation of AVL system benefits for operations monitoring and control. Some researchers, however, have commented on the challenges of obtaining adequate spatial and temporal resolution of the AVL data to monitor service quality (Furth, 2000; Strathman et al., 2001). Greater spatial resolution, at least at the level of the bus stop (rather than timepoints), and greater temporal resolution (under the typical one- to two-minute resolution of archive AVL data) may be necessary.

In the area of operations control, there is a continuing need for better decision support tools that use AVL data to determine effective real-time control measures. Dispatchers and field supervisors may better manage operations if they have decision support tools. Computational methods to assimilate AVL data and to evaluate potential operations control measures are lacking, both in the research community and in the industry at large. Also, most of the simulation studies to date, as highlighted in Table 2, have examined benefits at the level of the route. When passenger transfers are involved, or where buses are interlined or use dead-heads between routes, the effects of operations control measures must be evaluated on a systemwide basis. It remains an open research question how to model and evaluate the network effects of operations control actions.

5.2.3 Service Planning

Many of the analytic methods for service planning are reasonably mature (Furth, 2000). Nonetheless, the review by Furth suggests a number of important research and implementation issues in the use of AVL data within service planning. Consistent with the AVL data resolution issues mentioned above, there is a need for better statistical methods for summarizing AVL data. Because of the wealth of data, especially at high spatial and temporal resolution, determining statistically useful information from the AVL data requires sampling and data mining capabilities. Research is needed to determine the statistical quality of AVL data and the appropriate sampling and data mining procedures for service planning. Schedule adherence monitoring and scheduling analysis are just two of the potential application areas that can benefit from better statistical methods.

The longer-term benefit of AVL data in service planning also depends in part on its integration with other data at the agency. Geographic information systems (GIS), passenger counts, farebox information, schedules, and passenger survey data are just a few of the databases that are used in service planning. The interfaces between these data are needed to allow for better data retrieval and integration. Since many of the service planning activities rely on different sources of data, the data definitions (schema), interfaces, and computer tools are needed to integrate these data together (Furth, 2000; Hickman, Tabibnia, and Day, 1998).

5.2.4 Other Areas

This chapter has focused on some of the most direct and easily quantified benefits of AVL for bus transit. The social benefits of AVL are largely unknown. For this reason, we do not yet know the magnitude of these impacts, and they deserve further research. Most notably, the air quality impacts of bus transit may be affected by AVL. There should be further investigation of bus running cycles, emissions under these running cycles, and the impacts of operational and schedule improvements on bus operations. The more indirect effects of changes in ridership resulting from AVL, and the indirect effects on air quality, also deserve further study; however, our current inability to measure ridership improvements will represent a significant challenge.

The safety and security benefits of AVL also deserve further study. Given that a major motivation for AVL systems are the potential security and safety enhancements provided by vehicle location systems and silent alarms, this is a notable gap in the existing research.

ACKNOWLEDGMENTS

This research was supported in part by NSF grant CMS-9984906. Parts of the section on passenger information benefited greatly from joint work of the author with Charles River Associates and Ankerbold International on a project for the Transit Cooperative Research Program (TCRP), referenced within this chapter as Charles River Associates (2000).

NOTES

1. Note that this omits bus signal priority as a control strategy, due to the significant complexity of its evaluation. The reader is referred to the recent report by Gardner Systems (1998) for more information on this control strategy.
2. As a complement, an informative evaluation of control actions for light rail is given in Wilson et al. (1992). This study documented the effectiveness of a variety of control actions for high-frequency light rail service in Boston using automatic vehicle identification data.

3 These references deal with bus operations control. Optimal strategies for light rail operations control are discussed extensively in the work of Eberlein (1997) and Eberlein et al. (1998, 2001).

4 This model ignores the possible effects of interlining or dead-heading to reduce excess slack time. The number of buses may not be integer-valued in these cases. Nonetheless, the model described here provides a basic description of the nature of reductions in the bus fleet that can be achieved by reducing excess layover time.

REFERENCES

Abdel-Aty, M., Kitamura, R., Jovanis, P. "Investigating Effect of Advanced Traveler Information on Commuter Tendency to Use Transit," *Transportation Research Record* No. 1550, 1996a, 65–72.

Abdel-Aty, M., Kitamura, R., Jovanis, P. "The Impact of Advanced Transit Information on Commuters' Mode Changing," *ITS Journal*, Vol. 3, No. 2, 1996b, 129–146.

Abdel-Aty, M. "Using Ordered Probit Modeling to Study the Effect of ATIS on Transit Ridership," *Transportation Research – Part C*, Vol. 9, 2001, 265–277.

Abkowitz, M. "The Impact of Service Reliability on Work Travel Behavior," Ph.D. dissertation, Massachusetts Institute of Technology, Department of Civil Engineering, 1980.

Abkowitz, M., Eiger, A., Engelstein, I. "Optimal Control of Headway Variation on Transit Routes," *Journal of Advanced Transportation*, Vol. 20, No. 1, 1986, 73–88.

Abkowitz, M., Engelstein, I. "Methods for Maintaining Transit Service Regularity," *Transportation Research Record*, No. 961, 1–8, 1984.

Abkowitz, M., Lepofsky, M. "Implementing Headway-Based Reliability Control on Transit Routes," *Journal of Transportation Engineering*, Vol. 116, No. 1, January 1990, 49–63.

Abkowitz, M,. Tozzi, J. "Transit Route Characteristics and Headway-based Reliability Control," *Transportation Research Record,* No. 1078, 1986, 11–16.

Andersson, P. A., Hermansson, A., Tengvald, E., Scalia-Tomba, G.-P. "Analysis and Simulation of an Urban Bus Route," *Transportation Research – Part A*, Vol. 13A, 1979, 439–466.

Atkins, S. "Passenger Information at Bus Stops (PIBS): Report on Monitoring Studies of Route 18 Demonstration," London Transport Report, January 1994.

Ball, M. "Economic and Policy Considerations of Advanced Public Transportation Systems," Technical Report, National Urban Transit Institute, Center for Urban Transportation Research, University of South Florida, October 1994.

Barnett, A. "On Controlling Randomness in Transit Operations," *Transportation Science*, Vol. 8, No. 2, May 1974, 102–116.

Ben-Akiva, M, Bowman, J. L., Gopinath, D. "Travel Demand Model System for the Information Era," *Transportation*, Vol. 23, No. 3, August 1996, 241–266.

Ben-Akiva, M., Lerman, S. *Discrete Choice Analysis,* Cambridge, MA: MIT Press, 1985.

Bowman, L., Turnquist, M. "Service Frequency, Schedule Reliability and Passenger Wait Times at Transit Stops," *Transportation Research – Part A*, Vol. 15A, No. 6, 1981, 465–471.

Brand, B. "Intelligent Vehicle Highway System Benefits Assessment Framework," *Transportation Research Record,* No. 1408, 1994, 1–7.

Cambridge Systematics. "Travlink Operational Test Evaluation Report," prepared for the Minnesota Department of Transportation, August 1996.

Casey, R., Labell, L., Moniz, L., Royal, J., Sheehan, M., Sheehan, T., Brown, A., Foy, M., Zirker, M., Schweiger, C., Marks, B., Kaplan, B., Parker, B. "Advanced Public Transportation Systems: The State of the Art – Update 2000," Technical Report FTA-MA-26-7007-00-1, Federal Transit Administration, 2000.

Charles River Associates. "Strategies for Improved Traveler Information," Transit Cooperative Research Program (TCRP), Revised Draft Interim Report for Project A-20A, National Academy Press, Washington, DC, November 2000.

Eberlein, X.-J. "Real-Time Control Strategies in Transit Operations: Models and Analysis," Ph.D. Dissertation, Massachusetts Institute of Technology, Department of Civil and Environmental Engineering, 1995.

Eberlein, X.-J., Wilson, N., Barnhart, C., Bernstein, D. "The Real-Time Deadheading Problem in Transit Operations Control," *Transportation Research – Part B*, Vol. 32B, No. 2, 1998, 77–100.

Eberlein, X.-J., Wilson, N., Bernstein, D. "The Holding Problem with Real-time Information Available," *Transportation Science*, Vol. 35, No. 1, February 2001, 1–18.

ECONorthwest and Parsons Brinckerhoff Quade & Douglas, Inc. "Estimating the Benefits and Costs of Public Transit Projects: A Guidebook for Practitioners," Transit Cooperative Research Program (TCRP) Report 78, National Academy Press, Washington, DC, 2002.

Fu, L., Yang, X. "On Design and Implementation of Bus Holding Control Strategies under Real-time Information," paper presented at the 81st Annual Meeting of the Transportation Research Board (No. 02-2325), January 2002.

Furth, P. "Data Analysis for Bus Planning and Monitoring," Transit Cooperative Research Program (TCRP), Synthesis Report No. 34, National Academy Press, Washington, DC, 2000.

Gardner Systems. "Improved Traffic Signal Priority for Transit," Transit Cooperative Research Program (TCRP), Interim Report for Project A-16A, National Academy Press, Washington, DC, December 1998.

Gillen, D., Chang, E., Johnson, D. "Productivity Benefits and Cost Efficiencies from ITS Applications to Public Transit: The Evaluation of AVL," California PATH Working Paper, UCB-ITS-PWP-2000-16, September 2000.

Goeddel, D. "Benefits Assessment of Advanced Public Transportation Systems," Technical Report DOT-VNTSC-FTA-96-7, Federal Transit Administration, 1996.

Goeddel, D. "Benefits Assessment of Advanced Public Transportation Systems, Update 2000," Technical Report DOT-VNTSC-FTA-00-02, Federal Transit Administration, 2000.

Hall, R. "Traveler Route Choice Under Six Information Scenarios: Transit Level of Service Implications," Ph.D. Dissertation, Department of Civil Engineering, University of California, Berkeley, 1982.

Hall, R. "Traveler Route Choice: Travel Time Implications of Improved Information and Adaptive Decisions," *Transportation Research – Part A*, Vol. 17A, No. 3, 1983, 201–214.

Hall, R. "The Fastest Path through a Network with Random Time-Dependent Travel Times," *Transportation Science*, Vol. 20, No. 3, August 1986, 182–188.

Hansen, M., Qureshi, M., Rydzewski, D. "Improving Transit Performance with Advanced Public Transportation Technologies," California PATH Research Report, UCB-ITS-PRR-94-18, August 1994.

Hickman, M. "An Analytic Stochastic Model for the Transit Vehicle Holding Problem," *Transportation Science*, Vol. 35, No. 3, August 2001, 215–237.

Hickman, M. "Robust Passenger Itinerary Planning Using Transit AVL Data," Proceedings of the IEEE Intelligent Transportation Systems Council (ITSC) Conference, Singapore, September 2002.

Hickman, M., Tabibnia, S., Day, T. "Evaluating Interface Standards for the Public Transit Industry," *Transportation Research Record,* No. 1618, 172–179, 1998.

Hickman, M. ,Wilson, N. "Passenger Travel Time and Path Choice Implications of Real-Time Transit Information," *Transportation Research – Part C*, Vol. 3C, No. 4, August 1995, 211–226.

Khattak, A., Hickman, M. "Automatic Vehicle Location and Computer Aided Dispatch Systems: Commercial Availability and Deployment in Transit Agencies," *Journal of Public Transportation*, Vol. 2, No. 1, 1998, 1–26.

Kimpel, T., Strathman, J., Dueker, K., Griffin, D., Gerhart, R., Turner, K. "Time Point-Level Analysis of Passenger Demand and Transit Service Reliability," project report submitted to *TransNow*, July 2000.

Koffman, D. "A Simulation Study of Alternative Real-time Bus Headway Control Strategies," *Transportation Research Record,* No. 663, 1978, 41–46.

Levinson, H. "Supervision Strategies for Improved Reliability of Bus Routes," National Cooperative Transit Research and Development Program (NCTRP) Synthesis of Transit Practice No. 15, 1991.

Lin, G., Liang, P., Schonfeld, P., Larson, R. "Adaptive Control of Transit Operations," Technical Report FTA-MD-26-7002, Federal Transit Administration, 1995.

Maclean, S., Dailey, D. "Wireless Internet Access to Real-Time Transit Information," *Transportation Research Record,* No. 1791, 2002, 92–98.

Mitretek Systems, "Transit ITS Impacts Matrix", on the World Wide Web at: http://web.mitretek.org/its/aptsmatrix.nsf. Accessed October 30, 2002.

Morlok, E., Bruun, E., Blackman, K. "Advanced Vehicle Monitoring and Communication Systems for Bus Transit: Benefits and Economic Feasibility," Technical Report DOT-T-94-03, Federal Transit Administration, March 1993.

NextBus Web site, http://www.nextbus.com. Accessed February 8, 2003.

Okunieff, P. "AVL Systems for Bus Transit," Transit Cooperative Research Program (TCRP) Synthesis Report No. 24, National Academy Press, Washington, DC, 1997.

Reed, T. *Waiting for Public Transit: The Utility of Real-Time Schedule Information*, Ph.D. Dissertation, University of Michigan, Department of Urban Planning, 1994.

Reed, T., Levine, J. "Changes in Traveler Stated Preference for Bus and Car Modes Due to Real-Time Schedule Information: A Conjoint Analysis," *Journal of Public Transportation,* Vol. 1, No. 2, 1997, 25–47.

Rossetti, M., Turitto, T. "Comparing Static and Dynamic Threshold Based Control Strategies," *Transportation Research – Part A*, Vol. 32, No. 8, 1998, 607–620.

Senevirante, P. "Analysis of On-time Performance of Bus Services Using Simulation," *Journal of Transportation Engineering*, Vol. 116, No. 4, 1990, 517–531.

Sheikh, M. "Approaches to Customer Information for Public Transportation: Application to the San Juan Metropolitan Area," master's thesis, Massachusetts Institute of Technology, 1998.

Small, K. *Urban Transportation Economics*, Harwood Academic Publishers, 1992.

Smith, R., Atkins, S., Sheldon, R. "London Transport Buses: ATT in Action and the London COUNTDOWN Route 18 Project," *World Congress on Applications of Transport Telematics and Intelligent Vehicle-Highway Systems: Toward an Intelligent Transport System*, Vol. 6, 1994, 3,048–3,055.

Strathman, J., Dueker, K., Kimpel, T., Gerhart, R., Turner, K., Taylor, P., Callas, S., Griffin, D. "Automated Bus Dispatching, Operations Control, and Service Reliability: The Initial TriMet Experience," project report submitted to *TransNow*, October 1999.

Strathman, J., Dueker, K., Kimpel, T., Gerhart, R., Turner, K., Taylor, P., Callas, S., Griffin, D. "Service Reliability Impacts of Computer-Aided Dispatching and Automatic Vehicle Location Technology: A TriMet Case Study," *Transportation Quarterly*, Vol. 54, No. 3, Summer 2000, 85–102.

Strathman, J., Kimpel, T., Dueker, K., Gerhart, R., Turner, K., Griffin, D., Callas, S. "Bus Transit Operations Control: Review and an Experiment Involving TriMet's Automated Bus Dispatching System," paper presented at the 80th Annual Meeting of the Transportation Research Board, January 2001.

Strathman, J., Kimpel, T., Dueker, K., Gerhart, R., Callas, S. "Evaluation of Transit Operations: Data Applications of TriMet's Automated Bus Dispatching System," Paper presented at the 81st Annual Meeting of the Transportation Research Board, January 2002.

Transportation Management and Design. "Transit Scheduling: Basic and Advanced Manuals," Transit Cooperative Research Program (TCRP) Report No. 30, National Academy Press, Washington, DC, 1998.

Turnbull, K. "The Use of Information Generated from Transit AVL Systems," Proceedings of the IVHS America 1993 Annual Meeting, 1993, 82–88.

Turnquist, M. "A Model for Investigating the Effects of Service Frequency and Reliability on Bus Passenger Waiting Times," *Transportation Research Record,* No. 663, 1978, 70–73.

Turnquist, M. "Strategies for Improving Reliability of Bus Service," *Transportation Research Record,* No. 818, 1981, 7–13.

Turnquist, M., Blume, S. "Evaluating Potential Effectiveness of Headway Control Strategies for Transit Systems," *Transportation Research Record*, No. 746, 1980, 25–29.

Vandebona, V., Richardson, A. "Effect of Checkpoint Control Strategies in a Simulated Transit Operation," *Transportation Research – Part A*, Vol. 20A, No. 6, 429C436, 1986.

Welding, P. I. "The Instability of a Close-Interval Service," *Operational Research Quarterly*, Vol. 8, No. 3, 1957, 133–148.

Wellman, M., Ford, M., Larson, K. "Path Planning Under Time-Dependent Uncertainty," Proceedings of the Eleventh Conference on Uncertainty in Artificial Intelligence, 1995, 532–539.

Wilson, N., Macchi, R., Fellows, R., Deckoff, A. "Improving Service on the MBTA Green Line through Better Operations Control," *Transportation Research Record*, No. 1361, 1992, 10–15.

Zhao, J., Dessouky, M., Bukkapatnam, S. "Distributed Holding Control of Bus Transit Operations," Proceedings of the IEEE Intelligent Transportation Systems Council (ITSC) Conference, Oakland, CA, August 2001.

Chapter 6

CASE STUDY: IMPACTS OF ADVANCED TECHNOLOGY ON A SMALL CITY BUS SYSTEM

Edward Sullivan and Jeffrey Gerfen
Department of Civil and Environmental Engineering, Cal Poly State University

Cal Poly State University is carrying out a project funded by the Caltrans Division of Research and Innovation to develop, demonstrate, and evaluate an open architecture, low-cost, Advanced Public Transportation System (APTS) suitable for small and medium-sized transit properties. This chapter describes the APTS technology demonstration on San Luis Obispo (SLO) Transit and presents some findings on the evaluation of the new technologies with regard to system performance and user satisfaction. The evaluation includes an analysis of bus operations prior to and after deployment of the new technologies, and surveys with riders.

During the period 2000–2002, APTS technologies known as the Cal Poly Smart Transit System were deployed on San Luis Obispo Transit (SLO Transit) buses. The system provides:

- GPS-based location of buses;
- Emergency silent alarms for use by drivers;
- On-board display of real-time schedule adherence to drivers;
- Real-time transmission of bus locations;
- Solar powered Smart Transit Signs at key bus stops at Cal Poly and in San Luis Obispo to notify riders about the status of arriving buses.

Most equipment was fabricated from relatively low cost, off-the-shelf components.

Although the technology is still new and the settling-in process still underway, findings to date are encouraging regarding the benefits of deploying appropriately scaled APTS technologies in such semi-rural settings.

1. INTRODUCTION

The Cal Poly Smart Transit System project responds to the needs of small and medium-sized transit properties to improve operations and ridership with a minimum of resources. This approach to deploying APTS uses a minimum amount of technology to generate the maximum possible improvements. The approach relies on open architecture and modular solutions to provide real-time information to customers, help drivers and managers keep on schedule and handle anomalies, expedite fare collection, supply improved data for system planning, and enhance operational safety.

The San Luis Obispo City Transit (SLO Transit) service operates six principal routes serving a university community and regional business center of approximately 43,000 residents. All six routes stop downtown at City Hall and at Cal Poly State University, providing single transfer service between all origins and destinations in the 10.7-square-mile city. Maintaining on-time performance is critical to providing efficient transfers and maintaining ridership levels. SLO Transit also connects with countywide bus services at both City Hall and Cal Poly.

Most transit users are affiliated with Cal Poly State University, whose 16,500 students and 2,500 staff enjoy "free" rides by showing university identification. University ID cards will soon be read electronically and verified for validity at boarding. In compensation, the university pays SLO Transit about $200,000 annually, mostly from parking citation revenues. When Cal Poly is in session, the university community makes more than two-thirds of about 100,000 monthly rides on the system. Summer and December patronage is about half that which occurs during the school year.

Prior to June 30, 2001, the six SLO Transit routes operated on schedules that repeated every hour and were designed to have buses stop at City Hall either on the hour or half-hour in order to facilitate easy and predictable transfers. Maintaining schedules on this pulsed system became increasingly difficult due to increasing traffic congestion.

On March 4, 2001, a storm severely damaged a major culvert under a main arterial near Cal Poly. This occurred at a road section where all six SLO Transit bus routes operated. The city promptly banned all heavy vehicles, including buses, from the damaged road section. This situation continued until mid-2002. Buses were temporarily rerouted, in most cases to a longer itinerary, further impacting the system's schedule adherence performance.

New bus schedules were implemented in July 2001, in order to restore on-time performance, although the routes remained unchanged. The repeating hourly schedules were eliminated and the predictable hour and half-hour stops at City Hall and elsewhere in the system no longer occur. Also, an experimental evening service (after 7 p.m.) was dropped due to low ridership.

Obvious concern existed about adverse reactions of SLO Transit customers to the new more complicated and more limited schedules. Against this background, in October 2001, seven new Smart Transit Signs entered service. This made the newly installed APTS technologies visible to the public through the provision of real-time information about bus arrivals and other operational issues.

2. DETAILS OF THE APTS TECHNOLOGY AND ITS OPERATION

Smart Transit System Mobile Data Terminals (MDTs) are installed throughout the SLO Transit fixed-route fleet. These MDTs include a keypad and display mounted beside the driver, an integrated GPS receiver, a magnetic swipe card reader, an emergency silent alarm button, and an interface to the data radio system. The MDTs:

- Calculate schedule adherence for departures from scheduled stops. This information is displayed to the drivers, transmitted to dispatch, and used to notify drivers when they should depart following rest stops.
- Receive emergency button input from the driver's hidden silent alarm and transmit a "Mayday" message to dispatch for response.
- Receive ID information from the magnetic stripe card reader when Cal Poly students or staff swipe their ID cards upon boarding transit vehicles. The IDs are checked against a master list of good and bad ID numbers to validate the boardings.The emergency button and ID checkout features are being implemented.

The MDTs communicate with dispatch via a radio link that is shared with the voice channel. This shared voice/data communications system is economical to operate. Monthly radio service charges are approximately $15 per month per vehicle.

The Smart Transit System software on the central computer:

- Displays schedule adherence information for all buses for all stops during all hours of each day.
- Receives emergency messages transmitted from buses and alerts the dispatcher with audio and visual alarms, requiring the dispatcher to take action.
- Tracks and displays the locations of the buses. This information is archived and also provided to an on-line map display.
- Transmits bus locations and schedule adherence status to the Smart Transit Signs via wireless links.
- Receives valid ID number lists from Cal Poly and transmits these ID lists to the MDTs via wireless links. ID lists may be transmitted as a complete list or as an update to the list.
- Receives Cal Poly ride information from the MDTs via wireless links, presents it graphically, and generates ride usage reports. Seven Smart Transit Signs are installed within the City of San Luis Obispo and on the Cal Poly Campus. The Smart Transit Signs are solar powered,

controlled by wireless links, and meet ADA visibility requirements. The Smart Transit Sign at each stop cycles through messages showing the estimated minutes to arrival for the bus routes that stop at that location.

The Smart Transit System is written to be consistent/compliant with both the National ITS Architecture and TCP/IP Standards. The Smart Transit System is open-source and non-proprietary.

Figure 1. Mobile Data Terminal Mounted in Bus

Figure 2. A Smart Transit Sign

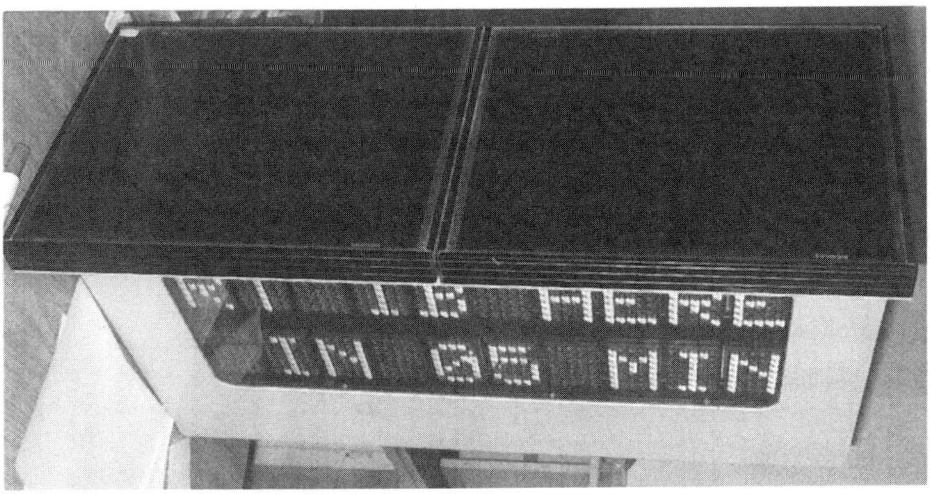

Figure 3. Solar Panel Mounted on a Smart Transit Sign

3. EARLY OPERATING EXPERIENCE

ATMS has the potential to improve transit system productivity, on the one hand through increased ridership in response to improved information dissemination and better service quality, and on the other hand, through improved operational efficiency in both day-to-day system management and responding to special situations. With regard to the latter, real-time data on schedule adherence is expected to be used by SLO Transit management for:

- Route and schedule planning, and to adjust portions of routes which regularly deviate from schedules;
- Dispatching assistance to buses experiencing mechanical difficulties;
- Adjusting service in real time when conditions warrant, such as during bad weather;
- Providing immediate feedback to drivers regarding schedule adherence;
- Identifying the need for further training for drivers who consistently deviate from schedules.

Drivers' reactions are positive about the availability of real-time information on schedule adherence, especially in light of the new complicated schedules which vary hour by hour. Drivers view the MDT as an accurate, easy-to-use, electronic "cheat sheet," a tool they appreciate for helping them do their jobs well.

As yet, the new technologies have not been fully integrated into the day-to-day administration of SLO Transit. Therefore, the full benefit of implementing these technologies remains unrealized. Eventually, the ongoing gathering and archiving of real-time bus location data should be useful for assessing the effectiveness of the schedule changes implemented in July 2001. Figure 4 illustrates the nature of the information obtained from the system, showing mid-day arrival times at a particular bus stop during a two-week period in March 2001. These particular data clearly show a systematic schedule-keeping problem at this location—with actual arrival times typically 6 to 15 minutes after the scheduled arrival time of 38 minutes past the hour. Delay patterns like this were common throughout the system prior to the new schedule's implementation in June, 2001.

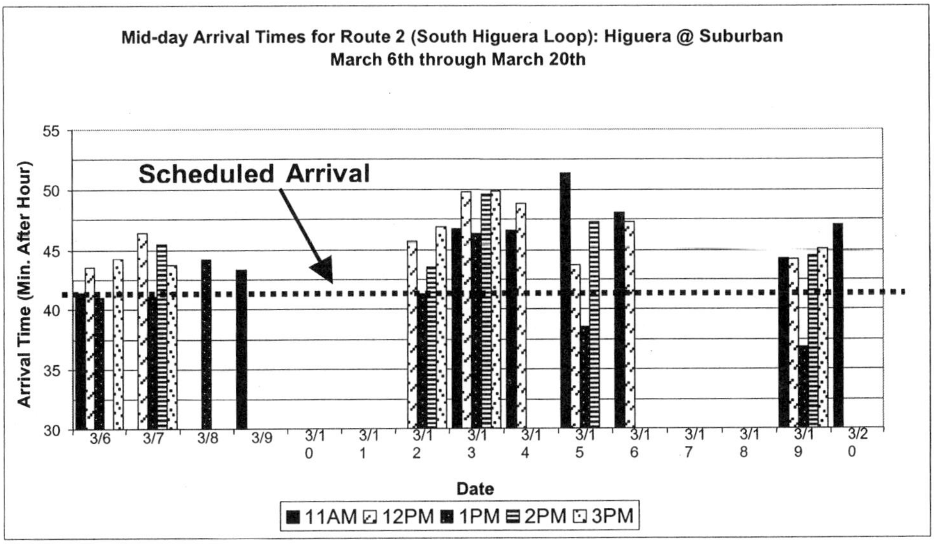

Figure 4. Typical Stop On-time Performance Comparison

Archived schedule-keeping data provide a valuable tool for detailed longitudinal evaluation of performance at selected locations, as seen Figure 4, as well as for easy estimation of overall route performance for selected days or using averages over days, as illustrated in Figure 5.[1]

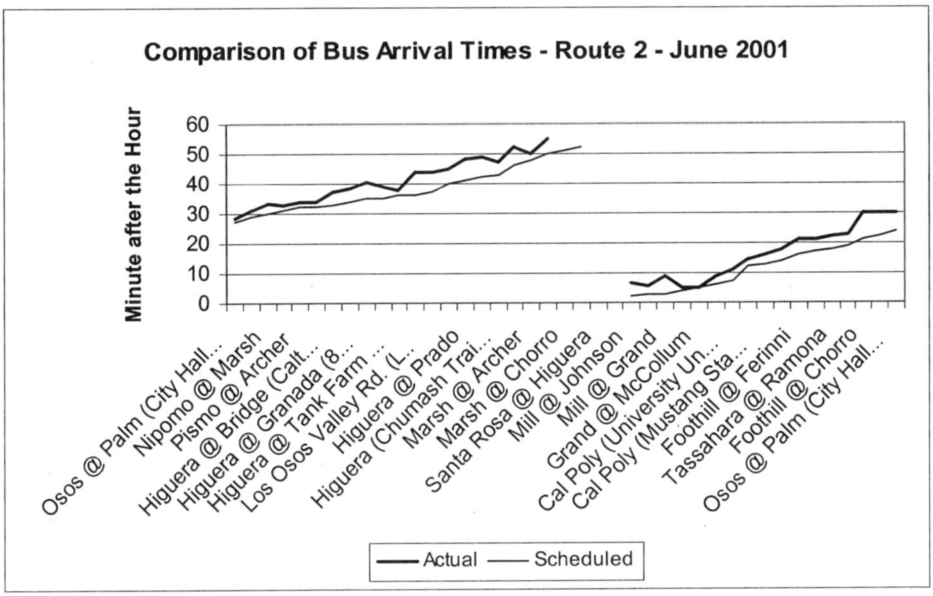

Figure 5. Typical Route On-Time Performance Comparison

4. INITIAL USER RESPONSE

A small-sample, on-board travel survey was conducted in November 2001, during the afternoon peak period, to assess bus riders' opinions concerning the recent service changes and the seven new Smart Transit Signs which began operating about a month earlier. One hundred and forty-eight surveys were completed, of which 120 reported riding SLO Transit at least once a week. Seventy of these 120 frequent riders are affiliated with Cal Poly, most (67) being students.

Among the 120 frequent riders (who ride at least once a week), 102 reported noticing the new Smart Transit Signs. Of these, 78 (77 percent) reported they had obtained information about their buses from one of these signs, and 28 (28 percent) specifically reported that a Smart Transit Sign had helped them make a transfer. As shown in Figure 6, these frequent riders are overwhelmingly positive about the Smart Transit Signs with 89 percent indicating that the new signs enhance SLO Transit service. A small number of infrequent bus users (17) who also had noticed the Smart Transit Signs were equally positive about the impact.

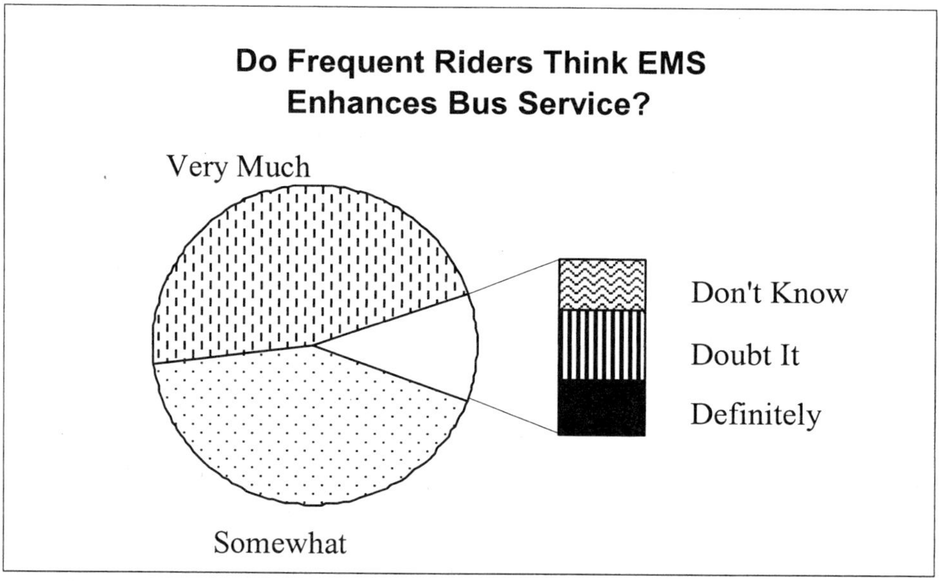

Figure 6. Frequent Riders' Opinions of the Impact of Smart Transit Signs

It is interesting that the positive opinions about the new Smart Transit Signs do not reflect riders' overall opinions about recent changes to local bus service. Among 74 frequent riders who responded to questions about schedule-keeping, 47 (64 percent) said they saw no change in on-time performance following July 2001, with 25 of these reporting that their buses had been and still are usually on schedule. The rest said their buses had been and still are sometimes late (18) or usually late (4). Among the 74 frequent riders, 11 said their buses had usually been on time before July but now were sometimes or usually late, while 9 said their buses were sometimes or usually late before July but now were usually on time. Figure 6 summarizes the general opinions of 86 frequent riders regarding the recent service changes. These views are surprising since the July schedule changes were implemented specifically to improve system on-time performance. One wonders whether these mixed opinions about schedule adherence actually reflect customers' discontent about the new complicated schedules and about the elimination of evening service. More in-depth interviews are needed to explore these issues further.

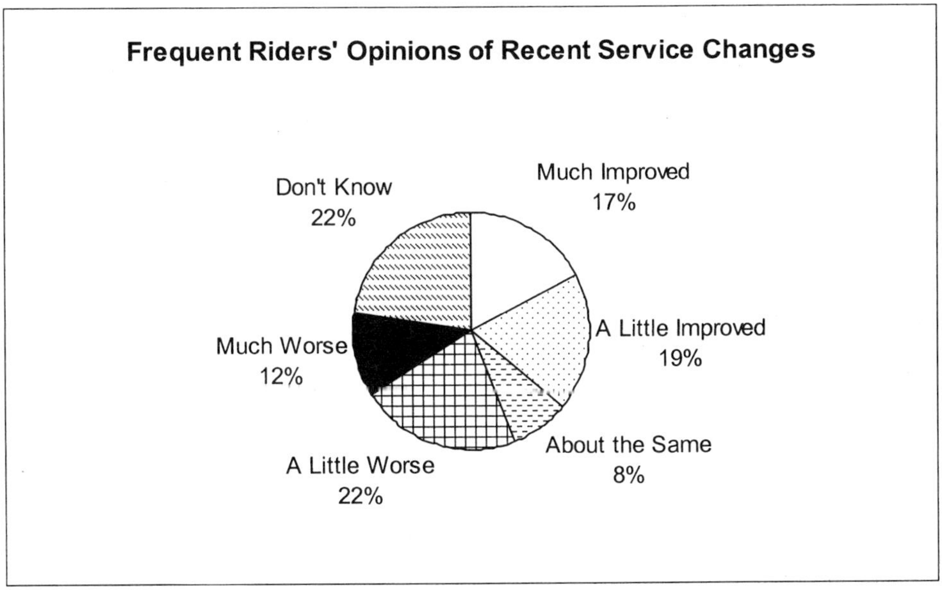

Figure 7. Frequent Riders' Overall Evaluation of Recent Service Changes

To summarize, although SLO Transit riders expressed mixed opinions about recent service changes in general, the introduction of real-time information via Smart Transit Signs appears to have been very well received.

5. SUMMARY AND CONCLUSION

SLO Transit was chosen by Caltrans to demonstrate low-cost Advanced Public Transportation System (APTS) technologies designed specifically for small transit systems. Mobile data terminals with GPS locators were installed on all vehicles, with real-time bus location and emergency alarm data transmitted via radio modems using previously existing voice radios. Besides providing useful data for system planning, the real-time bus location data are used to advise drivers regarding schedule adherence and to generate messages regarding impending bus arrivals employing Smart Transit Signs at principal bus stops throughout town.

The project has demonstrated the feasibility and positive impacts of applying APTS technologies to enhance small transit operations. Indications to date are that both the operators and bus customers perceive significant benefits from the deployment of this new technology. Although these early impacts are gratifying, the full significance of deploying Smart Transit technologies in this operating environment will take additional time to understand completely, as the operator fully integrates its new capabilities into its standard operating and marketing procedures.

NOTES

1 Note that some points near the change of hour are omitted from due to the inconvenience of averaging.

Chapter 7

BEYOND BENEFITS AND COSTS

Understanding Outcomes of ITS Deployments in Public Transit

Genevieve Giuliano and Thomas O'Brien
University of Southern California

Intelligent Transportation Systems technology is promoted as a means for improving public transit services. The intended benefits of ITS include better and more regular information, seamless transportation services, and improved productivity. A necessary condition of realizing these benefits is operational technology. However operational technology does not necessarily lead to successful projects. Rather, institutional issues drive project outcomes. This chapter presents results from six case studies of recent ITS tests to illustrate both conditions for successful ITS deployment and the consequences of not meeting these conditions. We close with some suggested strategies for improving ITS implementation outcomes.

1. INTRODUCTION

The 1991 Intermodal Surface Transportation Efficiency Act (ISTEA) launched extensive efforts to use Intelligent Transportation Systems (ITS) technology to improve public transit. ITS was intended to improve transit productivity, safety, accessibility, and mobility as well as increase service quality (Casey et al., 2000). The federal government has encouraged ITS adoption via funding of transit Field Operational Tests (FOTs) and other deployments around the U.S. Outcomes of these deployments have been varied, some reporting significant success and leading to permanent adoption of the new technology, others experiencing problems. What accounts for successful deployment of ITS technology in public transit? We conduct six case studies of public transit technology tests to identify determinants of outcomes. ITS technology is often seen as a means for accomplishing service integration in public transportation, e.g., via integrated fare media or coordinated scheduling. We find technical performance of the technology is a necessary but not sufficient condition for effective deployment. Rather, effectiveness depends on institutional capacity, functional relationships among all partners, and other organizational factors. These factors are particularly important in service integration projects.

This chapter is organized in four parts. First, we provide some background on the institutional context of ITS in public transit. We discuss the legislative context of FOTs as well as issues associated with public transit deployments. Second, we survey the methodologies being used to evaluate ITS deployments and briefly review the results of some of the first deployments. Third, we present an overview of six different ITS experiments within public transit. The case studies involve electronic payment and fare integration (San Francisco Bay Area TransLink, Washington DC SmarTrip, Chicago SmartCard), automated trip scheduling (Santa Clara SMART), and more ambitious service integration that may or may not include fare integration (San Gabriel Valley Smart Shuttle, Ventura Smart Card). Finally, we consider the policy implications of our findings and make recommendations for future policy action.

2. INSTITUTIONAL CONTEXT OF ITS APPLICATIONS IN PUBLIC TRANSIT

Despite billions of dollars in federal subsidies, public transit's market share has continued to decline (Lave, 1991; Pucher, Evans, and Wenger, 1998; Kain, 1999). Massive investments in new rail systems and capital stock as well as heavily subsidized fares eventually stabilized ridership. In the late 1990s ridership increased, though market share has either remained constant or declined. According to Bureau of Transportation statistics, public transit systems recorded nine billion trips in 1999, a 20 percent increase over 1995 figures. Over the same period, however, the percentage of work trips made on public transit actually decreased from 5.1 percent to 4.9 percent, while automobile use for the same purpose increased from 86.5 percent to 87.7 percent. The 2000 census commuting data indicate that public transit's share of overall work trips has returned to 1995 levels, at 5.2 percent. Automobile use is at 87.5 percent.

This moderate increase in transit share is occurring at an increased cost to the public. While the percentage of operating expenses recovered through fare revenues has remained relatively stable over the past decade (just shy of 39 percent in 2000), the subsidy per passenger has increased 22 percent over the same period. Between 1997 and 2000, the rate of increase alone was 19.4 percent (American Public Transportation Association, 2001)[1]. Efforts to use new technology to improve public transit service are the latest in a long series of federal policy initiatives aimed at more cost effectively reversing the long-term decline of the industry.

2.1 ISTEA, the ITS Program, and the Changing Role of MPOs

The passage of ISTEA in 1991 overhauled the transit funding process. Highway Trust Fund dollars, once dedicated to highway construction and improvements, became available for transit purposes.[2] Through ISTEA and the 1990 Clean Air Act (CAA), regional planning organizations received new authority to direct federal, state, and local funds toward transit and to determine conformity with regional air quality plans. ISTEA also launched the various ITS programs, including the Advanced Public Transportation Systems Program (APTS). APTS field tests are meant to help implement overall program goals and objectives, including enhanced customer satisfaction through technology and improved system productivity (Casey and Collura, 1994).

ISTEA marked a turning point in transportation policy. No longer was the answer to traffic congestion more highway capacity; rather the emphasis shifted to a more integrated approach that included managing demand and increasing the efficiency of the existing transportation system. Public transit was a key element in demand management, hence the shift to funding flexibility. It was argued by smart growth groups such as the Surface Transportation Policy Project that more efficient, better quality transit would attract more passengers, reducing congestion and air pollution, and ultimately resulting in more efficient urban form. New technology was viewed as one important means for developing better public transit. The Intelligent Transportation Society of America (ITSA) was mandated by Congress in conjunction with ISTEA to promote public/private partnerships in support of new technologies, including APTS.

The U.S. Department of Transportation has funded Field Operational Tests (FOTs) and the Transit IDEA program as a means of gauging the possibility of deploying ITS within public transit. Since the adoption of TEA-21 in 1998, the focus of national ITS policy has shifted from research to deployment. Two implementation issues were identified: shared technical standards and multi-agency coordination. Rules calling for shared standards and formal interagency agreements in FOTs were outlined in 2000 (Casey et al., 2000).

State and local agencies have played a critical role in the national ITS program. FOT funding is channelled through the state. Individual states have also developed their own APTS programs. The State of California has supported the application of advanced technologies through its Advanced Transportation Systems Program Plan.

Metropolitan Planning Organizations (MPOs) also have a larger voice in the development of APTS programs. ISTEA required that the federal government certify the transportation planning process (and the planning agencies) in metropolitan areas with populations greater than 200,000 people. MPOs, through certification, become eligible to receive federal highway and transit funds. ISTEA also gave MPOs new authority to establish budgetary priorities for already-approved projects (Lam and Miller, 2002).

The renewed focus on integrated planning efforts has also meant renewed efforts to organize planning at the metropolitan level and to include all affected parties in the planning process. Since MPOs tend to represent multiple jurisdictions, they have enjoyed a greater role in ITS deployments and have become implementing (and not merely planning) agencies.

One result of the federal legislation then is a complex institutional context for ITS deployment generally and for technology tests specifically. The typical transit test involves federal and state oversight, a variety of local partners, the transit operator(s), as well as private sector vendors and consultants. It takes place within a different setting and under a different process than everyday transit management. The test's success is therefore dependent upon effective negotiation within the new organizational context.

2.2 Expected Benefits of ITS in Public Transit

Transit funders and providers see ITS technology as a means for improving efficiency, increasing service quality, and ultimately attracting more choice riders. Technology such as automated passenger counters (APC) and automated vehicle location (AVL) systems may allow transit operators to better balance supply and demand and improve schedule adherence, providing more reliable service. These systems may also improve fleet management and hence reduce operating costs. Electronic fare cards may reduce dwell time and make fare payment more convenient, and also reduce losses from fare evasion. Traveler information services can expedite trip planning and provide real-time schedule information to travelers. In demand-responsive transit, AVL and automated dispatching may increase productivity and reduce passenger travel time. Signal priority systems can reduce travel time by reducing the amount of time the transit vehicle spends stopped at signalized intersections.

New technology also makes possible coordination between services—seamless integration of transit from the perspective of the passenger. When used by multiple agencies within a region, electronic fare cards make it possible to coordinate fares and transfers across different providers. When combined with AVL, coordination between services is possible, reducing transfer wait time for the passenger. As regional solutions are sought to the problem of decreasing mode share, technological integration allows for disparate systems to work together using the same ITS architecture.

2.3 The Structure of Public Transit

It is clear that the expected benefits of ITS for public transit are large. However, public transit has some inherent barriers to successful implementation. The first is the organizational structure of the industry. Large public transit organizations are heavily subsidized and subject to restrictive labor contracts. Heavy public subsidies place transit in the public arena, with service decisions often made on the basis of political imperative, rather than service demand (Jones, 1985; Fielding, 1995; Smerk, 1991). Transit labor contracts limit management flexibility in work assignments, work schedules, and in changes that could result in a loss of jobs. Therefore technology applications that increase productivity by substituting capital for labor may not be feasible, and the expected gains from technology may not be realized. In addition, public transit agencies do not have the profit motive that often drives innovation adoption in the private sector.

Small transit operations (e.g., municipal demand-responsive services) typically do not have the restrictive labor environment of large agencies, but often employ a labor force with limited technical knowledge. In these cases the complexity and technical sophistication of the new technology is itself a barrier.

The second barrier is the institutional structure of public transit. Public transit services are organized as spatial monopolies. Each operator has exclusive rights to operate a given type of service within a specified service area. Fares and service parameters are set by management and governing boards. As a result, local transit services are geographically segmented. Cities and counties have an incentive to protect their services from competition and to limit their provision to the local residents responsible for generating funds. While there is an economic argument for spatial monopolies, these boundaries are an artefact of transit subsidies.[3] Federal and state subsidies are allocated to political divisions. Local subsidies make up a growing share of subsidies, and these are tied directly to local jurisdictions.

Geographically or functionally segmented services are often not consistent with patterns of travel demand. Therefore, the traveler must negotiate between systems that do not accept one another's transfers and do not coordinate operating schedules. The lack of integration discourages transit use. The geographic proximity of competing or complementary services (as when different transit and paratransit services operate within the same jurisdiction) calls for multi-agency coordination; however, without changes in the structure of transportation funding, transit operators have little to gain from coordination. Coordination may require schedule adjustments or other changes that might increase operating costs, but are unlikely to realize compensating increases in revenue. Integrated fare mechanisms require competing agencies to share data, negotiate sharing of fare revenues, and perhaps share the maintenance of related equipment, further adding to agency costs. In sum, service coordination makes sense as a response to travel patterns; but it may generate substantial additional costs in an institutional environment that encourages segmented services.

3. EVALUATING NEW TECHNOLOGY IN PUBLIC TRANSIT

Federal FOTs and many state ITS deployments include a requirement for independent evaluation. The ITS program began in 1991, but the USDOT did not begin collecting information on the various tests until 1994. It was not until the end of the decade that the agency began to conduct more formal assessments of the ITS program's benefits. Consequently the literature on FOT results is limited.

3.1 Lessons from Deployments Under ISTEA and TEA-21

In 1997, the USDOT evaluated the 84 FOTs that it had funded since 1991 (USDOT, 1997). These FOTs addressed seven different areas of ITS implementation: traveler information, traffic management, public transit, rural transit, commercial vehicles, vehicle control and safety, and integrated systems. Data was still incomplete or non-existent for some tests, and the study more systematically approached the development of measurements for ITS benefits instead of measuring the benefits themselves. It focused on time savings, crashes, fatalities, throughput, cost savings, and customer satisfaction. The study attempted to measure benefits where feasible and make predictions for similar deployments; it also recognized the importance of anecdotal findings that could become guideposts for future evaluations.

TEA-21 brought about new guidelines for the evaluation of operational tests and other deployment projects, and by 1999, the USDOT had modified its list of assessment areas to include effective capacity improvements, emission/fuel savings, and "other." (Proper, 1999) The update also expanded upon the notion of integrated services by presenting preliminary findings from coordinated transit and corridor management tests in Houston, San Antonio, and New York. In the same year, a more thorough evaluation of integrated regionwide approaches to transportation management identified nine favorable conditions for ITS deployment (DeBlasio et al., 1999). They include a number of institutional-related factors that are increasingly deemed necessary to successfully integrate technology into an organization's standard operations. The nine conditions are:

- Developing a regional perspective
- Making ITS visible
- Understanding the nuances of partnering
- Planning for long-term operations and management
- Developing a regional management structure
- Facilitating ITS within the organization
- Identifying appropriate procurement methods
- Addressing intellectual property rights early
- Developing written policies

As individual FOTs were completed in the late 1990s, independent third-party evaluations were released. They provided in-depth analysis of the technological, fiscal, and institutional factors contributing to the success or failure of a test. In Ann Arbor, where an integrated APTS was deployed on fixed route buses and paratransit vehicles, the evaluators found some improvement in on-time departures, but only modest changes overall (Levine et al., 1999). In Denver, the deployment of an AVL system did not result in more efficient scheduling as intended. Problems resulted from an inability to integrate new and existing software applications (Weatherford, 2000). In Atlanta, an ambitious ITS deployment including AVL, APC, in-vehicle signage, wayside information devices, and information kiosks was never fully deployed as intended. MARTA, the regional transit authority, had hoped to coordinate the deployment with the 1996 summer Olympics. Ultimately, one-third of the system's buses were equipped with AVL and even fewer with APCs by the time the Games took place. The deployment of an integrated ITS system is on-going (Monahan et al., 2000).

Other evaluations have identified contracting arrangements, project management, and lack of clear objectives as major issues in FOTs (Hall, 1999; MacCarley et al., 2000). In at least one case, with an FOT discussed below, the USDOT has re-evaluated the test focusing on institutional capacity (Moniz, 2001).

Some recent studies have attempted to quantify regional aggregate benefits of ITS by using production function models and estimating impacts on total factor productivity (Gillen and Haynes, 2001; Thill and Rogova, 2001). In a study of paratransit operations, Pagano et al. (2001) determined that the use of computer-aided scheduling and dispatching systems do not show wide scale changes in efficiency; furthermore, the authors concluded that training plays a critical role in the adoption of new technology-based systems.

3.2 Evaluating the Impacts of Transit Integration Projects

Transit integration continues to play a more prominent role within the federal ITS deployment program. Of the 49 planned electronic fare payment systems in the U.S. in 2000, more than half were being designed to support multi-carrier fare integration (Goeddel, 2000). The USDOT has developed guidelines specifically for the ITS integration component (USDOT, 2001). The program's goals include providing incentives for institutional integration, and evaluations are required to address inter-agency cooperation. However, project funding is more dependent on the formulation of architectural and other technical standards, and not procedures for the integration of operations. There is a developing awareness that certain institutional factors play a role in successful inter-agency coordination (Lam and Miller, 2002), including shared goals and vision, but less of a consensus surrounding the means to measure institutional integration.

One difficulty is that the term "integration" comprises both technological integration via architectural standards and the integration of services through formal and informal agency agreements. There is a spectrum of integration that moves from compatibility (the case when one agency accepts the fare card of another) through interoperability of equipment and ends at complete service integration[4]. While technology-based integration efforts often have the latter as a goal, many only achieve something closer to technology compatibility. This is to be expected. Technology integration is more dependent upon vendor interoperability than on actual agency integration. Agency integration is much more difficult to achieve because it encompasses issues such as security, budgetary matters and governance, and often requires changes in the cultures of one or several agencies. It is not surprising that many of the early technology deployments and field tests focused on electronic fare payment. Fare payment systems provide a platform upon which to build technology integration programs but they do not automatically result in integrated services.

As evaluation guidelines develop, they will more accurately assess the impacts of technology deployments on safety, efficiency, cost, and customer satisfaction, i.e., the accepted evaluation measures. We propose an additional measure: a deployment's success at moving further along the integration spectrum if service integration is in fact the objective. We review previous deployments to determine if the tests result in new technology interfaces (such as fare card readers or common data platforms), compatible applications, or whether they actually result in the development of data exchange agreements, revenue sharing agreements or shared governance structures. In some cases, these tests have already undergone formal evaluation. It is our intent to contribute to those findings through further institutional analysis.

4. CASE STUDIES

This brief review suggests that while technical performance is essential, it does not guarantee FOT success. Many non-technical factors seem to play a role, particularly if service integration is the objective. Understanding the role of institutions and organizations in FOT outcomes requires detailed case studies, and relatively few have been conducted. We have chosen to revisit six different public transit technology tests to determine if they reveal new lessons about the relationship between technology performance and institutional performance. The exercise is beneficial because it allows us to consider the results from more recent phases of technology deployment not completed at the time of the original evaluation. Our approach also allows us to consider findings from a number of different tests; most evaluations are performed for a single FOT.

We have chosen both single agency tests and multi-agency tests as case studies. In attempting to move beyond benefits and costs as measures of effectiveness, it is important to consider the institutional context in which a test occurs. Single agency tests occur in the absence of pressures for service integration. The same technology deployed in both single agency and multi-agency settings may reveal the role that institutions play in the likely success of a deployment.

The case studies are not all in the same phase of deployment. In all cases at least the initial phase has been completed, but some have either begun or completed a second phase. Clearly the latter have the advantage of correcting their mistakes and showing progress in meeting identified objectives. We are interested in how the nature of the test, i.e., whether it involves a single agency or multiple agencies, contributes to the likelihood that agencies will use this advantage.

4.1 Description of Case Study FOTs

The case studies were selected in part on the basis of our own previous evaluation research, and in part to provide a reasonable cross-section of public agencies, technical complexity of the test, and as already discussed, requirements for inter-agency coordination. The case studies involved a review of all available reports on each FOT, as well as ex-post site visits and in-depth interviews with key participants where feasible. In two cases, the authors conducted the original FOT evaluations. Table 1 gives basic information on the case study FOTs. Each is briefly summarized below.

1. WMATA SmarTrip Smart Fare Card System

The Washington DC Metropolitan Area Transit Authority (WMATA) implemented its SmarTrip program in the spring of 1999. It is an extension of WMATA's magnetic stripe cards in use since 1976. SmarTrip is a permanent, rechargeable farecard system designed for use on WMATA's subways and in transit facility park-and-ride lots. The cards can be used to pre-purchase simplified fares for the agency's buses, but the buses themselves are not yet smart card-ready.

The transit agency adopted the smart card technology as a means of increasing passenger throughput, centralizing fare system bookkeeping, and for remote card tracking and fare enforcement. WMATA can place automatic blocks on lost or stolen cards. The agency intends to expand the system so that cards are accepted at local retailers.

The new contactless cards are embedded with an integrated circuit chip and read/write memory. Wireless communications are used to register the smart card when it comes within three inches of the fare reader. Data is recorded at WMATA headquarters. After the initial purchase of the smart card, passengers are able to continually refresh the card's cash value via currency, debit cards, or credit cards.

WMATA began development of a smart card fare system in 1995 as part of an earlier FOT (WMATA, 1996). The result was a cumbersome, battery-dependent card. The newly designed program uses a single vendor for the cards and fare equipment. The same vendor integrated the fare card system with the WMATA computer system using Windows-based software.

WMATA is using an incremental approach to system rollout. It tested the cards with agency employees and then with a small pool of 1,000 metro riders. It first tested only fare debits and has moved to add other card options at irregular intervals. WMATA has also entered into agreements with First Union Bank and Flexcar for tests of the smart card as a bank card and as an access card for car rentals.

Federal funding limitations meant that SmarTrip has not yet undergone formal evaluation. However various press reports indicate that WMATA sold 150,000 SmarTrip cards between May 1999 and March 2001, and agency personnel report that 250,000 cards are in use as of the spring of 2002 and that 7,000 new cards are being sold per month.

As a single agency test, SmarTrip did not require a platform compatible with other agencies' technology. The next step of this incremental approach is to integrate WMATA buses into the deployment. However, long-range goals include a regional smart card involving transit agencies in Washington DC, Maryland, and Virginia.

2. *CTA SmartCard Smart Fare Card System*

The Chicago Transit Authority debuted its SmartCard in 2000. Using the same technology and developer as the DC SmarTrip, SmartCard is a contactless, rechargeable fare card. It is being deployed on all CTA buses and at CTA rail stations as well as on buses run by the Pace bus system. As a whole, the system covers over 3,000 vehicles. The goal is to bring about more seamless transit within a single area.

Both CTA and Pace are divisions of the greater Northern Illinois Regional Transportation Authority (RTA). The RTA is responsible for financial oversight for CTA's city bus and rail service, Pace's six-county suburban bus system, and for Metra, a regional commuter rail line. Pace and CTA have some joint routes and share the same fare system. Metra is run on a zone-based fare system using different technology and has not taken part in the test.

The test allows fares to be deducted based on point of entry, resulting in more efficient fare reconciliation. Three thousand, five hundred cards were deployed in 2000 during the field test. CTA has authorized the deployment of 100,000 cards by the end of 2002. The initial goal of 300,000 was reduced in order to modify the card design.

SmartCard is the next step in the RTA's development of an ITS system. In the mid-1990s, it began implementing the Smart Intermodal Field Operation Test. The project was sponsored by RTA in conjunction with the City of Chicago Department of Transportation. It was designed to test two-way data communications in the service of improved bus operations. CTA tested computer-aided dispatching and enhanced data reporting as part of the FOT. The agency planned for expansions to include electronic fare payments and automated fare collection.

In 1997, CTA completed a 27-month deployment of an Automated Fare Collection (AFC) System on the agency's 141 rapid transit stations and 129 bus routes (Foote et al., 1999). The AFC is a magnetic stripe fare card that stores monetary value and decreases that value electronically with each ride or transfer. The CTA's Customer Service Division was reorganized as part of the deployment; some ticket agents became customer assistants with special training in answering complaints tied to automated fare cards. CTA also developed special units to process refunds.

Foote reported that CTA riders found the switch to fare cards difficult because of the initial cash outlay. Reduced fare riders, i.e., students, seniors, and the disabled, also indicated a low rate of conversion, at least initially. Cash remains an important fare medium. However, the CTA is using AFC technology as an important foundation on which to develop fare policy innovations, even with price insensitive riders. The agency used it in designing a university pass program capable of recording school and dates of validity. CTA also tested a transit fare system for disabled passengers in 1998. The system proved popular with users, and CTA reported \$11 million worth of savings—money that would normally be lost as a result of theft, human error, fraud, and fare evasion.

3. *San Francisco TransLink Smart Fare Card System*

TransLink debuted in the San Francisco Bay Area in 1993. It was one of the first on-board, computer automated fare collection programs using magnetic strip technology in the United States. The system was designed by the regional Metropolitan Transportation Commission, the local MPO, to allow transit passengers to use a single ticket to pay fares on Bay Area Rapid Transit (BART) trains, BART express buses, and buses run by the Central Contra Costa Transit Authority (CCCTA). The program underwent a formal evaluation in 1995 (Mundle and Associates, 1995).

Coordinated services have long been considered important in the Bay Area, where 21 different transit agencies are in operation. Some agencies established informal working arrangements as a result of the need to modify routes when BART rail service was begun (Lam and Miller, 2002).

BART, BART Express, and CCCTA had previously used paper passes as a means of coordinating fares. TransLink was designed to allow the operators to monitor ridership more effectively. BART's fare collection system recorded the number of transfers from CCCTA and BART buses at its fare gates. It was also hoped that TransLink would divide fare revenues more equitably. BART invoiced CCCTA for transfers from bus to BART and BART Express; CCCTA invoiced BART for all trips taken on its buses using TransLink.

The TransLink system included Bus Ticket Validators, a data storage module and fare gates. Electronic readers processed the data generated by the fare readers. BART was the equipment manager for all participants, although a third-party sales vendor assisted the agency with ticket orders.

Project design was done in phases with a planned extension of the service to Alameda County (AC) Transit in the East Bay. MTC first introduced the idea of a universal Bay Area ticket in the late 1970s and worked with local transit providers to develop multi-modal and multi-system passes. TransLink was its first attempt at a multi-agency magnetic fare card.

The MTC and the three participating agencies contributed members to a steering committee to oversee the project. MTC contracted with two different consultants; one to develop the technology, the other to review the organizational structures required for program support. The technology consultant's scope of work included working with AC Transit to secure compatible fareboxes in anticipation of joining the program, but AC Transit did not ever join the program. BART and CCCTA also entered into an inter-operator agreement covering roles and responsibilities, information reporting, public information, and pricing and revenue sharing.

The Mundle Report also suggests that TransLink's phased approach to system rollout, while limiting technological complexities, may have limited the effectiveness of the program. In surveys taken as part of the FOT, regional transit riders displayed an interest in transferring between BART and the San Francisco Municipal Railway (MUNI). MUNI was not part of the original TransLink system and its fare gates currently do not accept BART tickets. Surveys also indicated that TransLink users enjoyed pricing mechanisms that came with it but were not interested in transfers at all.

In the end, it was not possible to determine if TransLink truly facilitated transfers between BART services and CCCTA buses. System hardware and software problems resulted in unusable data. During a majority of the evaluation period, total CCCTA TransLink ridership as reported by the Central Contra Costa Transit Authority was less than the number of transfers reported by BART.

MTC remained interested in service coordination after the completion of the TransLink test. In 1996, state legislation authorized the commission to pursue consolidated transit service throughout the Bay Area; in 1999, the MTC awarded a 10-year, $110-million contract to a private sector consortium to make TransLink a universal transit ticket system for rail, ferry, and bus systems in 100 cities throughout northern California. This new test is being conducted in two phases; the pilot began in February 2002.

4. *Ventura County Smart Card Smart Fare Card System*

The Ventura Smart Card FOT implemented an integrated fare system across seven small transit operators in Ventura County (Giuliano, Moore, and Golob, 2000). The FOT was sponsored by the USDOT through Caltrans. The fare system involved smart fare cards, APCs, AVL, and related communications systems. The goals of the FOT were to provide seamless connections between the seven services (hence increasing ridership) and to provide reporting statistics (including passenger counts) for the seven operators.

The Ventura County Transportation Commission (VCTC) was the lead agency; partners in the FOT also included the seven operators (the county and six municipal services), the technology developer/integrator (who contracted with various hardware vendors), and state and federal contract monitors.

The technology system was complex and required data communication systems at garage facilities of each operator, as well as at each of the participating municipalities. Fare readers and APCs were installed on a variety of vehicles, often requiring customization. The fare system required a comprehensive database capable of monitoring sales and balances on all fare cards in near real-time.

The common fare system required agreements among all operators regarding fare sharing, treatment of transfers, policies regarding lost or stolen cards, etc. In addition, "seamless service" implied service coordination, e.g., ease of transfers between systems. The services, in fact, were not coordinated in any way, nor were there any institutional history of common transit policy within the county.

The FOT was beset with a variety of technical and institutional problems, and the system never operated as intended during the FOT. The FOT was made more complex by the inability of participants to agree on common policies, which placed additional burden on the technology. Few smart cards were sold and used, ridership was not positively affected, and the reporting data were never delivered. Nevertheless, the smart cards were retained after the end of the FOT, owing to the strong commitment of a now wiser VCTC. Eventually (2002) the system was replaced with newer generation cards and equipment built upon the previous iteration's prototype. The lessons also proved valuable to the industry in general, which, prior to the Ventura FOT, had little experience with this type of transportation payment system technology.

5. *Santa Clara County FOT Automated Dispatching System*

The Santa Clara Valley Transportation Agency (SCVTA), as part of its service to disabled persons, took part in a test of advanced paratransit capabilities. The test, sponsored by Caltrans, was conducted between 1994 and 1996 (Chira-Chavala et al., 1997). This test was motivated by the challenge of a vastly expanded clientele for the service due to Americans with Disabilities Act accessibility requirements. SCVTA's ADA service was run by a non-profit contract operator that screened eligible clients, entered into agreements with taxi and van companies covering specific service areas, dispatched ride requests, and monitored the quality of the service provided. This same contractor saw the opportunities afforded by new technology to improve productivity and thus become ADA compliant. Its objectives were the driving force behind the field test.

The FOT was designed to test automated trip scheduling systems, AVL equipment, and the flexibility of a digital geographic database in accommodating an increase in the demand for paratransit services. While ATSS was not new, software modifications were required to work within the paratransit environment. The contractor was already in the process of developing a technology program for its services and had both the technical and operational expertise to oversee the deployment on behalf of the SCVTA.

Limiting the scope of the FOT to a single paratransit application by a single agency with clear project objectives facilitated an implementation program based on those objectives. As a result, SCVTA successfully used AVL to limit the need for dispatch personnel to phone van and taxi providers about changes on the day of service, to facilitate monitoring on-time performance and real-time vehicle status in scheduling return trips, and to improve productivity without clients perceiving a degradation in service quality.

6. San Gabriel Valley Smart Shuttle Automated Dispatching System

The San Gabriel Valley (Los Angeles County) Smart Shuttle FOT took place from April 1997 until June 2000 (Giuliano, Moore, and O'Brien, 2001). The Federal Highway Administration, through the State of California Department of Transportation (Caltrans), funded a pilot project whose primary goal was to facilitate interoperability between two Dial-A-Ride shuttle services, a free localized fixed route shuttle service and two fixed route bus lines operated by a regional transit agency. The project featured automatic dispatching software meant to efficiently match riders and shuttle vans within individual transit services. It also used global positioning systems (GPS) to automatically track vehicle locations to more efficiently schedule trips in real time and to effectuate transfers

The FOT was administered at the local level by a regional association of governments (the MPO) and required the cooperation of three municipalities, a regional transit agency, as well as the private contract service operators. The relevant governing bodies approved participation in the FOT; however, there were no formal contractual arrangements, and no formal scope of work was defined for participation. Standard service contracts, the norm for many government agencies, were used for agreements between the MPO and a technology integrator. The technology integrator formalized contracts with software, hardware and communications vendors.

The participants in the San Gabriel Valley FOT began the project with differing levels of technological capacity in their operations. One Dial-A-Ride was run by hand; another was already using automated dispatching software and AVL. While this meant that a certain level of customization was required, the time frame of the FOT did not allow it. The legacy of a failed technology test in the FOT's previous incarnation (called ATHENA) placed added political pressure on the federal, state, and local authorities to deliver a project that showed some sort of favorable return on the public's investment.

As a result, parts of the system were deployed, but only limited integration was accomplished. A sufficient amount of hardware and software was deployed to show demonstration of data sharing, automated scheduling and, dispatching and system monitoring; but no real tests of coordinated transfers occurred. The FOT system was dismantled shortly after the end of the FOT, and there has been no further attempt to integrate these services.

4.2 Discussion

Table 2 summarizes the results of the case study FOTs. Based on the data we were able to collect, the technology was deployed and functioned as intended in Santa Clara. Washington deliberately reduced the scope of the smart card application to avoid technical problems. Chicago has successfully tested a smart card using an incremental approach, albeit on a limited scale. TransLink functioned from the perspective of the passenger, but card system data were unreliable. Ventura County, using leading-edge smart card technology, experienced many technical performance problems: equipment breakdowns were high, APC data was unreliable, and reporting data were not delivered. In the San Gabriel Valley, some equipment was deployed but never used, reporting data were not delivered, the automated dispatching system was not used as intended, and transfer capability was tested but not implemented. San Gabriel Valley used the same dispatching software as Santa Clara, but attempted to customize it to allow coordination and communication between transit agencies.

Table 2 shows a similar pattern for accomplishment of FOT objectives. Chicago and Washington were successful in implementing a fare system that allows the passenger seamless transfer between modes. TransLink made transfers between BART and one local bus system easier, and served as a proof of concept for eventual adoption of a common fare system throughout the region. In Ventura and San Gabriel Valley, the intended service coordination never took place, although Ventura did retain the smart cards.

The findings suggest that it is possible to deploy all the technological elements of a test and still not meet a given set of objectives. This is particularly the case with service integration. In the San Gabriel Valley and in Ventura County, AVL, GPS, APCs, and other technologies were installed on vehicles as intended but without any discernible positive impact on operators or system users. There were observable negative impacts on operators. On the other hand, the tests also show that it is possible to only partially meet a test's technological objectives and still show some progress toward overarching service objectives. Operational tests in general can be valuable without being entirely successful because of the lessons they offer. In Washington, the lack of deployment on buses limited systemwide impacts of the smart card, but successful deployment on the subway and in the park-n-ride lots did result in an integrated fare mechanism and increased passenger throughput. It also set the stage for system expansion. In the Bay Area, despite some unreliable data, TransLink did result in a single fare ticket mechanism that is further being tested as part of an expanded TransLink in 2002.

How do we explain the disparate outcomes from FOTs using similar (and in some cases identical) technologies? Although each case study is unique, there are some tentative conclusions to be drawn. In general, single agency tests like the ones in Washington and Santa Clara benefit from a lack of competing objectives. In the case of multi-agency tests, objectives are more likely to be met where technology is deployed in conjunction with the development of operating agreements covering security, data exchange, and revenue sharing (Figure 1). The limited effectiveness of the San Gabriel and Ventura tests is the result of too much attention paid to technology integration and not enough to service integration. Our findings suggest that transit agencies must address both the technical and institutional complexity of proposed deployments and the capacity of the parties involved to overcome those complexities.

4.2.1 Technical Complexity

Part of the explanation for functional outcomes lies with the technology itself. FOTs using more mature technology in a standard way had better outcomes. In Chicago, a deliberately incremental strategy was followed, and smart cards were introduced after they had been tested in other places (including Ventura County). Smart cards were used in a very basic way, as a standard debit card. Washington learned from previous unsuccessful smart card experiments, and limited use of the cards until performance was reliable. Public transit buses are particularly hostile environments for sensitive equipment. After encountering these problems, Washington elected not to place card readers on buses at the start of the SmarTrip deployment. This dramatically affected the capability of the cards, but assured more reliable performance. Santa Clara used the state-of-the-art commercial dispatching software in a standard application. Although several contract operators were involved, each service was operated independently, with economies coming from joint management and oversight. In contrast, efforts to customize the same software to allow real-time location of fixed-route transit vehicles and coordinated transfers in San Gabriel Valley resulted in extensive technical problems.

Multi-agency FOTs are far more technologically complex, because of communications and data exchange requirements. A smart card common fare system requires a central database that keeps track of card status, and a communications system to link participating transit operators and provide near real-time information on-board the transit vehicles. Fare payments must be recorded and allocated to participants. If service coordination is involved, real-time, inter-agency communications links must be established. In addition, the system must provide adequate reporting for all participants. Technical complexity increases more than proportionately with the number of participating agencies for all these reasons.

4.2.2 Multiple Partners and Service Integration

As a group, the FOTs with multiple partners were less successful than those within a single agency. There are several explanations. First, the FOTs with multiple operating partners had more technical problems than those housed within a single agency. Although the intent of TransLink was to include AC Transit, the technical problem of compatible fareboxes could not be resolved. In other FOTs, card readers were installed adjacent to the farebox; hence it is likely a feasible solution existed. It seems likely that resistance from AC Transit was a key factor. In Ventura County, lack of agreement among the participating transit operators added greatly to the complexity of the system, and this in turn led to many software and hardware problems. For example, one operator wanted invalid cards locked out of the system, while others wanted a message to the driver so that the passenger could be warned. Operators also insisted on different fare policies and different methods for uploading and downloading system data.

Second, management and project control are more straightforward in a single agency. When several agencies are involved, either decision-making must take place via consensus, a time-consuming and sometimes ineffective process, or some agency must take the lead (multi-agency FOTs require a lead agency). The latter is less time consuming but the resulting relationships are more likely to be horizontal in nature, and this is itself problematic. In the San Francisco TransLink case and in the San Gabriel Valley, the MPO took the lead. In Ventura, it was the Ventura County Transportation Commission, which also operated one of the participating transit services. In all cases decision-making was shared at least to some extent. However, areas of disagreement tended not to be resolved or were resolved by the lead agency and not the operators.

Chicago is a hybrid case. While the smart card fare applies to both CTA and Pace, both agencies are part of the RTA, which performs funding and oversight for all regional public transportation services. Relationships between the three operating agencies (Metra is the commuter rail operator) are well established, and fare policies between operators were already in place before the FOT.

Third, multi-agency FOTs are less likely to have common, agreed-upon objectives. When a single agency makes the decision to test a new technology, the objectives the new technology are expected to achieve are clear and are more likely to be designed in support of a business strategy. If there is not a good reason to invest in the risks of a new technology test, the agency is unlikely to do so. In Washington, WMATA wanted better integration between the various services it provides, and the smart fare card fare was one way to accomplish this integration. All benefits of integration would accrue to WMATA. In contrast, when several agencies are involved, common objectives are less likely to exist. As we noted earlier, most transit agencies have little incentive to coordinate services. A new farecard might cause revenue losses or increased administrative costs for a participating transit agency.

Fourth, our case studies suggest that multi-agency FOTs are motivated by regional interests when spearheaded by MPOs, but these interests are not necessarily shared by the local transit operators. FOTs, by definition, are risky: the FOT will have unanticipated effects on the operating agencies; therefore the agency should have a clear reason for taking these risks (e.g., increasing productivity, reducing costs). When the MPO defines the project objectives, the result is a "top-down" decision-making process, where operating agencies are urged to participate in FOTs aimed at producing regional benefits that may not produce internal benefits. Political expediency encourages participation, but the incentive structure mitigates against it. The result may be passive participation that minimizes the agency's expected losses. This passivity is reinforced when participating agencies have no financial stake in the FOT, as is frequently the case.

4.2.3 Technical Capacity

FOTs implicitly assume a level of technical competence among all participants, but it is often the case that drivers, dispatchers, maintenance workers, and clerical staff have little experience with computers or other technology. Using an automated dispatching system, for example, presumes basic computer literacy for a semi-skilled, low-wage worker. Card readers, AVL, communications devices, and APCs are highly sophisticated technologies requiring constant monitoring and regular maintenance by qualified technicians. The typical bus driver or dispatcher is not trained to use or maintain such equipment, and the FOT may have a very limited budget, as was the case in Ventura and San Gabriel Valley. In Ventura, bus drivers turned off the driver messaging units because they could not be read in the glare of the sun, not knowing that turning these units back on would require rebooting the entire system. City staff charged with selling smart cards were incapable of entering data with sufficient accuracy. The problem was solved by reverting to faxes sent to VCTC, where the data was entered into the system. In the San Gabriel Valley, some dispatchers had no computer experience, and training began with such basics as turning the computer on and using a mouse, taking up time that had been budgeted for training on the automated dispatching system. Some drivers did not use the Mobile Data Terminals (MDTs) because they found it difficult and time-consuming to do so.

Communications between the technology developers and project participants also depends on technical capacity. Project planners who are not familiar with new technology have a difficult time conveying operational information and questions to the technology developers. Drivers, dispatchers, maintenance workers, and others may be overwhelmed by the technical jargon and unable to communicate basic information to the technology developers. Finally, managers and planners may underestimate the complexity of the performance specifications they require if they have limited technical training.

4.2.4 Institutional Capacity

Technology reinforces underlying strengths and weaknesses. The ability to integrate technology into an agency's operations suggests an internal flexibility that was not evident in all of the cases. This is easier in a single agency setting. All of the FOTs took advantage of expert contractors, but software and hardware technicians were only successful where effective business processes and organizational management were already in place. Santa Clara Valley Transit Authority had an existing relationship with a contractor and merely expanded its scope of work. The contractor had already proven adept at coordinating the services of other sub-contractors and vendors. As a result, ATSS was a component of that service, not its sole objective. This stands in sharp contrast to the experiences of San Gabriel Valley and Ventura County. In both cases, technology was deployed with the assistance of a third party. The third-party integrator in the San Gabriel Valley was unable to overcome the ineffectiveness of the local MPO and the lack of commitment to the FOT by some of the participants. The third-party project manager in Ventura County did not have the technical expertise to effectively manage the technology developer. Despite the best efforts of these integrators, the objective of service integration was not met.

Pre-existing agreements also facilitate good management because they provide a framework in which to negotiate change. The unique nature of the RTA in Chicago may have contributed to the flexibility of its member agencies. CTA and Pace had the benefit of RTA-coordinated cross-agency agreements. These agreements resulted in a working shared fare system prior to the adoption of an AFC or smart card system. CTA management also responded to customer reaction to the AFCs by reorganizing its customer service division.

The ability to recognize limitations is an institutional strength. In Washington's SmarTrip, one of the most effective decisions may have been to integrate the smart card system with WMATA's centralized computer system using Windows-based software. This reduced the need for agency personnel to become expert at entirely new systems. In the cases where institutions took on tasks outside their areas of expertise, the tests were more likely to be unsuccessful.

Finally, good management also plays a role in setting realistic goals for the FOT. In Santa Clara, Chicago, and Washington, technology implementation was an incremental process. Management had a good sense of what the technology could do, and the technical objectives were consistent with larger organizational objectives. With TransLink, despite some success at developing an integrated fare mechanism, the MTC did not have any actual control over the participating operators. The responsibility for project coordination did not include financial control of the project. MTC therefore could encourage vigorous participation by all parties or recruit other possible participants like AC Transit that did not see the benefits of taking part in the test. In Ventura, VCTC lacked similar powers.

In Ventura and the San Gabriel Valley, entirely new systems were attempted. Problems were ignored or minimized, as the primary goal of the FOT was to get the technology installed and operating. Lack of communication between participants, limited understanding of the complexity of the technical system, and the absence of any clear goals beyond the FOT itself contributed to the outcomes of these FOTs.

5. LESSONS LEARNED

The purpose of a technology test is to determine whether the given technology application is appropriate for adoption on a larger scale. The lessons we take from an FOT or any other test should lead to better outcomes in future tests. When significant findings are repeated in different settings, then the lessons are even more valuable. Our case studies suggest that single agency FOTs are quite different from multi-agency FOTs. Single agency FOTs were characterized by clear goals and objectives, an incremental approach to the technology, and effective management. These helped the agencies to make modifications to the technology as needed and appear to be requirements for all successful FOTs. Our lessons learned focus on the multi-agency tests, as these have had more mixed outcomes. It is our hope that these cautionary tales prove useful to both the TransLink and Ventura projects as they begin their second phases.

1. *Goals and objectives should be clear, appropriate, understood by all parties, and agreed upon by all parties, especially those charged with carrying out the FOT. The proposed solution should match the goals and objectives.*

ITS is effective only when it is an appropriate solution to an existing problem. It cannot be a solution in search of a problem. Particularly if multiple agencies are involved, the development of objectives should proceed incrementally so that participants have time to respond to changing situations. The difficulties of developing even incrementally new applications are generally underestimated. In the case of FOTs, small projects that are actually implemented will prove more cost effective and useful than larger scale projects that deploy technology without results.

In some cases, agencies should be prepared to accept a non-technological solution if it accomplishes what it is intended to do. For example, radio has proven effective as a means for communication within transit agencies (i.e., dispatcher to driver) and for communication of transit information to the public. To date, more complex systems have not demonstrated sufficient value added to effectively substitute for the radio.

2. *Institutional arrangements should be formal, clearly specified and should allocate responsibility and risk appropriately. Similarly, technology works best in the context of pre-existing institutional relationships.*

Not all institutional issues can be anticipated but they can be minimized if goals are clear and roles defined. Technology integration is not the same as service integration. Service integration can precede technology integration and involve formal contracts, service standards, and fare agreements. These institutional arrangements establish a framework by which service partners negotiate conflict and change. Pre-existing institutional relationships explain in part the differences between Chicago and Ventura. In the absence of formal agreements, it is possible for participants to drop in and out of the project and to change decisions on key matters. The adoption of technology requires the same framework to address licensing, procurement, performance and system modifications. It is easier to modify an existing agreement to incorporate technology than to bring about a new partnership tied to that technology.

3. *Technology adoption occurs within a more comprehensive systems framework. The adopting agency must exhibit a certain degree of technological capacity and organizational flexibility.*

It is clear that the ultimate users of the technology (transit employees, passengers) must have a minimal level of technical competence. This seems to be more of an issue for small municipal services that often rely on low-cost contractors. However, even in large agencies like WMATA, many problems were encountered in the earlier experiments. FOTs should consider the technical capacity of users and invest in the necessary training to ensure proper use and maintenance of all software and hardware.

Technological capacity is also necessary for effective project management, e.g., selecting reliable vendors and determining system technical requirements. Finally, only agencies that have successfully deployed technology internally will be able to successfully take part in regional projects aimed at technology and service integration. The same agencies must also show a willingness to respond to the changes brought about by technology adoption, including changes in personnel needs

TransLink, Ventura, and San Gabriel Valley all attempted to use technology to bring about some integration in regional transit services. In the San Francisco Bay Area, efforts to integrate fares had been pursued by MTC for over 15 years, yet resistance still existed. It is not surprising that the bus service that did participate with BART was one where a large share of their ridership came from BART commuters. In Ventura, VCTC had launched a new regional service, and therefore had an interest in trying to link this new service with the pre-existing local services. The local service providers had no such incentive. The smart card itself was not the problem, but rather the concept of common fare policies. In the San Gabriel Valley, there was neither the interest nor the need for service integration, and the technology was incapable of creating such a need. The lesson here is that institutional problems must be resolved before technology implementation.

Effective leadership can play a critical role in resolving institutional problems, establishing an agency's objectives, and encouraging effective multi-agency coordination. At the same time, there are risks to unchecked or unquestioned leadership. The decision of an elected official in the San Gabriel Valley to take on a multi-agency FOT was not made in consultation with the truly affected parties, i.e., the operators. As a result, the test was largely a failure.

4. *New technology tests should be as incremental as possible.*

This is an obvious conclusion. Because of the internal changes in procedures required with new technology, as well as the technical capacity requirements cited earlier, incremental implementation minimizes the burden on participants. It allows more effective troubleshooting and problem solving, and probably leads to better long-term outcomes. Washington is the best illustration of incremental strategy.

Multi-agency tests almost preclude incremental approaches. The number of participants requires customization and complex solutions to software and hardware compatibility from the start. As a result, deployments tend to focus on the integration of technology and not the integration of service that is usually the ultimate goal.

5. *The FOT should provide benefits to all participants.*

In exit interviews at San Gabriel Valley, we asked one of the participating operators what it would take to achieve inter-agency cooperation. The answer was acknowledgement that a problem existed and could be solved to the benefit of all parties by cooperative action. In single agency FOTs, this process of problem identification and solution takes place "in house." All the costs and all the benefits of the proposed action will accrue to the agency. Consequently, there are some built-in checks. If an FOT is generating serious problems, it will be downscaled, or perhaps even abandoned. When several agencies are involved, the distribution of benefits and costs are less clear. In our three multi-agency case studies, it was a perceived lack of benefits to the agency that was cited as a primary reason for non-participation or dissatisfaction with FOT outcomes.

ITS has significant potential to increase the efficiency and effectiveness of public transit. Use of AVL is now widespread among large transit agencies, and various types of smart fare cards have moved beyond the major rail transit systems. ITS applications have been particularly successful in single agency settings, where the purpose of using the technology is clear and where there exists sufficient technical and organizational capacity. ITS applications have to date been less successful in multi-agency settings, in part because developing multi-agency systems is far more complex, and in part because they demand substantial institutional capacity. Our case studies have shed some light on what may be required for more effective ITS applications in multi-agency settings.

Table 1. Case Study Summaries

FOT Name	Location	Time Period	Technology	Goal	Participants
SmarTrip	Washington DC	1999–2000	Contactless electronic payment	Fare integration for bus, rail and parking lots	WMATA, card and fare equipment vendor
Smart Card	Chicago	2000–2001	Contactless fare payment	Integration of bus and rail fare systems	CTA, Pace, smart card developer
TransLink	SF Bay Area	1993–1994	Automated fare card	Bus and rail fare coordination	MTC, BART, BART Bus and Central Contra Costa TA, card vendor, technology developer, organizational consultant
Smart Card III	Ventura County, CA	1995–1997	Smart fare cards, Automated Vehicle Locator Systems (AVL), Automated passenger counters (APC), Comm. Systems	Seamless county-wide transit	SCAT, VCTC, Ojai, Camarillo, Fillmore, Moorpark, Santa Paula, Simi Valley, Thousand Oaks, tech developer/ integrator
SMART	Santa Clara, CA	1994–1996	Automated trip scheduling (ATSS), AVL	Improve paratransit productivity	Santa Clara Valley TA, contract service provider
Smart Shuttle	San Gabriel Valley, Los Angeles County	1998–2000	AVL, ATSS, Comm.	Interoperability between transit and paratransit	Monrovia Transit, Arcadia Transit, Duarte, Foothill Transit, tech. integrator, software vendor

Table 2. Case Study Results

FOT	Elements Deployed	Elements Not Deployed	Functioning Elements	Non-Functioning Elements	Objectives Achieved	Objectives Not Achieved
DC SmarTrip	Contactless smart card with circuit chip, read/write memory, and radio frequency antenna	Card readers on buses; non-transit based debits	Smart Card integrated with WMATA centralized computer system		Coordinated fare mechanism for bus, metro and parking lots; increase passenger throughputs, customer convenience, (no card swiping); remote card tracking/fare enforcement; eliminate exit fares	
Chicago Smart Card	Contactless smart card with circuit chip, read/write memory, and radio frequency antenna		Smart Card and touchpad system		Intermodal inter-agency smart card; point-of entry fare deduction	
Bay Area TransLink	AFC on trains and buses (Bus ticket validators, data storage module and fare gates)		Bus ticket validators and fare gates	System software to read data (unreliable)	Single ticket fare mechanism	Increased transfers (undetermined)
Ventura County Smart Card III	Fare readers and APCs, smart cards, AVL, comm. systems, fare system database		Communications system	Unreliable APC counts, high rate of fare trans VMS equipment failure (post processing)		Coordinated service/transfers; increased ridership; fully automated collection

Table 2. Continued

FOT	Elements Deployed	Elements Not Deployed	Functioning Elements	Non-Functioning Elements	Objectives Achieved	Objectives Not Achieved
Santa Clara SMART	Automated trip scheduling software (ATSS), AVL, geographic database		ATSS, AVL, database		Improved productivity, on-time performance; maintained level of service	
San Gabriel Valley Smart Shuttle	ATSS, GPS/AVL, mobile data terminals		Computer-based client records, mobile data terminals (sporadic)	AVL, ATSS (relied upon dispatcher overrides)	Computer-based trip requests	Coordinated transfers/service integration, route deviation

	Technology Integration ⟶ Service Integration							
	Front-end interface	**Back-end interface**	**Applications compatibility**	**Formal data standard and exchange agreement**	**Formal security management agreement**	**Cost and revenue sharing agreement**	**Formal operations agreement**	**Shared governance and administration**
San Gabriel Valley		√						
Chicago	√	√	√	√	√	√	√	√
Ventura	√	√	√					
SF Bay Area	√	√	√	√		√	√	

Figure 1. The Integration Spectrum

NOTES

1. Between 1991and 2000, the rate of inflation was 27 percent.
2. Use of the Highway Trust Fund for non-highway purposes actually began in the early 1980s on a very limited basis. It was not until ISTEA that significant portions of the Fund became flexible (Dunn, 1998).
3. Transportation economists have argued that public transit is subject to economies of scale and density, and thus is a natural monopoly. Under such conditions a single regulated (and subsidized) provider is efficient (Small, 1992).
4. The authors are grateful to Michael Dinning, Chief of the Infrastructure Protection and Operations Division at the USDOT Volpe Center, for first suggesting the steps along the integration spectrum.

REFERENCES

American Public Transportation Association. *National Transit Summaries and Trends.* Washington, DC: American Public Transportation Association, 2000.

Casey, R. F., Collura, J. "Advanced Public Transportation Systems: Evaluation Guidelines," Report No. DOT-T-94-10, Washington DC: Office of Technical Assistance, Federal Transit Administration, 1994.

Casey, R. F., Labell, L. N., Moniz, L., Royal, J. W., Sheehan, M., Sheehan, T., Brown, A., Foy, M., Zirker, M., Schweiger, C. L., Marks, B., Kaplan, B., Parker, D. "Advanced Public Transportation Systems: The State of the Art Update 2000," Report No. FTA-MA-26-7007-00-1, Washington DC: U.S. Department of Transportation, 2000.

Chira-Chavala, T., Venter, C., Gosling, G. "Advanced Paratransit System: An Application of Digital Map, Automated Vehicle Scheduling and Vehicle Location Systems," Report No. UCB-ITS-RR-97-1, Berkeley, CA: University of California Institute of Transportation Studies, 1997.

DeBlasio, A. J., Jackson, D., Tallon, A., Powers, G., O'Donnell, J. "Successful Approaches to Deploying a Metropolitan Intelligent Transportation System," Report No. FHWA-JPO-99-032, Cambridge, MA: Volpe National Transportation Systems Center, 1999.

Dunn, J. A. *Driving Forces: The Automobile, its Enemies and the Politics of Mobility.* Washington, DC: Brookings Inst. Press, 1998.

Fielding, G. J. "Transit in American Cities," in *Geography of Urban Transportation,* S. Hanson, ed., New York: Guilford Press, 1995.

Foote, P. J., Patronsky, R. T., Stuart, D. G. "Transit Customer Acceptance of Automated Fare Collection Systems," *Journal of Public Transportation* 2(3), 1999, 1–20.

Gillen, D, Haynes, M. "Measuring Aggregate Productivity Benefits from Intelligent Transportation System Applications: The California Experience," *Transportation Research Record: Journal of the Transportation Research Board* 1774, 2001, 52–59.

Giuliano, G., Moore J. E., Golob, J. "Integrated Smart-Card Fare System: Results from Field Operational Test," *Transportation Research Record: Journal of the Transportation Research Board,* 1735, 2000, 138–146.

Giuliano, G., Moore J. E. II, O'Brien, T. "Advanced Technology and Integrated Public Transit: The San Gabriel Valley Smart Shuttle Field Operational Test," *Transportation Research Record: Journal of the Transportation Research Board,* 1774, 2001, 44–51.

Goeddel, D. L., "Benefits Assessment of Advanced Public Transportation System Technologies, Update 2000," Report No. DOT-VNTSC-FTA-00-02, Washington, DC: U.S. Department of Transportation, Federal Transit Administration, 2000.

Hall, R. "Institutional Issues in Traveler Information Dissemination: Lessons Learned from the TravInfo Field Operational Test," *ITS Journal,* 5, 1999, 3–38.

Jones, D. *Urban Transit Policy: An Economic and Political History.* Englewood Cliffs, NJ: Prentice Hall, 1985.

Kain, J. "The Urban Transportation Problem: A Reexamination and Update," *Essays in Transportation Economics and Policy,* J. Gomez-Ibanez, W. Tye and C. Winston, eds., Washington, DC: Brookings Inst., 1999.

Lam, A., Miller, M. A. "Investigating Institutional Aspects of Multi-Agency Transit Operations-Review of the Literature," Report No. UCB-ITS-PWP-2002-3, Berkeley, CA: University of California Institute of Transportation Studies, 2002.

Lave, C. "Measuring the Decline in Transit Productivity in the U.S.," *Transportation Planning and Technology* 15(2/4), 1991, 115–124.

Levine, J., Hong, Q., Hug Jr., G. E., Rodriguez, D. "Evaluation of the Advanced Operations System of the Ann Arbor Transportation Authority: Impacts of an Advanced Public Transportation System Demonstration Project," Report No. EDL 13193, Washington, DC: U.S. Department of Transportation, 1999.

MacCarley, C. A., Mattingly, S., McNally, M., Moore, J., Mezger, D. "Lessons Learned From the Irvine Integrated Freeway Ramp Metering/Arterial Adaptive Signal Control FOT," paper No. 01-3354 presented at the Transportation Research Board, 80th Meeting, Washington DC, January 2001.

Monahan, P., Schweiger, C.,. Buffkin, T. "Evaluation of the Metropolitan Atlanta Regional Transit Authority Intelligent Transportation System, Report No. FTA-MA-26-7007-2000-3, Washington, DC: U.S. Department of Transportation," 2000.

Moniz, L. "Promoting Seamless Regional Fare Coordination: Ventura County Fare Integration," Report No. FHWA-OP-01-033, Washington, DC: U.S. Department of Transportation, 2001.

Mundle & Associates, Inc. "Final Report:TransLink Monitoring Program," Report No. DTUM60-91-C-41020, Washington, DC: U.S. Department of Transportation, 1995.

Pagano, A., Metaxatos, M. P., King, M. "How Effective are Computer-Assisted Scheduling and Dispatching Systems in Paratransit?: Results from a Sample of Operators," paper No. 01-22094 presented at the Transportation Research Board, 80th Meeting, Washington DC, January 2001.

Proper, A. T. "ITS Benefits: 1999 Update," Report No. FHWA OP-99-012, Washington, DC: U.S. Department of Transportation, 1999

Pucher, J., Evans, T., Wenger, J. "Socioeconomics of Urban Travel: Evidence from the 1995 NPTS," *Transportation Quarterly*, 52(3), 1998, 15–33.

Small, K. A. *Urban Transportation Economics,* Vol. 51 of Fundamentals of Pure and Applied Economics series, Newark, NJ: Harwood Academic Publishers, 1992

Smerk, G. *The Federal Role in Urban Mass Transportation.* Bloomington, IN: Indiana University Press, 1991.

Thill, J.-C., Rogova, G. "Benefits Evaluation of Basic Information Dissemination Services," *Transportation Research Record: Journal of the Transportation Research Board* 1774, 2001, 60–70.

USDOT, *Guidelines for Participation in the FY02 ITS Integration Component of the ITS Deployment Program*, Washington, DC: FHWA, ITS, 2001.

USDOT. *ITS Benefits: Continuing Successes and Operational Test Results,* Washington, DC: FHWA, ITS, 1997.

Weatherford, M. "Assessment of the Denver Regional Transportation District's Automatic Vehicle Location System," Report No. FTA-MA-26-7007-2000-2, Washington, DC: U.S. Department of Transportation, 2000.

WMATA. *Uniform Fare Technology Test Program Report: February 1995–February 1996,* Washington, DC: Washington Metropolitan Area Transit Authority, 1996.

Chapter 8

TRAFFIC SIGNAL CONTROL SYSTEMS

Alex Skabardonis
Institute of Transportation Studies, University of California, Berkeley

Signal timing optimization of existing systems, signal coordination, and advanced traffic control, all have been proposed as components of Intelligent Transportation Systems (ITS) measures. However, quoted benefits are based on limited data. This chapter presents the findings from the analysis of the impacts of signal control improvements based on a large number of real-world implemented projects. Three major types of signal control improvements were analyzed: optimization of existing signal timing plans, signal coordination, and traffic responsive control. The study quantified both the level of, and the factors affecting, the improvements in traffic performance. Also, some key issues in performing benefit-cost analyses are discussed.

1. INTRODUCTION

Efficient traffic signal control has been recognized as an important component of the Advanced Traffic Control and Information Systems (ATMIS) element of Intelligent Transportation Systems (ITS), currently pursued as a way for improving the efficiency of existing transportation facilities. Synchronizing traffic signals along arterials or in a network, and optimizing the signal settings, result in smoother traffic flows, reducing idling and stopping. This, in turn, reduces fuel use, saves motorists travel time, diminishes wear and tear on vehicles, and cuts vehicular emissions.

Continuous traffic growth and difficulties in building new highway facilities through developed areas will mean that existing arterials and networks controlled by traffic signals will have to carry a higher portion of anticipated traffic increases. Transportation management centers (TMCs) incorporating freeway ramp metering and other access restrictions designed to protect mainline freeway capacity will introduce additional traffic on surface streets. New federal, state, and regional programs (e.g., transit priority) also may provide an impetus for greater attention to signal systems, particularly along major arterials.

A number of ITS-related publications report the benefits of "advanced" signal control systems in terms of reductions in travel times, delay, number of stops, and fuel consumption (1, 2, 3). Most of the cited benefits however, are based on limited data and do not relate to the geometric, traffic, and control characteristics of the specific project areas. Furthermore, reporting different measures of benefits from multiple sources could be misleading (e.g., "time savings of 41 percent and fuel consumption savings of eight percent"). More important, there is limited information on the monetary benefits and costs associated with the deployment of such systems.

In this chapter, we analyze the impacts of signal control improvements based on the results of actual real-world projects undertaken as part of the California's Fuel Efficient Traffic Signal Management (FETSIM) Program (4). We also discuss the effectiveness of traffic responsive control based on real-world data from the Los Angeles Advanced Traffic Control and Surveillance System (ATSAC) (5) and experiences from other agencies (6). We hope that this ongoing work will contribute to a better understanding of the level of, and the factors affecting the expected benefits, from improved signal control systems.

Sections 2 and 3 of the chapter briefly describe the FETSIM and Los Angeles ATSAC databases used in the analysis of benefits from signal timing optimization, signal coordination, and traffic responsive control. Section 4 presents the findings from the analysis of the results. Next, we discuss the issues involved in determining the benefit-cost (B/C) ratio of signal control improvements from the savings in travel time, fuel, and other measures of effectiveness (MOEs). The last section summarizes the key study findings along with recommendations for future work.

2. THE FETSIM PROGRAM: OVERVIEW AND DATABASE

The California's FETSIM Program provided financial assistance, training, and technical support to local agencies to optimize the timing of their signal systems over an 11-year period (1983–1993). The program's primary objective was to reduce stops, delays, and fuel consumption through the implementation of more effective signal timing plans. A second objective of the program was to enhance the capability of local traffic engineers to continue to manage their traffic signals effectively.

A total of 163 local agencies (154 cities and nine counties) participated in the FETSIM program in 334 projects retiming 12,245 signals at a total cost of \$16.1 million, or \$1,091 per signal. Most of the participants were located in the urbanized San Francisco Bay Area, Los Angeles, San Diego, and Orange counties. Thirty-nine projects (536 signalized intersections) also involved replacement of signal controllers, and installation of time-based coordination units to allow previously uncoordinated signals along arterials to function as a coordinated system.

Figure 1 shows the key characteristics of the FETSIM project areas. About 73 percent of the systems retimed were single or crossing arterials with a total of 5,364 (44 percent) traffic signals. The average size of arterial systems retimed was 15 signals, and the average size of grid systems was 51 signals. Signal systems' hardware ranged from electromechanical fixed-time controllers to state-of-the-art central control systems. Fifty-six percent of all the signals were traffic actuated; on single arterial systems 90 percent of the signals had actuated controllers. Most of the pretimed signals were located in the downtown areas of the larger cities. Coordination was mostly provided through hardwire interconnect, with phone lines used in about five percent of the signal systems. A significant proportion of the arterial systems are using on-street masters with time-based coordination units. Optimal signal timing plans were developed using the TRANSYT-7F computer model (7). TRANSYT was selected because it is publicly available, capable of handling complicated networks, it has been thoroughly field-tested, and it directly produces estimates of delay, stops, and fuel consumption to determine the savings from signal timing optimization.

TRANSYT includes a macroscopic (platoon-based) deterministic model that simulates existing conditions along signalized arterials or grid systems and estimates degree of saturation, travel time, delay, stops, fuel consumption, queue lengths, and other performance measures. Use of TRANSYT requires coding the network into links and nodes, and data on turning movements, saturation flows, speeds, and existing signal settings. The model outputs are compared to observed field conditions (normally travel times, delays, and queue lengths) and the model parameters are adjusted until the model reasonably replicates field conditions in the project area. TRANSYT then is used to optimize the timing plans (cycle length, splits, and offsets) for each time period (normally a.m., mid-day, and p.m. peak periods). The alternative plans are evaluated using the stop, delay, and fuel consumption estimates, and the best ones are implemented in the field. The estimation of benefits is based on the model estimates and "before" and "after" field studies.

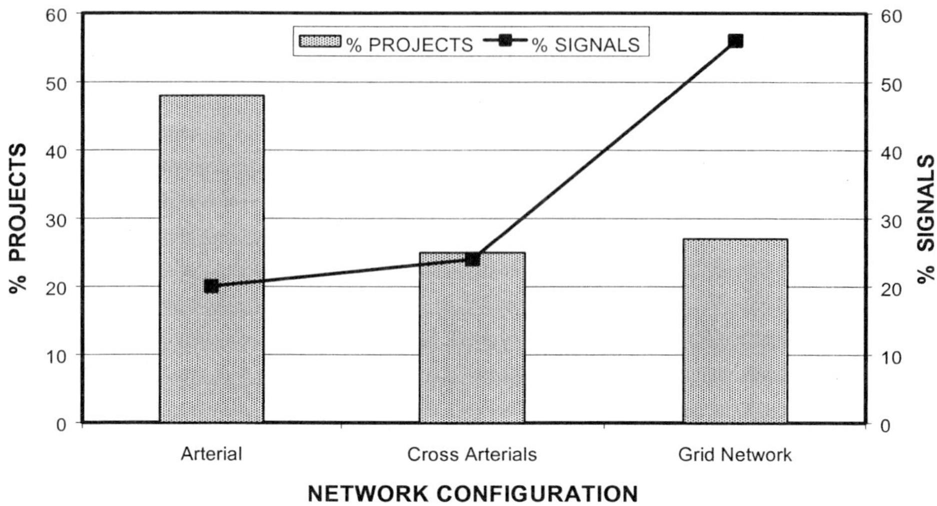

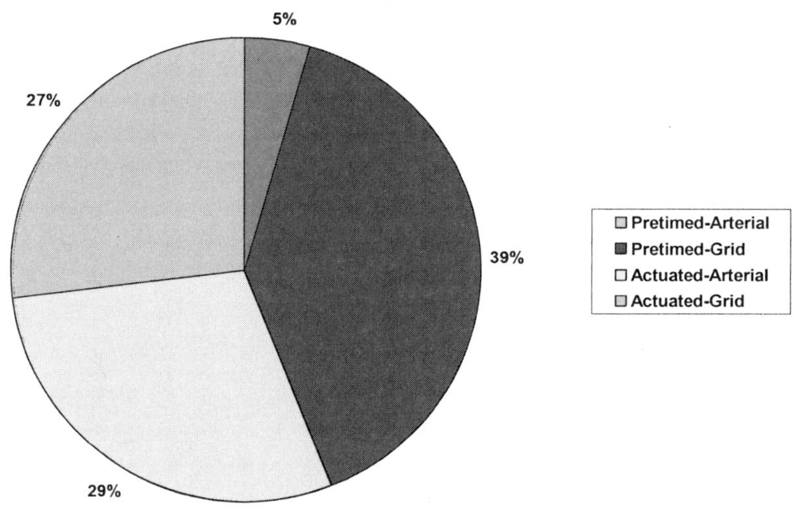

Figure 1. The FETSIM Database

Training was provided to the local agencies' staff and their consultants through a series of workshops designed to provide step-by-step guidance through lectures and laboratories in the application of the TRANSYT model. Follow-up technical support and review of interim products was also provided to ensure the successful completion of each project.

3. LOS ANGELES ATSAC CIC CONTROL

A real-time traffic control system can use vehicle detectors to collect cyclic traffic counts, which can be used to determine the best signal timings for each cycle. This allows the green times to never be more than one cycle behind the actual traffic conditions, which seems superior to optimal fixed-time control that is based on average hourly volumes. The Critical Intersection Control (CIC) is designed so that at a critical intersection, the green demand for each phase is calculated every cycle, while the cycle length and offsets remain fixed to maintain coordination. The CIC control software implemented in the LADOT ATSAC control system allocates the green times in each cycle to the conflicting movements based on volume and occupancy data from detectors located all the conflicting critical approaches.

The effectiveness of the CIC control strategy in improving the operational performance at signalized intersections was evaluated at seven real-life intersections, part of the ATSAC control system. Real-time detector data were obtained from the ATSAC *Detector Analysis Report*. The corresponding CIC timing splits was obtained from the ATSAC *Real Time Split Monitor Report*. The existing fixed-time time-of-day signal settings were obtained from the existing timing charts. These timing plans have all been recently optimized, so any improvements obtained from the CIC control due to obsolete fixed-time timing plans were expected to be minimal.

4. ANALYSIS OF THE PROJECT RESULTS

4.1 Benefits from Signal Timing Optimization

Based on TRANSYT model estimates, signal timing optimization of coordinated signal systems produced an average of 7.7 percent drop in travel time, 13.8 percent reduction in delays, 12.5 percent reduction in stops, and 7.8 percent decline in fuel use. The values represent the average percentage changes for an 11-hour weekday, unless specific volume adjustment factors were available from the individual cities. These average improvements are based on 163 projects (49 percent) of the total 334 projects in the FETSIM program and 6,701 signalized intersections (55 percent of the total retimed.)

Because the TRANSYT model often overestimates savings at intersection approaches when oversaturation occurs, such links were eliminated (based on the model outputs when available) in calculating the average improvements for each project. This may result in a slight underestimation of the total benefits.

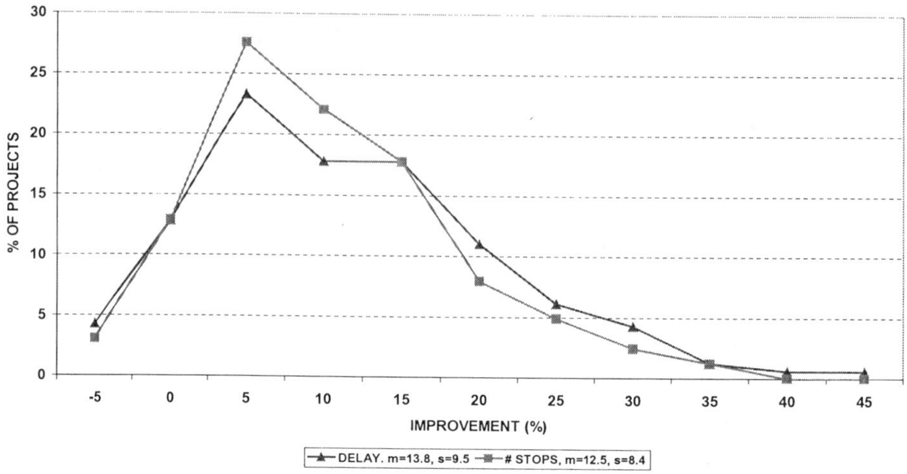

Figure 2. Distribution of Benefits–Signal Timing

Field studies were performed "before" and "after" the implementation of the optimized timing plans to measure the improvements in traffic flow using floating cars. The average measured savings for coordinated systems were 7.4 percent reduction in travel time, 16.5 percent reduction in delay, and 17 percent reduction in stops. These measured benefits are generally in agreement with the TRANSYT model estimates. The difference between TRANSYT and field results is due to the selected survey routes, number of test runs, and definitional differences. Most of the agencies that did field tests selected survey routes that followed the major arterials of their systems (or the through traffic for systems involving a single arterial.) They usually covered less than half of the total number of street segments (but more than half of the total vehicle-miles traveled) and in general undersampled turning movements.

Figure 2 shows the distribution of the percentage savings in delay and stops. The level of improvements in traffic performance varied considerably among the retiming projects. Some agencies found little or no improvement, and other reported gains of over 30 percent in delay and stops, and a 20 percent reduction in fuel consumption. The analysis of the results indicates that the following factors account for most of the variability in the estimated savings:

Quality of Existing Timing Plans (Baseline Conditions): Of the agencies that obtained little benefits, the majority reported that the existing timings were quite good, so the lack of substantial improvement appears to represent efficient operations "before" the signal timing optimization. Larger cities (Los Angeles, San Francisco) obtained somewhat lower percent savings in performance than smaller cities, which probably is due to better timings in the "before" case.

Network Configuration: Larger savings were realized on arterials than on grid networks (by an average of about five percent in delay and stops). Small improvements were obtained on simple systems (e.g., equally spaced arterials, one-way streets) that had been well timed with traditional methods (e.g., time-space diagrams). Also, several systems that had to be coordinated with other adjacent systems did not gain significant benefits because the timing optimization, particularly the cycle length, was constrained to maintain compatibility with the other systems.

Traffic Patterns: Larger savings were obtained on high-volume systems with predominant through movements. The improvements were small on systems with low volumes and no predominant platoons (e.g., networks with minimal activity outside the peak periods). Also, marginal savings were found on systems with several congested intersections that are in need for capacity improvements.

Signal Equipment: Higher benefits were obtained on systems with actuated signals and flexibility in choosing control parameters/options. The improvements on those systems depend on the understanding of the signal operations and implementation of the TRANSYT optimal settings into the actuated controllers. Equipment limitations (e.g., single dial controllers that permit only one cycle length and green times to be implemented) reduced the level of possible improvements in a number of projects. On average the benefits on arterials and grid networks with actuated signals were higher by five to seven percent than the improvements on pretimed signal systems.

Figure 3 shows the relationship between the savings in travel time and savings in fuel consumption based on the TRANSYT model results. The results indicate that the benefits in fuel use are generally linearly related to the travel time improvements. Thus, the travel time savings estimates could be used as a proxy for determining the improvements in fuel use, if direct estimates of fuel consumption savings are not available. It should be noted, however, that fuel savings are generally higher than the travel time savings (by up to five percent on the average) on arterial systems with closely spaced intersections.

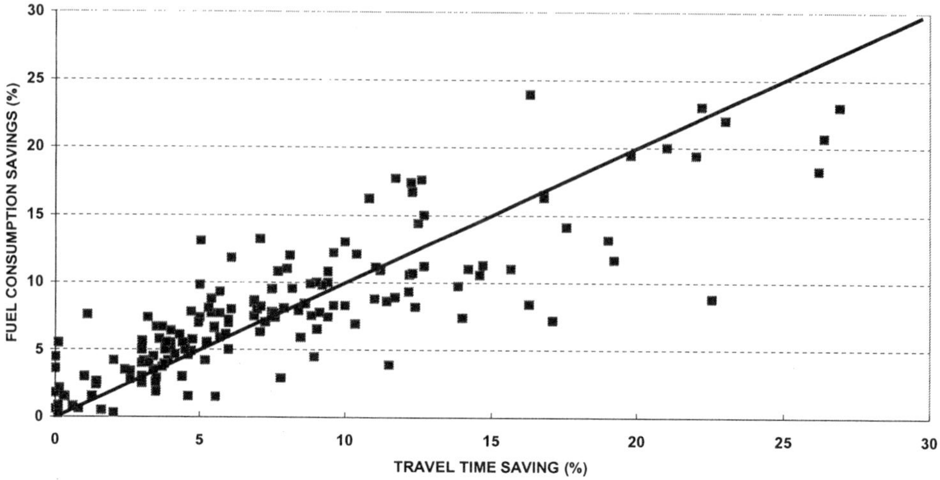

Figure 3. Fuel Consumption vs. Travel Time Savings

4.2 Benefits from Signal Coordination

The benefits from signal coordination were assessed based on "before" and "after" field studies using floating cars. The analysis of the field measurements from 76 projects (that obtained statistically significant results) show that on average the travel time was reduced by 11.4 percent, delay was cut by 24.9 percent, and stops were decreased by 27 percent. Figure 4 shows the cumulative distribution of the percentage improvements in traffic performance. Approximately 65 percent of the projects had benefits within the 10 to 35 percent range.

Signal coordination produces major benefits for the through traffic for signal spacing up to 0.5 mile and moderate to heavy traffic volumes (volume/capacity ratio $\geq$ 0.6). The variation in intersection spacing, proportion of turning traffic, and signal phasing are the main factors that influence the expected benefits between sites under the same overall traffic volume levels and average intersection spacing.

Signal coordination generally worsened the traffic performance on the systems' entry links. The increase in delay on those links depends on the difference between the system cycle length and the optimal cycle length for isolated signal operation, the traffic volume on the approach, and the type of control (pretimed or actuated).

The trade-offs between the improvements on the through traffic and the disbenefits on the entry links of a network should be carefully assessed before assuming that signal coordination is the preferred strategy. The evaluation should consider both the relative percent change and the absolute differences in the delays and stops.

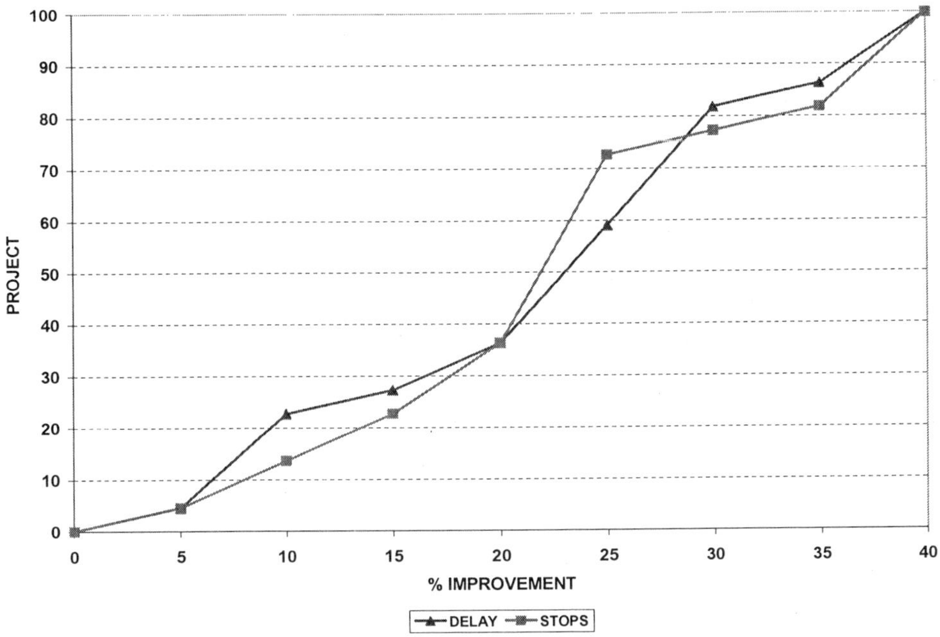

Figure 4. Distribution of Benefits—Signal Coordination

4.3 Benefits from Traffic Responsive—CIC Control

Table 1 shows the evaluation of the CIC control strategy in improving the operational performance at seven real-life intersections, part of the ATSAC control system in Los Angeles. The results indicate that CIC control generally improved intersection performance in terms of average delay and level of service (LOS) compared to the optimized fixed-time timing plans.

The effectiveness of CIC depends on the intersection geometric, traffic, and control characteristics. Significant reductions were realized on two-phase intersections with exclusive turning lanes, and/or unbalanced critical volumes. The flexibility of adjusting the green splits with CIC becomes limited on multiphase signals (because of the constraints of minimum phase times) and on intersections with more than one critical lane group during the same period of the day (i.e., all conflicting critical lane groups are close to saturation). Under such situations, CIC split adjustments are usually small because any improvements to one intersection approach results in disbenefits to the rest of the intersection approaches.

Table 1. Impacts of CIC Control – Los Angeles ATSAC System

Intersection	(v/c) Reduction (%)	Delay Reduction (%)	LOS (% of cycles) Improved	Same	Worsened
Melrose/Fairfax	8.3	13.2	41	59	0
Olympic/Sepulveda	1.8	4.0	0	100	0
National/Overland	0.0	3.1	0	100	0
6th Street:**					
-Broadway	14.0	10.8	53	42	5
-Spring	-4.7	4.9	0	100	0
'-Main	13.5	17.7	55	40	5
-Los Angeles	12.5*	16.2*	27	73	0

**Data for 10 cycles were not used-invalid volumes*

5. BENEFIT-COST ANALYSIS

There are several issues to be addressed in performing a benefit-cost (B/C) analysis of improved signal control strategies and systems, including but not limited to the MOEs to be considered, the monetary values for translating the MOE savings into benefits, and the time period for calculating the benefits and costs. Some of the issues are discussed below:

Monetary Values Assigned to the Savings in MOEs: Typically the savings in travel time (vehicle-hours) and fuel (gallons) are translated into monetary values for calculating the benefits from the signal control improvements. Several agencies have established such monetary values for evaluating alternative transportation improvements, e.g., construction of new highway facilities. These values may be adjusted to account for the drivers' perception of time benefits. Signal control improvements on average result in savings of one to two minutes/vehicle. Thus, the choice of monetary values for performing B/C analyses of control improvements should consider that the time-savings cannot be readily perceived by individual travelers.

Savings in MOEs vs. Monetary Benefits: High percentage improvements in traffic performance do not necessarily translate into large amounts of hours of time and gallons of fuel savings. The benefits depend on the baseline amounts of excess delay and fuel consumption. For example, a strategy that reduces delay by 10 percent in a heavily traveled system for a net benefit of 200 veh-hrs, would be more cost effective than a strategy which reduces delay by 20 percent, or a net benefit of 100 veh-hrs, in a system with light traffic volumes.

Baseline Conditions: Advanced signal control strategies that update the signal timing plans on-line based on detector data require significant investments in signal equipment and communications. The evaluation of benefits from such systems should consider the baseline conditions, i.e., was the previous system optimally timed or were the improvements due to signal optimization that could be achieved without additional capital signal improvements? The analysis methodology should determine a) the existing system performance, b) the system performance of the existing system with optimal signal settings, and c) the system performance with the new system. The difference in MOEs between (a) and (c) provides the change in total benefits, of which the difference between (b) and (c) is the incremental benefit due to the installation of the advanced control system.

Time Period for Estimation of Benefits and Costs: The improvements in traffic performance from signal timing optimization usually last three years on average. Several studies have reported that the performance degradation of optimal signal timing plans is about three percent per year in urban areas (8). The performance degradation is due to traffic growth and changes in traffic patterns. Therefore, it can be assumed that the benefits last three years for a one-time cost of signal retiming. However, the time periods for estimating benefits and costs for improved signal control with new signal hardware is more complicated. Hardware costs (signal controllers, communications) are much higher but their useful life is typically 10 to 15 years. The benefits however, last considerably less and may not depend entirely on the improved hardware, as discussed above (baseline conditions).

Additional Benefits: Improved signal control strategies produce several additional benefits; those include a substantial decrease in air pollutant emissions on project areas. Smoother traffic flows contribute to reduction in accidents. Bus operators and their riders benefit from better signal timing, since operating costs are reduced and average speeds improve. Such benefits are difficult to quantify for inclusion in the B/C analysis and strongly depend on the "base case" conditions in each project area. Air pollution reductions, for example, are more important in non-attainment areas than in cities with clean air; bus savings accrue when bus routes are affected. Nevertheless, these additional benefits could be significant at the local level and should be kept in mind in assessing the results from signal control improvements.

6. DISCUSSION

Signal timing optimization of existing systems, signal coordination, and advanced traffic control all have been proposed as components of ITS measures. However, quoted benefits are based on limited data. This chapter presents the findings from the analysis of the impacts of signal control improvements based on a large number of real-world implemented projects. Three major types of signal control improvements were analyzed: optimization of existing signal timing plans, signal coordination, and traffic responsive control. The study quantified both the level of, and the factors affecting, the improvements in traffic performance.

Based on results from over 163 implemented projects, signal timing optimization of coordinated signal systems produced an average of eight percent drop in travel time and fuel use, 14 percent reduction in delays, and 13 percent reduction in stops for a typical weekday. The major factors affecting the benefits include quality of existing timing plans, network configuration, traffic patterns, and signal equipment (pretimed vs. traffic actuated). Signal timing optimization is a highly cost/effective strategy because of its low cost. The estimated average B/C cost ratio in the FETSIM project areas is 17:1 based on the methodology recommended by AASHTO (9). Annual fuel savings alone outweigh the total program costs by more than 5:1.

Signal coordination produces significant reductions in delay, stops, and fuel consumption. The average improvements include an 11 percent reduction in travel time, 25 percent reduction in delay, and 27 percent reduction in the number of stops. The greater benefits occur on closely spaced arterials with high through volumes. The variation in intersection spacing, proportion of turning traffic, and signal phasing are the main factors that influence the expected benefits between sites under the same volumes and average intersection spacing. Signal coordination worsens the performance on entry (uncoordinated) movements in the system, typically side streets, and the trade-offs should be carefully assessed. The B/C ratio of signal coordination depends on the costs of signal control equipment.

The detailed evaluation of one traffic responsive control strategy (Los Angeles CIC) indicates it generally improved the intersection performance over the optimized fixed-time timing plans. The effectiveness of the CIC strategy depends on the intersection geometric, traffic and control characteristics. Significant reductions were obtained on two-phase intersections with exclusive turning lanes, and/or unbalanced critical volumes.

The assessment of the signal control improvements in this chapter considered the total system benefits. Benefits would be higher (or lower) on subsystems or individual links than the systemwide estimates as was already discussed for the case of signal coordination. Several other studies have reported benefits only on subsystems (e.g., through traffic on arterials) which makes it difficult to assess if the proposed strategies produced net efficiency gains or simply transferred the impacts to the rest of the system links.

There is a need to carefully quantify the benefits of other traffic signal systems and strategies that have been developed to respond to on-line changes in traffic volumes and adjust to current changes in traffic demand. Examples of such systems include SCOOT and SCATS plus recently proposed adaptive systems (RT-TRACS). The estimation of the expected benefits should be based on carefully undertaken field studies and simulation modeling.

ACKNOWLEDGMENTS

The chapter was based on the work in support of the FETSIM Program performed by the Institute of Transportation Studies, UC Berkeley under a series of contracts to the California Department of Transportation (Caltrans) and the California Energy Commission (CEC). Richard Macaluso of Caltrans Headquarters provided guidance and support. The collaborative work with the Los Angeles Department of Transportation was sponsored by the California PATH program at UC Berkeley.

The contents of this chapter reflect the views of the author, who is responsible for the facts and the accuracy of the data presented herein. The contents do not necessarily reflect the official views of or policy of the California Department of Transportation. This chapter does not constitute a standard, specification, or regulation.

REFERENCES

USDOT. "Intelligent Transportation Infrastructure Benefits: Expected and Experienced," Washington, DC, 1996.

USDOT. "Intelligent Transport Systems: Real World Benefits," Report FHWA-JPO-98-018, Washington, DC, 1998.

Chen, K., ed. "ITS Handbook 2000," PIARC Committee on Intelligent Transport, 2000.

Skabardonis A. "Evaluation of the Fuel Efficient Traffic Signal Management (FETSIM) Program: 1983–1993," Research Report UCB-ITS-RR-94-11, University of California, Berkeley, 1994.

Skabardonis, A., Gallaher, B., Patel, K. "Determining the Capacity Benefits of Real-Time Signal Control at an Intersection," *Transportation Research Record*, No. 1634, 1999.

Transportation Research Board. "Adaptive Signal Control Workshop," Traffic Signal Systems Committee, 80th TRB Annual Meeting, Washington DC, 2001.

Wallace, C. E., et al., "*TRANSYT-7F User's Manual*," prepared for the Federal Highway Administration, Office of Traffic Operations, 1983 (updated 1988/91/98).

Bell, M. C., Bretherton, R. D. "Ageing of Fixed-Time Traffic Signal Plans," Second International Conference on Road Traffic Control, London, 1986.

American Association of State Highway and Transportation Officials. "A Manual on User Benefit Analysis of Highway and Bus Transit Improvements," Washington, DC, 1977.

Chapter 9

EVALUATING EFFECTIVENESS OF RAMP METERS

Evidence from the Twin Cities Ramp Meter Shut-off

David Levinson
Department of Civil Engineering, University of Minnesota

Lei Zhang
Department of Civil Engineering, University of Minnesota

Ramp meters in the Twin Cities have been turned off for eight weeks in fall 2000 in an experiment testing their effectiveness. This chapter analyzes the data collected during the experiment on several representative freeways during the afternoon peak period. Several performance measures for ramp metering including mobility, equity, consumers' surplus, productivity, accessibility, and travel time variation are developed and applied to the studied freeways. It is found that ramp meters are particularly helpful for long trips relative to short trips. On TH169, trips more than three exits in length benefit, while those three exits or less are hurt by ramp meters. Ramp metering, while generally beneficial to freeway mainline, may not improve trip travel times (including ramp delays). Reduction in travel time variation with the presence of ramp metering is observed as another important benefit from ramp meters. The results are mixed, suggesting a more refined ramp control algorithm which explicitly considers ramp delay is in order.

1. INTRODUCTION

In what may be the single most comprehensive experiment in the history of surface transportation, ramp meters in the Twin Cities of Minneapolis and St. Paul, Minnesota, were turned off for eight weeks in October, November, and December 2000. This chapter presents the detailed results of an analysis of observed data of several representative freeways (Trunk Highway (TH) 169 northbound and southbound, I-94 eastbound, I-494 outer-loop/inner-loop and

TH62 westbound) during the afternoon peak period, and considers a variety of measures of effectiveness (MOE) resulting with and without ramp meters to control freeway traffic in the Twin Cities area. Earlier research (1)(2) identified a number of alternative performance measures. These include accessibility, mobility, equity, productivity, consumers' surplus, travel time variation.

The first ramp meter was installed in the Twin Cities in 1970 on southbound I-35E north of downtown St. Paul. Now, after 30 years of evolution, meters are standard on many freeways. There are currently 443 meters regulating ramp entrance flows throughout the metropolitan area. Figure 1 displays the number of ramp meters that were put into operation each year. Since the first installation of ramp meters, which operated as an isolated system, there has been sustained improvement in the system. Now, most of the ramp meters are controlled centrally in real-time. Also, initially there were single lane ramp meters, but to better utilize the system so that it does not affect the arterial or connecting roads, the usual practice now is to have two-lane ramp meters, which increases the storage capacity of ramps.

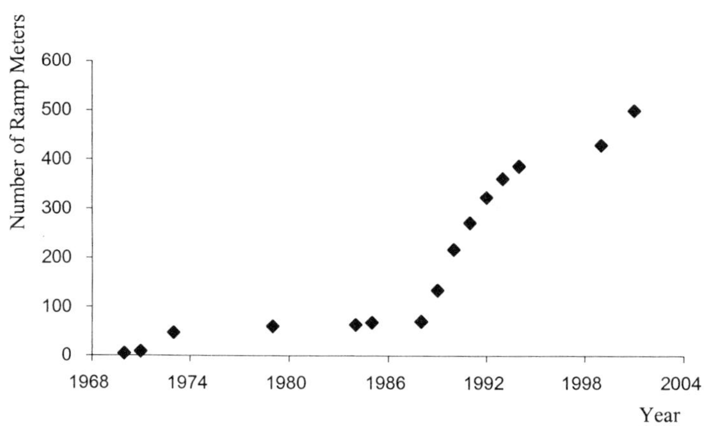

Figure 1. Ramp Meter Deployment in the Twin Cities Metro Area

Ramp meters in the Twin Cities were intended "to optimize flow in metro area freeway corridors by making efficient use of available transportation facilities" (3). The Minnesota Department of Transportation made this goal operational through a control strategy that divided freeways into zones terminating at bottlenecks. The control strategy was based on the concept of balancing the volume of traffic entering the zone with the volume of traffic leaving the zone, so as to ensure the capacity of the zone bottleneck would not be exceeded. Ramp metering was used to limit those vehicles entering the zone. The control algorithm has evolved into a real-time, volume-based, metering zone equation (subject to incident and occupancy override):

$$A + U + M + F = X + B + S \tag{1}$$

Where
A upstream mainline volume (measured variable)
U sum of unmetered entrance ramp volumes (measured variable)
M sum of metered local access ramp volumes (controlled variable)
F sum of metered freeway-to-freeway ramp volume (controlled variable)
X sum of exit ramp volumes (measured variables)
B downstream bottleneck volume at capacity (constant)
S space available within the zone (volume based on a measured variable)

For more details on the Minnesota algorithm, readers may refer to reference (3)(4)(5).

However, controversy arose when a state senator from rural Minnesota challenged the conventional wisdom of the state Department of Transportation. The long delays at some ramps (at times, though not generally, in excess of 20 minutes) to ensure that the freeway remained free-flowing drew the ire of some commuters, who believed the system was at best inefficiently managed. The state legislature passed a bill in spring 2000 requiring a ramp meter shut-off experiment. This chapter is an analysis of the data collected with and without metering. All data used in this study has passed the Mn/DOT Traffic Management Center continuity test for detector readings, which is an algorithm based on flow conservation to check the accuracy of detector data.

The next section details the method used to measure travel times on ramps and freeway segments from the data available. The following section outlines the various performance measures and shows how they are computed. Then results are presented for representative freeways for each of the performance measures. Recommendations and conclusions are delivered at the end of this chapter.

2. MEASURING TRAVEL TIMES

This section summarizes the calculation methodology required to measure travel times (and speeds) on entrance ramps, freeway segments, and origin-destination (OD) pairs on a highway with and without ramp meters. The computation of various performance measures to be introduced in the next section is based on measured travel times.

The data collected for entrance ramps come in two types of paired data in five-minute intervals:

a) Departure rate (Q_k) arrival rate (q_k) pair in each time interval (k) obtained from volume detectors.

b) Departure rate (Q_k) queue length (n_k) pair for each time interval obtained from volume detectors and periodic visual observation of queue length by remote cameras.

The second type of data can be transformed to the first type by Equation 2:

$$q_k = Q_k + 12(n_k - n_{k-1}) \tag{2}$$

Where
q_k the arrival rate in time interval *k* (vehicles/hour)
Q_k the departure rate in time interval *k* (vehicles/hour)
n_k the queue length in time interval *k* (number of vehicles)

Throughout the studied peak periods, all ramp upstream detectors have low occupancy readings and videotapes (at ramps without upstream detectors) don't show any queue spillover effects to local connecting streets. This assures that the delays at on-ramps represent total delays caused by ramp meters.

Using the I/O queuing diagram shown in Figure 2, it is possible to find the total travel time every individual vehicle spends at ramps: (t_2-t_1). This travel time contains two parts, the free flow travel time from ramp upstream detector to the departure detector and ramp delay. Since ramps are short in distance and the free flow travel time at ramps can be neglected, the time duration (t_2-t_1) will just be called ramp delay for the remainder of this chapter (A discussion on distinguishing "delay" and "waiting time in a queue" can be found in Lawson et al. (1997) (6) and Lovell and Windover (1999) (7) among others). The same method can be used to obtain arrival time, but assuming a uniform arrival at the back of the queue is not as accurate as assuming a uniform departure from the front of the metered queue, and is discussed more below.

The data are collected in five-minute intervals (5 minutes = 300 seconds). So, the average time headway for time interval k equals $300/Q_k$ (sec). Then the departure time of the first vehicle is t_1 which is equal to h_1. The departure time of the second vehicle is t_2 which is equal to (h_1+h_2). As the time headway is accumulated, the departure time (T_v) for every individual vehicle can be calculated. The arrival time (t_v) can also be obtained by the same methods. The delay (d_v) of every vehicle can be calculated by Equation 3:

$$d_v = T_v - t_v \tag{3}$$

Where
t_v arrival time for vehicle v
T_v departure time of vehicle v
d_v delay of vehicle v (sec)

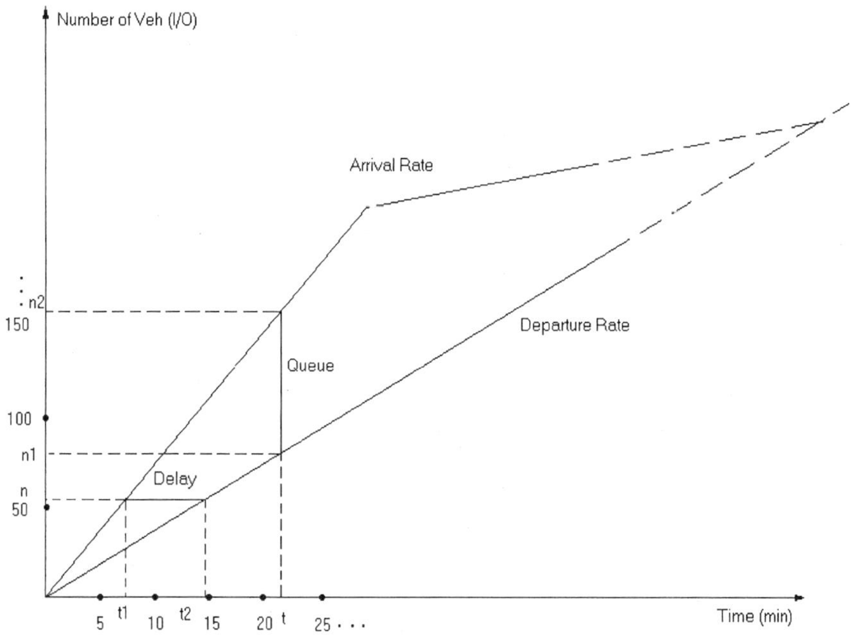

Figure 2. Queuing Diagram

The departure rate within the window is still assumed to be uniform due to the presence of ramp meters. An assumption must be made about the arrival rate of vehicles at the back of the queue. Observed data is only available in five-minute traffic counts. A uniform arrival rate would give a lower bound for delay estimation; a more reasonable assumption is to use a Poisson arrival process, which allows for bunching of vehicles. If the number of vehicles arriving at a queueing system has a Poisson distribution with a mean of q_k customers per unit of time, the time between arrivals has an exponential distribution with a mean of $1/q_k$. With the data collected by departure rate detectors, arrival rate detectors and queue length cameras at these ramps, the ramp delay for each vehicle and the average delay in each five-minute time interval are obtained. The Poisson arrival process at each entrance ramp is simulated for 50 times. The resulting individual vehicle headways of each simulation run are computed using Equation 3 and then averaged over all simulation runs.

$$\bar{u}_{s,k1} = 2.76 \times 10^{-5} (\frac{Q_{k1} L_v}{K_{k1}}) \quad (4)$$

Where
space mean speed of detector l in time interval k (km/sec)
Q_{kl} volume of detector l in time interval k (vehicles/hour)
L_v average vehicle length plus the length of the loop detector (m)
K_{kl} time occupancy of the 1st (2nd) detector in time interval k (%)

Average vehicle length plus detector length, L_v, commonly known as the effective vehicle length, is a crucial factor in estimating speed from inductive loop detector flow and occupancy readings. Average vehicle length estimates were taken from the Mn/DOT Traffic Management Center effective loop detector length calibration/normalization study. Since there is more than one loop detector at each station (multiple lanes), there are multiple space-mean speeds at one station derived from Equation 4. The density-weighted mean of all lanes will be used as the speed at each station, which is, e.g. for a two-lane freeway section:

$$\bar{u}_{s,k} = \frac{K_{k_1} \bar{u}_{s,k_1} + K_{k_2} \bar{u}_{s,k_2}}{K_{k_1} + K_{k_2}} \quad (5)$$

Assume that this speed is the average speed within this segment (that is, speeds within a segment are uniform). If there is no detector in a segment, the speed of the nearest station will be taken as the average speed in this segment (this kind of situation is very rare). Then the travel time of each time interval can be obtained:

$$\tau_k = L / \bar{u}_{s,k} \quad (6)$$

Where
τ_k travel time in time interval k (sec)
L length of the section (km)

We define that the free flow travel time (F) of a specified freeway segment as the shortest travel time on this segment of all the five-minute intervals (k) with and without ramp metering. The computed free flow travel speeds range from 93 to 123 km/hour depending on the freeway segment.

$$F = \min(\tau_k) \quad (7)$$

Delay during time interval k is defined as the difference between the free flow travel time (F) and the actual travel time (τ_k).[1]

$$d_k = \tau_k - F \tag{8}$$

Once delays at entrance ramps and travel times on freeway mainline segments in each time intervals are obtained, it is possible to build an OD travel time matrix. However, this requires that the ramp delays and freeway segment travel times be synchronized. A database which records the ramp delays and segment travel times for each five-minute period can be built using the above equations. The travel time for each OD pair (from ramp i to ramp j), by synchronizing the database, is:

$$\tau_{i,j,k} = d_{r,k} + \tau_{i,k+x1} + \tau_{i+1,k+x2} + \ldots + \tau_{j-1,k+x(j-i)} \tag{9}$$

Where

$\tau_{i,j,k}$ travel time from origin i to destination j departing in time interval k

$d_{r,k}$ delay on ramp r in time interval k

τ_{k+x1} travel time in the freeway segment i in time interval $(k+x_1)$

x synchronization coefficients; x is equal to the integer part of the quotient of the travel time from the origin to the beginning of the current segment divided by the time interval (300sec)

Similarly, an OD delay matrix can be obtained by synchronizing ramp delays and freeway mainline delays. Finally, combined with OD distance information, the OD travel time matrix generates an OD speed matrix.

3. PERFORMANCE MEASURES

3.1 Mobility

A number of performance measures are used to evaluate the ramp meters. Mobility, or ease of movement, can be measured on ramps, freeway segments, and for the system as a whole. Total delay, number of vehicles being delayed, average delay through the whole observation period, and average delay of each time interval are computed for each ramp. The travel time and delay for each freeway segment are measured. They are combined through synchronization into a series of OD matrices containing different mobility measures (travel time, travel delay, speed).

3.2 Equity

The Gini Coefficient of concentration (developed by Corrado Gini in 1936 (8)) and the Lorenz Curve (developed by Max O. Lorenz in 1905 (9)) have been used in economic studies to analyze income inequality. They are applied here to analyze travel time, delay, and speed inequalities. The distribution of the total delay is represented by the Lorenz curve and the statistical analysis is done using the Gini Coefficient, a measure of inequality. Figure 3 illustrates the Lorenz Curve for the case of Valley View Road entrance ramp on TH169, shown as the line separating A_1 and A_2 (the heavily shaded and lightly shaded areas respectively). The Lorenz Curve relates the proportion of the population receiving a given proportion of delay. While the bottom 100 percent of the population gets 100 percent of delay by definition, the bottom 50 percent may only get 30 percent of the delay. A Gini Coefficient of 0.0 indicates perfect equality, and 1.0 indicates perfect inequality (the most delayed person suffers all the delay). The Gini Coefficient (G) is defined as

$$G = A_1 / (A_1 + A_2) \tag{10}$$

Where

A_1 area between Lorenz Curve and 45-degree line

A_2 the rest of triangle defined by Lorenz Curve, x-axis, and vertical line projecting from 100 percent of the population in question

For each mobility measure OD matrix, corresponding spatial equity, temporal equity, and temporal-spatial equity are evaluated. The equity analysis is illustrated for the speed OD matrix, shown in Table 1. If the equity measures are calculated by the speeds in all the time intervals for just one OD pair (e.g. *speed 11, speed 21, ... , speed m1*), the temporal equity can be evaluated. Temporal equity measures the differences between drivers who travel on the same route but arrive at the origin (entrance ramp) at different times. On the other hand, if the equity measures are obtained with respect to the speed in the same time intervals but different OD pairs (e.g. *speed 11, speed 12, ... , speed 1n*), spatial equity results. These equity measures tell the differences between drivers who arrive at the different entrance ramps at the same time. Also, to evaluate the equity for the whole network throughout the observation period, the temporal-spatial equity measures can be used which are calculated by all the m × n speed values.

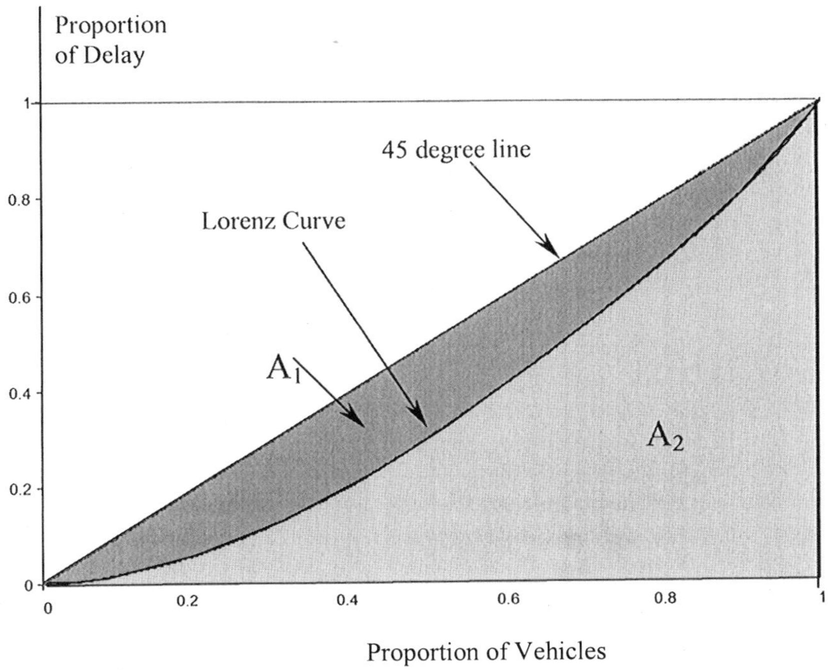

Figure 3. Lorenz Curve for Valley View Road Entrance Ramp on TH169

Table 1. Sample OD Speed Matrix

Speeds	OD pair *1*	OD pair *2*	…	OD pair *n*
Time Interval *1*	Speed *11*	Speed *12*	…	Speed *1n*
Time Interval *2*	Speed *21*	Speed *22*	…	Speed *2n*
…	…	…	…	…
Time Interval *m*	Speed *m1*	Speed *m2*	…	Speed *mn*

3.3 Consumers' Surplus

Consumer surplus measures the difference between the market price of a particular good and the price the buyer is willing to pay for that good. Because the willingness to pay varies between individuals, the consumer surpluses for two persons will not be the same. However, consumer surplus can be aggregated across individuals into consumers' surplus. In general, change in consumers' surplus is used rather than using consumers' surplus as an absolute measure, because it is more readily measured. In travel behavior, the price in this case is the travel time while the quantity of the good is the number of vehicles using the road network. As the travel time across a certain stretch of the traffic network decreases, there will be more vehicles willing to access the same stretch pushing the flow up. Mathematically, this can be approximated as:

$$\Delta CS = 0.5(Q_{off} + Q_{on})(\tau_{off} - \tau_{on}) \tag{11}$$

Where

Q_{on}, Q_{off} flows when the ramp meters are on, off respectively

τ_{on}, τ_{off} travel times when the ramp meters are on, off respectively

If the travel time when the ramp meters are switched off is greater, then there is a gain of consumer surplus with metering.

3.4 Productivity

Productivity is the ratio of the output of any product to the input that was required to produce that output. For freeway networks, vehicle kilometers traveled (*VKT*) is the main output and vehicle hours traveled (*VHT*) is the main input. In this case, a partial productivity factor (*P*) of a freeway network is equivalent to a measure of network average speed:

$$P = \frac{output}{input} = \frac{\sum VKT}{\sum VHT} = \frac{\sum QL}{\sum Q\tau} \tag{12}$$

The ratio of *VKT* and *VHT* is measured for each freeway segment and ramps separately and then combined to obtain the productivity of the system for both the metering-on and metering-off cases. Ramp metering is considered beneficial if the productivity with its presence is higher.

3.5 Accessibility

From the transportation planners' perspective, accessibility is defined as the ease of reaching destinations. Weibull (1980) (10) suggests that accessibility is a measure of an individual's ability to participate in activities in the environment. Areas with high congestion often have high accessibility. Three different functions of travel time are used; these are described in the results section. Freeway accessibility is computed both with and without ramp metering.

$$A_i = \sum_j Q_j f(\tau_{ij}) \tag{13}$$

Where

A_i accessibility of zone *i*

Q_j opportunities at zone *j*, measured using exit volumes

τ_{ij} travel time between *i* and *j*

3.6 Travel Time Variation

Travel time variation is simply the standard deviation of travel times. Travel time reliability is also used to quantify travel uncertainties, but in general defined in other ways (e.g., probability that the actual travel times will be less than a particular travel time). Here we look at two ways to calculate travel time variation: inter-day and intra-day (11). Equation 14 is used to calculate inter-day travel time deviation of all trips with the same OD pair starting at the same time interval across different days. Thus V_t stands for the *inter-day travel time variation* of this particular OD pair at time interval t:

$$V_t = \sqrt{\frac{\sum_{n=1}^{N} (\tau_{t,n} - \bar{\tau}_t)^2}{N-1}} \tag{14}$$

Where

V_t inter-day travel time variation of trips starting at time interval t

$\tau_{t,n}$ travel time of trips starting at time interval t in day n

$\bar{\tau}_t$ average travel time of trips starting at t across all N days

Then inter-day travel time variation difference (D_t) between metering-on ($V_{t,on}$) and metering-off ($V_{t,off}$) can be obtained by simply subtracting metering-on values from metering-off values:

$$D_t = V_{t,off} - V_{t,on} \tag{15}$$

Then for trips with the same OD pair, we acquire a vector of inter-day travel time variation differences across different time intervals during the p.m. peak: D_1, D_2, ... , D_t. By repeating this process, we acquire the same type of vectors for all OD pairs. The ranges (lower/upper bound) and median values of those vectors can be illustrated graphically with a range/median plot. Different from the previous performance measures, computation of inter-day travel time requires a multi-day data set. We select the last six weeks of the shut off period and the corresponding weeks in year 1999 with metering on to avoid the impacts of seasonal demand fluctuation. Some dates within these periods are excluded for further considerations such as bad weather or construction work on the studied freeways.

On the other hand, V_n is the *intra-day travel time variation* of all p.m. peak trips with the same OD in day n only. The equation for calculating V_n is:

$$V_n = \sqrt{\frac{\sum_{t=1}^{T}(\tau_{t,n} - \bar{\tau}_n)^2}{T-1}} \quad (16)$$

Where

V_n intra-day travel time variation of trips in day n

$\bar{\tau}_n$ average travel time of trips in day n throughout all T time intervals

Because of the criteria in selecting days described in the above paragraph, we couldn't get a perfect one-to-one match for intra-day travel time variation (for instance, days excluded from metering-on case may not be excluded from metering-off case and vice versa). Rather than showing travel time variation differences between metering-on and metering-off cases directly (as equation 15 for inter-day travel time variation), the averages of travel time variation are first computed separately for metering-on and metering-off cases. Then by comparing these two average values ($\bar{V}$), we ascertain whether ramp metering control reduces or increases intra-day travel time variation.

$$\bar{V} = \frac{\sum_{n=1}^{N} V_n}{N} \quad (17)$$

4. RESULTS

4.1 Mobility, Equity, Consumers' Surplus, Productivity, and Accessibility

TH169 northbound is divided into 16 freeway segments that are served by 16 entrance ramps. The analysis section begins at Valley View Road and continues until Medicine Lake Road. However, for the segment between TH62 eastbound and TH62 westbound, the data were unavailable and so the ramps were reduced to 15 in total. The data for the analysis include the five-minute flows and travel times on the freeway segments and the ramps for both the metered and the unmetered cases. The date, times (2:55 p.m.–6:10 p.m.), and locations of this analysis are the same across all performance measures for TH169. In order to make the results comparable, the data used for the analysis were collected on Tuesdays: March 21 (metering-on) and November 7 (metering-off), 2000. November 7 is the third Tuesday after ramp lights were shut down. The reason to choose a day in the third week of the shut-off experiment is to avoid the noisy and unrepresentative travel behaviors immediately after shut down and in the holiday season. Entrance ramp delays are only analyzed for March 21, as in the absence of ramp metering there should be no significant ramp delay. However, ramp volumes for both dates are considered.

First the relationship between mobility and equity for OD pairs on TH169 with and without ramp meters is estimated. Figures 4 and 5 illustrate the trends in the change of the mobility and equity with and without metering. Note that in Figure 4, the shortest trips (those on the right side of the graph) actually are hurt in mobility terms by ramp metering, while the longest trips (those on the left side) benefit the most. Figure 5 looks at the equity across time periods, and shows improving equity and worsening mobility as the peak is reached. Both results suggest that equity is increased when ramp metering is off.

What ramp meters deliver in term of mobility and equity can be shown by the comparison of the two cases in Table 2. Previous research indicates that ramp meters can increase the mobility of freeway networks, which is confirmed here. With ramp metering, the average travel speed (taking ramp delay into account) of the network increases from 37 to 62 km/hour; travel delay per km decreases from 82 sec to 68 sec and the average travel time for one trip decreased from 610 sec to 330 sec. No previous results can be relied to guide the analysis of equity. When looking at trips, a drop in the Gini Coefficient in the absence of metering is found. This suggests the system becomes fairer when meters are removed. This drop is observed for three primary measures: travel time per mile, travel speed, and travel delay per km, as shown in Table 2.

Table 3 shows productivity, the vehicle kilometers of travel per vehicle hours of travel on freeway segments and ramps. The freeway segments have productivity of 102 km/hour with metering and 52 km/hour without meters. The net productivity of the ramps themselves is 5.76 km/hour with meters and (by assumption) 40 km/hour without meters. Combining freeway segments with ramps gives a system productivity measure. The system productivity improves immensely with ramp metering. In fact the percentage increase in system productivity is 64 percent.

The changes in consumers' surplus for each individual segment are summed to get a benefit from metering of 3,531 vehicle hours. The change in consumers' surplus on ramps is found to be 639 vehicle hours. As expected, ramp meters significantly reduce the productivity and consumers' surplus of the ramps. The change in consumers' surplus of the system with ramp metering is overall positive, the ramp meters benefit the freeway segments more than they hurt the ramp segments, so an overall positive change in consumers' surplus of 2,893 vehicle hours is recorded.

Three different accessibility models were applied to TH169. The first is a classic gravity model, the second a model estimated for freeways in the Twin Cities, and the third from a regional gravity model estimated for Washington DC (Levinson and Kumar, 1995 (12)). For all the three cases, accessibility increases with the ramp metering, as shown in Table 4. However, there may be accessibility functions for which this is not the case.

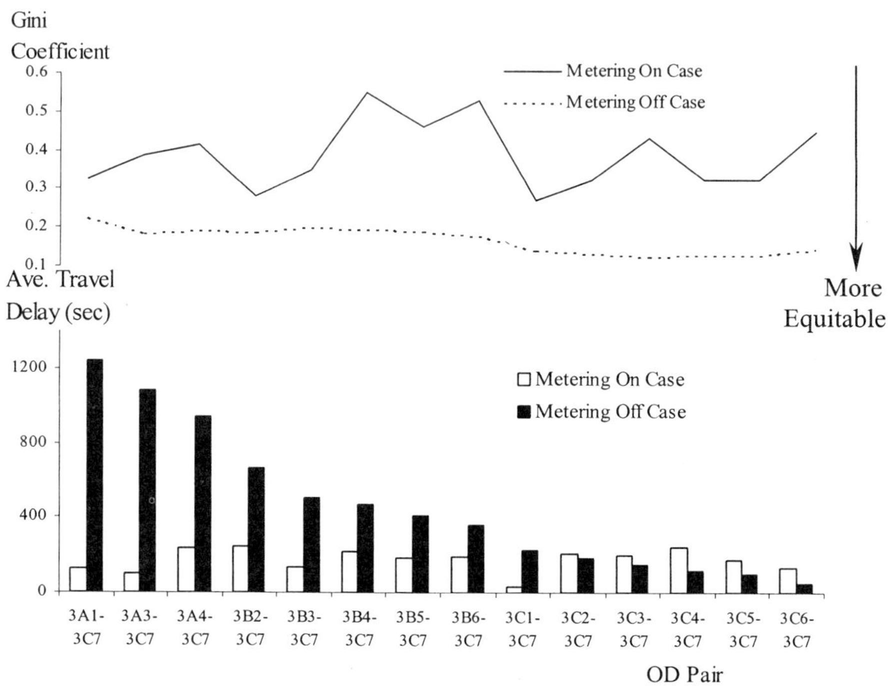

Figure 4. Temporal Equity and Mobility (Travel Delay) TH169

I-94 eastbound is divided into eight freeway segments from Olson Highway to Marion Street which consists of nine entrance ramps and eight freeway segments. Again, we are working with the afternoon peak period from 2:55 p.m.–6:10 p.m. Analyzing I-94 paints a somewhat different picture than TH169. In order to make the results more comparable, the data used to calculate in both cases were collected on Wednesdays (Mar. 29 metering-on and Nov. 01, 2000 metering-off (the third Wednesday of the shut-off experiment)).

Surprisingly, on I-94, the network mobility measures decrease slightly as the result of the ramp meter control. The average travel speed (taking ramp delay into account) of the network decreases from 87 km/hour (without control) to 79 km/hour (with control). Travel delay per mile increases from 27.9 sec (without control) to 42.1 sec (with control) and the average travel time for one trip increases from 285 sec (without control) to 299 sec (with control). In terms of temporal-spatial (network) equity: the ramp metering-off case is more equitable. Because the ramp off case has higher mobility, there is a negative relationship between mobility and equity.

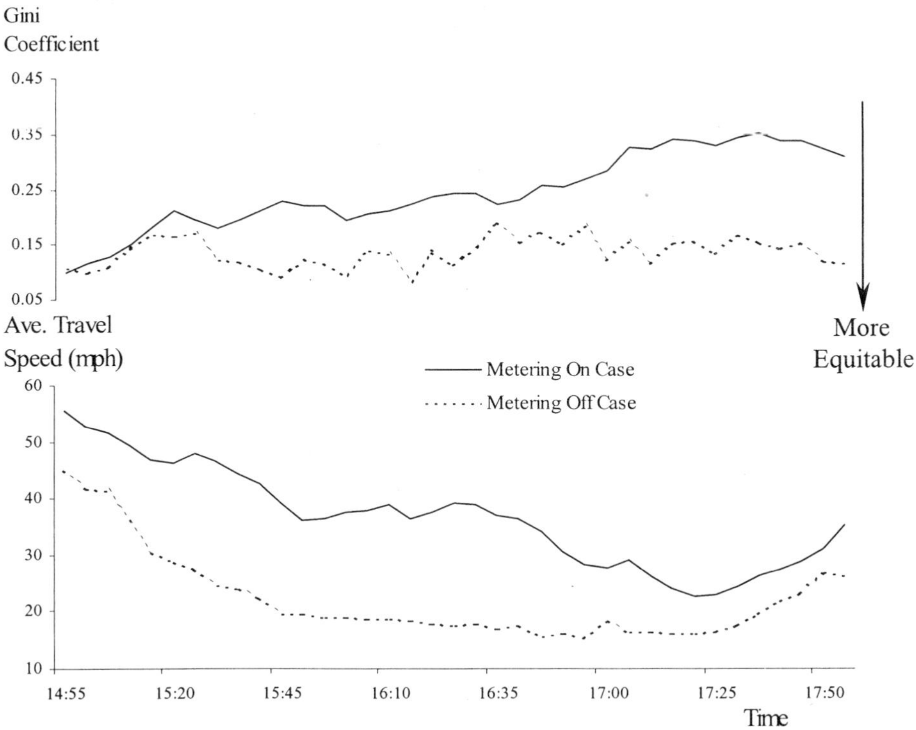

Figure 5. Spatial Equity and Mobility (Speed) TH169

Figure 6 shows temporal equity: overall ramp metering is less efficient and equitable than no metering. Also, the different effect of ramp control on long trips and short trips can be demonstrated by the figure—long trips are better off, short trips are worse off with metering. Figure 7 illustrates spatial equity: it seems that the relationship between spatial equity and mobility is positive, but this is not always the case.

Despite the seeming poor performance on the mobility measure, weighting the data differently, in Table 3, suggests an increase in the productivity of the system by 8.26 percent. The net change in the consumers' surplus of the whole system (including freeways and ramps) equals the sum of the individual changes of 481 vehicle hours.

The accessibility measures for I-94 are shown in Table 4. Unlike TH169, but consistent with our mobility measures, these results are mixed. In one of the three cases, accessibility falls with metering.

Table 2. Temporal-Spatial Equity and Mobility

			Travel Speed	Travel Time	Travel Delay
With Meters	TH169	Mobility Measures	62 km/hour	99 sec/km	68 sec/km
		Gini Coefficient	0.28	0.46	0.68
	I-94	Mobility Measures	79 km/hour	89 sec/km	42 sec/km
		Gini Coefficient	0.17	0.24	0.49
Without Meters	TH169	Mobility Measures	37 km/hour	113 sec/km	82 sec/km
		Gini Coefficient	0.23	0.21	0.28
	I-94	Mobility Measures	87 km/hour	75 sec/km	28 sec/km
		Gini Coefficient	0.14	0.16	0.39

Table 3. Productivity

		Segment VKT	VHT	Ramps VKT	VHT	Productivity (km/hour)
With meters	TH169	339822	3341	3994	703	85
	I-94	539286	5494	3785	264	94
Without meters	TH169	271388	5214	3815	95	52
	I-94	523027	5940	3819	95	87

Table 4. Accessibility Measures

Model	TH169			I-94		
	With Meters	Without Meters	% Change	With Meters	Without Meters	% Change
$f(C_{ij}) = 1/t_{ij}^2$	2.9	2.5	16%	12.5	8.5	46 %
$f(C_{ij}) = e^{-0.00189 \times t_{ij}}$	58932	34502	71 %	42977	43597	-1.4 %
$f(C_{ij}) = e^{-0.08 \times t_{ij}}$	93.2	63.772	46%	822.5	456.9	80 %

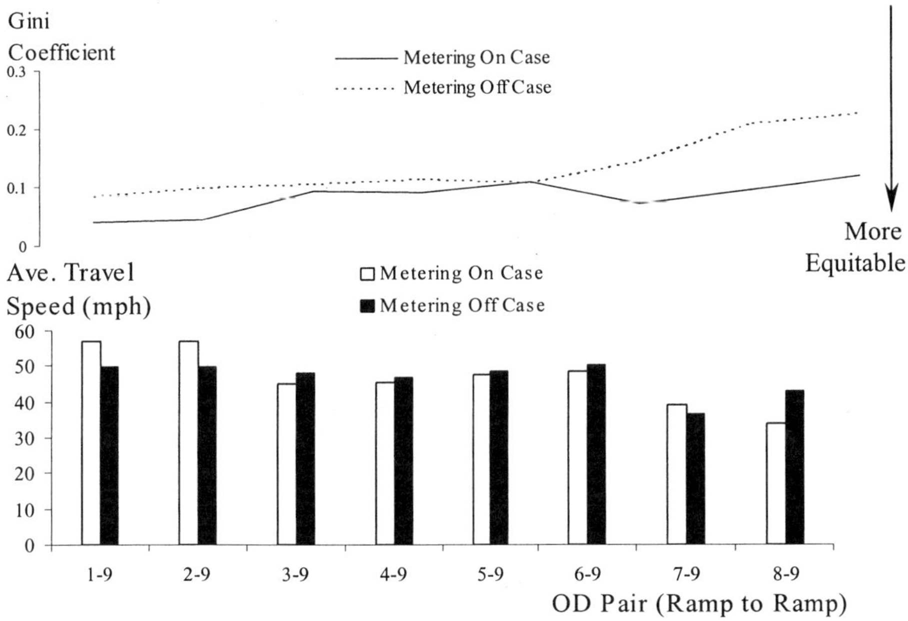

Figure 6. Temporal Equity and Mobility (Speed) I-94

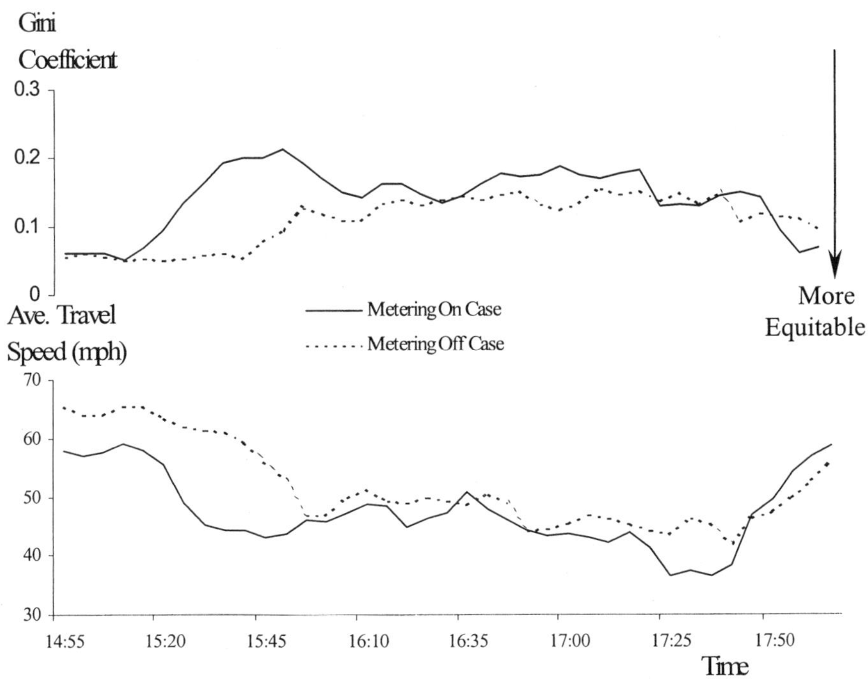

Figure 7. Spatial Equity and Mobility (Speed) I-94

4.2 Travel Time Variation

Inter-day travel time variation results for one (TH169) of the four studied freeways are shown graphically in Figure 7, which is representative. It is obvious that for most OD pairs, inter-day travel time variability is reduced by implementation of the ramp metering system (null hypothesis V_{off}–V_{on} > 0 cannot be rejected at level 0.01). Freeway peak hour travel reliability increases with ramp metering. One can find that for extremely short trips (≤5 km), it is hard to say whether ramp meters improve or reduce travel time variations. Figure 9 illustrates intra-day travel time variation results with two curves representing metering-on and metering-off cases respectively. It is clear that ramp meters play a positive role in reducing intra-day travel time variation. Just as the inter-day results, intra-day travel time variation of long trips is reduced more significantly than those of short trips.

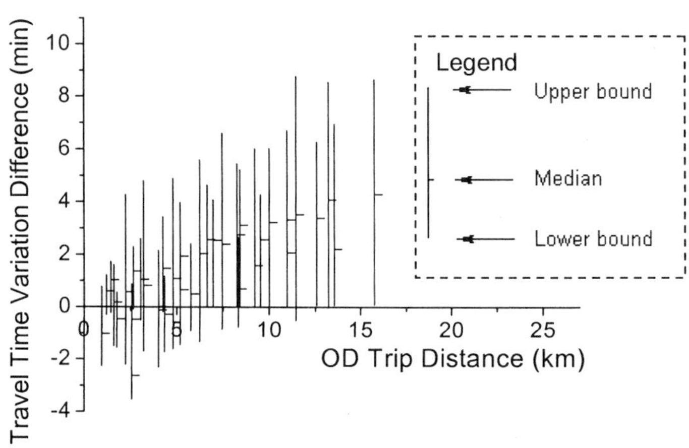

Figure 8. Inter-day Travel Time Variation Differences (Voff – Von) TH169

By assuming that all OD pairs have the same number of trips, overall average inter-day travel time variation differences can be obtained, which is 1.82 minutes. That means the implementation of ramp metering control can reduce 1.82 minutes of travel time standard deviation. Black and Towriss, 1993 (13), Small, 1995 (14) and Small et al., 1999 (15) estimated so-called "reliability ratio" (ratio of cost of standard deviation to mean travel time when scheduling costs are not separately considered) and consensus results of 0.7, 1.27, and 1.3 were obtained. Using the unit cost of travel time uncertainty—$0.21 per minute of standard deviation which was estimated by Small et al., (1999) (15) from a stated preference passenger survey in Los

Angeles, CA, ramp metering in the Twin Cities can save $0.38 for each freeway trip in terms of increased travel certainty.

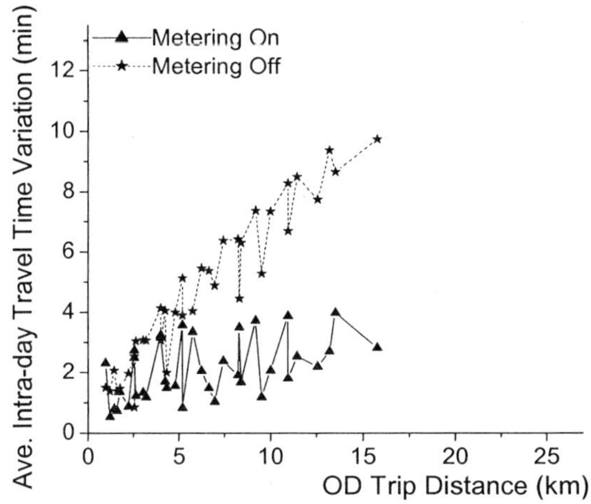

Figure 9. Intra-day Travel Time Variation with/without Ramp Metering TH169

5. CONCLUSIONS

This chapter dealt with a number of measures of effectiveness. In general, the findings were favorable to ramp metering on TH169. These findings are limited in scope as they are based on only one representative day of each of the metering and no-metering period. Different sections change the results of some performance measures. Analysis of I-94 for instance, tempers some of the glowing results for ramp metering, suggesting a larger proportion of origin-destination (OD) pairs are worse off with meters than without, though other overall measures of effectiveness are still generally positive.

The theory underlying the Minnesota zonal ramp metering strategy argues that maximized flows on the freeway mainline guarantees lowest travel time for the whole freeway system including ramps. Following this logic, the ramp meters were intended to maximize throughputs at selected freeway bottlenecks. This study of TH169 shows that the facility performs better in the presence of operating ramp meters than in their absence, judged by a majority of the measures of effectiveness (MOE). The change in consumers' surplus was positive and the productivity of the system almost doubled. Freeway speeds and flows are consistently higher with ramp metering on than without. Furthermore, TH169 shows better trip speeds with metering. These gains by ramp metering are logical when the intention is to maximize freeway throughput. However, this metering objective does not necessarily maximize user satisfaction of the system due to unevenly distributed ramp delays. In contrast, I-94 shows improvements to the operations of freeway mainline do not always offset the additional ramp delay. Metering must be used finely with a chisel, rather than coarsely with a sledgehammer.

Looking at the consistency of various performance measures developed in this chapter, it is found that mobility, consumers' surplus, productivity, and accessibility tend to provide the same conclusions on the effectiveness of ramp meters. However, equity trades off with other MOEs. When ramp metering is present, long trips benefits while short trips are hurt, suggesting a more inequitable situation than without metering. If a ramp metering objective only pays attention to mobility (efficiency), its poor equity indications will inevitably lead to an important public policy debate—should we reserve the freeways for long trips. If the answer is no, a more refined ramp metering theory, which considers both efficiency and equity, is in order. Future theoretical studies should pursue alternative objective functions. For instance, efficiency can be defined more broadly as maximizing the utility of travelers, recognizing a non-linear value of time (one-minute ramp delay is more onerous than one minute free-flow travel). A practical way to satisfy equity considerations is also suggested here: setting a constraint on individual ramp delay, even at the expense of overall freeway efficiency.

Any attempt to balance efficiency and equity of ramp meters must consider ramp delay in addition to freeway throughput. Unfortunately, current data do not permit any such strategies. Aside from a few spotty locations, there exists no accurate measure of the number of vehicles waiting in queue at a ramp meter at any given time in the Twin Cities. This study attached here uses data from special data collection efforts carried out by Mn/DOT's Traffic Management Center on a few freeway facilities. Unfortunately, such data collection efforts are not routine. Additional data collection systems to measure queue lengths in real time are required.

Ramp metering was designed to improve freeway traffic flow, and safety. While it generally does both, the analysis of travel time variation on all four studied freeways confirms that it also has the affect of improving travel time reliability for long trips. On average, ramp meters save $0.38 for each freeway trip in terms of increased travel certainty. Multiplying this figure by total annual peak hour trips, the resulting annual savings would exceed the monetized absolute travel time savings estimated in another parallel study (16)[2]. This huge gain of more reliable travel should be captured in the analysis of ramp metering benefits.

Finally, it must be kept in mind that ramp metering alone cannot be expected to mitigate traffic growth. Given the under-investment in highway capacity relative to growth in demand, and the current unwillingness to affect demand through pricing or other measures, congestion is inevitable. While ramp meters can help at the margins, by delaying the onset of freeway breakdowns and making freeways flow smoother, they cannot eliminate congestion entirely.

NOTES

1 Alternatively, freeway delay could have been defined as the difference between the actual travel time, and the desired travel time (the travel time with the speed limit). In that case, reducing speed from 120 km/hour to 110 km/hour increases travel time, but still counts as zero delay, as the speed remains above the speed limit.

2 A discussion of safety effects of ramp metering is also provided in this reference.

REFERENCES

1. Levinson, D. M. "Perspectives on Efficiency in Transportation," presented at the 81st TRB Annual Conference in Washington, DC, January 2002.
2. Levinson, D. M. "Identifying Winners and Losers in Transportation," (in press) *Transportation Research Record,* 2002.
3. Minnesota Department of Transportation. "Traffic Management Program Overview: Twin Cities Metro Area," Report Number TMC07043-0196, February 1996.
4. Minnesota Department of Transportation Metro Division. *Traffic Management Center (1998) Ramp Metering by Zone – The Minnesota Algorithm*, Working Report.
5. Bogenberger, K., May, A. D. "Advanced Coordinated Traffic Responsive Ramp Metering Strategies," California PATH Working Paper UCB-ITS-PWP-99-19, 1999.
6. Lawson, T. W., Lovell, D. J., Daganzo, C. F. "Using the Input-Output Diagram to Determine the Spatial and Temporal Extents of a Queue Upstream of a Bottleneck," *Transportation Research Record,* 1572, 1997.
7. Lovell, D. J., Windover, J. R. "Analyzing Freeway Traffic under Congestion: Traffic Dynamics Approach," discussion by D. J. Lovell and J. R. Windover. *Journal of Transportation Engineering*, July/August 1999.
8. Gini, C. *On the Measure of Concentration with Especial Reference to Income and Wealth*, Cowles Commission, 1936.
9. Lorenz, M. O. *Methods of Measuring the Concentration of Wealth*, Publication of the American Statistical Association, 9, 1995, 1905, 209–219.
10. Weibull, J. W. *On the Numerical Measurement of Accessibility. Environment and Planning A*, Vol. 12, 1980.
11. Bates, J., Dix, M., May, A. D. "Travel Time Variability and its Effect on Time of Day Choice for the Journey to Work Transportation Planning Methods," Proceedings Seminar C, PTRC. 1987, 299–311.
12. Levinson, D. M., Kumar, A. "A Multimodal Trip Distribution Model: Structure and Application," *Transportation Research Record*, 1466, 1995, 124–31.
13. Black, I. G., Towriss, J. G. *Demand Effects of Travel Time Reliability. Center for Logistics and Transportation*, Cranfield Institute of Technology, 1993.

14. Small, K. A., Noland, R. B., Koskenoja, P.-M. "Socio-economic Attributes and Impacts of Travel Reliability: A Stated Preference Approach," California PATH Report, MOU-117, 1995.
15. Small, K. A., Noland, R. B., Chu, X, Lewis, D. "Variation of Travel-Time Savings and Predictability in Congested Conditions for Highway User-Cost Estimation," NCHRP Report 431, 1999.
16. Cambridge Systematics. "Mn/DOT Ramp Metering Study Final Report," 2001 Web access http://www.dot.state.mn.us/rampmeterstudy/. Accessed on May 30, 2002.

Chapter 10

ELECTRONIC TOLL COLLECTION AND VARIABLE PRICING

Mark W. Burris
Texas A&M University

This chapter examines the incremental, societal, costs and benefits associated with (1) incorporating electronic toll collection (ETC) into an existing toll plaza, (2) replacing an existing toll plaza with electronic open road tolling, and (3) replacing the flat toll structure with a variable toll rate. Benefits resulting from the increased throughput of ETC included reduced delay, reduced fuel consumption, and reduced emissions. Costs included the purchase price, installation, and operation and maintenance costs. The analysis was based on a hypothetical toll road with three, 12-lane toll plazas and used empirical cost figures from toll plazas around the United States and Canada. Travel time benefits were derived using discrete event simulation modeling of the toll plazas. Fuel and emissions reductions were also developed via modeling. The incremental benefits of ETC were found to exceed costs in various traffic scenarios, increasingly so as traffic increased. Variable pricing was found to have significant net benefits in high traffic volumes, but costs exceeded benefits in uncongested traffic conditions.

1. INTRODUCTION

Electronic toll collection (ETC) made its debut on U.S. highways in Dallas in 1989 and, as of 2001, over 40 toll authorities in 19 states had implemented ETC (Kolb, 2002). Many of these toll authorities converted their existing toll plazas to incorporate ETC (Mitretek Systems Inc., 1999), since it can reduce traffic congestion, reduce queue lengths, and improve traffic flow (Al-Deek et al., 1997; Pietrzyk and Mierzejewski, 1993; Wilbur Smith Associates, 2001). The use of ETC has also been shown to significantly reduce harmful emissions and reduce fuel consumption (Sisson, 1995; Gillen et al., 1999; Saka et al., 2001, Levinson and Chang, 2003). This chapter examines these benefits and compares them to the costs of installing, operating, and maintaining two types of ETC systems: standard retrofitting of a plaza and open road tolling (ORT).

Incorporating a variable toll rate with ETC is another technique designed to decrease peak period congestion on the roadway. Agencies set toll rates that vary with the congestion level of the toll facility to reduce traffic demand during peak times. This demand shifts to off-peak periods with excess capacity, thereby improving the overall flow of traffic. Although only 19 such facilities currently exist (Burris and Pendyala, 2002), results indicate significant changes in traffic patterns can result from even small changes in toll price (Cain et al., 2001). This chapter will also examine the potential costs and benefits of implementing variable toll rates along with the ETC system.

Whereas much literature exists on the operational benefits of ETC, there have been few cost-benefit analyses performed on the implementation of such a system. In this chapter, results are presented from empirical data gathered on the cost of components required for the incorporation of ETC into a conventional toll plaza environment that previously offered only manual and automatic coin machine (ACM) toll collection. Next, the change in traffic flow resulting from ETC was derived from simulation models. This change in traffic flow resulted in an overall decrease in vehicle operating costs, a decrease in total travel time, reduced fuel consumption, and reduced emissions. These reductions were quantified to produce a monetary estimate of the benefit of ETC (for both standard retrofitting and ORT). Finally, a variable toll rate was introduced, and the resulting changes in traffic flow were analyzed to determine the additional benefits derived from this variable toll rate.

1.1 Electronic Toll Collection

To pay tolls electronically, a small transponder with a unique identification code must be attached to the toll-paying vehicle. In most cases this transponder is mounted to the front windshield of the vehicle. When the vehicle enters the toll plaza area, a reader identifies the transponder and the toll plaza computer system deducts the appropriate toll from the corresponding account. This process takes less than a second, and therefore vehicle speed through the plaza is limited only by safety concerns. This appeals to drivers because it eliminates the need for cash payments and removes the need to come to a complete stop to pay the toll. The majority of ETC systems are simply added to an existing toll plaza (retrofitted ETC). In the case of ORT, the plaza is removed and a gantry with readers and video enforcement systems is placed across the highway, allowing for the uninterrupted free flow of traffic at highway speed.

Typically, toll patrons obtain a transponder from the toll agency and are required to open an ETC account from which the tolls will be deducted. The primary method of opening an account is with a credit card. However, many agencies sell transponders and open accounts to patrons paying with cash, thereby allowing anonymous accounts. In this manner drivers have the convenience of ETC without the concern that the government will track their movements through their transponder.

ETC increases the benefits users derive from traveling by lowering the average variable cost (AVC) of driving (see Figure 1). Benefits are defined as the area above the generalized cost of travel and below the demand curve. The point at which the AVC intersects the demand curve indicates the generalized cost of travel (C_0) and flow of vehicles (Q_0). Traditional flat-rate tolls, fuel costs, vehicle operating costs, and travel time costs are the main components of the generalized cost.

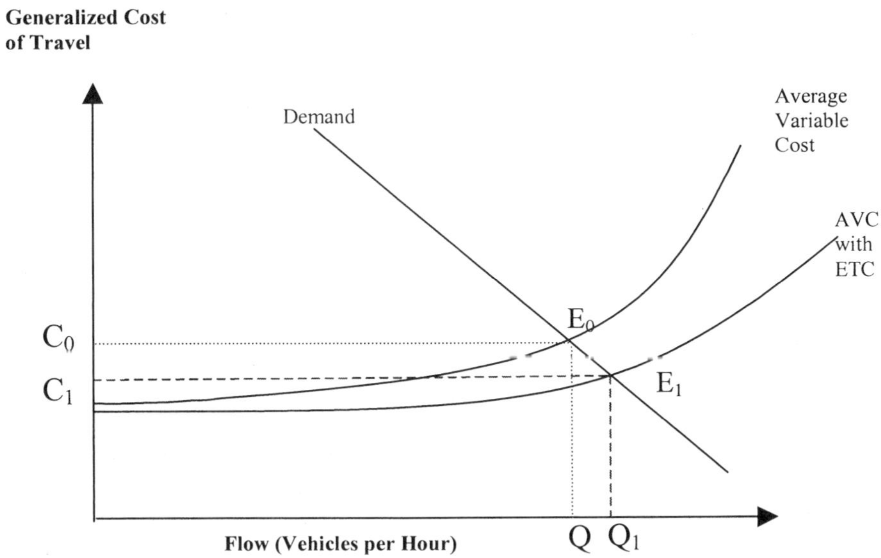

Figure 1. Change in AVC due to ETC Implementation

Tolls, vehicle operating costs, and fuel costs remain relatively constant with greater traffic flow, whereas travel time costs increase substantially as the flow of traffic nears the capacity of the facility. Therefore, under low flow conditions, the AVC remains relatively low as vehicles travel at or near the speed limit of the facility and spend the minimal amount of time traversing the facility. As the flow increases, congestion worsens, and travel times increase resulting in an increased cost of travel. The implementation of ETC can lower travel time through reduced queueing and nonstop toll transactions. Travel time reduction lowers the AVC and increases driver benefits by the area $C_0C_1E_1E_0$.

1.2 Variable Pricing

A similar demand graph illustrates the costs and benefits of variable pricing (Mohring, 1999) (see Figure 2). Without variable pricing, a flow of Q_0 vehicles can be expected at a price of C_0. Under these circumstances, the net societal benefit of travel is defined as the difference between user benefits (the area $a + b + c + d$) and welfare loss (the triangular area h). Welfare loss occurs under congested conditions because drivers do not pay the marginal cost of using the facility. Under congested conditions, the addition of a single vehicle can increase the travel time of all vehicles, yielding a high marginal cost. This cost is external to the driver and is not accounted for when deciding to travel, resulting in inefficient use of the facility.

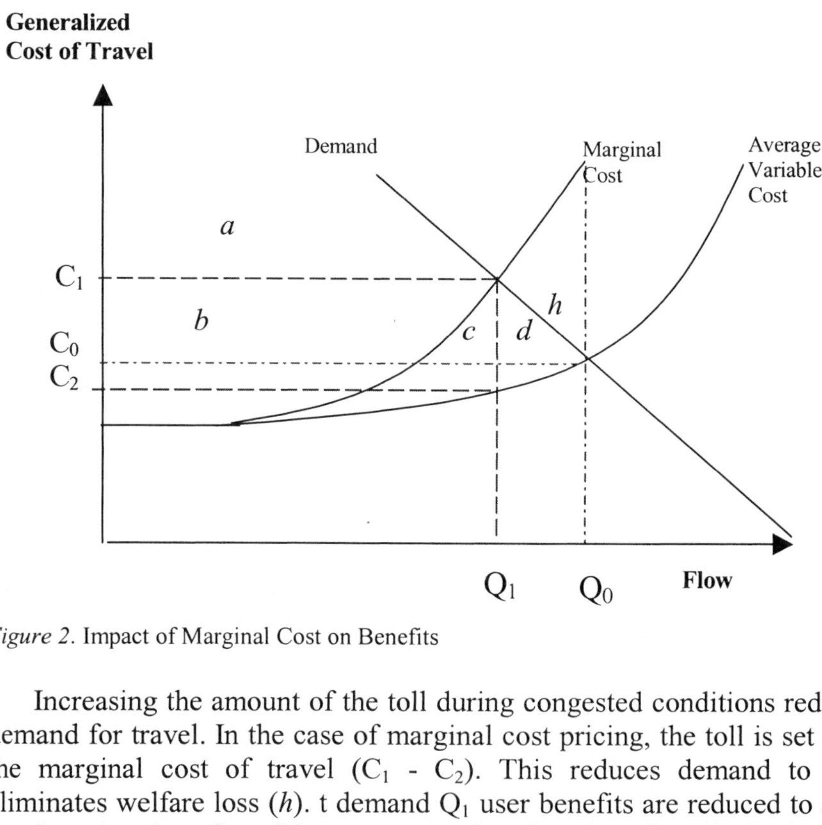

Figure 2. Impact of Marginal Cost on Benefits

Increasing the amount of the toll during congested conditions reduces the demand for travel. In the case of marginal cost pricing, the toll is set equal to the marginal cost of travel (C_1 - C_2). This reduces demand to Q_1 and eliminates welfare loss (h). t demand Q_1 user benefits are reduced to a, while previous user benefits of $b + c$ are transferred to the toll authority in the form of increased toll revenue. The benefits (d) are lost as some users (Q_0 - Q_1) forego the trip on the toll facility. Therefore, the change in net societal benefit is equal to h - d. As congestion worsens, the marginal cost and AVC curves diverge and the potential benefits of marginal cost pricing increases.

2. BENEFIT-COST ANALYSIS METHODOLOGY

This research followed standard practices used in the benefit-cost analysis of a transportation project (Federal Highway Administration, 2000; Li et al., 1999). Actual costs and benefits were used wherever possible. In some cases, such as the value of travel time savings, the time saved was estimated analytically and the value of that time savings was estimated using the latest research available. All values were estimated for the entire 10-year evaluation period and then reduced to a net present value. The present value of all incremental costs and benefits were compared to find the incremental benefit of implementing the ETC system. The benefit-cost ratio for the alternatives examined was found using Equation 1.

$$BCR = \frac{\text{benefits}}{\text{costs}} \tag{1}$$

A benefit-cost ratio greater than one indicated that the benefits of installing the system outweighed the costs over the evaluation period. In this research, a 10-year evaluation period was used based on the expected life of the ETC technology (U.S. Department of Transportation, 2002). The equipment was assumed to have no salvage value. The present value of most annual costs were found using Equation 2, with a real discount rate (r) of 3.1 percent (Office of Management and Budget, 2002).[1]

$$PV = \sum_{y=1}^{10} A \cdot \left[\frac{1}{(1+\mathrm{r})^{y-1}} \right] \tag{2}$$

where:

PV = present (year 1) value
A = annual cost
r = real interest rate (3.1%)
y = year of evaluation period (1 to 10)

This analysis did not include three costs: interest on toll deposits, the cost of violation processing, and the cost of increased crash rates. Users were required to open and maintain an account with the toll agency with a minimum balance in the account at all times. Drivers lost the interest that could have been earned if this money were invested rather than placed into an ETC account. However, although this was a cost to the user, it was a benefit to the toll authority, and was simply a transfer of wealth.

The cost of violation processing was also not included in this research. This analysis assumed that the revenue gained from the fines would meet or exceed the cost of prosecuting violators and collecting fines. To obtain a conservative estimate of net benefits this potential benefit was not included.

Finally, the possibility of an increased number of crashes resulting from ETC implementation was not included in the analysis. Abdelwahab and Abdel-Aty (2002) found that the use of ETC increases the probability of crashes at toll plazas. However, a literature review found no other examples of a statistically significant increase in crashes. Some research addressed the issue directly and found no significant correlation between ETC implementation and crash rates (Gillen et al., 1999; Li et al., 1999). Considering the speed differential between ETC vehicles and other vehicles it would not be surprising if further research revealed a significant increase in crashes after the installation of ETC. However, at this time the evidence on crash rates is unclear and the cost of crashes was not included.

Additionally, one direct potential benefit of ETC was not explicitly addressed. The addition of ETC in a toll plaza greatly increases the capacity of the plaza, thus delaying or eliminating the need for costly expansion of the plaza. This, in turn, would result in a cost savings for the toll authority. In all scenarios analyzed here except ORT, each toll plaza remained at 12 lanes for the life of the analysis.

Indirect benefits of installing ETC were also not addressed. For example, the ability to use ETC vehicles as probe vehicles for traffic data collection (such as Houston TranStar providing travel speeds in Houston: http://traffic.tamu.edu/incmap/incmap.aspx) was not included in benefit calculations. However, the incremental cost of these other ETC functions is significantly reduced due to installing ETC on the toll roads.

For this analysis, a model toll plaza system consisting of three toll plazas on a toll highway was developed. In this manner certain costs (such as transponders and the customer service center) were distributed across all three plazas. Each plaza initially had a total of 12 lanes, with eight automated coin machine (ACM) lanes and four manual lanes. A second model with each plaza consisting of four dedicated ETC lanes, four ACM/ETC lanes, and four manual/ETC lanes was used for the benefit-cost analysis of ETC, both with flat rate and variable rate tolls. ETC was installed in all lanes since toll authorities commonly provide ETC in all lanes, providing ETC paying patrons additional flexibility in lane use (Spock, 1998). For the evaluation of ORT, a four-lane toll road was assumed with readers mounted on overhead gantries at three locations.

3. QUANTIFYING COSTS AND BENEFITS

3.1 Baseline Costs

The baseline costs were the costs incurred by maintaining and operating the current toll plaza system for the evaluation period. The net costs were found by subtracting these baseline costs from the cost of purchasing, installing, operating, and maintaining the two types of ETC systems.

3.2 Costs of ETC

The incremental costs of adding an ETC system fell into six categories: lane equipment, installation, computer equipment, transponders, customer service, and operation and maintenance. Most costs were determined on a per lane basis. However, only one plaza computer was needed at each plaza. Also, both the host computer system and the customer service center served the entire toll plaza system, and only one of each was required. Table 9 shows a summary of all costs (see Note 2 for complete cost data and references).

Lane Equipment

The equipment necessary for ETC in a toll lane included automatic vehicle identification (AVI) equipment, automatic vehicle classification (AVC) equipment, a video enforcement system (VES), and other items such as display signs. The AVI equipment in an ETC lane typically includes an antenna and a reader. The antenna receives the signal from the vehicle transponder. The reader identifies the driver by the unique transponder identification number. AVC equipment automatically determines the classification of the vehicle (automobile, three-axle truck, four-axle truck, etc.) in order to charge the correct toll. Most toll plazas use a post-classification system that classifies the vehicle after the transponder has been read. A VES is necessary to prosecute violators. A VES usually consists of two video cameras that capture photographs of each violator's license plates. Cost data obtained during this research found an average lane cost of $30,000 for AVI, AVC, and signage, excluding the VES. The average cost for a VES was an additional $30,000 (see Note 2). Therefore, total lane equipment costs were estimated to be $60,000 per lane, or $2,160,000 for the entire 36-lane system.

For an ORT system, only two lanes are needed in each direction due to the very large throughput. This yields an equipment cost of $720,000. However, overhead gantries are necessary to mount the equipment. Cost data found an approximate gantry cost of $24,000. Therefore, the total lane equipment cost for the ORT system was estimated to be $792,000.

Installation

All installation costs associated with adding ETC equipment to a lane were included in this category. This includes installation of AVI hardware, AVC equipment, a VES, computer hardware, and computer software. The agency itself may perform installation, or it may contract the installation to another party. In most cases, the ETC equipment vendor handles installation. In this analysis, an approximate installation cost of $2,000 per lane was found (R. Harrington, North Texas Tollway Authority, personal communication, 2002). Additionally, several static road signs are necessary to direct drivers into the appropriate lanes at the correct speeds. This was estimated to be an additional $5,000 per lane. Multiplying this by the 36 lanes to be equipped with ETC systems yields a total installation cost of $252,000.

Installation costs of an ORT system are much higher due to the geometric modifications necessary. In order to install an ORT system, the existing toll plaza must be completely converted into a simple four-lane roadway. These costs include demolition, repaving, asphalt removal, and sod. Total costs were estimated to be $1,905,582 for the installation of the ORT system (Reich and Davis, 2001; Texas Department of Transportation, 2002).

Computer Equipment

Each toll plaza facility required a host computer and the accompanying software. Additional hardware was necessary to install in each ETC lane. The system also required additional data storage because of the large amount of information that must be kept regarding the toll users. Also included in the cost of computer equipment were auxiliary items such as printers, modems, and cables. The cost of computer equipment varied considerably depending on the quality of existing equipment. Those plazas with newer ACM systems would not need to invest as much capital in computer equipment as those with less state-of-the-art technologies. Research found average costs of $500,000 and $250,000 for host and plaza computer systems, respectively. This toll plaza system for both retrofitted ETC and ORT required one host computer and three plaza computers for a total cost of $1,250,000.

Transponders

Each vehicle paying the toll electronically required a transponder. There are currently three types of transponders commonly used in the U.S. Type I transponders are read-only, Type II transponders (such as E-Z Pass) can be read plus they can have information written onto them, and Type III transponders can be read and written to like the Type II tag plus they can communicate information to the driver (such as SUNPASS) (Pietrzyk and Mierzejewski, 1993). The majority of transponders used in the U.S. are Type I or II. Examination of various toll agencies found an average transponder cost of $30. Agencies must consider whether or not to pass the cost of transponders on to drivers. Examining the ETC programs around the U.S., most agencies absorbed the cost themselves, provided the driver enrolled in the account and prepaid their tolls using a credit card (which most users do). Therefore, this analysis assumed the cost of the transponders would be paid by the agency at the average cost of $30.

In order to determine the number of transponders that were required, data from Lee County, Florida, were analyzed. In Lee County there were three toll plazas in close proximity all using the same transponders, and therefore experience in Lee County could be applicable to the analysis performed here. In Lee County, the number of transponders in circulation was approximately twice the average workday volume of ETC transactions at all three plazas. Volume and market share assumptions for the scenarios examined here (to be discussed later in the chapter) found an average daily ETC volume per plaza of 38,948 for the low traffic volume scenario, 44,610 for the medium traffic volume scenario, and 67,012 for the high traffic volume scenario. This resulted in transponder costs of $7,017,120, $8,029,800, and $12,062,160 for the low, medium, and high traffic volumes, respectively.

For analysis of an ORT system, ETC market shares were assumed based on values from Highway 407 in Toronto (407 International Inc., 1999). Data showed the daily traffic volume in Toronto to be approximately 62 percent ETC. The daily ETC volume was doubled and multiplied by the average transponder cost of $30 to obtain total transponder costs of $8,715,960 and $9,977,040 for the low and medium traffic volumes.

Customer Service

A customer service center was necessary to handle the administration of ETC accounts, customer relations, and distribution of transponders. A small budget was also included for marketing, training of toll plaza attendants, Web site development and maintenance, and informational fliers.

Implementation of the customer service center involves the cost of the facility and staffing costs. Some of these staffing costs may be offset by reduced toll collection staffing with ETC. However, the Oklahoma Turnpike Authority (MITRE Corp., 1996) and Lee County, Florida (S. Hopwood, LeeWay Service Center, personal communication, 2002), did not reduce the number of toll collection employees. These findings, combined with the fact this plaza retrofit assumed no manual lanes were converted to dedicated ETC lanes, meant that in this analysis none of the service center staffing costs could be assumed to be offset by staffing reductions elsewhere. Research found the cost of opening a customer service center to be approximately $1,000,000, with annual staffing costs of $1,100,000. These staffing costs increased annually by the average wage increase of 5.1 percent (U.S. Social Security Administration, 2001).

In the case of ORT, the savings due to a reduction in staffing was estimated as part of the operation and maintenance cost savings of eliminating the manned lanes.

Operation and Maintenance

Operation and maintenance costs of $176,000 per year for a manual lane and $15,800 for an ETC lane (MITRE Corp., 1996) were used. This analysis assumed that the operation and maintenance cost of an ACM lane was approximately the same as those of an ETC lane. Using this information, a net present value operation and maintenance cost of $21,797,817 for the existing (non-ETC equipped) plaza was calculated for the evaluation period

The operation and maintenance costs of the toll plaza changed after the installation of ETC. The operation and maintenance costs of the four ACM lanes that were converted to ETC lanes did not change. The changes resulted from the addition of ETC hardware into the four remaining ACM lanes and the four manual lanes. With the addition of ETC in all lanes, a net present value of the operation and maintenance costs totaled $25,115,789. Subtracting the baseline costs from this value gives an incremental operation and maintenance cost of $3,317,972 for the ETC-equipped plaza.

After all costs had been calculated, the total was divided by the estimated number of ETC transactions over the evaluation period to get an average transaction cost. Dividing the total cost of approximately $50 million[3] (depending on traffic volume scenario) by the estimated number of ETC transactions over the 10-year period yielded transaction costs ranging from $0.12 for the low traffic volume scenario to $0.08 for the high traffic volume scenario. This value corresponded well to other research, which showed transaction costs to range between $0.05 and $0.15 with an average value of $0.10 (P. Samuel, Toll Roads Newsletter, personal communication, 2002; CRSPE Inc., 2001; Smith, 2002; M. Daughtry, Virginia Department of Transportation, personal communication, 2002). Therefore, the costs used in this analysis appeared reasonable.

Calculation of operation and maintenance costs for the ORT system was made difficult by the very small number of ORT systems currently in operation. Analysis of financial data from Highway 407 in Toronto found an approximate cost per transaction of $0.20 based on 62 percent ETC transactions and 38 percent by visual inspection of the license plate. Multiplying this by the total number of transactions yielded a net present value operation and maintenance cost of $157,584,000 for the low volume and $180,274,800 for the medium volume scenarios. Subtracting baseline costs from these figures found additional operation and maintenance costs to be $135,786,183 and $158,476,983 for the low and medium volumes, respectively.

These costs were significantly higher than those of a standard ETC system. This was due to the high cost of billing drivers via their license plate numbers. While a computer program can read most of the license plates, some must be read by humans, creating a significant operating cost. One source estimated the cost of these transactions to be between $7 and $8 per transaction (Leshinsky and Fielding, 2002). There are two caveats to this estimate: the first is that if only ETC transactions are allowed the cost of the system would decrease dramatically; the second is that recent literature suggests that the cost of this type of toll collection is decreasing as companies gain experience in the area (McManus, 2002).

3.3 Discrete Event Model Development

To determine the amount of travel time saved by the installation of ETC, discrete event stochastic computer simulation models of the toll plaza were developed. The models were developed using the general-purpose simulation software ARENA (Rockwell Software Inc., 2001). Several assumptions were made to assure conservative estimates of the benefits and to allow for relatively straightforward modeling. First, only automobiles were modeled. Trucks generally comprise only a small percentage of the total traffic volumes[4]. In addition, they produce more pollutants and generally take longer to pay the toll. Therefore, excluding trucks provided a conservative estimate of the benefits of ETC.

The analysis assumed that vehicles arrived at the toll plaza following a negative exponential distribution (Burris, 1995; Drew, 1968; Gerlough and Barnes, 1971) with the mean time between arrivals equal to the reciprocal of the traffic flow. Each vehicle was then assigned a payment type based on the percentage of each vehicle type in the scenario being modeled (see Table 1). The percentage of manual and ACM transactions in the base case were based on the percentages that could be handled efficiently by the toll plaza. In this manner, we make the logical assumption that the toll plaza is operating in an efficient manner to begin with. In the scenarios with ETC, typical ETC participation rates from around the U.S. were used to develop the percentages of each transaction type.

Table 1. Percentage of Transaction Types

Model	Time Period	Manual Transactions (%)	ACM Transactions (%)	ETC Transactions (%)
Base	Peak	20	80	0
	Off-Peak	20	80	0
	Low	20	80	0
ETC	Peak	13	22	65
	Off-Peak	13	42	45
	Low	13	42	45

Source: Author's calculations

The vehicles then randomly joined one of the queues for a lane that served that type of vehicle. If the selected queue was two vehicles longer than another available queue that also served that specific type, then the vehicle switched to the shorter queue. In two cases the vehicle would switch to a lane that served slower vehicle types (for example an ETC vehicle using an ACM lane). If the queue in the slower lane was shorter by three or more vehicles or if it was empty the vehicle that would normally choose the lane with the faster payment type would switch to the slower lane (see Note 5 for a flow chart of the model). Vehicles moved up in the queue as vehicles at the front of the queue were processed.

The transaction times for manual and ACM toll collection were assumed to follow a negative exponential distribution. The mean service rate for a manual toll transaction was 9.6 seconds, or 375 vehicles per hour (vph). The mean service rate for an ACM transaction was 5.3 seconds or 650 vehicles per hour (vph)[6]. These values, particularly the values for the manned lanes, can fluctuate significantly from toll plaza to toll plaza. Confounding factors included the percentage of trucks, the percentage of vehicles with the correct change, the familiarity of drivers with paying the toll, the difficulty level of paying the toll (for example, a $1 toll was collected faster than a $1.50 toll), and the percentage of vehicles in each lane paying with large bills, tokens, tickets, or by ETC. For example, in Halifax, Nova Scotia, drivers crossing two toll bridges during the peak traffic periods were primarily commuters and were well acquainted with paying the 75-cent toll to cross a bridge. The toll was paid using either three quarters or, more frequently, a token. At this facility, the ACM lanes would occasionally serve 1,000 vph—an amount approaching that of a low-speed ETC lane.

Examination of several toll agencies found speeds in retrofitted ETC lanes ranging from 5 to 45 mph (see Table 2). The average ETC lane speed was approximately 30 mph, and, therefore, vehicle speeds in the ETC lanes were assumed to follow a normal distribution with a mean of 30 mph and a standard deviation of five mph. A two-second spacing between vehicles was also assumed. Using these assumptions, a mean transaction time of 2.40 seconds and an average processing rate of 1,500 vph was obtained. This rate corresponds well with the literature (Pietrzyk and Mierzejewski, 1993; Al-Deek et al., 1997).

Table 2. ETC Lane Speeds

Toll Authority	Speed in Retrofitted ETC Lanes (mph)
Georgia Tollway Authority	45
Harris County Toll Road Authority	45
Kansas Turnpike Authority	20
Lee County	25 and 35 depending on facility
Maine Turnpike Authority	10
Maryland Transportation Authority	5
Massachusetts Turnpike Authority	15
Oklahoma Transportation Authority	30
Orlando Orange County Expressway Authority	35
South Jersey Transportation Authority	15

Examination of several toll plazas found that market penetration of ETC was generally greater during peak periods than in other periods. Average market share of ETC was found to range from 19 to 76 percent, but in all cases was greater in the peak times. Therefore, the largest ETC market share was during the peak periods (see Table 1). Note that all of the traffic volumes described the amount of traffic at one toll plaza in one direction. All calculated benefits were then doubled to determine the benefit for both directions of travel at one toll plaza and then tripled to find the benefits of the entire toll system.

Two scenarios were developed, a low level of traffic and a medium level of traffic. The two levels of traffic were developed to represent the average traffic volume during the 10-year evaluation period. Values were calculated for both workdays and non-workdays. A distribution of 250 workdays and 115 non-work days per year was assumed. Assuming typical peaking characteristics on urban roadways, daily workday volumes were also divided into three time periods: peak, off-peak, and low. On non-workdays, only two hourly volumes were used for the analysis: off-peak and low (see Table 3). Most models were run 20 times, and the analysis used the average result. In four cases either the resulting average number of ETC toll-paying customers or the average delay per vehicle had a standard error (at the 95 percent level) greater than 10 percent of the mean value. These four models were run additional times to reduce the standard error to a maximum of five percent of the mean value.

Table 3. Traffic Volumes in the Models

Scenario	Day	Period	Length of Period (hours in each direction of travel)	Traffic Volume (vph in one direction of travel)
Medium Volume	Work	Peak	3	3,650
		Off-Peak	13	2,350
		Low	8	400
	Non-Work	Off-Peak	14	1,940
		Low	10	630
Low Volume	Work	Peak	3	3,200
		Off-Peak	13	2,050
		Low	8	350
	Non-Work	Off-Peak	14	1,700
		Low	10	550

Source: Traffic volumes and the number of peak, off-peak, and low volume hours per day were estimated using data from Fort Myers, Florida and the Traffic Engineering Handbook (Institute of Transportation Engineers, 1999).

To check the validity of the model results, a spreadsheet was developed to estimate the queueing delays experienced by vehicles. The spreadsheet used standard M/M/m stochastic queueing theory formulas (Mannering and Kilareski, 1998) to estimate vehicle delay for all periods of the work and non-work days. For low volumes of traffic the spreadsheets corresponded well to the simulation models. However, at higher volumes (nearing the capacity of the toll plaza) the spreadsheets could not consider the spillover of vehicles from one peak hour to the next and the additional waiting time that a developed queue causes. Standard queueing formulas could not analyze scenarios with very high traffic volumes, as the toll plaza was over capacity during the peak period. Therefore, the standard queueing models could only verify the results from low traffic scenarios.

3.4 Benefits of ETC in a Retrofitted Toll Plaza

The implementation of electronic toll collection yielded numerous benefits (Pietrzyk and Mierzejewski, 1993; Gillen et al., 1999; Saka et al., 2001), primarily travel time savings, fuel reduction, and emissions reduction. This section quantifies the value of these benefits for the toll plaza systems previously outlined.

Another potential option may be the elimination of tolls entirely. This would maximize the time and operational cost savings. However, this may not be feasible as there may be no other funding options available. Also, removing the tolls may prove both inequitable and inefficient. The toll restricts the use of the road to those drivers who feel the benefit of travel exceeds the cost, including the toll. Removing the toll reduces this direct cost and encourages inefficient use of the road. The most likely replacement for the lost toll revenue would be from the gas tax. This transfers the cost of the road from users to all drivers, whether they use that particular road or not. Removing the toll also has the potential to shift the cost from more affluent commuters (those who could afford and found it worthwhile to take a toll road) to all commuters.

Benefits from Travel Time Savings

Travel time savings were typically the largest contributor to benefits (Leviäkangas and Lähesmaa, 2002). The implementation of ETC impacted travel time savings in two ways. The first was by shortening queues at toll plazas. ETC lanes had higher service rates than manual and ACM lanes and could therefore process vehicles more efficiently. Implementing electronic toll collection also reduced travel times by reducing the time spent decelerating and accelerating. Toll patrons using ETC lanes had to decelerate to a moderate speed (30 mph in this analysis), whereas those using manual and automatic lanes had to come to a complete stop.

First, the time savings obtained from the increase in approach and departure speeds of ETC vehicles was determined. The travel times of an ETC vehicle and an ACM or manned lane vehicle were compared over an arbitrary distance longer than that needed to completely decelerate and accelerate. All drivers were assumed to drive at 65 mph and then rapidly decelerate as they approached the toll plaza[7]. ETC drivers decelerated to 30 mph while other drivers decelerated to 0 mph. Drivers then accelerated rapidly back to 65 mph after paying the toll. Calculations were performed using published deceleration and acceleration rates (American Association of Street and Highway Transportation Officials, 2001) and uniform acceleration and deceleration equations (Mannering and Kilareski, 1998). Subtracting these two values and multiplying by the total number of annual ETC users in the ETC lanes generated annual time savings. The few ETC paying drivers who used an ETC/ACM or ETC/manned lane (due to larger queues in the ETC lanes) were assumed to slow to 0 mph because of safety reasons, vehicles in front of them, or gates in the toll lanes. Therefore, these vehicles were not included in this calculation.

Second, the amount of time vehicles spent in the toll plaza system, both in the queue and paying the toll, was found using the simulation model. This analysis was performed for both work and non-work days, both with and without ETC installed. These results gave the annual reduction in time spent at the toll plaza resulting from implementing ETC.

The two travel time savings, reduced acceleration/deceleration time and reduced delay in the plaza, were combined and converted to a monetary value. Research has shown the value of a driver's time to be approximately 50 percent of his or her hourly wage rate (Small, 1992). The average national wage was found to be $15.46 per hour based on a 40-hour work week (U.S. Social

Security Administration, 2001). However, the average occupancy of vehicles must also be considered in the value of travel time per vehicle. For this analysis, average passenger time was valued at 30 percent of the national average wage (Waters, 1992). To find the average number of passengers an average vehicle occupancy was needed. This was calculated using highway statistics from the FHWA (Federal Highway Administration, 2001). Dividing the total number of person-miles traveled by the total number of vehicle-miles traveled gives an average occupancy of 1.6. The value of travel time was therefore calculated to be $10.51 per vehicle-hour. This value was inflated yearly according to an average wage index (U.S. Social Security Administration, 2001) of 5.1 percent to calculate values for the entire 10-year evaluation period.

Benefits from Reduced Emissions

Electronic toll collection reduced emissions because of the reduced idling time in the queue and the reduced deceleration and acceleration. Two computer models were used to measure emissions reduction for three types of pollutants: nitrogen oxides (NO_x), volatile organic compounds (VOC), and carbon monoxide (CO). The models used were the Comprehensive Modal Emissions Model (CMEM) (University of California, 2000) and a model developed by Ahn, Rakha, Trani, and Van Aerde (Ahn et al., 2002). Unfortunately, there was some disparity between the two results, so the average values of the two results were used in the final calculations (see Table 4).

Table 4. Emissions Outputs (Per Vehicle)

	NO_x		VOC		CO	
	CMEM	Ahn et al.	CMEM	Ahn et al.	CMEM	Ahn et al.
Vehicle Using the Manual or ACM Lane	0.274 g	0.852 g	0.0428 g	0.321 g	1.38 g	8.62 g
Vehicle Using the ETC Lane	0.242 g	0.761 g	0.0395 g	0.309 g	1.27 g	8.63 g
Reduction by Using ETC	0.032 g	0.091 g	0.0033 g	0.012 g	0.11 g	-0.01 g
Value Used in Analysis	0.062 g/vehicle		0.0077 g/vehicle		0.05 g/vehicle	

The behavior of a vehicle traveling from a point 1,000 feet in advance of the toll plaza to a point 3,000 feet past the plaza was modeled. Speed, fuel use, and emission calculations were performed on a second-by-second basis for a vehicle traveling through both an ETC lane and a manual/ACM lane. The difference in the two results was the reduced emissions from a vehicle paying via ETC. The annual emissions reduction was found by multiplying the annual number of ETC transactions in the dedicated ETC lanes by this reduction per vehicle.

Emissions reduction resulting from shorter queue times was found using idling emission rates (see Table 5). The reduced amount of time spent in the plaza area under the ETC scenario was multiplied by these values to determine the idling and queueing delay emission reductions.

Table 5. Average Idling Emission Rates (Grams/Hour)

Pollutant	Summer	Winter	Average
NO_x	4.72	6.16	5.44
VOC	16.1	21.1	18.6
CO	229	371	300

Source: U.S. Environmental Protection Agency, 1998

Mobile emissions account for significant amounts of NO_x, VOC, CO, O_3 (ozone), SO_x (sulfur oxides), and PM_{10} (particulate matter). However, for multiple reasons, this research dealt with only three criteria pollutants NO_x, VOC, and CO. The literature on emissions reduction resulting from ETC usage (Sisson, 1995; Saka et al., 2001; Gillen et al., 1999) contained little information or costs of the other pollutants. Also, because of limitations of the computer models used, NO_x, VOC, and CO were the only three pollutants that could be evaluated. This is an unfortunate shortcoming of this analysis, particularly because emissions of particulate matter and sulfur oxides could not be obtained. Some research has shown that the health effects of these two pollutants to be greater than those of the three analyzed in this report (Delucchi, 2000). However, the overall costs of SO_x and PM_{10} emissions are probably quite small. Other research has shown the emission rates of PM_{10} and SO_x to be significantly lower than those of the three pollutants examined here (Small and Kazimi, 1995). Additionally, due to federal emissions standards, SO_x and PM_{10} emissions from vehicles will eventually be negligible (Small and Kazimi, 1995). Obtaining emission data for ozone was also difficult, because it is an indirect product of motor vehicle exhaust. Ozone is formed when hydrocarbons react with nitrogen oxides in the presence of sunlight. Because ozone forms from other motor vehicle pollutants, the amount of ozone from mobile emissions cannot be directly measured.

To convert these emission reductions to a monetary value, the costs associated with these pollutants were obtained from research conducted by Delucchi (2000) and Small and Kazimi (1995) (see Table 6). Both of these sources based their cost of emissions on the health cost of motor vehicle pollution. The values used in this analysis were on the conservative end of the estimates. In addition, this analysis did not include reductions in particulate matter 10 (PM_{10}) and sulfur oxides (SO_x) emissions. Including these pollutants would further increase the benefits of ETC. These costs were primarily based on the cost of health care to treat diseases related to these emissions. Therefore, costs were inflated according to an average health care index (+3.5 percent per year, U.S. Health Care Financing Administration, 2001) to calculate values for the entire evaluation period.

It is important to note that this area of research is in debate and the values presented here in Table 6 can only be considered reasonable approximations within an order of magnitude. However, this uncertainty does not impact the overall results as emissions savings are much smaller than travel time savings.

Table 6. Values of Emission Reductions

Pollutant	Delucchi (2000)		Small and Kazimi (1995) as modified by Levinson (2002)	Values Used in This Analysis
	Low	High		
NOx	\$1.59/kg	\$23.34/kg	\$1.33/kg	\$1.59/kg
VOC	\$0.13/kg	\$1.45/kg	\$1.71/kg	\$1.45/kg
CO	\$0.01/kg	\$0.10/kg	\$0.0063/kg	\$0.01/kg

Benefits from Reduced Fuel Use

Similar to reductions in emissions resulting from ETC, ETC decreases overall fuel consumption by:

- reducing the time spent idling in the queue and paying the toll, and
- reducing the amount of deceleration and acceleration required.

The two emission estimation models and the literature (Biggs and Akcelik, 1986) provided the rate of idling fuel consumption. All three sources indicated the average idling rate of fuel use was 0.475 gallons per hour. Next, the total delay that vehicles experienced in the queues and paying the toll for both the base and ETC models were obtained from the simulation models. The difference in the total delay was multiplied by the idling rate of fuel use to determine the amount of fuel saved because of reduced vehicle delay with the installation of ETC.

Fuel reduction from shortened deceleration and acceleration was derived directly from the outputs of the two models. The two models estimated that the fuel saved by ETC vehicles slowing to 30 mph and not having to come to a complete stop was 0.0053 gallons and 0.0065 gallons. This analysis used an average of these two results, 0.0059 gallons per transaction. To determine the total volume of fuel saved, the total number of ETC transactions in the dedicated ETC lanes was multiplied by this savings per transaction.

The two fuel savings estimations were combined to get a total volume of fuel saved for each scenario examined. To convert this volume of fuel saved to a monetary value, a gasoline price of \$1.502 per gallon was used (American Automobile Association, 2002). Next, both the federal tax on fuel (18.4 cents per gallon) and the average state tax on fuel (20.7 cents per gallon) were removed from the price of fuel since the taxes are transfers of wealth and not costs or benefits. The resulting price was then inflated using an average fuel index (2.6 percent per year) to calculate values for the entire evaluation period (U.S. Department of Energy, 2002). Based on these many assumptions, the year-one benefits of ETC for this scenario can be summarized as follows[8]:

$$Benefits = \#ETC \times \$0.0543 + \Delta time \times \$11.076 \tag{3}$$

where:
ETC = the number of ETC transactions in the dedicated ETC lanes
Δtime = the change in total time spent by all vehicles in the queues and paying the tolls

Benefits of Open Road Tolling

The benefits gained from ORT were significantly higher than those gained from conventional ETC. By allowing drivers to travel at highway speeds without slowing down, the service rate becomes equal to the capacity of the toll road, eliminating all forms of delay associated with a standard toll plaza system. Delay is further reduced due to the elimination of the deceleration and acceleration processes. These reductions in delay greatly increased the travel time savings. Fuel use and emissions were also significantly reduced due to the free flow of traffic.

3.5 Costs of Variable Pricing

The incremental cost of adding a variable toll rate to a new ETC system can be minimal. The costs include marketing the concept to the public, training of toll collection staff, software development, and signage.

In this analysis, ETC and variable pricing were installed simultaneously. Therefore, the costs of marketing and printing informational flyers for variable pricing was included in the costs of those same activities undertaken to introduce the public to ETC (see ETC service center costs). Similarly, minimal staff training would be required to explain the intricacies of variable pricing, and this cost was incorporated into the cost of staff training for ETC. Variable pricing software can be extremely simple (for example, the code would check the time of day and simply adjust toll rates by a percentage during specific time periods), and no additional costs were included. Finally, the cost of signage for variable pricing was included in the cost of the new signs required to delineate the toll plaza lanes for ETC.

Therefore, in theory, an authority could develop a variable pricing program for little cost in addition to the cost of installing ETC. In practice, this is difficult. Experience has shown that extensive public outreach and marketing campaigns are necessary to educate the public with regard to the benefits of variable toll rates (Harrington et al., 2001; Transportation Research Board, 1994). Even with these efforts, variable pricing (also referred to as value or congestion pricing) projects can face intense public pressure, and many have been terminated prior to operation. In the future, this may not be as large an issue as the public learns more about successful value pricing projects around the U.S. However, for the purpose of this analysis, a public awareness and marketing effort of $600,000[9] undertaken in the first year was assumed to be the only incremental cost of variable pricing.

3.6 Benefits of Variable Pricing

As stated previously, the objective of variable pricing was to manage the demand for the toll facility. Shifting some of the demand from the congested peak period to the less congested off-peak (or shoulder) period reduces the societal welfare loss caused by congestion. This results in improved traffic flow, reduced travel times, reduced emissions, and reduced fuel usage during the peak period with minimal impact on the off-peak period traffic.

This examination of costs and benefits is limited to the toll plaza area itself. However, with variable tolls impacting driver behavior, the benefits from variable tolls would likely extend far beyond the toll plaza. Traffic congestion both upstream and downstream from the toll plaza will be reduced due to drivers' shifting their time of travel to less congested periods. For example, peak period congestion at an intersection downstream of the plaza will be reduced during the peak period, improving travel for all drivers using the intersection, including those who had not driven through the toll plaza.[10]

To estimate the benefits derived from variable pricing, the discrete event simulation models were run again using modified traffic volumes. The changes in overall delay and the number of vehicles paying via ETC in a dedicated lane were then entered into Equation 3 to determine the benefits from ETC with variable pricing. Subtracting the benefits found for ETC yields the incremental benefits of variable pricing.

The difficulty was to determine the number of drivers that would alter their time of travel as a result of the variable toll. Examination of the few facilities in the world with variable tolls indicated toll-price travel-demand elasticities ranging from –0.02 to –1.0 (see Table 7). Elasticity is defined as the percentage change in traffic volume divided by the percentage change in price (see Equation 4).

$$E = \frac{(q_2 - q_1)/q_1}{(p_2 - p_1)/p_1} \tag{4}$$

where:
E = price elasticity of demand
q = volume
p = price (toll)

Table 7. Toll Price Elasticities on Facilities with Variable Toll Rates

Location	Elasticity	Source
Lee County (Cape Coral and Midpoint Bridges)	-0.02 to -0.36	Cain, et al., 2001
California (SR 91)	-0.9 to -1.0	Sullivan, 2000
	-0.7 to -0.8	Yan et al., 2002
California (I-15)	-0.02 to -0.16	Dahlgren, 1999
	-0.34 to -0.42	San Diego Association of Governments, 1999
Houston (Hardy Toll Road)	-0.4 to -0.8	Spock, 1998
France (A-1)	-0.16 to -0.28	Small and Gomez-Ibanez, 1997
Singapore (City Center)	-0.25	Menon et al., 1993

For this example it was assumed there existed limited potential for mode and route diversion and no abandoned trips. This would likely result in an elasticity at the low end of the range found in Table 8. The elasticity used was –0.20. This analysis also assumed a 50 percent increase in toll rate during the peak period on all work days. Also, during the three-hour peaks, only drivers in the first or last hour of the peak were willing to change their time of travel to the hour immediately before or the hour immediately after the peak period (see Cain et al., 2001, for traffic response to a similar variable toll rate). Therefore, 10 percent of drivers on either end of the peak period shifted to the shoulder period. This resulted in a traffic pattern shown in Table 8. This traffic pattern was then modeled in ARENA (Rockwell Software Inc., 2001) to obtain vehicle queues and delays.

Table 8. Traffic Volumes in the Variable Pricing Models

Scenario	Day	Period	Length of Period (hours in each direction of travel)	Traffic Volume (vph in one direction of travel)
High Volume*	Work day – with variable tolls	Peak	1	5500
		Reduced Peak	2	4950
		Shoulder	2	4075
		Off-Peak	11	3525
		Low	8	600
	Work day – without variable tolls	Peak	3	5500
		Off-Peak	13	3525
		Low	8	600

* Note that initial models were developed using similar volumes as shown in Table 3. However, variable tolls were found to provide little benefit. This was not surprising since there was little congestion at the plaza where ETC was installed. Therefore, the higher traffic volumes were developed to examine how variable tolls can produce benefits in congested conditions.

In practice, the number of drivers altering their time of travel because of the variable toll rate is difficult to predict. Many factors are involved in the decision-making process for each driver. Primarily, there is the penalty for arriving to a destination early, a penalty for arriving late, and the cost of travel (Small, 1992). These factors differ for each driver and differ spatially and temporally for an individual as well. The method used in this analysis to predict driver reaction to a variable toll, and therefore incorporate all of these variables, is probably the most straightforward. However, this method requires judgment regarding the similarities between the scenario under investigation and the various facilities with variable toll rates.

Another method would be to estimate how drivers in an area value their travel time and the penalties they place on early or late arrival. Based on these values, a model could be developed that would predict mode use, route use, and time of travel based on maximizing the utility of each driver. A third method would be to build a transferable model of the impact of variable tolls based on driver socioeconomic and commute characteristics using empirical results from one of the facilities employing variable tolls. Then the model could be run on the socioeconomic and commute characteristics of local drivers facing a similar variable toll (Burris, 2002).

In theory, prices could be set such that traffic never exceeded a defined volume—possibly just beneath where the marginal and average price curves diverge (see Figure 2). This would require a rapidly fluctuating toll rate. The operational facility with the most dynamic pricing is currently the I-15 high-occupancy/toll (HOT) lane in California, which can change toll rate as frequently as every six minutes.

4. RESULTS

The incremental costs and benefits of retrofitting a plaza with ETC are shown in the second and third columns of Table 9. Not surprisingly, as congestion worsens, savings increase dramatically while costs show little change. In both the low and medium traffic scenarios the benefits of a plaza retrofitted with ETC outweighs the costs. Travel time savings account for approximately 90 percent of the benefits. Savings in fuel are the next largest portion of savings, whereas savings from reduced emissions account for less than one percent of savings.

Table 9. Results (Total NPV from 10-Year Evaluation)

Category	Incremental Costs and Benefits of ETC (Thousands of Dollars)		Incremental Costs and Benefits of Variable Pricing* (Thousands of Dollars)
	Low Traffic Volume	Medium Traffic Volume	High Traffic Volume
Lane Equipment	$2,160	$2,160	$0
Installation	$252	$252	$0
Computer Equipment	$1,250	$1,250	$0
Transponders	$7,017	$8,030	$0
Customer Service Center	$1,000	$1,000	$0
Service Center Staffing	$11,000	$11,000	$0
Operation and Maintenance	$3,318	$3,318	$0
Marketing	$0	$0	$600
Travel Time Savings	$31,592	$157,600	$20,218
Fuel Savings	$2,862	$8,781	$951
Emissions Savings	$86	$139,887	$69
TOTAL (Benefits – Costs)	$8,543	$142,172	$20,638
B/C Ratio	1.33	5.18	35.40

* These costs were incurred when adding variable pricing to an existing retrofitted ETC system.

Column 4 of Table 9 shows the incremental costs and benefits of applying a variable toll rate to the congested toll facilities. The application of variable pricing provides a high incremental benefit-cost ratio (35.8 to 1) and a positive net present value. In contrast, when variable tolls were applied to the medium traffic level, which did not suffer from congestion with ETC, there were few incremental benefits found and a negative net present value was obtained. Therefore, even though the expense of adding variable pricing can be minimal, direct benefits are obtained only when there is congestion at the facility (as shown in Figure 2)[11].

The incremental benefit-cost results were compared to the results obtained for the New Jersey Turnpike System (Wilbur Smith Associates, 2001). On a savings per vehicle basis, the incremental benefits found in this analysis for the high traffic volume scenario were twice those found on the New Jersey Turnpike. For the low traffic volume scenario, savings per vehicle was only 18 percent of the savings found in New Jersey. Therefore, results from the New Jersey Turnpike were in the range of results found in the scenarios examined here.

The values found in Table 9 change substantially based on the assumptions in the models. For example, if a single toll facility were modeled, discounted aggregate costs would decrease by approximately 20 percent while discounted aggregate benefits would decrease by 66.7 percent. In this event, the low volume scenario would have an incremental benefit-cost ratio of less than one. The incremental benefit-cost ratio for the medium traffic volume in this single toll facility scenario would still be greater than three.

Next, the incremental costs and benefits of ORT over the existing (non-ETC) plaza were examined (see Table 10). The incremental benefit-cost ratios for these scenarios were not as large as for the standard ETC plaza. However, these results were based on the very limited data available on transaction costs of ORT. These costs may have dropped significantly over the last few years as companies gained experience in this area. Additionally, these costs were based on the assumption that vehicles with and without transponders could use the road. The incremental benefit-cost ratios of ORT would be significantly higher if the method of charging drivers via their license plate numbers was eliminated. By requiring drivers to have a transponder before using the toll road, costs would be greatly reduced, thus increasing the benefit-cost ratios.

Incremental benefits from installing an ORT system were 187 percent higher than those gained from installing a standard ETC system for low volumes and 45 percent higher for medium volumes. However, due to the large operation and maintenance costs associated with an ORT system, the incremental benefits do not outweigh the incremental costs for the low traffic volume scenario, with the incremental benefit-cost ratio being 0.62. A ratio of 1.31 was calculated for the medium traffic volume. The incremental benefits outweigh the costs in this scenario, but the incremental benefit-cost ratio is still significantly lower than that calculated for the same traffic volume with a standard ETC system.

Costs for such items as sod and repaving were obtained by using Texas DOT unit cost estimates (see Notes) plus design specifications in the Toll Plaza Design report from NCHRP (Schaufler, 1997).

Table 10. Results (Total NPV from 10-Year Evaluation)

Category	Incremental Costs and Benefits of ORT (Thousands of Dollars)	
	Low Traffic Volume	Medium Traffic Volume
Lane Equipment	$720	$720
Installation	$84	$84
Computer Equipment	$1,250	$1,250
Transponders	$8,716	$9,977
Customer Service Center	$1,000	$1,000
Service Center Staffing	$11,000	$11,000
O&M Difference	$135,786	$158,477
Demolition	$1,440	$1,440
Asphalt Removal	$79	$79
Repaving	$67	$67
Sod	$118	$118
Overhead Gantries	$72	$72
Travel Time Savings	$83,239	$217,994
Fuel Savings	$15,233	$22,994
Emissions Savings	$716	$1,242
TOTAL (Benefits-Costs)	-$61,144	$57,946
B/C Ratio	0.62	1.31

5. CONCLUSION

This researched analyzed the incremental costs and benefits of retrofitting a toll plaza with electronic toll collection for low and medium traffic congestion scenarios. In both cases, a positive net present value was found. The majority of costs were the responsibility of the toll authority, whereas drivers obtained the majority of the benefits. Benefits were dominated by the value of travel time savings, followed by savings in fuel use, and, finally, savings from reduced emissions.

Next, the incremental costs and benefits of installing an open road tolling system were examined. Benefits were found to be significantly larger than those associated with a standard ETC system. However, due to the large operation and maintenance costs of ORT, the benefit-cost ratios were actually smaller, with the costs outweighing the benefits in the low volume scenario.

Finally, the incremental costs and benefits of incorporating a variable toll rate with ETC were examined. We found that under congested conditions variable pricing provided a positive, incremental net present value. However, under uncongested conditions, benefits were minimal and a negative net present value was found.

Although this particular analysis found positive net incremental benefits of ETC, ORT, and ETC with variable pricing, this was based on the scenarios examined. The cost and benefit values used in this analysis were obtained from empirical evidence collected at toll roads and variable pricing projects around the country. Using these values in the scenarios modeled here yielded average transaction costs that appeared reasonable when compared to results from around the country.

Therefore, this research could be used as a framework for benefit-cost analysis. A toll agency interested in evaluating the potential costs and benefits of implementing ETC (with or without variable tolls) would need to apply the specifications of its toll facilities to this framework to obtain an estimate of their potential costs and benefits.

ACKNOWLEDGEMENTS

The author gratefully acknowledges the assistance of several toll authorities, notably the North Texas Tollway Authority, the Lee County Department of Transportation, and the Kansas Turnpike Authority. Additionally, Justin Winn, a civil engineering student at Texas A&M University, provided valuable assistance in obtaining the data required for this analysis. However, all errors and omissions are the sole responsibility of the author.

NOTES

1 The use of the real discount rate removes the effect of inflation from the calculations. The real discount rate accounts for the difference between the nominal discount (n) rate and the inflation rate (i). In three cases (the cost of emissions, the cost of fuel, and the cost of service center staffing) prices were know to grow at a rate other than the nominal rate of 5.1 percent provided by the Office of Management and Budget. In these cases the prices were inflated at their nominal rate minus the rate of inflation (i) = 1.9 percent. See Small, 1999, for further discussion and the relationship between i, n, and r.

2 Cost data used in estimations

Item	Cost	Source
AVI Equipment	$8,568 per lane	Kansas Turnpike Authority
AVI Equipment	$8,664 per lane	Transcore iServer
AVI Equipment	$10,839 per lane	Lee County, Florida
AVI Equipment	$11,000 per lane	North Texas Tollway Authority
Variable Message Sign	$2,600	Mark IV
Vehicle Classification System	$8,000 per lane	North Texas Tollway Authority
VES (w/ 3 cameras)	$40,000 per lane	North Texas Tollway Authority
Violation Camera (average)	$7,500	ITS Unit Cost Database
Computer Equipment/Software	$6,954	Kansas Turnpike Authority
Host Computer Equipment	$100,000	North Texas Tollway Authority
Software Development	$2,000,000	North Texas Tollway Authority
ETC Software (low)	$5,000	ITS Unit Cost Database
ETC Software (high)	$10,000	ITS Unit Cost Database
Service Center	$1,050,444	Lee County, Florida
Service Center Staffing	$1,081,029 per yr.	Lee County, Florida
Plaza Computer Subsystems	$25,887 per lane	Gillen et al., 1999
Host Computer Subsystem	$588,724	Gillen et al., 1999
Computer Equipment/Software	$128,300	NCHRP Synthesis 194
Host Computer Equipment	$307,400	NCHRP Synthesis 194
Operating Cost of ETC Lane	$15,800 per year	Oklahoma Turnpike Authority
Operating Cost of Manual Lane	$176,000 per year	Oklahoma Turnpike Authority

Source	Cost of ETC Equipment (AVI, AVC, VES, etc.) per lane
Kansas Turnpike Authority	$16,909 (low)
Kansas Turnpike Authority	$32,405 (high)
Gillen et al., 1999	$92,772
Pietrzyk and Mierzejewski, 1993	$15,400
North Texas Tollway Authority	$62,800

Item	Cost	Source
Asphalt Removal	$2 per square yard	Texas Department of Transportation
Hot Mix	$38 per ton	Texas Department of Transportation
Sod	$3 per square yard	Texas Department of Transportation
Overhead Gantries	$24,000 each	Texas Department of Transportation
Demolition of Toll Booths	$30 per square foot	Reich and Davis, 2001

Using these unit costs plus design specifications in the Toll Plaza Design report from NCHRP (Schaufler, 1997) the costs for redesign of the plaza as an ORT system (in Table 10) were derived.

3 Note that this total does not equal that shown in Table 9, since Table 9 indicates the incremental costs of ETC.

4 In one extreme example, the truck percentage on two toll bridges in Lee County, Florida, is less than one percent.

5.

Flow Chart of Toll Plaza Simulation Model

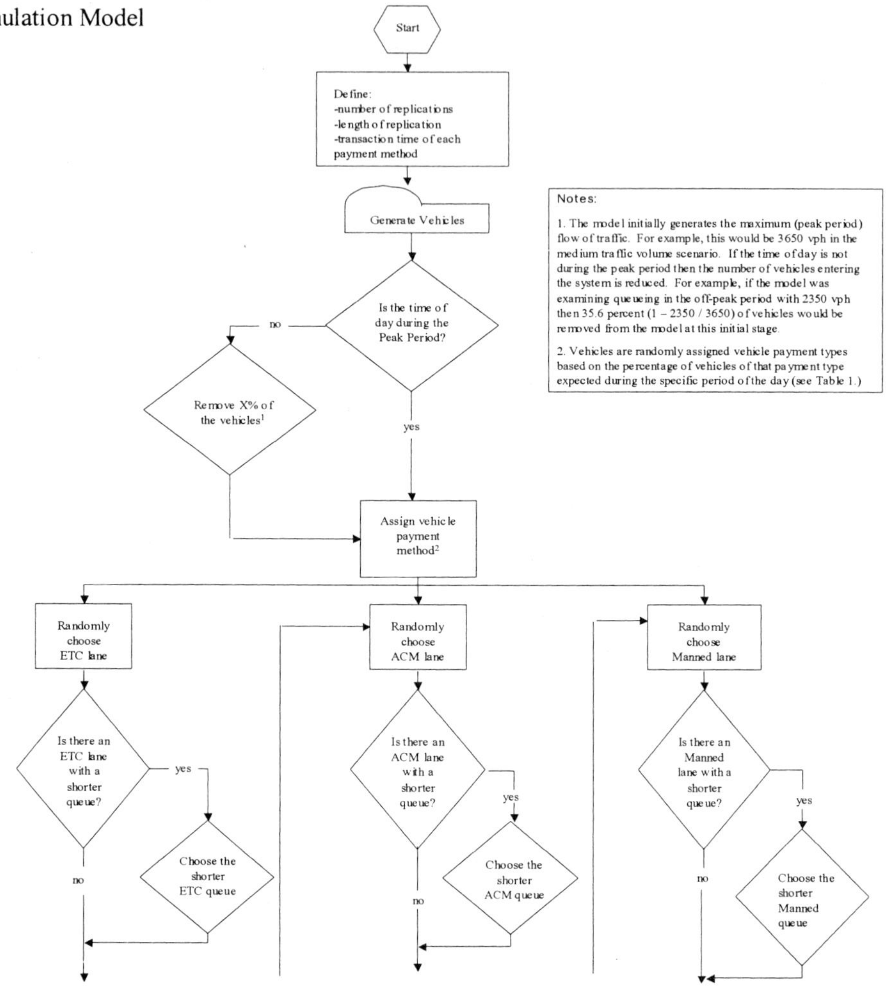

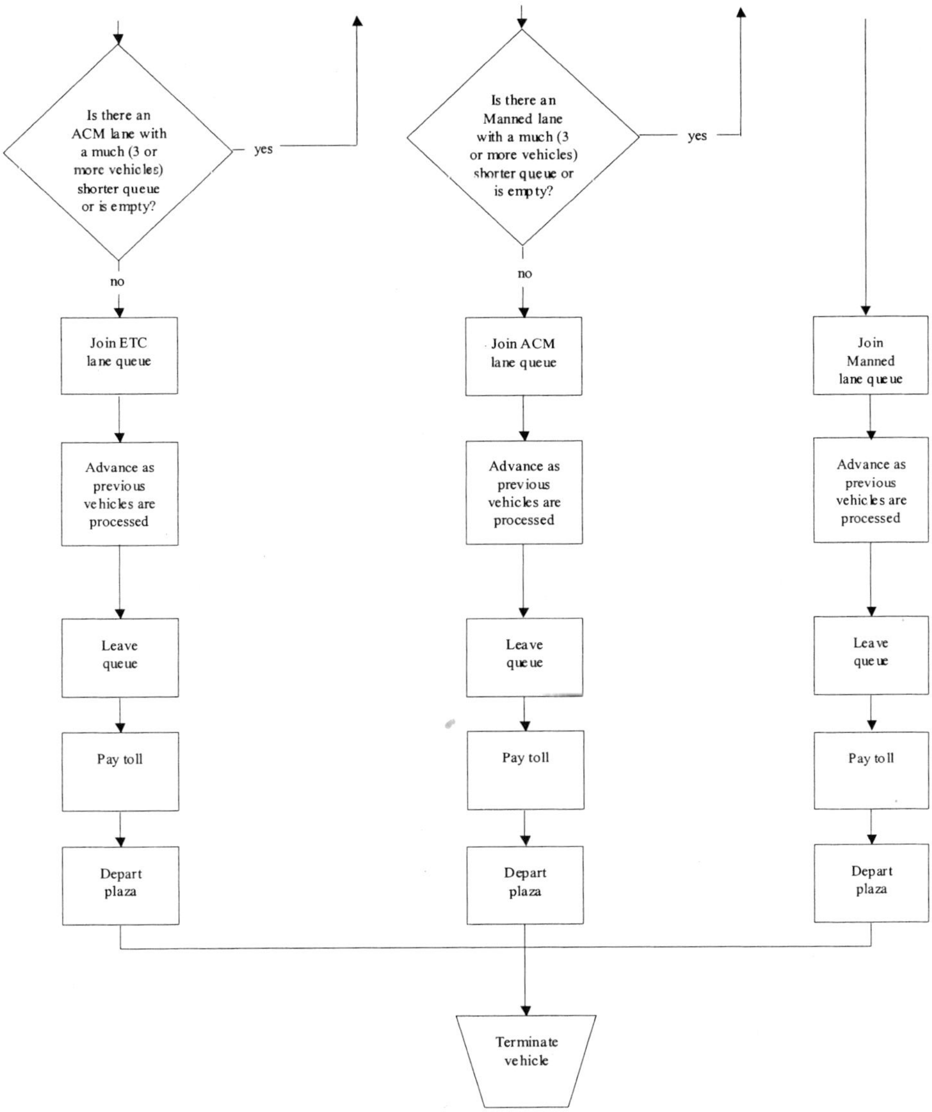

Is there an ACM lane with a much (3 or more vehicles) shorter queue or is empty?
yes
no
Is there an Manned lane with a much (3 or more vehicles) shorter queue or is empty?
yes
no
Join ETC lane queue
Join ACM lane queue
Join Manned lane queue
Advance as previous vehicles are processed
Advance as previous vehicles are processed
Advance as previous vehicles are processed
Leave queue
Leave queue
Leave queue
Pay toll
Pay toll
Pay toll
Depart plaza
Depart plaza
Depart plaza
Terminate vehicle

6 These service rates were obtained from several sources. The author's investigation of two toll plazas in Halifax, Nova Scotia, resulted in determining a maximum sustainable transaction rate of approximately 380 vph in a manned lane and 900 vph in an ACM lane. The author's investigation of two toll plazas in Lee County, Florida, resulted in determining a maximum sustainable transaction rate of approximately 380 vph in a manned lane and 700 vph in an ACM lane. The distribution of transaction times were not best described as negative exponential, but were close. Therefore, assuming a negative exponential distribution would not cause significant error in this example. Al-Deek et al. (1997) examined Orlando Orange County Expressway facilities and found a transaction rate of approximately 400 vph in a manned lane and 600 vph in an ACM lane. Pietrzyk and Mierzejewski (1993) found a transaction rate of approximately 350 vph in a manned lane and 500 vph in an ACM lane.

7 Based on this author's experience (scientific spot speed studies, qualitative observations, and personal driving experience), drivers familiar with the toll plaza generally ignore the speed limit signs posted on the approach to the plaza that would mandate a slow deceleration.

8 These benefits were calculated in a similar manner for all 10 years and then reduced to a net present value (see Table 9).

9 Similar in size to the one for the Lee County Variable Pricing Project.

10 For an example of calculating the benefits from variable pricing extending citywide see Mohring, 1999.

11 However, as mentioned previously, there is potential for substantial indirect benefits outside of the immediate toll plaza area.

REFERENCES

407 International Inc. Highway 407 Prospectus for Initial Public Offering, 1999.

Abdelwahab, H. T., Abdel-Aty, M. A. *Traffic Safety Analysis for Toll Plazas Using Artificial Neural Networks and Logit Models,* prepared for the Transportation Research Board Annual Meeting. Transportation Research Board. National Research Council. Washington, DC, 2002.

Ahn, K., Rakha, H., Trani, A., Van Aerde, M. "Estimating Vehicle Fuel Consumption and Emissions based on Instantaneous Speed and Acceleration Levels," *Journal of Transportation Engineering,* 28(2), 2002, 182–190.

Al-Deek, H. M., Mohamed, A. A., Radwan, A. E. "Operational Benefits of Electronic Toll Collection: Case Study," *Journal of Transportation Engineering*, 123(6), 1997, 467–477.

American Automobile Association. *2000 Fuel Gauge Summary*. http://www.aaa.com/news12/. Releases/Fuel/fuel00sum.html. Accessed July 9, 2002.

American Association of Street and Highway Transportation Officials. *A Policy on Geometric Design of Highways and Streets*, Fourth Edition, Washington, DC, 2001.

Biggs, D., Akcelik, R. *An Energy-Based Model of Instantaneous Fuel Consumption,* ARRB, Australian Road Research Board, 1986.

Burris, M. "Modeling Electronic Toll Collection's Effect on Traffic at the A. Murray MacKay Bridge Toll Plaza," thesis, University of New Brunswick, Fredericton, NB, Canada, 1995.

Burris, M., Pendyala, R. "Discrete Choice Models of Traveler Participation in Differential Time of Day Pricing Programs," *Transport Policy*, 9(4), 2002. 67–77.

Burris, M. "Application of Variable Tolls to a Congested Toll Road," *ASCE Journal of Transportation Engineering.* Accepted for publication.

Cain, A., Burris, M., Pendyala, R. "The Impact of Variable Pricing on the Temporal Distribution of Travel Demand," *Transportation Research Record*, 1747, TRB, National Research Council, Washington, DC, 2001, 36–43.

CRSPE Inc. *Lee County Toll Transaction Costs*, Lee County Department of Transportation, Lee County, FL, 2001.

Dahlgren, J. "High Occupancy Vehicle/Toll Lanes: How Do They Operate and Where Do They Make Sense?," California PATH Working Paper, University of California, Berkeley, CA, 1999

Delucchi, M. A. "Environmental Externalities of Motor-Vehicle Use in the U.S.," *Journal of Transport Economics and Policy*, 34(2), 2000, 135–168.

Drew, D. *Traffic Flow Theory and Control,* McGraw-Hill, Inc., U.S., 1968.

Federal Highway Administration. "Highway Economic Requirements System Technical Report," FHWA, U.S. Department of Transportation, Washington, DC, 2000.

Federal Highway Administration. "Annual Vehicle Distance Traveled in Miles and Related Data–2000," U.S. Department of Transportation, 2001, http://www.fhwa.dot.gov/ohim/hs00/vm1.htm. Accessed June 10, 2002.

Gerlough, D., Barnes, F. *Poisson and Other Distributions in Traffic,* ENO Foundation for Transportation, Inc., Saugatuck, CT, 1971.

Gillen, D., Li, J., Dahlgren, J., Chang, E. "Assessing the Benefits and Costs of ITS Projects: Volume 2, An Application to Electronic Toll Collection," California Partners for Advanced Transit and Highways Research Report UCB-ITS-PRR-99-10. Institute for Transportation Studies, University of California, Berkeley, CA, 1999.

Harrington, W., Krupnick, A., Alberini, A. "Overcoming Public Aversion to Congestion Pricing," *Transportation Research,* 35A, 2001, 93–111.

Institute of Transportation Engineers. *Engineering Handbook*, 5th edition. Washington, DC, 1999.

Kolb, M. "Electronic Toll and Traffic Management on the Web," 2002. http://www.ettm.com. Accessed June 5, 2002.

Leshinsky, P., Fielding, R. E. "Getting There Faster," *ITS International*, 8(4), 2002, 55–56.

Levinson, D, *Financing Transportation Networks*. Northampton, MA: Edward Elgar Publishing, 2002.

Levinson, D., Chang, E. "A Model for Optimizing Electronic Toll Collection Systems," *Transportation Research Part A* 37(4), 2003, 293–314.

Leviäkangas, P., Lähesmaa, J. "Profitability Evaluation of Intelligent Transport System Investments," *Journal of Transportation Engineering*, 128(3), 2002, 276–286.

Li, J., Gillen, D., Dahlgren, J. "Benefit-Cost Evaluation of the Electronic Toll Collection System: A Comprehensive Framework and Application," *Transportation Research Record*, 1659, TRB, National Research Council, Washington, DC, 1999, 31–38.

Mannering, F., Kilareski, W. *Principles of Highway Engineering and Traffic Analysis*, Second Edition. John Wiley & Sons, Inc., USA, 1998.

McManus, S. "Freeflow Tolling Crosses Oceans," *ITS International*, 8(4), 2002, 48–49.

Menon, G., Lam, S., Fan, H. "Singapore's Road Pricing System: Its Past, Present and Future," *Institute of Transportation Engineers Journal*, 63(12), 1993, 43–48.

MITRE Corporation. *Intelligent Transportation Infrastructure Benefits: Expected and Experienced*, Washington, DC, 1996. http://www.its.dot.gov/tcomm/itibeedoc/etcs.htm. Accessed June 25, 2002.

Mitretek Systems Inc. *Intelligent Transportation Systems Benefits: 1999 Update*. Washington, DC, 1999.

Mohring, H. *Congestion: Essays in Transportation Economics and Policy*. Brookings Institution Press, Washington, DC, 1999, 181–221.

Pietrzyk, M., Mierzejewski, E. "Electronic Toll and Traffic Management (ETTM) Systems," National Cooperative Highway Research Program, Synthesis of Highway Practice 194, Transportation Research Board, National Research Council, Washington, DC, 1993.

Reich, S., Davis, J. *The Feasibility of Open Road Tolling in Florida*, Center for Urban Transportation Research, University of South Florida, 2001.

Rockwell Software Inc. Arena. Version 5. Sewickley, PA, 2001.

Saka, A. A., Agboh, D., Ndituru, S., Glassco, R. " Estimation of Mobile Emissions Reduction from Using Electronic Tolls," *Journal of Transportation Engineering*, 127(4), 2001, 327–333.

San Diego Association of Governments. *Fastrak Users' Response to Toll Pricing Change: A Time Series Analysis of Time of Travel.* San Diego, CA, 1999.

Schaufler, A. E. *Toll Plaza Design*, National Cooperative Highway Research Program, Synthesis of Highway Practice, 240, Transportation Research Board, National Research Council, Washington, DC, 1997

Sisson, M. "Quality Benefits of Electronic Toll Collection," *Transportation Quarterly*, Vol. 49, 1995, 93–101.

Small, K. *Urban Transportation Economics*, Chur, Switzerland: Harwood Academic Publishers, 1992.

Small, K. A., Gomez-Ibanez, J. A. "Road Pricing for Congestion Management: The Transition from Theory to Policy," *Transport Economics*. Amsterdam, Netherlands Harwood Academic Publishers, 1997, 373–403.

Small, K., Kazimi, C. "On the Costs of Air Pollution from Motor Vehicles," *Journal of Transport Economics and Policy*, January 1995, 7–32.

Smith, L. *ITS Decision Report: Electronic Toll Collection*, Partners for Advanced Transit and Highways, University of California, 2002, http://www.path.berkeley.edu/~leap/EP/Electronic_Payment/electron_toll.html. Accessed June 4, 2002.

Spock, L. *National Cooperative Highway Research Program Synthesis of Highway Practice 262: Tolling Practices for Highway Facilities*, Transportation Research Board, National Research Council, Washington, DC, 1998.

Sullivan, E. *Continuation Study to Evaluate the Impacts of the SR 91 Value-Priced Express Lanes: Final Report*, Cal Poly State University, San Luis Obispo, CA, 2000.

Texas Department of Transportation. *Average Low Bid Unit Price*, 2002. http://www.dot.state.tx.us/business/avgd.htm. Accessed September 13, 2002.

Transportation Research Board. *Curbing Gridlock, Peak-Period Fees to Relieve Traffic Congestion*, Vol. 1, National Research Council Special Report # 242, Washington, DC, 1994.

University of California. Comprehensive Modal Emissions Model, 2000.

U.S. Department of Energy. Energy Information Administration, 2002 http://www.eia.doe.gov/oil_gas/petroleum/data_publications/wrgp/mogas_history.html>. Accessed July 20, 2002.

U.S. Department of Transportation. *ITS Unit Cost Database*, 2002, http://www.benefit cost.its.gov/its/benecost.nsf/ByLink/CostHome. Accessed June 25, 2002.

U.S. Environmental Protection Agency. *Emission Facts: Idling Vehicle Emissions*, Report EPA420-F-98-014, Washington, DC, 1998.

U.S. Health Care Financing Administration. *Index Levels of Medical Prices: 1997-2001*, 2001. http://www.hcfa.gov/stats/indicatr/tables/t8.htm. Accessed June 15, 2002.

U.S. Social Security Administration. *National Average Wage Index*, 2001. http://www.ssa.gov/OACT/COLA/AWIgrowth.html. Accessed July 5, 2002.

Waters, W. *The Value of Time Savings for the Economic Evaluation of Highway Investments in British Columbia*, British Columbia Ministry of Transportation and Highways, Canada, 1992

Wilbur Smith Associates. *Operational and Traffic Benefits of E-ZPass to the New Jersey Turnpike*, 2001, http://www.state.nj.us/turnpike/execsum.pdf. Accessed July 15, 2002.

Yan, J., Small, K., Sullivan, E. "Choice Models of Route, Occupancy, and Time-of-Day with Value Priced Tolls," *Transportation Research Board Annual Meeting*, National Academy Press, Washington, D.C, 2002.

Chapter 11

FREEWAY SERVICE PATROLS

A Stated Preference Analysis of Insurance Values

David Levinson
Department of Civil Engineering, University of Minnesota

David Gillen
University of California-Berkeley and Wilfrid Laurier University

Pavithra Parthasarathi
URS

In this chapter, a Stated Preference (SP) analysis was carried out to identify the factors that influence people to choose highway assistance services (FSP) over private assistance services (PAS). The Los-Angeles FSP was used as a test case and the B/C ratios were also calculated based on the utility the FSP provides to an individual. Different values were chosen for the average time of waiting of the FSP and the B/C ratios were calculated in each case. The results indicate that the probability of an individual choosing the highway assistance services depends on the attributes of the program like the time of waiting for assistance and cost of waiting for assistance. The B/C ratios for the Los Angeles FSP were in the range 6.2–6.3.

1. INTRODUCTION

Highway assistance services, also called highway helpers, freeway service patrols (FSPs), and a variety of other names, are one of the main approaches used by incident management programs. The main goals of Freeway Service Patrols are to identify incident locations, reduce incident duration time, restore full freeway capacity, and reduce the risks of secondary accidents to motorists (Fenno and Ogden, 1998). These programs use vehicles to patrol heavily traveled segments and congested sections of the freeways that are prone to incidents (MnDOT, 2000). The role of the patrols is to clear the majority of incidents without any assistance from the other agencies. During major incidents, the patrols help assess the equipment and manpower needed to clear the incidents, coordinate with the other agencies involved, provide the needed traffic control, and act as a buffer between the workers and traffic. They also help detect and verify incidents like major accidents and pass on the required information to the transportation management centers (TMCs). This helps reduce delay, congestion, wasted fuel, emissions, and potential for secondary accidents.

The goal of this paper is to determine the value that people place on the benefits offered by freeway service patrols in comparison to private assistance services. This is done by estimating how much they would be willing to pay to avoid being stranded when their vehicles break down on the freeway. The factors that contribute to people choosing to rely on the highway assistance services in comparison to the private assistance services are investigated. In addition, the effectiveness of freeway service patrol for their insurance value only was analyzed using a benefit-cost analysis. A range of values was tested for the average time of waiting of the freeway service patrol and benefit-cost ratios were calculated for each.

The first part of the paper reviews studies that have been carried out on FSP programs. The second section outlines the theory of value that is used in this paper. The next part of the paper details the methodology of the stated preference analysis. Hypotheses about the study are put forth and the choice model results discussed. The subsequent section estimates a cost model, applies it to the Los Angeles freeway service patrol. The estimates of benefits from the choice model are presented. The final section calculates benefit-cost ratios based on the value users place on having the service available.

2. BACKGROUND

The first service patrol was started in the early 1900s. Early patrols were positioned at locations where incidents were expected to have a major impact on the traffic flow. The first patrol that was operated on a regular basis was the Chicago Emergency Traffic Patrol (ETP) in 1960.

The patrols are generally sponsored by public agencies but sometimes involve a combination of agencies and private organizations. Most of the funding comes from State Departments of Transportation (DOTs), local and state police, and metropolitan transportation agencies. Private towing companies are contracted to provide the patrols and supply the required vehicles, trained drivers, and equipment.

Patrols vary greatly in their temporal and spatial extent, as well as the frequency of coverage. The timespan may be 24 hours, daytime, peak period, or peak hour. The frequencies of the patrols range between one vehicle every 10 minutes to one vehicle every hour and is usually decided based on a trade-off between the area of coverage and intensity of coverage. The network coverage can be focused or broad. Patrols use a variety of vehicles including pickup trucks, vans, tows, trucks, cars, and utility vehicles. Certain patrols have special on-call support vehicles like changeable message signs (CMS) trailers, crash-cushion trailers, dump trucks, and sanders. The primary goal of these patrols is to remove the vehicles stalled in the freeway routes. Other services include changing flat tires, providing a needed gallon of gasoline, moving the vehicle to a safe location away from traffic, jump-starting a battery, or duct taping a hose.

In addition to the public highway assistance services like the freeway service patrols, there are also private emergency services, often operated by auto clubs, which provide similar services. These offer services to stranded motorists who are members of their club. The largest auto club is the Automobile Association of America (AAA). AAA is a non-profit federation of 90 motor clubs with offices in the United States and Canada, originally formed by nine motor clubs in Chicago in 1902.

California PATH (Partners for Advanced Transit and Highways) undertook two studies that evaluated the effectiveness of freeway service patrols in California. The first study (Skabardonis et al., 1995) evaluated the effectiveness of the freeway service patrols operating on a 7.8-mile test section of the I-10 (Beat 8) freeway in Los Angeles. The evaluation methodology estimated the incident delays before and after the freeway service patrols were introduced in that test section. The benefit-cost ratio was calculated using the delays and fuel savings due to reductions in incident duration and was found to be greater than 5:1 for reduction in duration of about 15 minutes. The results of the study showed that introduction of the freeway service patrol in the test section increased the number of incidents assisted and reduced the detection and response time of the incidents.

The second examined a San Francisco Bay Area freeway section (Skabardonis et al., 1998). Two hundred and seventy-six hours of "before" and "after" data were collected and processed for the section. The study found that, based on the savings in incident delay and fuel consumption, the introduction of the freeway service patrol was cost-effective at the test site.

A study carried out by the Texas Transportation Institute (Fenno and Ogden, 1998) showed that these patrols have a high benefit-to-cost ratio that varied from 2:1 to over 36:1. The patrols have become highly popular among the motorists and have proved to be very effective in aiding in the removal of congestion causing accidents.

The studies conducted so far have focused on the effectiveness or economic efficiency of the freeway service patrol. In the benefit-cost analysis the benefits have been measured as savings in expenses rather than consumer valuations of the service. Our study makes a contribution in two ways. First, it analyzes the factors that influence people in choosing to rely on the freeway service patrol vs. an auto club and also the benefits to an individual due to the presence of the freeway service patrol. Second, it develops measures of consumer valuations of the freeway patrol service and therefore provides the basis for accurate benefit measurement.

3. INSURANCE VALUE

A good or service is comprised of both Use value and Non-Use values. The total value of a good, from an individual's perspective, is the summation of both these values and is a function of the psychological, moral, ethical, and altruistic satisfaction obtained from the good.

Use value (or active value) is defined as the value an individual obtains from actually using the good or service. Non-use value (or passive value) is the value that an individual places on something although he does not intend to use it. Non-Use value is comprised of the following categories:

1) Existence value is the value obtained by an individual from the knowledge that a good exists (or is protected as in the case of an important resource).
2) Vicarious value is the value than an individual obtains from the indirect consumption of a resource.
3) Option value is the value that an individual obtains from having an option to enjoy the resource later.
4) Quasi-option value is the opportunity value that an individual obtains by delaying a decision that may result in irreversible losses otherwise.
5) Bequest value is the value that an individual in the current generation gets from preserving the good for the use of future generations.

The insurance value of a good is much like an option value. By paying for insurance, you are allowing the option of enjoying the insurance coverage at a later time. An auto club membership can be considered as insurance for individuals against being stranded on a freeway when their vehicles break down.[1] Breakdown insurance is simply a pooling of risks; the subscriber pays a small fee, and most of the time loses money (by not actually taking advantage of the service), but on occasion gets a large reward (by having the service available when needed).

Freeway service patrols are in many respects a public version of that component of the auto club service dealing with roadside assistance. The pooling of risk is done through tax dollars, and so all motorists are members. While the traditional private auto club limits its service to members, it may provide a positive network externality by clearing incidents faster than in its absence. Freeway service patrols are justified on the basis of this positive network benefit, but also provide the private benefit of aiding the broken down vehicle in addition to helping traffic flow better. Our study aims to measure this private "insurance" benefit, to complement the public benefit that has previously been measured by Fenno and Ogden (1998) and Skabardonis et al. (1995 and 1998).

4. METHODOLOGY

A stated preference survey questionnaire was developed at the University of Minnesota, Minneapolis to find the value of the highway assistance services. The pilot survey was carried out on a sample of 16 individuals, mostly college students at the University of Minnesota, Minneapolis in spring 2000. After this pilot study, a revised Internet-based survey was carried out at UC-Berkeley and at UC-San Diego with a sample size of 1,008 (Gillen et al. 2001).[2]

The survey was designed to provide measures of how people value the range of service both temporally as well as geographically and the type of service offered. The three key categories of service were when it was offered, where it was offered and the quality of service that was offered. The conjoint model was used to elicit responses to measure willingness to pay. The survey instrument is given in Appendix 1.

An analysis of the data from the Internet-based survey was carried out using the logit model. The aim of the analysis was to estimate the probability of an individual choosing a set of characteristics associated with the highway assistance services given certain breakdown related characteristics and individual characteristics.

5. HYPOTHESIS AND RESULTS: PRIVATE VS. PUBLIC HIGHWAY ASSISTANCE SERVICES

The survey consisted of series of questions in which the respondents had to choose between characteristics representative of (1) freeway service patrols (FSP) and (2) private assistance services (PAS).

The hypothesis was that the probability of an individual choosing the public assistance services or alternative (1) compared to alternative (2) is a function of the difference in the time of waiting between the alternatives (1–2), difference in the cost of assistance between alternatives (1–2), time of breakdown on the freeway (morning/evening/night), and the socio-demographic characteristics: age, sex, income, auto age, maintenance expenses, commute to work, cell phone ownership, and towing coverage.

Individuals choosing alternative (1) were coded as one and individuals choosing alternative (2) were coded as zero. Dummies were used for sex, cell phone ownership, and towing coverage ownership.

The results show that the probability of an individual choosing alternative (1) decreases with an increase in the time of waiting between the alternatives and an increase in the cost of assistance. Also it is seen that men are more likely to choose alternative (1) rather than alternative (2). Women more strongly favor a briefer wait than men. The results of the binary logit model are given in Table 1. All the variables considered are significant and influence the choice probabilities.

Table 1. Freeway Service Patrol Choice Model

Choice of Relying on Freeway Service Patrol

Logit estimates		Number of obs	=	9728
		LR chi2(12)	=	1511.04
		Prob > chi2	=	0.0000
Log likelihood = -5983.0931		Pseudo R2	=	0.1121

Variable	Coefficient	Std. Error	z	P>|z|
ΔTime waiting*	-0.033	0.016	-2.110	0.035
ΔCost *	-0.048	0.00423	-11.410	0.000
Sex* (Male=1)	0.292	0.046	6.380	0.000
Age*	-0.010	0.002	-5.390	0.000
Income*	-8.70e-06	9.71e-07	-8.960	0.000
Autoage*	0.016	0.004	4.050	0.000
Maintenance expenses*	-1.76e-04	5.46e-05	-3.220	0.001
Commute*	0.014	0.002	6.550	0.000
Cell phone* (Own=1)	-0.118	0.048	-2.470	0.013
Towing coverage*	0.128	0.065	1.950	0.051
Morning time*	1.230	0.055	22.480	0.000
Evening time*	1.251	0.055	22.830	0.000
_cons	-0.616	0.197	-3.130	0.002

* Indicates significance at 95 percent confidence level

The age and income variables show that as the age and income of individuals increase they are less likely to opt for the public assistance services. This indicates that older and higher income individuals would prefer a shorter wait even at a higher price.

The commute variable, which refers to the length of an individual's commute to work in miles, is significant and contributes positively to the individual choosing the public assistance services. Further an individual owning a cell phone is less likely to choose to rely on public assistance services. The time of day dummies indicate that compared to midnight, individuals stranded on the freeway in the morning or evening would prefer the public assistance services.

Surprisingly, individuals having towing coverage are more likely to wait for the public assistance services. This can perhaps be explained by the risk-averse nature of some individuals who not only are members of auto club but also prefer government provided highway assistance service. This suggests that public and private assistance services serve as complements to risk-averse individuals rather than substitutes. This makes sense when one considers that private coverage is broader in both time and space than public assistance offered by freeway patrol services.

The analysis shows that the probability of an individual choosing the public assistance services depends on the attributes of the program like the time of waiting and the cost of assistance. The heterogeneity of the sampled group and larger sample size has helped indicate the importance of socio-demographic characteristics compared with our initial pilot study.

6. COST ANALYSIS

The cost model used here was developed using data for highway assistance services operating in the various states (Fenno and Ogden, 1998), shown in Table 2. The data contained the name and location of the patrol, centerline kilometers, number of routes and vehicles for each patrol, the year the patrol was started, the annual incidents, the weekday hours of operation, sponsorship and funding agencies for the patrols. The population data were obtained to be consistent with the program areas. (Bureau of the Census, 1999; Negative Population Growth, 2000; Northern Indiana Regional Planning Commission 2000; California Department of Finance, 2000).

The independent variables considered to affect the cost of the program are the number of vehicles used by the patrol, number of routes that the patrol operates, and the population of the area in which the program operates. The annual budget of the patrol is taken to be the dependent variable.

A simple OLS regression, reported in Table 3, reveals whether the variables considered are significant. The results indicate that the variables considered are significant and influence the annual cost of the program. The annual cost of the program increases with the number of vehicles and number of routes that the program operates, that is, the size of the program. The incremental cost of adding routes is larger than that of adding vehicles. As population coverage increases, the incremental cost goes down, this can be viewed in some respects as the effect of density.

The Los Angeles FSP was used as a test case for the cost analysis. The data for the Los Angeles FSP were used in the cost model developed to get the annual cost of the program. The Los Angeles FSP operates on 41 routes and uses 150 vehicles. The model shown in Table 3 predicts the total cost of operation of the Los Angeles FSP is $18,687,338, consistent with the $20,000,000 estimate obtained by Fenno and Ogden (1998).

7. BENEFIT ANALYSIS

The logit model developed in the survey analysis is used for the benefit analysis. The analysis considers two scenarios. The "before" scenario has just the private assistance service operating. The "after" scenario has both the PAS and FSP operating in the area.

The PAS was assumed to have a constant average wait time and cost of assistance in both the "before" and "after" scenarios while the FSP average wait time was varied.

The assumptions used here are:

a) The average wait time for the PAS was assumed to be one hour in both the "before" and "after" scenarios
b) The average cost of assistance for the PAS was assumed to be $25 in both the "before" and "after: scenarios

The utility of a particular alternative to an individual was considered to be a function of the average time of waiting of the alternative, average cost of assistance of the alternative and other related socio-demographic characteristic. The utility for the "after" and "before" scenarios were calculated as given below:

$$V_{After} = V_{PAS} + V_{FSP}$$

$$V_{Befire} = V_{PAS} + V_{NoFSP}$$

V_{After} is the utility to an individual in the "after" scenario

V_{Befire} is the utility to an individual in the "before" scenario

V_{PAS} is the utility of the PAS alternative to an individual

V_{FSP} is the utility of the FSP alternative to an individual

V_{NoFSP} is the utility of the No FSP alternative to an individual

Table 2. Freeway Service Patrol Data

Patrol Location	Patrol Name	Hours	Annual Incidents	Annual Budgets	Year Started	Centerline Kilometers	Number routes	Number Vehicles
Albany ,NY	Samaritan	6	8200	NA	1983	NA	2	12
Atlanta,GA	Highway Emergency Response	16.5	16900	400000	1995	105	5	12
Austin,TX	Courtesy Patrol	16	NA	350000	1996	48	2	3
Boston,MA	Motorist Assistance Patrol Samaritan	6	72000	NA	1994	NA	16	16
Charlotte,NC	Incident Management Assistance Patrol	16	12000	410000	1990	26	1	6
Chicago,IL	Emergency Traffic Patrol	24	100000	3500000	1960	127	12	56
Cincinnati,OH	Samaritan	6	18200	NA	1992	NA	3	3
Columbia,SC	State Highway Emergency Patrol	4	4200	200000	1996	32	2	3
Dallas,TX	Courtesy Patrol	16	20000	750000	1987	564	7	17
Denver ,CO	Mile High Courtesy Patrol	5.5	18000	700000	1992	61	5	10
Detroit,MI	Freeway Courtesy Patrol	10	7080	NA	1994	68	4	5
El Paso,TX	Courtesy Patrol	15	18000	186000	1993	31	2	6
Fresno,CA	Freeway Service Patrol	4	1650	241600	1993	35	2	2
Ft.Lauderdale,FL	I-95 Service Patrol	13	24000	1000000	1995	81	6	7
FT.Worth,TX	Courtesy Patrol	24	10200	400000	1973	338	3	7
Greeley,CO	State Patrol Coutesy Patrol	7	NA	30000	1996	19	1	2
Greensboro,NC	Incident Management Assistance Patrol	16	3800	283000	1993	39	3	4
Greenville,SC	State Highway Emergency Patrol	4	NA	165000	1996	48	2	3
Haywod Co.,NC	Incident Management Assistance Patrol	24	4500	180000	1969	32	1	2
Houston,TX	Motorist Assistance Program	16	33500	1400000	1986	270	9	16
Indianapolis,IN	Samaritan	6	3800	NA	1991	NA	1	1
Kansas City.,MO	Motorist Assist.	13	40000	20000	1992	97	2	4
LosAngeles,CA	Metro Freeway Service Patrol	8	250000	20000000	1991	650	41	150
Miami,FL	I-95 Service Patrol	13	NA	400000	1997	27	4	4
Minneapolis,MN	Highway Helper	16	11000	610000	1987	145	7	8
New Jersey,NJ	Courtesy Patrol	8	3580	115000	1989	81	3	5
NeW York,NY	Highway Emergency Local Patrol	8	23570	2905000	1990	217	7	21
Norfolk,VA	Safety Service Patrol	24	12000	700000	1992	31	2	6
Northwestern IN	Hoosier Helper	24	13375	NA	1991	26	1	3
Oakland,CA	Freeway Service Patrol	7	97000	6000000	1991	354	20	51
Orange Co., CA	Freeway Service Patrol	7.5	80000	2000000	1992	145	10	30
Philadelphia,PA	Incident Management team	24	NA	NA	1989	815	20	15
Pittsburg,PA	Penn Licoln Parkaway Patrol	6	6000	245000	1996	42	3	4
Providence,RI	Samaritan	6	4400	NA	1978	NA	1	1
Raleigh,NC	Incident Management Assistance Patrol	14	8500	237000	1993	48	2	4
Richmond ,VA	Motorist Assistance Program	15	64500	1075000	1989	NA	NA	7
Riverside Co.,CA	Freeway Service Patrol	6	16000	700000	1993	40	4	8
Sacremento,CA	Freeway Service Patrol	6.5	11700	NA	1992	82	4	8
San Antonio,TX	Courtesy Patrol	24	6250	475000	1978	229	6	4
San Diego,CA	Freeway Service Patrol	6.5	18500	2000000	1993	250	7	7
Southern Connecticut	Samaritan	6.5	4800	NA	1985	NA	1	1
Springfield,MA	Motorist Assistance Patrol Samaritan	6	72000	NA	1995	NA	1	1
St.Louis,MO	Motorist Assistance Patrol	16	NA	NA	1993	161	10	14
Tampa,FL	I-4 Service Patrol	14	NA	NA	1996	32	4	7

Source: (Fenno and Ogden, 1998)

Table 3. Freeway Service Patrol Cost Model

Dependent Variable = Budget

Variable	Coefficient	Std. Err	t	P>|t|	Los Angeles Data	Total
Vehicles*	102603	19819	5.17	0.000	150	15,390,450
Routes*	143769	67812	2.12	0.044	41	5,894,561
Population*	-0.588	0.237	-2.48	0.020	3597556	-2,115,170
Constant	-483	221831	-2.17	0.039	1	-482,503
N	30				Total Cost for LA	$18,687,338
Adj. R-square	0.9631					

* Indicates significance at 95 percent confidence level

Using the coefficients obtained in the survey analysis model, the individual utility for both the scenarios was calculated for each of the 1,008 respondents of the survey as given above and then averaged to obtain the average utility. Four different time of waiting of the FSP were chosen and the calculation repeated for each time of waiting of the FSP.

The difference in the utilities was calculated using the log-sum formula given below (6):

$$\text{Logsum} = \frac{1}{m}\ln \sum_{i \in C_n^2} e^{mV_{in}^2} - \frac{1}{m}\ln \sum_{i \in C_n^1} e^{mV_{in}^1}$$

where C_n refers to the choice set

m is a scale parameter

V_{in} is the utility of alternative i to individual n

The superscripts 1 and 2 refer to the "before" and "after" scenarios considered. The scale parameter was taken to be one since the model used is a binary logit model.

The difference in the average utilities for each case was calculated using the above formula. This difference in utilities was divided by the coefficient of travel cost to convert it into monetary terms. The monetized difference was multiplied by the population of Los Angeles, taken as 3,823,000, to calculate the total benefits due to the FSP. The total benefits obtained are divided by the total cost of operation of the Los Angeles FSP obtained in the cost model to obtain benefit cost ratios. The results of the analysis are shown in Figure 1.

Figure 1. Benefit-Cost Analysis

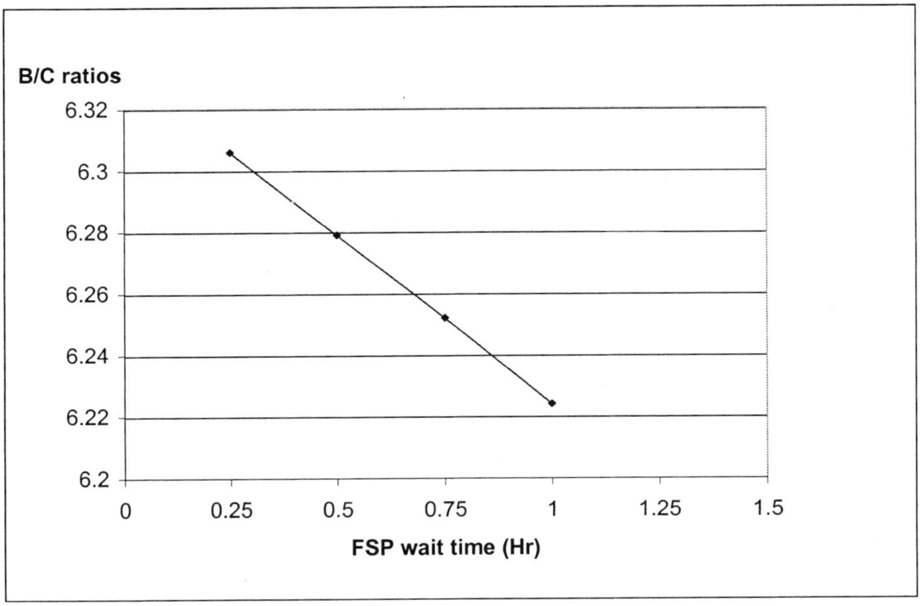

8. CONCLUSIONS

This research has made two important contributions to the ITS literature. First, we have developed an instrument that provides a more accurate measure of the benefits, measured by willingness to pay, attributable to freeway patrol services. Second, we have used our measures to calculate for a representative jurisdiction (Los Angeles) the net benefits of providing freeway patrol services and how these net benefits change as the service level changes. This offers an important tool for decision-makers, as the issue is not simply whether to offer freeway service patrols but how much, where, and how should the service attributes be designed.

We have found that freeway service patrols have value in improving traffic flow and safety by clearing incidents quickly. They also have value for the individuals who are helped by the patrols, who otherwise would have to wait for a private assistance service through their auto club or by calling a tow truck. This study performed a stated preference survey of over 1,000 individuals to ascertain the insurance value of freeway service patrols. The results indicate that freeway service patrols provide insurance benefits for their customers when they save time and money over private assistance services. The benefit-cost ratios decrease as the time of waiting for the FSP increases (freeway service patrols become less competitive).

APPENDIX

This survey is being conducted as part of a research project. The aim of this project is to find out how people look at the benefits and services of highway assistance and the value people place on such programs. The primary focus of highway assistance services is to remove stalled vehicles from the Freeways. The services provide include towing the vehicle to a safe location away from traffic, changing tires, providing a gallon of gas, jumpstarting a battery, etc. These services operate only at certain times and on certain critical routes.

Your participation in this survey will help identify the value of such services. All answers are strictly confidential, and no name identification will be recorded.

Thank you for your participation. Please circle your choices.

1) If your vehicle breaks down on an urban freeway at 7:30 in the morning:
Would you prefer:
a) To be towed by the highway assistance service to a safe location away from the traffic with a waiting time of 15 minutes on the road,
(or)
b) To be towed to the nearest garage or to a place from where you can make arrangements to get your vehicle repaired with a waiting time of 60 minutes on the road.
Circle a or b

2) If your vehicle breaks down on an urban freeway at midnight:
Would you prefer:
a) To be towed by the highway assistance service to a safe location away from the traffic with a waiting time of 20 minutes on the road,
(or)
b) To be towed to the nearest garage or to a place from where you can make arrangements to get your vehicle repaired with a waiting time of 40 minutes on the road.
Circle a or b

3) If your vehicle breaks down on an urban freeway at midnight:
Would you prefer:
a) To wait for 30 minutes on the freeway with your vehicle, paying no cost to get assistance from the highway assistance service,
(or)
b) To wait for 10 minutes and pay $10, for you to get assistance from the highway assistance service.
Circle a or b

4) If your vehicle breaks down on an urban freeway at 7:30 in the morning:
Would you prefer:
a) To wait for 20 minutes on the freeway with your vehicle, paying no cost, for you to get assistance by the highway assistance service,
(or)
b) To wait for 10 minutes and pay $5, for you to get assistance by the highway assistance service.
Circle a or b

5) If your vehicle breaks down on an urban freeway at 7:30 in the morning:
Would you prefer:
a) A highway assistance service that helps to tow the vehicle to a safe location away from traffic, at no cost with a waiting time of 15 minutes,
(or)
b) A highway assistance service that tows the vehicle to the nearest garage or to a place from where you can make arrangements to get your vehicle repaired, with a waiting time of 20 minutes and a cost of $50.
Circle a or b

6) If your vehicle breaks down on an urban freeway at midnight:
Would you prefer:
a) A highway assistance service that helps to tow the vehicle to a safe location away from traffic, at no cost with a waiting time of 15 minutes,
(or)
b) A highway assistance service that tows the vehicle to the nearest garage or to a place from where you can make arrangements to get your vehicle repaired, with a waiting time of 25 minutes and a cost of $30.
Circle a or b

7) If your vehicle breaks down on an urban freeway at 7:30 in the morning:
Would you prefer:
a) A highway assistance service that helps to tow the vehicle to a safe location away from traffic, at no cost, away from the traffic, with a waiting time of 30 minutes,
(or)
b) A highway assistance service that tows the vehicle to the nearest garage or to a place from where you can make arrangements to get your vehicle repaired, with a waiting time of 15 minutes and a cost of $15.
Circle a or b

8) If your vehicle gets a flat tire on an urban freeway at midnight:
Would you prefer:
a) To pay a $50 fee and be assisted in changing the tire,
(or)
b) To pay no fee but to be towed just to a safe location away from the traffic after which you make the necessary arrangements to fix the tire.
Circle a or b

9) If your vehicle gets a flat tire on an urban freeway at 7:30 in the morning:
Would you prefer:
a) To pay a $50 fee and be assisted in changing the tire,
(or)
b) To pay no fee but to be towed just to a safe location away from the traffic after which you make the necessary arrangements to fix the tire.
Circle a or b

10) If your vehicle gets a flat tire on an urban freeway at midnight:
Would you prefer:
a) To pay a $30 fee and be assisted in changing the tire,
(or)
b) To be towed just to a safe location away from the traffic after which you make the necessary arrangements to fix the tire, at no cost.
Circle a or b

11) If your vehicle gets a flat tire on an urban freeway at 7:30 in the morning:
Would you prefer:

a) To pay a $30 fee and be assisted in changing the tire,

(or)

b) To be towed just to a safe location away from the traffic after which you make the necessary arrangements to fix the tire, at no cost.

Circle a or b

As a general user of the roadway:

12) Would you prefer:

a) That you pay an annual fee of $50 for highway assistance services and not pay a fee if the vehicle actually breaks down on the freeway,

(or)

b) That you pay no annual fee but $25 for assistance, when your vehicle actually breaks down.

Circle a or b

13) Would you prefer:

a) That you pay an annual fee of $75 for highway assistance services and not pay a fee if the vehicle actually breaks down on the freeway,

(or)

b) That you pay no annual fee but $50 for assistance, when your vehicle actually breaks down.

Circle a or b

14) Would you prefer:

a) That you pay an annual fee of $100 for highway assistance services and not pay a fee if the vehicle actually breaks down on the freeway,

(or)

b) That you pay no annual fee but $150 for assistance, when your vehicle actually breaks down.

Circle a or b

15) Would you prefer:

a) That you pay an annual fee of say $25 for highway assistance services and not pay a fee when the vehicle actually breaks down on the freeway,

(or)

b) That you pay no annual fee but $100 for assistance, when your vehicle actually breaks down.

Circle a or b

16) Suppose the highway assistance service being provided now operates only on interstate highways.
Would you prefer:

a) That everyone pays an annual fee of $75 so that the highway assistance service operates on all major highways, not just interstates,

(or)

b) That everyone pays an annual fee of $50 but that the highway assistance service operates only on interstate freeways.

Circle a or b

17) Suppose the highway assistance service being provided now operates only on interstate highways.
Would you prefer:
a) That everyone pays an annual fee of $50 so that the highway assistance service operates on all major highways, not just interstates,
(or)
b) That everyone pays an annual fee of $30 but that the highway assistance service operates only on interstate freeways.
Circle a or b

18) Suppose the highway assistance service being provided now operates only during morning and evening rush hours.
Would you prefer:
a) That everyone pays an annual fee of $75 so that the highway assistance service operates at all times,
(or)
b) That everyone pays an annual fee of $50 but that the highway assistance service operates only at certain fixed times.
Circle a or b

19) Suppose the highway assistance service being provided operates only during morning and evening rush hours.
Would you prefer:
a) That everyone pays an annual fee of $50 so that the highway assistance service operates at all times,
(or)
b) That everyone pays an annual fee of $30 but that the highway assistance service operates only at certain fixed times.
Circle a or b

Please answer the following questions
1) Your age:

2) Sex: Male Female

3) Occupation (Check all which apply):
Full-time Student
Part-time Student
Working
Part-time Working

4) What is your annual income (Check all which apply)
Less than $5,000
$5,000–$10,000
$10,001–$20,000
$20,001–$30,000
$30,001–$40,000
$40,001–$50,000
$50,001–$60,000
$60,001–$70,000
$70,001–$80,000
Over $80,001

5) Do you own or lease a vehicle?
   Yes
   No

6) If you do have an automobile, what is the make, model, and year of the automobile?
   YEAR ____________________________
   MAKE ____________________________
   MODEL ___________________________

7) Is the automobile in a good repair?
   Yes
   No
8) Is the recommended maintenance for the automobile being done regularly?
   Yes
   No

NOTES

[1] It is true that auto clubs offer a bundled service whereby members have a range of services from breakdown assistance to travel planning to insurance.

[2] The survey was carried out for all staff at UC-Berkeley and UC-San Diego. In order to encourage people to participate, all participants were entered into a drawing for a Personal Digital Assistant.

REFERENCES

Ben-Akiva, M., Lerman, S. *Discrete Choice Analysis: Theory and Application to Travel Demand*, Cambridge, MA: MIT Press, 1989.

Bowles, S., Gintis, H. "Risk Aversion, Insurance and the Efficiency–Equality Tradeoff," NBER, 1998.

Bureau of the Census. (MA-99-1) "Metropolitan Area Population Estimates for July 1, 1999 and Population Change for April 1, 1990 to July 1, 1999" (includes April 1, 1990 Population Estimates Base) http://eire.census.gov/popest/archives/metro/ma99-01.txt

California Department of Finance. "City/County Population Estimates with Annual Percent Change," January 1, 1999 and 2000 http://www.dof.ca.gov/html/Demograp/e-1table.htm

Fenno, D., Odgen, M. "Freeway Service Patrols A State of the Practice," *Transportation Research Record*, No.1634, 1998, 28–38.

Gillen, D., Levinson, D., Pavithra K. P., Johnson, D., Madhav, P. "Evaluation Methods for Measuring the Value of ITS Services and Benefits from Implementation: Part X Freeway Service Patrols," California PATH Research Report UCT-ITS-PRR-00-XX, 2001.

Levinson, D., Parthasarathi, K. P. "Evaluation Methods for Measuring the Value of ITS Services and Benefits from Implementation: Part X Freeway Service Patrols," California PATH Working Paper. UCB-ITS-PWP-2001-3, 2000

MacMinn, R. "Risk and Choice," The International Risk Management and Insurance Conference, Taipei, 1999.

Minnesota Department of Transportation, "Freeway Operations Section–Highway Helper Summary Report," January 2000.

Negative Population Growth, http://www.npg.org/states/va.htm NPG State Facts Virginia, 2000.

Northern Indiana Regional Planning Commission (2000) http://www.nirpc.org/demotrends.html

Skabardonis, A., Noeimi, H., Rydzweski, D., Varaiya, P. P., Petty, K., Al-Deek, H. "Freeway Service Patrol Evaluation," California PATH Research Report. UCB-ITS-PRR-95-5, 1995.

Skabardonis, A., Petty, K., Varaiya, P. P., Bertini, R. "Evaluation of the Freeway Service Patrol in Los Angeles," California PATH Research Report. UCB-ITS-PRR-98-31, 1998.

Chapter 12

ADVANCED TRAVELER INFORMATION SYSTEMS

Relationships to Traveler Behavior

Asad J. Khattak
Department of City and Regional Planning, University of North Carolina

Felipe Targa
Department of City and Regional Planning, University of North Carolina

Youngbin Yim
Department of Civil Engineering, University of California, Berkeley

Advanced Traveler Information Systems are becoming an integral part of urban transportation systems. This chapter discusses issues related to how people access, acquire, and use travel information. The perceived benefits and willingness to pay for dynamic information are also discussed. Empirical evidence from a major field operational test in the San Francisco Bay Area is examined to answer questions about why, how, and who uses travel information.

1. INTRODUCTION

Advanced Traveler Information Systems (ATIS) can potentially improve peoples' accessibility to economic and social activities through the use of technology. ATIS are intended to meet travelers' information needs, help them make more informed travel decisions, and moderate the effects of traffic congestion on both themselves and other travelers (Schofer, Khattak, and Koppelman, 1993). There are a range of technologies that allow people to access travel information, including radio, television, wireless and landline telephone, the Internet, and GIS-based in-vehicle dynamic navigation systems (Yim, Khattak, and Raw, 2002). In congested networks, dynamic information systems can support several traveler choices including the selection of destinations, modes, routes, departure times, intermediate stops, and parking.

Real-time information can also help with readjustments, e.g., diversions from the selected route to avoid unexpected traffic congestion (Heathington, 1969; Boyce, 1988; Al-Deek et al., 1988; Mahmassani and Jayakrishnan, 1991; Khattak, Schofer and Koppelman, 1993; Polydoropoulou et al., 1996; Liu and Mahmassani, 1998; Ben-Akiva, Bottom, and Ramming, 2000; Srinivasan, and Mahmassani, 2002). Emerging information technologies are likely to help people plan their trips, save them travel time, reduce navigational errors, and lower anxiety/stress due to route-finding or congestion. Though in some instances traveler information systems can distract drivers and increase their crash risk.

A limited number of studies have determined the feasibility, benefits, and risks of ATIS technologies. Specifically, conceptual models that characterize how people make their travel decisions and use travel information have been developed over the past decade (e.g., Khattak 1991; Ben-Akiva, Bowman, and Goupta, 1996). Furthermore, there is a growing body of empirical evidence regarding traveler decisions and the impacts of new and improved information systems acquired through federally sponsored field operational tests conducted in the U.S. One such effort is TravInfo, a regional traveler information system in the San Francisco Bay Area (Yim and Miller, 2002), which is the focus of this chapter. This test began in September 1993 with funding from the Federal Highway Administration and the California Department of Transportation, and has now moved to full deployment. The PATH Program in the Institute of Transportation Studies at the University of California, Berkeley conducted a behavioral evaluation of the field test, the results of which are reported in this chapter.

The outcomes of ATIS demonstrations depend on many factors; among them are:

- ATIS design, both the overall system and the human-machine interface
- Information system performance in terms of how well the data are collected, processed, and disseminated to the end user
- Attributes of the test location, particularly the availability of alternative modes and surplus capacity on alternate routes, and other network characteristics
- Institutional issues such as public and private sector support, clarity of objectives, organizational structures of the stakeholders involved, implementation of the test
- Economic, social, and technological environment
- The extent of individual and societal benefits.

Individual benefits may be tangible, such as travel time savings, or intangible, such as anxiety reduction. Society may benefit from ATIS through reductions in congestion (especially incident-induced) and pollution. ATIS designers are likely to focus on the benefits at the level of the individual user, and perhaps move the system closer to user equilibrium. While this may result in benefits for a wide range of the population, it is unlikely to lead us toward a social optimum.

Perhaps one of the most important factors in ATIS success is the extent of individual and social benefits, which are not really clear. They certainly depend on how individuals acquire, understand, and use information. Our purpose in this chapter is to describe how ATIS might impact travelers. First, we present a conceptual structure, based on our earlier work (Schofer, Khattak, and Koppelman, 1993; Yim, Khattak, and Raw, 2002), which discusses traveler behavior and information, factors affecting traveler response to ATIS, and evaluation issues. Then we present a brief description of TravInfo, its goals and objectives, and the structure of the evaluation project conducted when TravInfo was a field operational test. We conclude with a synthesis of the traveler response results based on TravInfo's empirical findings and documented in earlier studies (Khattak, Yim, and Stalker, 2002, 1999; Wolinetz, Khattak, and Yim, 2001; Yim, Khattak, and Raw, 2002).

2. CONCEPTUAL STRUCTURE

To understand the relationships between ATIS design and performance and traveler behavior, we must examine the effect of dynamic information on mode, departure time, route decisions, and diversions from habitual patterns (Figure 1). Beginning with such a foundation, we can then explore the effects of different ATIS configurations on traveler behavior.

2.1 Traveler Behavior and Information

Traveler behavior is the process of individual decision-making about what trips to make, where to go, when to depart, what mode of travel to use, and what route to follow. While individuals in congested urban areas often have considerable latitude in making these choices, making the decision processes more difficult to understand and predict, they are constrained by the spatial aspects of travel opportunities, network structure and transportation services, individual resources and capabilities, lifestyle requirements (to work, shop, etc.), and many other forces. Static and dynamic information about travel opportunities, services, network structure, and performance plays an important role in meeting traveler information needs and influencing their travel decisions. Conceptually, relevant and accurate dynamic information can contribute to choices that are more informed and perhaps better, either for the individual traveler, society as a whole, or both.

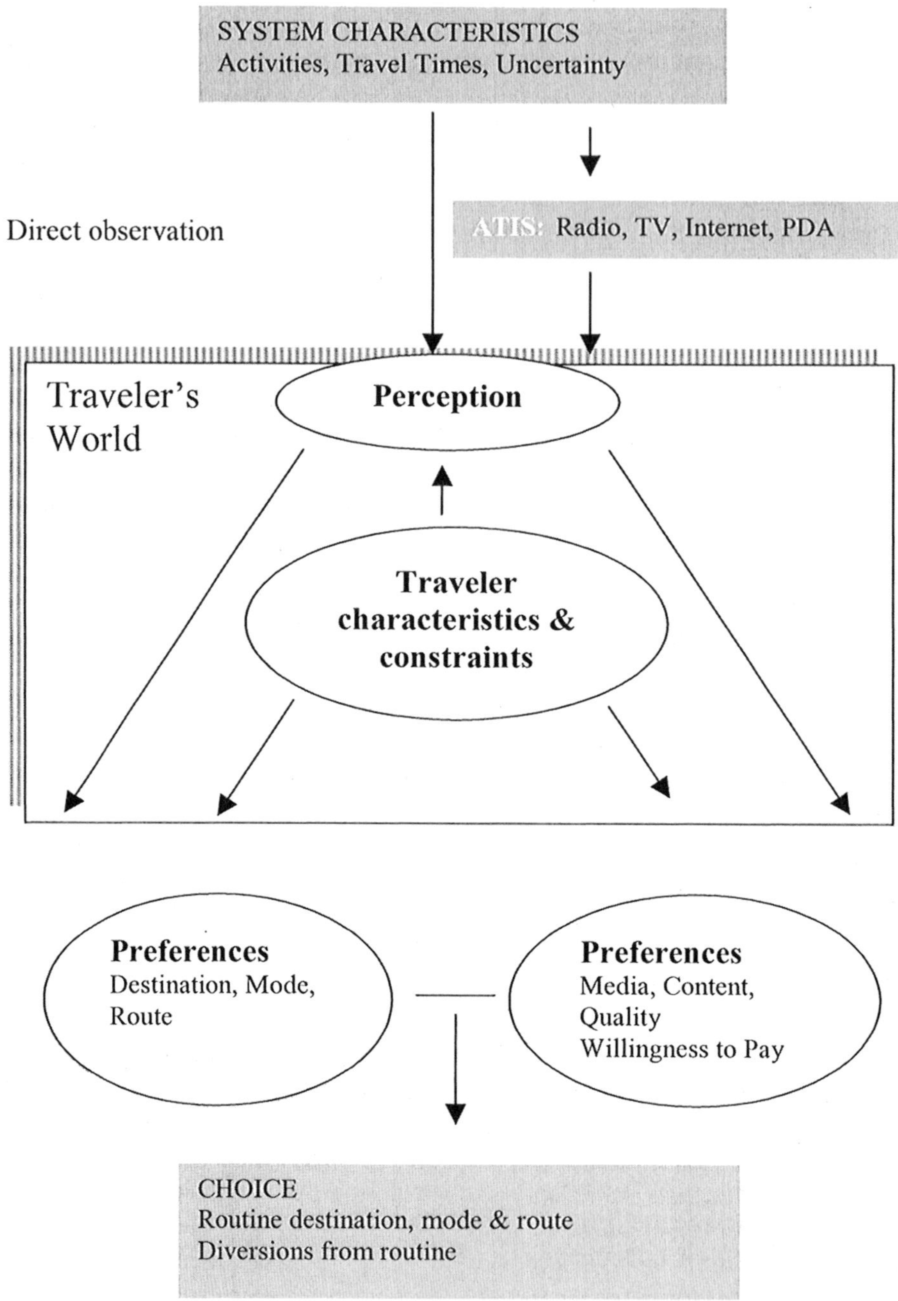

Figure 1: Conceptual Model of Traveler Behavior

Travel conditions on networks change over time, and thus what is a good choice now may be a poor decision tomorrow, or 10 minutes from now. Conditions vary regularly over daily, weekly, and seasonal cycles, and they can shift quickly and sporadically as a result of incidents such as accidents, breakdowns, load spills, special events, and extreme weather. ATIS can inform travelers about close-to-real-time roadway conditions, and this might influence short- and intermediate-term travel choices.

Information to support travel decisions is often acquired actively by searching (reading, seeing, asking, listening) from various sources, and it is used, along with stored knowledge, to make transportation choices, both long-term (e.g., auto purchase and mode choice) and short-term (e.g., departure time and route choice). Individuals have limited information-processing capabilities and resources, and as a result their typical decision-making processes use simple choice rules and they rely on limited search efforts, e.g., Simon's (1979) concept of "bounded rationality" to select satisfactory options (Mahmassani and Chang, 1985). In many urban areas, the search for options, such as the home-to-work or home-to-shop route, may be well short of the optimal route. The amount of time devoted to searching depends on the importance of the travel decision, the availability of salient information, the repetitiveness of the decision, and the expected costs and payoff of additional searching.

Often travelers cannot perform all the computations necessary for making their optimal choices and they do not have perfect ability to store and retrieve information. They do not always know the complete set of destination, mode, and route alternatives and the important attributes of their alternatives. Furthermore, they may not have the resources to reach an optimal solution in a dynamically changing network (de Palma, 1998).

Through surveillance and communications technologies, urban areas are continuously generating travel information that can fulfill travelers' information needs and support their travel choices, though the information is becoming increasingly complex in its structure and content. This information is then used by an advanced processor, the human brain, which has adapted to simplify choices so a large number of decisions can be made quickly (Tversky and Kahneman, 1974). Since many travel decisions are made repeatedly and become routine, experienced trip-makers have evolved strategies to cope with the stress and complexity of these choices. The challenge for ATIS is to intervene in these behavioral processes, to provide dynamic information that meets traveler needs, is accessed and used, and contributes to improved travel experience for individuals and the society.

Gathering, organizing, and conveying information about transportation network options and performance is complicated by the inherent spatial and temporal dimensions of such information. Human knowledge of the spatial environment, the cognitive map (Golledge and Stimson, 1997), is based on an often-limited mental representation of route locations and the physical environment. Cognitive maps influence travel behavior (Wenger et al., 1990;

Khattak and Khattak, 1998; Ramming, 2002); for example, the propensity to divert in the face of unexpected congestion is related to the number of alternate routes known to a person (Khattak, 1991; Polydoropoulou et al., 1996). People differ widely in their ability to understand and utilize spatial information. The potential for expanding and enriching cognitive maps through ATIS may be substantial, and the value of doing so needs to be explored.

2.2 Factors Affecting Traveler Response to ATIS

The development and evaluation of information systems requires an understanding of both short- and long-term traveler responses to information about travel conditions. These responses are likely to be influenced by the content of information, dissemination media, and by the attributes of information such as accuracy and relevance.

Information source. Given that people desire travel information, it can be acquired from an increasingly diverse array of media, including radio, television, computer (Internet), telephone, hand-held devices, personal digital assistants, and in-vehicle navigation devices. Depending on the value of information to them, people are expected to have different levels of access to and ownership of these devices and use them differently on various types of journeys and at different times.

Information content. The content of information is critically important for supporting travel decisions. For example, in selecting their destinations, people might value business and service directory information as well as the location and availability of parking at alternative destinations; they want to avoid unexpected congestion and therefore incident congestion and travel time information is likely to support their route choice. Information is further characterized by whether it is *static* or *dynamic*. The business directory information in the previous example is static, whereas incident information is dynamic. Where appropriate and possible, people are likely to prefer *quantitative* information to *qualitative* descriptions, e.g., qualitative descriptions of congestion, such as roadway "jammed" or "operation at posted speed limits," may be less informative than quantitative estimates of travel time delay in minutes (Durand-Raucher, 1992). Some presentation styles may be more useful and more effective than others, depending on the context. For example, travelers may prefer terse messages rather than a conversational style. Some travelers are likely to find map-based (pictorial) information more useful than others. Depending on the purpose of the trip, some travelers may find prescriptive information or route guidance very useful, and these would often be suggestions that help them escape delays.

Information attributes. People are likely to acquire and use information that they perceive to be credible, relevant, and accurate. The challenge is to develop an information system that is widely accessed and perceived as providing relevant and accurate information.

Since the 1990s demonstration studies have been designed to evaluate, in a structured manner, the effects of these aspects of information on traveler behavior. Repeated observations are necessary to separate the effects of differences in information media, content, and quality. In addition to the various aspects of information described above, peoples' utilization of travel information is also influenced by their own attributes, household characteristics, and situational constraints.

The magnitude of market penetration of ATIS technologies will influence their effect on travel conditions in the long term. The costs of these systems, as well as preferences for privatization, suggest that consumers will be asked to pay for all or part of ATIS equipment and services (Wolinetz et al., 2001). Since we can expect price to have an important influence on technology ownership, information acquisition, and use decisions, it becomes essential to understand consumers' willingness to pay for various ATIS attributes and services.

Willingness to pay is likely to be strongly differentiated across types of ATIS services, e.g., whether the information is customizable, whether users pay for the service on a monthly or per-call basis, whether the information provided is static and/or dynamic, and whether the information is bundled with others services such as safety and security. For example, Onstar is a service that has three plans with only static travel information for route guidance ranging from $16 per month to $70 per month. It is important to differentiate consumer responses to different services and media so that effective price structures can be identified and tested by the private sector companies. A map of the willingness-to-pay response surface, in terms of ATIS content and performance, management policies/subsidies, and individual characteristics, is important for supporting large-scale deployment decisions.

Note that in a rapidly changing information technology market, where the Internet allows nearly free access to information, willingness to pay is a moving target. Additionally, the price-performance mixes offered by ATIS are changing as the technologies mature. Price can be expected to drop as communications technologies become cheaper and the volumes of information increase; in addition, the installation of surveillance and travel data processing will become faster as the needs for greater security grows. ATIS effectiveness can be expected to rise over time, and the mix of service offerings is likely to become increasingly focused on what consumers truly value. Perhaps, successful travel information services will be those bundled with other travel services (Khattak, Yim, and Stalker, 2002).

A key issue is the public and private nature of information and the market penetration rate of subscriptions for information services. On the one hand, changeable message signs and highway advisory radios are public sources, which provide the same descriptive information to everybody about roadway conditions ahead. On the other hand, various information subscriptions do not provide the same information to all and they might provide both descriptive and prescriptive information about alternatives. Clearly, information (about incidents) is more valuable if a subset of people have it, since if it is widely available the benefits get more diffused—though this is likely to lead to user equilibrium. Therefore, market share of private travel information subscriptions, which presumably will provide more valuable information than that available for free, would affect willingness to pay since if only a subset of people have information they can gain more by altering their route or some other trip aspect.

2.3 Evaluation Issues

A key purpose of ATIS evaluation experiments is to understand the traveler behavior implications well enough to build a basis for designing future systems and making decisions about their implementation. To accomplish this, we must measure behavior and potentially causal factors so that the following types of questions can be answered:

How do people access travel information? One of the stages in making repetitive travel decisions relates to information device access and ownership. Access and ownership are not synonymous, because in some instances a person may have ownership but not access (e.g., access to home cable television while the person is at work), or access but not ownership (e.g., Internet at work may not be owned by the individual). Understanding behavioral responses to ATIS access and use requires that practitioners and researchers collect data on device access and ownership and travel information acquisition/use.

How do travelers use the dynamic information that they acquire? Use can be defined in several ways. Some travelers may feel reduced anxiety because of the information, but may not make direct use of its information for changing decisions. Others might find ATIS very valuable on their work trips, given the high value of time on such trips and the penalty often associated with late arrival (schedule delay). Others may review the information on a regular basis but make only limited use of descriptive information or available route guidance advice. Still others may use dynamic information frequently to adjust their travel decisions and accept advice without question. Utilization patterns can be expected to vary with traveler characteristics, including demographics (age, gender, education) and personality (Khattak, 1991; Schofer, Khattak, and Koppelman, 1993). Individual travelers may mix these various patterns of low to high levels of ATIS use. It will be important to capture all of these modes of ATIS utilization, because each may produce a different set of individual and social benefits. Relating use to traveler characteristics will contribute to projections of future market acceptance of ATIS.

How and when do travelers use ATIS? There are likely to be particular kinds of circumstances that promote or discourage ATIS use. These might be defined in terms of location on the network and the availability of routing options, travel conditions, weather, lighting, and situational factors (trip purpose, time of day, destination), moderated by traveler characteristics as described above. To the extent that ATIS is more useful under particular circumstances, perhaps high-uncertainty incident situations, it is important, albeit challenging, to fine-tune system design and performance for better functioning in such circumstances.

Why is dynamic information important to travelers? For the purposes of design and development, it is not sufficient to measure ATIS utilization; it also is important to understand the forces motivating ATIS use in terms of the benefits and of design and performance attributes. Exploring behavioral responses to ATIS media, content, and attributes will require variation of those attributes in experimental settings, for example, testing different human/machine interfaces, different services, and different performance levels. Such controlled experimentation may sometimes conflict with the operational orientation of private sector equipment suppliers wishing to market their proprietary products, and public sector agencies focused on providing good information to travelers and improving network performance. Though recent trends show that the private sector, encouraged by the willingness to pay by higher end consumers, is taking the lead in this human factors area.

How do travelers perceive ATIS? To anticipate future market response to these emerging technologies, it will be necessary to go beyond measures of observed behavior to explore how users feel about ATIS. Levels of user satisfaction, comfort, and traffic-related anxiety can be correlated with observable ATIS utilization, but they may also vary substantially across individuals as a function of demographics and personality. These perceptions will be important in service purchase decisions.

What are the consequences of using ATIS? The consequences are first observable at the level of the individual traveler, in terms of objective outcomes such as travel time reductions relative to unassisted navigation, as well as psychological impacts such as changes in stress/anxiety levels. Whereas individual consequences may affect market potential, public intervention in the development and implementation of ATIS must be justified in terms of social benefits, i.e., improvements in network performance. Although network performance changes due to ATIS are difficult to measure.

How much are travelers willing to pay for information? ATIS currently requires public subsidies to operate. Some ATIS are available free of user fees via radio broadcasts and phone-in services, while others are sold by automobile companies as part of a safety and security package. While there might be a high price elasticity of demand for information services, varying with different levels of information and different delivery sources (e.g., telephone, in-vehicle, pager), consumers might be willing to pay relatively modest sums for a better quality service that is perhaps bundled with other services that they perceive to be beneficial.

2.4 Evaluation Methods

There are several experimental approaches to evaluating ATIS behavioral responses. We can learn about behavioral responses to ATIS by asking people what they want and how they would react to different services and attributes. This is the stated preference approach, and it is useful for exploratory studies of new concepts and technologies or for understanding willingness to pay. Yet stated preference studies sometimes produce results that may not correspond to real behavior; respondents sometimes want to please the researcher by giving the "right" or expected answer, but this may not reflect their beliefs or future behavior.

More definitive results can be achieved, at considerably higher costs, through observational studies, in which people are given better travel information with ATIS technologies and services, and their responses are observed and reported (Schofer et al., 1993). Such observations can be conducted in a laboratory using simulations, or in the field with operational ATIS. The value of the observational approach is that it presents subjects with more realistic systems and allows researchers to record how people respond. The level of realism varies with the sophistication of the experiment, but it is always greater than that achievable in stated preference studies, because observational studies show preferences revealed through behavior. Conducting surveys to ask about revealed behavior is also popular among transportation professionals.

Observational studies conducted in the laboratory are generally less costly than field studies, and are more easily controlled, in the sense that ATIS attributes and services may be varied systematically, and subjects may be presented with a carefully managed set of test conditions. On the other hand, achieving a level of realism sufficiently high to support generalization of results is more difficult in the laboratory, because of both the limitations of simulation and the biases brought about by the observation procedures themselves. Field experiments are more costly and complex, but offer the potential to be more realistic and thus more readily generalized to other settings.

Observations of travel behavior, as well as surveys to capture peoples' perceptions and feelings, can provide a more realistic and comprehensive picture of behavioral responses to ATIS. Extended field experiments with this natural flavor and automated, unobtrusive measurement of traveler actions can reduce or even eliminate observational biases. On the other hand, natural field experiments require greater resource commitments, because they must be operated for extended time periods, and because of the need to measure potentially contributing phenomena such as weather, traffic conditions, and situational factors, which the researcher would control for in managed experiments.

Recently, transportation researchers have successfully combined Stated Preference (SP) experiments, where individuals choose from a given set of hypothetical scenarios, with Revealed Preferences (RP), which is how people (report they) behave in real-life situations. Revealed preference data are richer in information about observed behavior, whereas stated preference data provide information about how people might respond to a new alternative or how much they are willing to pay for a new service. A combination of the two types of data can give deeper insights.

3. TRAVINFO EVALUATION

TravInfo is one element in a growing body of empirical evidence (field observational studies) regarding traveler decisions and the impacts of new and improved information systems. We present a brief description of TravInfo, its goals and objectives, and the structure of the evaluation project conducted when TravInfo was a field operational test. Then, using TravInfo evaluation surveys, we will describe the traveler response results[1] and, provide some answers to the questions raised above about ATIS access, ownership, use, perceptions, and benefits and willingness to pay for information.

TravInfo's goal is to broadly disseminate accurate, comprehensive, timely, and reliable information on traffic conditions and multi-modal travel options to the public in the Bay Area. Funded by the U.S. Department of Transportation as one of the 16 field operational tests in 1993, TravInfo provided free dynamic information about traffic conditions and multimodal travel options.

The evaluation of the field test was performed using various data sources from field observations, focus group discussions, a series of telephone surveys with travelers, in-person interviews with project partners and Traveler Information Center staff, and field measurements. Significant resources were devoted to designing surveys and collecting behavioral data. The surveys were based on a contemporary understanding of traveler behavior and the factors that might influence it, including the availability and use of dynamic information. Particularly, the TravInfo assessment sought data in a number of areas including the importance of delays and congestion to traveler behavior in the short term; attributes of alternative routes and modes; attributes of individual travelers; the efficacy of various media, including new media such as the Internet, in delivering travel information; and willingness to pay for travel information. Evaluation surveys assessed traveler response to, and perception of, the TravInfo project and the various information sources and devices available to the public.

The evaluation surveys of travelers and system users were conducted between November 1995 and November 1998 (Figure 2). Although existing sources of dynamic information, including commercial radio and television reports for traffic and transit information, were not formally part of the

TravInfo system, the use of these sources by travelers was considered in the assessment surveys. The overall evaluation strategy was to study the response of the whole population, response of people more inclined to use information technology (early adopters), and traveler decision-making in high-benefit incident situations. For the traveler response part, the evaluation consisted of four coordinated studies, all of which used survey research. A "before and after" study design was used to understand traveler response. The large surveys were conducted before and after TravInfo implementation. The before study established "base" travel conditions. The surveys were conducted to study in-depth the changes in behavior over time.

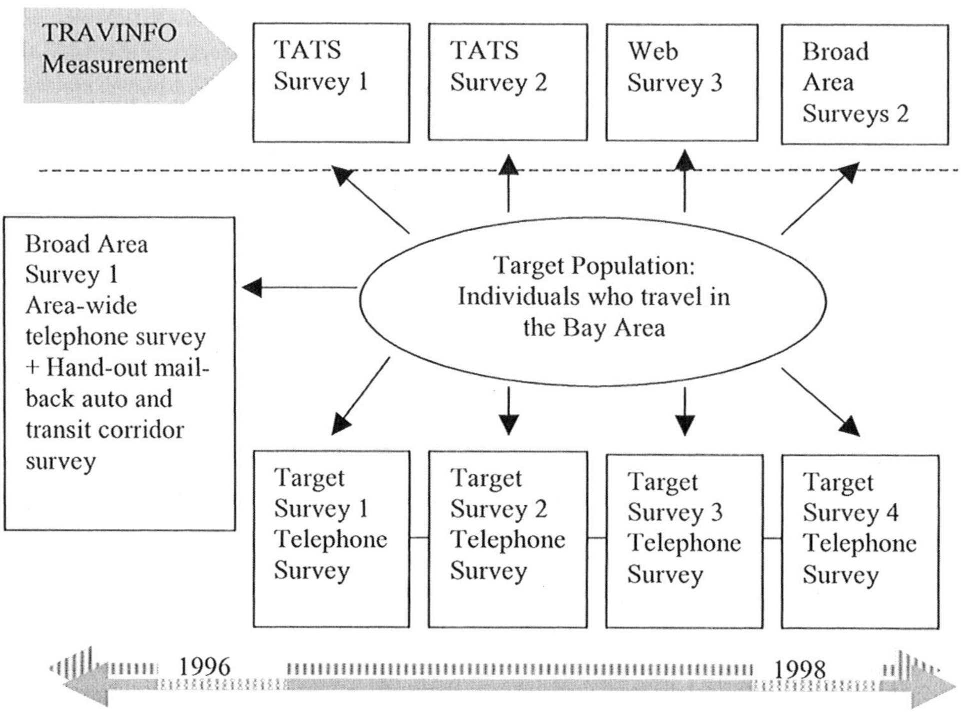

NOTES:
TATS = Traveler Advisory Telephone System
Target Surveys = Responses of a panel in the Bay Area I-580 corridor after the occurrence of a major incident.

Figure 2. TravInfo Traveler Behavior Surveys

The surveys asked respondents about their perceived uncertainty, incident delays, travel times and costs, revealed choices, and stated willingness to pay for information. Telephone surveys, conducted before, during, and after the field test included: two Broad Area surveys—BAS1 and BAS2 (Yim, Hall, and Weissenberger, 1997; Yim, 2000); four waves of surveys (Target) focusing on specific incidents that occurred on a heavily used freeway segment (Koo, Yim, and Hall, 1998, 2000); and two surveys of callers to the TravInfo Traveler Advisory Telephone System (TATS) (Yim et al., 1998; Koo and Yim, 2001; Khattak, Yim, and Stalker, 2002). In addition, a Web-based on-line survey was conducted of users of TravInfo information through Web sites maintained by private Information Service Providers (ISP) (Yim, 2000; Miller and Loukakos, 1998). Six focus groups provided initial insights and were helpful in survey design (Yim, 1999).

4. TRAVELER RESPONSE RESULTS

The surveys that are the basis of the empirical findings presented below were intended to evaluate the impacts of the TravInfo project. Each set of surveys targeted a different population, and reflected an evolving understanding of the factors influencing travel decisions in different situations. The purpose here is to integrate the survey results, interpret them, and draw suggestive inferences regarding preferences for information access devices, information acquisition and use, and willingness to pay for dynamic information. We do not perform statistical analysis/modeling of the data in this chapter. For empirical analysis of data, the reader is referred to TravInfo research reports, available from the PATH Program at University of California at Berkeley.

4.1 How do People Access Travel Information?

Both access and ownership of information devices and acquisition and use of travel information were investigated rigorously in the 1998 Broad Area survey (Targa et al., 2002). In this Broad Area survey, respondents were asked about (1) their access and ownership of information devices including cable television, cellular telephones, hand-held devices, pagers and personal digital assistants, computers at home and work with Internet access, and in-vehicle navigation devices, (2) the use of these devices for receiving travel information, and (3) changes in routine travel decisions due to dynamic information. The results show that 100 percent of respondents access or own at least one device (on average about four devices). This might be partly due to the survey methodology, i.e., respondents were contacted via telephone and therefore they had to have access to at least one device. This is not surprising given that people are likely to have radio, a television, and a telephone. The real issue is how many and what type of devices can they access, and whether greater access is associated with greater usage. Among all respondents 66.4 percent received travel information either regularly or occasionally, and 33.1 percent adjusted their travel decisions in response to that information. Information device access and ownership (captured by the number of devices) increased with higher income and certain professions. The use of these devices for acquiring travel information increased with access or ownership of more information devices, longer times residing in the study area, highway/freeway use, higher exposure to unexpected congestion, and longer travel time. More frequent use of dynamic travel information was associated with higher propensity to change routine travel behavior (e.g., route diversion).

4.2 What Sources of Information do People Access?

The Broad Area surveys indicate that most travelers receive some form of dynamic traffic information (Table 1.1). They also suggest that radio, and to a lesser extent, television, are the prevalent media through which information is provided during the pre-trip stage (Table 1.2). The predominant change between the two phases of the Broad Area Study is that radio reports were used less in the second study. Internet use increased as a source of pre-trip information (from one percent to four percent) and cell phone use doubled from one percent to two percent as a source of en-route information (Table 1.3). Telephone access to travel information was essentially constant. This suggests that new technologies (specifically cell phone and Internet) are the main growth markets for acquisition of travel information. The potential for these two media is further indicated by a more than ten-fold increase in cellular phone subscriptions, from nearly four percent in the first Broad Area survey to almost 57 percent in the second Broad Area survey. At the time of the second survey, 52 percent of respondents had Internet access either at home or at work or both. Clearly, there is great room for expansion in the use of these technologies for delivery of travel information.

Table 1. Selected Survey Results—Automobile Users

	BAS1	BAS2	Target	TATS 1	TATS 2	ISP
1.1 Users of dynamic information (freeway drivers)						
Regular [a]	33%	36%	N/A	80%	85%	64%
Occasionally	34%	38%	N/A	20%	15%	36%
Never	33%	26%	N/A	N/A	N/A	N/A
1.2 Source from which information was obtained (pre-trip)						
Radio	54%	30%	47%	N/A	N/A	N/A
Television	23%	22%		N/A	N/A	N/A
Telephone	19%	18%	N/A	69%	53%	N/A
Internet	1%	4%	N/A	N/A	N/A	100%
Cell Phone	N/A	N/A	N/A	N/A	N/A	N/A
1.3 Source from which information was obtained (en route)						
Radio	68%	48%	45%	N/A	N/A	N/A
Cell Phone	1%	2%	N/A	31%	47%	N/A
1.4 Reasons for not seeking information						
Do not listen	18%	18%	N/A	N/A	N/A	N/A
Info not relevant	55%	47%	N/A	N/A	N/A	N/A
No alternatives	5%	17%	N/A	N/A	N/A	N/A
Unreliable	2%	8%	N/A	N/A	N/A	N/A
Incomprehensible	2%	1%	N/A	N/A	N/A	N/A
Not sure	18%	9%	N/A	N/A	N/A	N/A
1.5 Travelers who changed plans due to information [b]						
Any Change	30%	53%	34%	48%	56%	84%
No Change	70%	47%	66%	52%	44%	16%
1.6 Types of travel decision changes (by travelers who changed plans (multiple response permitted)						
Departure Time	44%	44%	55%	16%	13%	37%
Route	71%	71%	70%	33%	29%	~50%
Mode	10%	10%	9%	1%	11%	1%
Cancel Trip	10%	2%	N/A	4%	6%	7%
1.7 Perceived benefits from dynamic information (multiple response permitted)						
Saves Time	21%	23%	15%	31%	23%	10%
Reduces Anxiety	18%	22%	24%	4%	3%	5%
Travel Plan	35%	49%	26%	53%	33%	24%
Other/Unsure	26%	6%	35%	12%	41%	27%
General Benefit	N/A	N/A	N/A	N/A	N/A	34%

[a] "Regular" in Broad Area means those who acquire information most of the time when they travel. "Regular" in TATS survey means at least once a week. "Regular" in ISP means at least once a week.

[b] Broad Area studies only considered travelers who changed decisions based on pre-trip information.

4.3 What Types of Information (Content) do People Desire?

A higher propensity for seeking travel information as indicated in the second Broad Area survey was significantly related to respondents who took longer trips, faced unexpected congestion, were female, employed, and owned a cellular telephone (Yim et al., 1999). That survey also indicated that the most desirable type of information in order of desirability is:

1. Current traffic conditions on radio or television that are updated every minute.
2. Detailed information about alternate routes around congestion, including where to exit and what surface streets to take, with comparative travel times.
3. An in-car navigational computer with a display showing highways and roads. The computer could show where congestion exists and map the fastest routes in terms of time around congestion.
4. An estimate of the time of delay on the usual route from unexpected traffic congestion.
5. An estimate of the travel time to get from the point of departure to the point of arrival on the usual route and any planned alternate routes.
6. Information about traffic conditions at specific locations, which a traveler could request over the telephone or on-line through a computer.
7. Detailed information about mass transit alternatives to avoid congestion, including up-to-the-minute bus, ferry, and train schedules and routes.
8. Automatic notification of unexpected traffic congestion on a traveler's usual route through a pager or cellular phone.

Of the travelers who did not receive traffic information, approximately half stated that the reports do not cover the route that they take (Table 1.4). Radio coverage is the most common source of dynamic information, yet the coverage was restricted. The morning peak hours typically received the widest traffic information coverage, with only a few radio stations reporting traffic conditions during afternoon peak and off-peak hours. Also, during 1996, radio reports ran no more than once every eight minutes, and only in half-minute segments. The area covered by traffic reports was limited to major freeways, and reporting was not consistent throughout the Bay Area and somewhat lacking in detail (Yim et al., 1996). These results suggest that the relevance of travel information is very important to travelers, both in making the decision to acquire travel information and in changing their actual travel decisions. Lack of alternate routes was also a significant consideration for travelers.

Though market penetration of TravInfo technologies was small (only nine percent of respondents in the second Broad Area study were aware that it existed), new users were attracted both to the telephone system and to travel

Web sites (Yim and Miller, 2002). Approximately one-third of phone callers and one-third of Web site visitors switched to TravInfo from radio/television reports. Other users who reported never listening to radio and television reports also began to use TravInfo, as did some users who continued to use radio reports and supplemented them with access to TravInfo. Those who switched were long freeway commuters and high-mileage drivers. The average commute time for both groups was 45 minutes, versus an average commute time in the Bay Area of 28 minutes (one-way). Traffic Web site users perceived the quality of Web site information to be far superior to radio/television traffic reports. Maps and verbal descriptions of freeway speeds and the locations of incidents were considered valuable for making travel decisions. The focus group participants also preferred obtaining information from the phone or the Internet compared to tuning in to radio or television reports, despite the effort required on their part.

4.4 What are the Changes to Travel Decisions (Behavioral Change) in the Presence of Information?

Based on the Broad Area 1 survey, the propensity to (ever) adjust pre-trip travel decisions on the basis of travel information was highest for respondents who reported that they commute to work compared with other travelers (Khattak, Yim, and Stalker, 2002). However, a significant portion (between 18 and 52 percent, depending on the mode and trip purpose) of trip-makers did not divert because of travel information. Individuals who experienced higher travel time uncertainty (measured by reported times of one-way automobile and transit commute when traffic congestion is severe) and reported the occurrence of unexpected delays (for automobile commuters and non-commuters) during the past month had a higher propensity to make pre-trip decision changes in response to travel information. Unexpected delays significantly increased the route change propensities of automobile commuters and non-commuters. Radio travel information seemed to increase the probability that the respondent will change route, departure time, or both.

One-third to one-half of users who acquired travel information made changes in their travel decisions (Table 1.5). The percentage increased from the first Broad Area study to the second. This may be partly due to the lower percentage of radio listeners appearing in the Broad Area study. The TATS and ISP studies revealed that users who actively seek information via telephone or Internet are more likely to change their travel behavior than travelers who relied on radio and television, as expected. At the same time, people who are more willing to change their travel decisions are more likely to access travel information.

Among travelers who changed their behavior, altering their route was the most frequent change (Table 1.6). The second most common change was altering departure time. Few travelers changed to transit despite the relatively good transit opportunities in the Bay Area, mainly because they perceived it to be inconvenient and more time-consuming than driving, even in congested conditions.

The Broad Area studies also revealed that non-commuting drivers changed their travel habits more than commuting drivers, perhaps reflecting the flexibility inherent in non-work trips. Among commuting drivers, those who sought travel information at work were more likely to leave earlier or take an alternate route.

4.5 Why is Information Important to Travelers?

Results regarding the reasons that travelers valued information suggested that time savings and the opportunity to plan the trip differently were most important (Table 1.7). An interesting result is the level of users who reported that travel information reduced their level of anxiety or stress. This percentage was much higher among Broad Area and Target study respondents than among telephone and Internet users. This is consistent with the observation that telephone and Internet users were more likely to seek information, since they had to be proactive in order to acquire it, and were more likely than the average user to change their travel decisions based on the information they received. This suggests that an important value of radio traffic reports is to help drivers feel in control of what is going on around them, perhaps because congestion that has an explanation is less stressful than congestion that is unexplained.

4.6 How Much are Travelers Willing to Pay for Travel Information?

Willingness to pay was investigated rigorously in the 1998 Broad Area survey (Wolinetz, Khattak, and Yim, 2001) as well as in the TATS surveys (Khattak, Yim, and Stalker, 2002). In the Broad Area survey, the vast majority of those who already had electronic devices such as personal computers or PDAs indicated that they would be willing to pay to subscribe to traffic information. Respondents were asked if they seek travel information, and, if so, about their willingness to pay for a hypothetical ATIS that provided: (1) Automatic notification of unexpected congestion on respondents' usual route, (2) Estimated time of delay from unexpected congestion on respondents' usual route, (3) Automatic alternate route planning around congestion, and (4) Estimated travel time on respondents' usual route and on any planned alternate routes. Sixty-six percent of the respondents sought travel information, and of these information seekers 71 percent (48.5 percent of the respondents) were willing to pay for ATIS. Those who preferred to pay on a per-call basis were 37.1 percent of the respondents, and they were willing to pay for ATIS as follows: \$1, 21.7 percent; \$0.75, 4.2

percent; $0.50, 6.8 percent; $0.25, 2.4 percent (average $0.74 per call). Those who preferred to pay on a monthly basis were 11.0 percent of the respondents and they were willing to pay as follows: $7, 8.3 percent; $5, 1.7 percent; $3 (average $3.84 per month). Increased willingness to pay for ATIS was related to respondents who altered their trips in response to information and stated a greater desire for dynamic information. Males and younger respondents were more inclined to pay for the service.

The survey of TravInfo callers indicated that the average use of the system would decline if a service charge was initiated without further improving the service (Khattak, Yim, and Stalker, 2002). Callers expressed a willingness to pay if the service could be customized to suit their information needs. Consumer response to purchasing travel information services seemed cost-sensitive, but the demand for information was relatively inelastic for travelers making longer trips. Trip characteristics and personal attributes seemed to play an important role in information acquisition, use, and willingness to pay. People who experience longer trips with greater travel time uncertainty and those who are younger and male seem to desire dynamic information. Higher willingness to pay for travel information received via telephone was associated with preference for customized travel information, longer trips, commuting, and listening to radio traffic reports. Fee-based information services are likely to be more successful in situations where the demand for information is relatively inelastic and improvement or customization of travel information is achievable.

Indeed the willingness to pay results do not account for a lower information value with increasing market penetration. In particular, as the market penetration of private information subscriptions increases, people might be less willing to pay for the service. This is because people can gain more by altering their routes or some other trip aspect if only a small subset of them know about incident-induced congestion ahead. While lower benefits are possible, Hall (1996) found that increasing market penetration of *accurate* information cannot harm network performance. Furthermore, the availability of dynamic travel information is often beneficial to both subscribers (who often gain by avoiding unexpected congestion) and non-subscribers (who gain because subscribers divert to avoid delays). Thus ATIS does not simply re-distribute benefits and their net effect is to lower network delays and improve the overall transportation system performance.

5. SUMMARY AND CONCLUSIONS

Understanding traveler response to new technologies is at the core of knowing which innovative traveler information systems will be successful. We have discussed the key traveler behavior issues surrounding ATIS and described findings from behavioral surveys. The following questions were answered:

How do people access travel information? Almost all people in the surveys had access to or ownership of at least one device (on average about four devices) that could be used to obtain dynamic travel information. Two-thirds of all respondents received travel information either regularly or occasionally, and one-third changed their travel decisions in response to that information. The main reason cited by those not seeking dynamic information was that it was not relevant to their travel patterns. The findings about access and ownership of information sources and about acquisition and use of travel information suggest that a significant gap exists between access and use. Also, decisions about access and ownership of information sources and about acquisition and use of travel information themselves should be analyzed explicitly in planning for advanced traveler information systems.

What sources of information do people access? The Broad Area surveys indicate that most travelers received some form of dynamic traffic information. Radio and, to a lesser extent, television, were the prevalent media through which information was obtained. Respondents used a variety of information sources to obtain travel information during the pre-trip as well as en-route stages, with cellular phones, the Internet, and in-vehicle devices representing important future growth markets; San Francisco surveys showed that their use had increased substantially during the TravInfo test.

What types of information do people desire? The most desirable types of information in order of desirability are: frequent updated traffic conditions on radio or television, detailed information about alternate routes around congestion, in-car navigational computer showing highways and roads, estimation of the time of delay and directions to get from the point of departure to the point of arrival, information about traffic conditions at specific locations, information about mass transit alternatives, and automatic notification of unexpected traffic congestion. The results also suggested that the relevance of travel information is very important to travelers, both in making the decision to acquire travel information, and in changing their actual travel decisions.

What travel decisions do people change in response to information? Dynamic information seekers who called TravInfo TATS or accessed dynamic information on the TravInfo-supported Internet Web sites were more inclined to change their travel decisions compared with Broad Area respondents, as expected. Clearly people who are predisposed to changing their travel decisions will seek out information from new sources implying simultaneity in their access and change decisions, which needs to be investigated. Those who changed travel plans due to dynamic information were more inclined to change routes and then departure times. Mode changes and trip cancellations due to dynamic travel information were rare, as expected.

Why is information important to travelers? Saved travel time and help with travel planning were the key perceived benefits of dynamic information. Interestingly, a reduction in anxiety was also cited by many respondents as a benefit. Respondents demanded high-quality information, and some were willing to pay for premium information services. While the new information services and media seemed to suffer from a lack of publicity during their initial stage of testing, they still appealed to information seekers and early adopters. Emerging technologies are likely to receive more publicity as automobile manufacturers and other technology companies market their products and services to larger segments of the population.

Are travelers willing to pay for dynamic information? There seems to be significant (latent) demand for personalized information services that would allow users to retrieve information when needed, to the point where a significant number of Bay Area travelers stated they would be willing to pay either on a per-call basis or a monthly subscription fee for a customizable service. However, the new information must be superior to that obtained for free through radio or television or other Internet outlets and services. The benefits from new information technologies may be limited due to competition with existing information sources such as the radio and television (but these benefits are likely to improve incrementally over time). Also, increasing market penetration of subscription travel information services is likely to reduce the benefits to the users.

Empirical evidence suggests that travel information helps individuals switch routes and departure time. The potential for information benefits is perhaps higher in cases of unexpected incidents, which are often a substantial portion of the congestion in urban areas. However, only small portions of the travelers change their travel decisions in response to incidents. The potential for demand reduction due to information seems to be substantial in such situations but the challenge is also greater mainly because the quality of information available in incident situations is relatively low. New information media can focus on providing dynamic information and improve the quality of information on routes that have high travel-time uncertainty.

NOTES

1 The evaluation project of the Field Operational Test included four principal elements: (1) Assessment of traveler response, (2) Institutional evaluation, (3) Technology assessment evaluation, and 4) System performance evaluation. However, our analysis is based on the traveler response component, which is concerned with acquisition and dissemination of TravInfo data.

ACKNOWLEGEMENT

We are grateful to the Carolina Transportation Program, UNC-Chapel Hill and PATH Program, University of California at Berkeley for support. We are grateful to Ms. Elizabeth Shay for proofreading this chapter.

REFERENCES

Al-Deek, H., Martello, M., May, A., Sanders, W. "Potential Benefits of In Vehicle Information Systems in a Real Life Freeway Corridor Under Recurring and Incident Induced Congestion," PATH Research Report UCB-ITS-PRR-88-2, Institute of Transportation Studies, University of California, Berkeley, 1988.

Ben-Akiva, M., Bowman, J., Goupta, D. "Travel Demand Model System for the Information Era," *Transportation*, Vol. 23, 1996, 241–266.

Ben-Akiva, M. E., Bottom, J., Ramming, M. S. "Route Guidance and Information Systems." Prepared for *Journal of Systems and Control Engineering, Special Issue on Road Traffic Modelling and Control*, Markos Papageorgiou and Christina Diakaki, eds., 2000.

Boyce, D. "Route Guidance Systems for Improving Urban Travel Demand and Location Choice," *Transportation Research*, 22A, 2X-281, 1988.

Durand-Raucher, Y. "Effect De L'Information Routiere Certifiee Sur Le Comportement Des Conducteurs," Programme de Recherche et de Developpement pour l'Innovation et la Technologie dans les Transports Terrestres, September 29–October 1, 1992, Versailles, France.

de Palma, A. "Individual and Collective Decision Making: Application to Travel Choice," *Theoretical Foundation of Travel Choice Modeling,* T. Garlang T. Laitila and K. Westin eds. Pergamon Press, 1998, 33–50.

Golledge, R., Stimson, R. *Spatial Behavior, A Geographic Perspective*, Guilford Press, New York: 1997.

Heathington, K. "On the Development of a Freeway Driver Information System," unpublished Ph.D. dissertation, Civil Engineering Department, Northwestern University, Evanston, IL, 1969.

Khattak, A. "Driver Response to Unexpected Travel Conditions: Effect of Information and Other Factors," unpublished Ph.D. dissertation, Department of Civil Engineering, Northwestern University, Evanston, IL, 1991.

Khattak, A., Schofer, J., Koppelman, F. "Commuters' En-route Diversion and Return Decisions: Analysis and Implications for Advanced Traveler Information Systems," *Transportation Research*, Pergamon Press, Vol. 27A, No. 2, 1993, 101–111.

Khattak, A. J., Khattak, A. J. "A Comparative Analysis of Spatial Knowledge and En-Route Diversion Behavior Across Chicago and San Francisco: Implications for ATIS," *Transportation Research Record*, 1621, Transportation Research Board, National Research Council, Washington DC, 1998, 27–35.

Khattak, A. J., Yim, Y., Stalker, L. "Does Travel Information Influence Commuter and Noncommuter Behavior? Results from the San Francisco Bay Area Travinfo Project," *Transportation Research Record*, 1694, Transportation Research Board, National Research Council, Washington DC, 1999, 48–58.

Khattak, A., Yim, Y., Stalker, L. "Willingness to Pay for Travel Information: Combining Revealed and Stated Preferences with a Random Effects Negative Binomial Model," forthcoming in *Transportation Research Part C*, Pergamon Press, 2002.

Koo, R., Yim, Y., Hall, R. "TravInfo Evaluation Traveler Response Element: the Target Study, Phase 1 Results," California PATH, UCB-ITS-PWP-98-24, University of California, Berkeley, September 1998.

Koo, R., Yim, Y. "TravInfo Evaluation Traveler Response Element: The Target Study, Final Results," California PATH, UCB-ITS-PWP-2000-3, University of California, Berkeley, March 2000.

Koo, R., Yim, Y. "TravInfo Evaluation Traveler Response Element: TravInfo 817-1717 Caller Study Phase 2 Results," California PATH, UCB-ITS-PWP-2001-07, University of California, Berkeley, 2001.

Liu, Y., Mahmassani, H. "Dynamic Aspects of Departure Time and Route Decision Behavior Under Advanced Traveler Information Systems (ATIS): Modeling Framework and Experimental Results," presented at the 77th Annual Meeting of the Transportation Research Board, Washington, DC, 1998.

Mahmassani, H., Chang, G. L. "Dynamic Aspects of Departure Time Choice Behavior in a Commuting System," *Transportation Research Record*, 1037, 1985, 88–101.

Mahmassani, H. S., Jayakrishnan, R. "System Performance and User Response Under Real-Time Information in a Congested Traffic Corridor," *Transportation Research*, 25A, 5, 1991, 293–307.

Miller. M., Loukakos, D. "TravInfo Evaluation (Technology Element) Traveler Information Center (TIC) Study: System Reliability and Communications Interface (9/96 –12/97)", California PATH, UCB-ITS-PWP-98-21, University of California, Berkeley, September 1998.

Miller. M., Loukakos, D. "Final Report for TravInfo Evaluation (Technology Element) Traveler Information Center (TIC) Study," to be published PATH Research Report.

Polydoropoulou, A., Ben-Akiva, M., Khattak, A., Lauprete, L. "Modeling Revealed and Stated En-route Travel Response to Advanced Traveler Information Systems," *Transportation Research Record*, 1537, 1996.

Ramming, S. M. "Network Knowledge and Route Choice," Department of Civil and Environmental Engineering, Massachusetts Institute of Technology, Ph.D. dissertation, 2002.

Schofer, J., Khattak, A., Koppelman, F. S. "Behavioral Issues in the Design and Evaluation of Advanced Transportation Information Systems," *Transportation Research C*, Vol. 1, No. 2. 199, 107–117.

Simon, H. *Models of Thought*. New Haven: Yale University Press, 1979.

Srinivasan. K. K., Mahmassani, H. S. "Trip Time Perception and Judgment Processes in Tripmaker Decisions under Real-time Traffic Information," presented at Transportation Research Board, 81st Annual Meeting. Washington, DC, CD-ROM, 2002.

Targa, F., Khattak, A. J., Yim, Y. B. "Understanding Access and Use of Dynamic Travel Information,." working paper, 2002.

Tversky A., Kahneman, D. "Judgments under Uncertainty, Heuristics and Biases," *Science*, 185, 1974, 1,124–1,131,.

Wenger, M., Spyridakis, J., Haselkom, M. D., Bartield, W., Conquest, L. "Motorist Behavior and the Design of Motorist Information Systems," *Transportation Research Record*, 1281, 1990, 159–167.

Wolinetz, L., Khattak, A., Yim, Y. "Why Will Some Individuals Pay for Travel Information When it Can be Free? Analysis of a Bay Area Travel Survey," *Transportation Research Record*, 1759, TRB, National Research Council, Washington, DC, 2001.

Yim,Y., Hall, R., Weissenberger, S. "TravInfo Evaluation Traveler Response Element: The Broad Area Study, Phase 1 Results," California PATH, UCB-ITS-PWP-97-9, University of California, Berkeley, March 1997.

Yim. Y., Hall, R., Koo. R., Miller. M. "TravInfo Evaluation: TravInfo 817-1717 Caller Study Phase 1 Results," California PATH, UCB-ITS-PWP-98-25, University of California, Berkeley, September 1998.

Yim. Y. "Consumer Response to Advanced Traveler Information Systems: Focus Group Results," ITS America, 9th Annual Meeting Conference Proceedings, April 19–22, 1999.

Yim. Y. "TravInfo Evaluation: Information Service Provider Study – Traffic Web Site Users and Their Travel Behavior," California PATH, UCB-ITS-PWP-2000-5, University of California, Berkeley, May 2000.

Yim, Y. "TravInfo Evaluation Traveler Response Element: the Broad Area Study, Phase 2 Results," unpublished working paper, 2000.

Yim, Y., Khattak, A. J., Raw, J. "Traveler Response to New Dynamic Information Sources: Analyzing Corridor and Area-B surveys," forthcoming in *Transportation Research Record*, 2002.

Yim. Y., Miller. M. A. "Evaluation Study of the TravInfo Regional Transportation Information System," presented at Transportation Research Board, 81st Annual Meeting. Washington, DC, CD-ROM, 2002.

Chapter 13

TRAVEL TIME RELIABILITY

Using Real-time Loop Detector Data to Estimate Mixed Logit Route Choice

Henry X. Liu
California PATH Program, University of California

Will Recker
Department of Civil and Environmental Engineering,
Institute of Transportation Studies, University of California

Anthony Chen
Department of Civil and Environmental Engineering, Utah State University

Travel time reliability has generally been surmised to be one of the more important decision factors in travelers' route choice. In this paper, we study the travelers' trade-offs among travel cost, time, and reliability using real-time loop data. Traveler's route choice is formulated as a mixed-logit model, with the coefficients in the model representing individual traveler's preferences or tastes towards travel time, reliability, and cost. We apply the methodology to newly collected data concerning route choice in the California State Route 91 value-pricing project, and are able to estimate how travelers value travel time and travel-time reliability. To find the distribution of the model coefficients and thereby uncover the contribution of travel time reliability in the dynamic route choice, we use a genetic algorithm to identify the parameter set that results in the best match between the aggregated results from traveler's route choice model and the observed time-dependent traffic volume data from loop detectors. We find that the estimated median value of travel time reliability is substantially greater than that of travel time, and that the estimated median value of degree of risk aversion indicates that travelers value a reduction in travel time variability more highly than a corresponding reduction in the travel time for that journey. Moreover, travelers' attitudes towards congestion are not homogeneous; substantial heterogeneity exists in travelers' preference of travel time and reliability. Our results validate results from some previous studies and demonstrate the applicability of the approach in travelers' behavioral studies.

1. INTRODUCTION

It is accepted that a wide range of factors influences the route choice of individual travelers. In addition to such factors as perceived travel time, monetary cost, comfort, and safety, the reliability of travel time has been generally conceded to be an important factor, particularly for trips, such as journey-to-work, where time constraints (e.g., arrival time) may impose significant penalties on an individual. Reliability, by its nature, implies something about the certainty or stability of travel time of any particular trip under repetition. As such, reliability is closely associated with the statistical concept of variability. Variability could result from the differences in the mix of vehicle types on the network for the same flow rates, differences in driver reactions under various weather and driving conditions, differences in delays experienced by different vehicles at intersections, and such random incidents as vehicle breakdown and signal failure, etc. Variability in network travel times introduces uncertainty for travelers in that they do not know with certainty when they will arrive at their respective destinations. This risk (or added cost) to a traveler making a trip may be manifest in a willingness to pay a premium (e.g., through use of toll roads or HOV lane) to avoid congestion and to achieve greater reliability in travel times.

Although travel time reliability ostensibly plays an important role in the traveler's route choice behavior, there has been little empirical work directed to an understanding of the effects of reliability on the route choice decision-making of the traveler; many questions remain unanswered. How do travelers value travel time and its reliability, how much does the travel time reliability contribute to travelers' route choice, and how much variation is there in travelers' preferences regarding the potential trade-off between reliability and travel time itself? Answering these questions can help in the design and evaluation of transportation planning and operation strategies, but requires that this attribute be accounted for explicitly in the modeling of travelers' choice.

The above questions could be studied either through direct or indirect methods (Jackson and Jucker, 1981). The direct method involves posing a series of questions to a sample of travelers in a certain population, usually either as a revealed preference (RP) survey, in which the actual behavioral response to the traffic condition is reported, or as a stated preference (SP) survey, in which a traveler's behavior in hypothetical scenarios is reported. The indirect method involves inferring the answers to these behavioral questions from observed data describing the flows on alternative routes connecting an origin-destination pair.

Most previous research that has attempted to address issues of reliability using direct methods has analyzed RP data and/or SP data. Abdel-Aty et al.

(1996) conducted a study to investigate effect of travel time variability on route choice using repeated measurement SP data. Their results indicated the significance of both the degree of travel time variation and traffic information on route choice. Bates et al. (2001) provided a comprehensive overview of the theory underlying the valuation of reliability, and discussed the empirical issues in data collection. Because of the difficulties of finding real choice situations with sufficient variation to allow statistically reliable estimates to be obtained for RP data, they acknowledged the value of SP data, and applied SP data in the study of valuation of reliability in passenger rail services. Although SP is usually de facto the only realistic possibility for data collection, Lam and Small (2001) leveraged the opportunity of a road pricing project and measured values of travel time and reliability from 1998 RP data on actual behavior of commuters on State Route 91 (SR91) in Orange County, California. Recently, Small et al. (2002) continued their previous studies by combining both RP and SP data on SR 91 to empirically identify the varied nature of traveler preference for travel time and reliability. They found that highway users exhibit substantial heterogeneity in their valuation of travel time and reliability.

However, both RP and SP data have drawbacks. Although a greater level of detailed data could be obtained from the survey from individual travelers, and these data may lead to a higher degree of accuracy for the estimation, data collection for the survey of large sample size and its following analysis are time-consuming and expensive. For SP data, it is not sufficient to say that the response to hypothetical situations really reflects traveler's behavioral choice to actual situations. For instance, because people tend to overstate the time delays they actually experienced, it is common that they respond more to a given actual time saving than to a hypothetical time saving of the same amount. Therefore, the estimated value of travel time may be lower than the actual. Although there is a general econometric tradition for favoring RP data, there are often serious problems in achieving the level of detail in data that is ideally required. For the study of travel time reliability, as noted in the paper of Bates (2001), it is virtually impossible to find RP situations where there is sufficient perceived variation to allow statistically reliable estimates—a notable exception to this is the paper by Lam and Small (2001).

Alternatively, advances in traffic surveillance and monitoring technologies, including real-time data from inductive loop detectors, can provide valuable aggregated information that ostensibly resulted from the disaggregated individual travel route choices. Instead of surveying motorists on their choices in the direct method, we propose an indirect method to answer some behavioral questions in such a way that the estimated choice probability resulting from route choice model matches the revealed probability exhibited in the real-time loop detector data. To the best of our knowledge, there are but a very few research studies that study behavioral issues using the indirect method, and this paper aims to fill this gap.

In this paper, we study the trade-off among travel cost, time, and reliability using real-time loop data. Traveler's route choice is formulated as a mixed-logit model, which extends the random utility model that underlies multinomial logit (McFadden and Train, 2000); the coefficients in the model representing individual traveler's preferences or tastes toward travel time, reliability, and cost. To find the distribution of the model coefficients and thereby uncover the contribution of travel time reliability in the dynamic route choice, we use a genetic algorithm to identify the parameter set that results in the best match between the aggregated results from traveler's route choice model and the observed time-dependent traffic volume data from loop detectors.

We apply the proposed approach to measure value of time (VOT), value of reliability (VOR), and degree of risk aversion (DORA) simultaneously using data on actual travel behavior drawn from a real pricing context. A recent value pricing project on a major commuting highway, State Route 91 (SR 91) in Orange County, California, gives travelers the option to travel free on the regular lanes or to pay a time-varying price for express travel on toll lanes situated along the median of the highway. Based on their respective choices of whether or not to pay a toll for the congestion-free travel, we observe the outcome from the choice probability between the two parallel routes in the form of loop detector data on 30-second averages of count and occupancy. We find that travel time reliability plays an important role in traveler's decision-making for route choice. Moreover, the results indicate that travelers value travel time reliability substantially higher than they do travel time savings. Our results validate results from some previous studies and demonstrate the applicability of our approach in the study of this particular traveler behavior.

The rest of the paper is organized as follows. The next section discusses the route choice formulation using mixed-logit model, and estimation procedure to identify the unknown parameters in the route choice model. We then apply the proposed methodology to the SR 91 data and describe empirical results in Section 3 and Section 4. The final section provides a summary of research findings.

2. ROUTE CHOICE FORMULATION AND ESTIMATION PROCEDURE

2.1 Route Choice Formulation

Travelers' route choice among the available options will reflect their perception of the costs and benefits associated with each option. If the costs or benefits are perceived to be uncertain, the choice will be influenced by the travelers' attitude to that uncertainty. We incorporate the stochasticity of route travel time as a measure of the risk associated with the selection of specific routes. On the basis of the perceived distribution of network travel times, travelers are assumed to behave differently when considering routes for which their perceived travel times have a probabilistic component. Some are risk averse, choosing routes with longer expected travel times but smaller variations. Others, the risk takers, may choose routes with shorter expected travel times but greater variations in travel time reliability.

In modeling this behavior, we assume that the individual traveler has a subjective probability distribution of travel time for each available route. Additionally, we assume that there exists an objective distribution of travel time based on actual measurement over a suitably defined time period. This stochastic travel time reflects the intrinsic fluctuations in the transportation network, as noted, due to particular weather conditions, unpredictable lane closures, traffic accidents, etc. It is not necessarily the case that the subjective and objective probability distributions over route travel time are identical. (They may differ, and when this is the case, the existence of perception errors is witnessed.) However, for travelers in peak-hour commuting trips it seems reasonable to assume that these two distributions are same, i.e., drivers have no misperceptions of either travel time or travel time variation. This is the case for the model considered here; we leave the incorporation of traveler's perception errors for future studies.

We assume that travelers consider travel time, travel time reliability (i.e., risk), and out-of-pocket monetary cost (such as toll) in their choice of route. Moreover, we assume that they value any trade-off between travel time and travel time reliability differently depending on individual tastes, and that such tastes are distributed in the population in a manner that covers a spectrum in terms of the degree of risk aversion. We further assume that drivers are rational and are maximizing some utility measure, and suggest a common disutility functional form, but with coefficients (disutility weights) that reflect individual's preference. Travelers' perceived disutility is a function of the route travel time, travel time variability, monetary cost, and the individual traveler's attitude toward these three variables at each time. Specifically, we assume that the traveler is faced with a choice among P^{rs} alternative freeway routes between a freeway on-ramp origin, r, and a corresponding freeway off-ramp, s. (In this formulation, we assume that surface street travel is irrelevant to the choice and that the freeway origin and destination are fixed.). Under these assumptions, the disutility to traveler n of travel, commencing at time t, along path p linking on-ramp origin r and off-ramp destination s is specified as:

$$U_{np}(t) = \beta_n^{'} x_{np}(t) + \varepsilon_{np} \tag{1}$$

where $x_{np}(t)$ is a vector of observed variables (including alternative specific constants), β_n is a corresponding coefficient vector that may vary over individuals but does not vary across alternatives or time, and ε_{np} is an unobserved extreme value random term that captures the idiosyncratic effect of all omitted variables that are not individual specific. ε_{np} is assumed to be identically and independently distributed across all choice occasions and independent of $x_{np}(t)$ and β_n.

Since only commuting trips are considered here and we assume that the traveler's subjective distribution is identical to the objective distribution of route travel time, n is omitted from the subscripts of $x_{np}(t)$. Therefore, $x_p(t)$ is a vector of observed variables based on the actual measurements from the field. Specifically, $x_p(t) = [T_p(t), R_p(t), C_p(t)]'$, where $T_p(t)$ measures route travel time, $R_p(t)$ measures travel-time reliability, and $C_p(t)$ is the monetary toll cost. Therefore, the value of travel time (VOT) and value of travel-time reliability (VOR) are defined as:

$$VOT_n = \frac{\partial U_{np}(t) / \partial T_p(t)}{\partial U_{np}(t) / \partial C_p(t)} = \frac{\beta^T}{\beta^C}; \tag{2}$$

$$VOR_n = \frac{\partial U_{np}(t) / \partial R_p(t)}{\partial U_{np}(t) / \partial C_p(t)} = \frac{\beta^R}{\beta^C}; \tag{3}$$

where $\beta_n = [\beta_n^T, \beta_n^R, \beta_n^C]'$, a vector of coefficients reflecting individual n's particular tastes toward travel time, reliability, and monetary cost. As the notation indicates, the models we consider are specified so that VOT and VOR depend on the individual traveler n but not on the choice instant t. From Equation (2) and (3), we can further define the degree of risk aversion (DORA) to reflect the degree of risk aversion, i.e., the extent to which travel time variability is undesirable to traveler n:

$$DORA_n = \frac{\partial U_{np}(t) / \partial R_p(t)}{\partial U_{np}(t) / \partial T_p(t)} = \frac{\beta^R}{\beta^T}. \tag{4}$$

The larger the value of DORA, the higher the perceived cost of uncertainty, and the more risk averse the traveler.

Preference heterogeneity is introduced by assuming that the coefficients β_n are random variables. These coefficients are assumed to vary over travelers based on individual characteristics in the population with density $f(\boldsymbol{\beta})$. This density is a function of parameters $\boldsymbol{\Theta}$ that represent, for example, the mean and the covariance of the β's in the population. This specification, known as "mixed" logit or "random coefficients" logit, is identical to standard logit except that $\boldsymbol{\beta}$ varies over decision-makers rather than being fixed. As such, the probability that traveler n will select path p, conditioned on $\boldsymbol{\beta}_n$, is given by:

$$L_{np}(\boldsymbol{\beta}_n;t) = \frac{e^{\beta' \mathbf{x}_{np}(t)}}{\sum_{\forall j \in P} e^{\beta' \mathbf{x}_{nj}(t)}} \tag{5}$$

The unconditional probability is the integral of $L_{np}(\boldsymbol{\beta}_n;t)$ over the distribution of all possible values of $\boldsymbol{\beta}_n$, i.e.,

$$P_{np}(t) = \int \frac{e^{\beta' x_{np}(t)}}{\sum_{\forall j \in P^{rs}} e^{\beta' x_{nj}(t)}} \cdot f(\boldsymbol{\beta}) d\boldsymbol{\beta} \tag{6}$$

Equation (6) is the general form for the so-called mixed-logit probability. Assuming that the parameters of $f(\boldsymbol{\beta})$ are $\boldsymbol{\Theta}$, the unbiased estimator $\breve{P}_{np}$ for P_{np} can be estimated using Monte-Carlo simulation to integrate the computational difficult parts of the preference distribution (Train, 2002).

Because the components of $\mathbf{x}_{np}(t)$ are strictly negative, and utility U_{np} is a monotonically decreasing function of these components, the corresponding distribution of parameters $\boldsymbol{\beta}_n$ is restricted to positive values for all n. As such, a logical candidate assumption for $f(\boldsymbol{\beta})$ is to specify $\ln(\beta) \sim N(b,W)$, where b and W are the mean and variance parameters to be estimated (Bhat, 2001; Train, 2002). Lognormal distributions are often specified when analyst wants to assure that the coefficient takes the same sign for all people. But we were unable to reach convergence since the lognormal distributed coefficients are exponentiated when they enter the utility function. So we assume the parameters $\boldsymbol{\beta}_n$ have independent normal distributions. If we further place the traveler in one of the M groups defined by their access to information (the assumption being that more risk adverse travelers may be more inclined to search out travel-time information). In this case, we would specify $\beta \sim N(b_m, W_m); m \in M$.

An issue of terminology arises with mixed-logit models (Train, 2002). There are two sets of parameters in a mixed-logit model. First, we have the parameters $\boldsymbol{\beta}$, which enter the logit formula. These parameters have density $f(\boldsymbol{\beta})$. The second set of parameters describe this density. For example, if we assume that $\boldsymbol{\beta}$ is normally distributed with mean b and covariance W, then b and W are parameters that describe the density $f(\boldsymbol{\beta})$.

With the assumption that the random parameters β^T, β^V, β^C for time, reliability and cost have normal distributions, i.e., $\beta^T \sim N(b^T, W^T)$, $\beta^V \sim N(b^V, W^V)$, $\beta^C \sim N(b^C, W^C)$, the parameter sets that need to be estimated are $\{b^T, W^T, b^V, W^V, b^C, W^C\} \subset \boldsymbol{\Theta}$. The estimation of $\boldsymbol{\Theta}$ will define VOT, VOR, and DORA, and thereby uncover the relative roles of travel time and travel time reliability in route choice, as well as identify the distribution of the population along the risk dimension. We let $\boldsymbol{\Omega}$, called the parameter space, denote the set of all possible values that parameters $\boldsymbol{\Theta}$ could assume. The estimation of $\boldsymbol{\Theta}$ is to search $\boldsymbol{\Omega}$ and find the best $\boldsymbol{\Theta}$ satisfying certain criteria. Traditionally, these parameters in the mixed-logit model are estimated based on RP and/or SP data by simulated maximum likelihood estimation (Bhat, 2001; Bhat and Castelar, 2002). However, since our observed data are aggregated responses in the form of loop counts rather than the individual responses of each traveler, we use a genetic algorithm to identify the parameter set that results in the best match between the aggregated results from traveler's route choice model and the observed time-dependent traffic volume data from loop detectors. We provide details of this procedure in the next section.

2.2 Estimation Procedure

Consider freeway trips originating from origin O located at on ramp r during time interval $t_0 - \Delta t_0$. The total number of such trips is evident from the 30-second loop counts Q at r as:

$$\overline{Q}_r(t_0) = \sum_{j=0}^{\Delta t_0/30} Q_r(t_0 - j) \tag{7}$$

Since the dynamic O-D matrix $O(t) \rightarrow D(t)$ is presumed to be known, the total number of trips originating at O = r, and bound for destination D = s, during time interval $t_0 - \Delta t_0$ is given as:

$$\overline{Q}_{rs}(t_0) = \frac{\sum_{j=0}^{\Delta t_0/30} O_{rs}(t_0 - j)}{\sum_{\forall k \in S} \sum_{j=0}^{\Delta t_0/30} O_{rk}(t_0 - j)} \cdot \overline{Q}_r(t_0); S = \{k \in \text{set of all off ramps}\} \tag{8}$$

Consider the observed loop count at some station i on the path p_{rs} over the time interval $t_0 - \Delta t_0$, i.e.,

$$\hat{Q}_i(t) = \sum_{j=0}^{\Delta t_0/30} Q_i(t - j) \tag{9}$$

For any loop station i on the path $p = \{1,2,...i,...s\}$, assume that the trips starting at time t_0 arrive at loop station i at time t. Then, an estimate of $\hat{Q}_i(t)$ is given by:

$$\hat{\hat{Q}}_i(t) = \sum_{\forall t_0 < t} \sum_{\substack{\forall p \in P^{rs} \\ i \in p}} P_p(t_0) \cdot \overline{Q}_{rs}(t_0) \tag{10}$$

where $P_p(t_0)$ is the mixed-logit probability given in Equation (6). Alternatively, using the unbiased estimate $\breve{P}_p(t_0)$ for $P_p(t_0)$ via Monte-Carlo simulation,

$$\hat{\hat{Q}}_i(t) = \sum_{\forall t_0 < t} \sum_{\substack{\forall p \in P^{rs} \\ i \in p}} \breve{P}_p(t_0) \cdot \overline{Q}_{rs}(t_0) \tag{11}$$

$\hat{\hat{Q}}_i(t)$ is a function only of known values and the unknown parameters of $f(\boldsymbol{\beta}/\boldsymbol{\Theta})$. A standard approach to selecting the values of $\boldsymbol{\Theta}$ is to minimize the mean square error (MSE) between the estimate $\hat{\hat{Q}}_i(t)$ and its true (observed) value $\hat{Q}_i(t)$ over some specified time period $t_1 \leq t \leq t_2$, i.e.,

$$\min_{\boldsymbol{\Theta}}(MSE) = \int_{t_1}^{t_2} \sum_{\forall i} [\hat{Q}_i(t) - \hat{\hat{Q}}_i(t)]^2 dt \tag{12}$$

or, for distinct 30-second counting intervals,

$$\min_{\boldsymbol{\Theta}}(MSE) = \sum_{t=1}^{t=\frac{t_2 - t_1}{30}} \sum_{\forall i} [\hat{Q}_i(t) - \hat{\hat{Q}}_i(t)]^2 \tag{13}$$

Because the search space of potential solutions is large, we employ an intelligent optimization technique to identify the parameter set for $\boldsymbol{\Theta}$ that satisfies the condition defined by Equation (13). Traditional optimization algorithms use an estimate of the gradient to identify potential search directions. However, because of well-known difficulties in obtaining such gradients in transportation applications, heuristic approaches have been adopted extensively. The so-called Genetic Algorithm (GA) is one such heuristic search algorithm that attempts to search the solution space in a "smart" manner on the basis of natural selection and natural genetics, and has been shown to be powerful and broadly applicable (Gen and Cheng, 2000). Various authors have studied the application of GA to different transportation problems including, for example, the parameter calibration of microscopic traffic simulation models (Cheu et al., 1998; Lam and Xu, 2000, Kim and Rilett, 2001, etc.).

GA models the parameter set as chromosome and each chromosome is evaluated by a fitness function that represents how well it fits a given problem. The fitness function used here represents how well the estimate volume $\hat{\hat{Q}}_i(t)$ and its true (observed) value $\hat{Q}_i(t)$ match. An exponential fitness function is used:

$$F = \exp(-S * (\sum_{t=t1}^{t2} \sum_{\forall i} \frac{\left| \hat{\hat{Q}}_i(t) - \hat{Q}_i(t) \right|}{\hat{Q}_i(t)}) / (NT * NL)) \tag{14}$$

where NT is the number of time intervals encompassing $[t_1, t_2]$, NL is the total number of observed stations in the network, and S is the scaling parameter. The expression inside the exponential is the mean absolute error ratio (MAER) for the all of the observed loop stations over time period $[t_1, t_2]$, which measures the difference between the observed volume and estimated volume.

To emulate the natural selection mechanism in genetic evolution, GA applies the rules of reproduction, crossover, and mutation to the chromosomes to create new chromosomes. Reproduction is an operation through which chromosomes are copied into the mating pool with a probability proportional to their fitness. In this study, a combination of tournament selection and elitism is adopted for the reproduction process. The elitism strategy keeps the chromosome that had the highest fitness value for comparison with the fitness values computed from the next generation's chromosomes. If the subsequent generation fails to improve the highest fitness value, the elite will be copied into the mating pool. The crossover operator provides search capability in the GA. We adopt the uniform crossover operator, in which two chromosomes in the mating pool will be randomly selected. At randomly and independently selected locations according to a predetermined crossover probability, the crossover operation exchanges the parents' chromosome values, and generates offspring chromosomes. Mutation is a process to overcome the local optimum problem. Each gene of a selected chromosome is allowed to mutate according to a predetermined mutation probability, thereby reducing the likelihood that the search process will get stuck in a local optimum. The goal is to pass beneficial and survival-enhancing traits to new generations. In this process, chromosomes that have high fitness values have opportunities to reproduce, by crossbreeding with other chromosomes in the population.

GA is considered robust because at any time step (or generation) of a search, GA progresses towards the optimal solution from a population of points, instead of starting the search at a single point, which increases the likelihood that the global, rather than a local, optimum will be found. The use of multiple points increases the robustness of search in a large, complex and poorly understood space, which is very typical for many transportation problems. Because of its robustness for this particular class of problems, we adopt GA in the estimation procedure used in this paper. The details of the GA approach for estimating the parameters in a mixed-logit model are given in Liu, Recker, and Chen (2002).

3. EMPIRICAL DATA COLLECTION AND PROCESSING

3.1 Study Site

We apply the proposed method to newly collected data concerning route choice in the California State Route 91 value-pricing project. The SR 91 toll lanes, located between the SR 91/SR 55 junction in Anaheim, CA, and the Orange/Riverside County Line, are the world's first fully automated privately operated toll lanes (Sullivan, 2000). The express lanes extend about 10 miles along the former median of the Riverside Freeway (SR 91), connecting the rapidly growing residential areas in Riverside and San Bernardino counties to job centers in Orange and Los Angeles counties to the west. SR 91 in eastern Orange County includes four regular freeway lanes (91F) and two express lanes (91X) in each direction. Motorists who wish to use express lanes must register and carry identifying electronic transponder (the so-called FasTrak) to pay a toll that varies hourly according to a preset schedule. Tolls in the express lanes vary hour-by-hour to regulate demand and maintain free flow traffic, in contrast to often-congested traffic conditions in the adjacent free lanes. Tolls on westbound traffic during morning commute hours ranged from \$1.65 (at 4–5 a.m.) to \$3.30 (at 7–8 a.m., Monday–Thursday). Within the SR 91 corridor, the Eastern Toll Road (ETR) competes with the 91X for trips to Irvine and vicinity. However, since the 91X has no entrance or exit between its starting and ending points, ETR users must use the highly congested 91F for access.

We regard the SR 91 toll road portion as a two-route network. One route is the 91X, and the other is 91F, both 10 miles in length. This gives motorists the option to travel free on regular roads or to pay a time-varying price for congestion-free express travel on a limited part of their journey. Because of the toll pricing structure, traffic consistently moves at a free-flow speed of approximately 75mph even during peak hours on this facility. Consequently, we assume that travel time on 91X is deterministic (reliable) and equal to eight minutes, corresponding to a speed of 75 mph. However, the free lanes are often congested during the morning peak hours (5–9 a.m.), and travel time on the 91F is rather stochastic and unreliable, presenting a relatively "clean" real-world experimental environment to study the relative contributions of travel time and travel time reliability in the route choice decision process.

3.2 Travel Time and Reliability Data Collection and Processing

Obtaining accurate measures of travel conditions, especially the appropriate measurement of travel time reliability, is a formidable task. We use actual field measurements (floating cars) of travel time on 91F taken at different times during morning peak period. Our data was obtained from the study of Small et al. (2002). The data consist of peak period travel time on 91F for 11 days: first on October 28, 1999, and then on July 10–14 and September 18–22, 2000. Data were collected from 4 a.m. to 10 a.m. on each day, and include a total of 210 observations of travel time along the 10-mile stretch of 91F at different times of day encompassing the morning peak period. Interested readers may refer to their paper for more details on the travel time data collection and processing techniques.

In order to construct measures of travel time and its reliability, we consider both the central tendency and the dispersion of the travel time distribution. Measures of central tendency include the mean and the median, and measures of dispersion include the standard deviation, the inter-quartile difference such as the 90th–50th or 80th–50th, ratio of standard deviation to mean, and percent of observations that exceed the mean by some specific threshold, etc. The nature of these measures is that they are positive, monotonically increasing functions of variability. We assume that motorists, especially commuters in the morning peak hours, are concerned with the probability of significant delay, and are likely to pay particular attention to the upper tail of the distribution of travel times. Among the candidate measures that capture this effect, we arbitrarily use the difference between the upper quartile and the median. To make our results comparable to Small et al. (2002), we use the same measures of central tendency and dispersion, i.e., median and the 80th–50th percentile differences.

Figure 1 shows the raw field observations of travel time savings (i.e., the difference between the 91F and 91X travel times over the 10-mile stretch). The non-parametric estimates of mean, median, and 80th percentile are calculated and displayed. Median time savings reach a peak of 5.6 minutes around 7:15 a.m. Figure 2 shows the median travel time savings and the 80th–50th percentile differences. The latter reaches a peak around 8:10 a.m. Correlations between these two measures are insignificant.

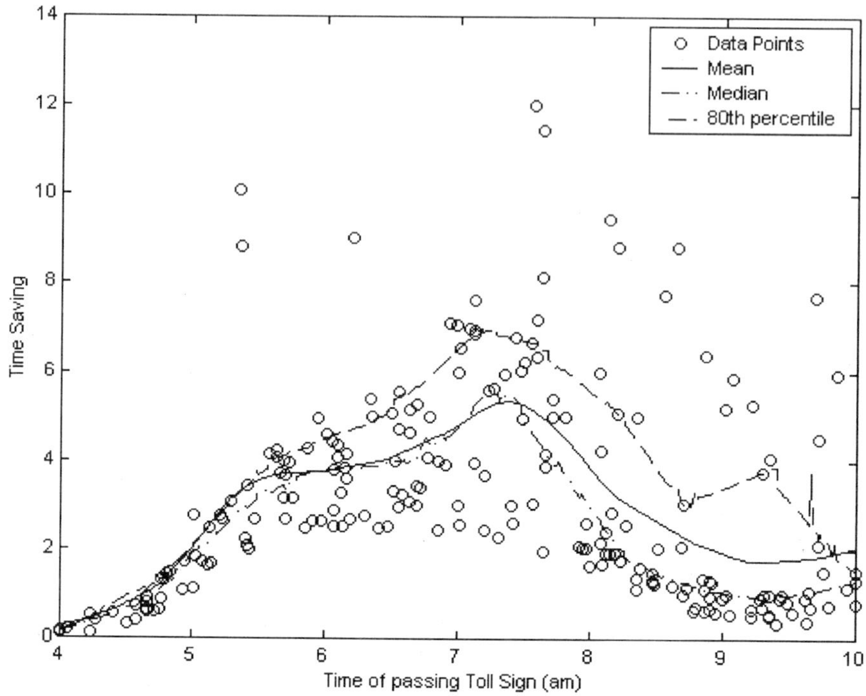

Figure 1. Travel Time Saving (From the Study of Small et al., 2002)

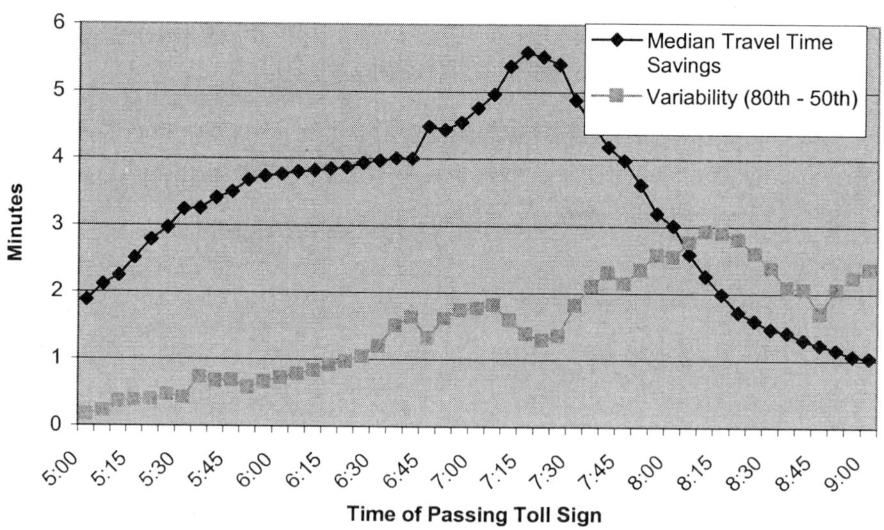

Figure 2. Measurements of Travel Time and ITS Variability

3.3 Volume Data Collection and Processing

Along the stretch of SR 91 under consideration, loop detector stations are spaced at a distance of every mile. Each loop detector station includes six loops covering all lanes of 91F and 91X. Volume data were collected using 30-second loop detector data and aggregated into five-minute interval. The data consist of volumes on 91X, 91F, and ETR for 30 weekdays from September 17 to November 16, 2001. Since our study is concerned with the traveler's choice probability between 91X and 91F, the volume data of ETR was subtracted from 91F because ETR users have no option but to use 91F. Figure 3 shows the traffic flow on both 91X and 91F. As shown in Figure 4, the percentage of travelers taking 91X reaches a peak at around 8 a.m.

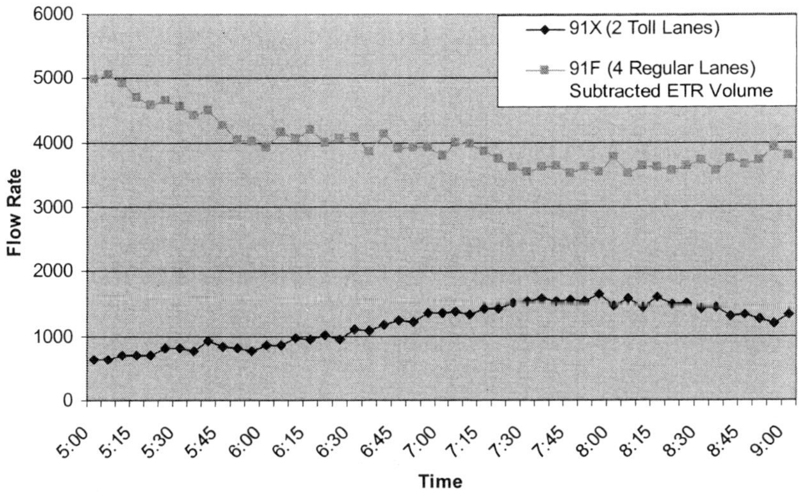

Figure 3. Traffic Flow on SR91 (September 18, 2001)

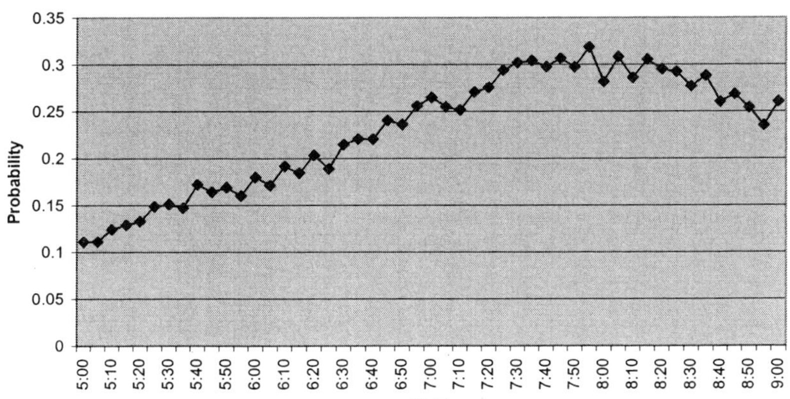

Figure 4. Percentage of Travelers Taking Toll Lanes from Loop Detector Data (September 18, 2001)

4. RESULTS AND ANALYSIS

After data collection and processing, we applied the GA procedure to identify the parameter set that produced the best match to the volume data revealed from the loop detectors. The parameters used in the GA procedure are shown in Table 1. To evaluate each chromosome, the choice probability estimated from mixed-logit was calculated using 2,000 random draws from a normal distribution of the components of $\boldsymbol{\beta}$ for the Monte-Carlo simulation. The convergence of the GA procedure is shown in Figure 5, which displays the decreasing MAER values with the number of generations.

To estimate the parameters $\boldsymbol{\Theta}$ with certain confidence level, we performed 30 GA runs with the volume data from 30 days, with each GA run corresponding to the volume data from one particular day. Figure 6 shows the identified values for parameters $\boldsymbol{\Theta}$ with 30 GA runs (The standard deviation Sd is given instead of variance W). The statistical estimates of parameters $\boldsymbol{\Theta}$ from these 30 GA runs are shown in Table 3.

Table 1. Control Parameters for the GA

Population size	20
Maximal Number of Generations	50
Chromosome Length Per Parameter	6
Crossover Probability	0.6
Mutation Probability	0.033
Elitism Flag	1

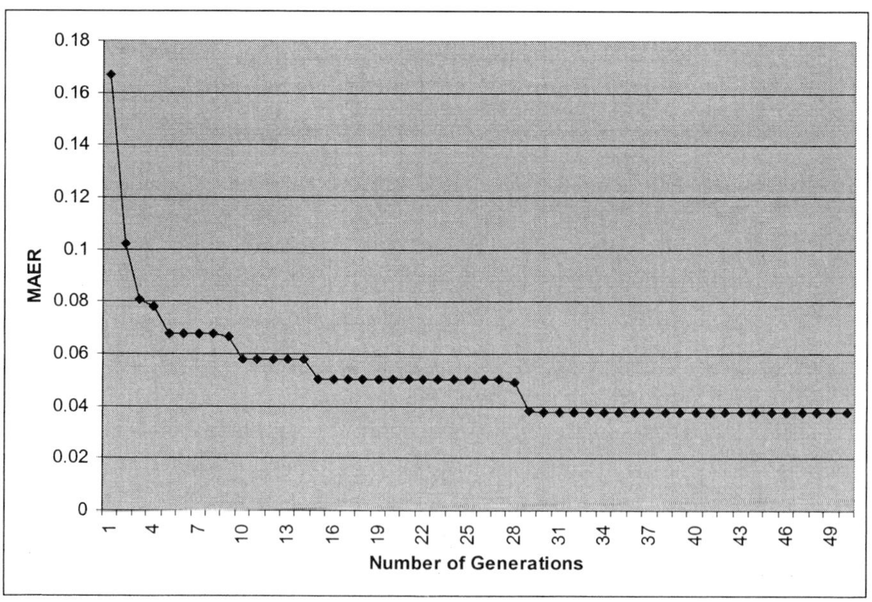

Figure 5. GA Convergence Curve with Best Fitness Values

Table 2. Estimated Parameter Values

Parameters	Range	Estimated Value (Median / [5%-ile, 95%-ile])
b^T	[10, 40]	15.39 / [11.05, 20.34]
Sd^T	[0, 10]	5.28 / [0.77, 9.07]
b^V	[10,40]	25.66 / [20.08, 29.38]
Sd^V	[0, 10]	6.14 / [2.54, 9.38]
b^C	[1, 2]	1.26 / [1.0, 1.81]
Sd^C	[0, 1]	0.55 / [0.04, 0.94]

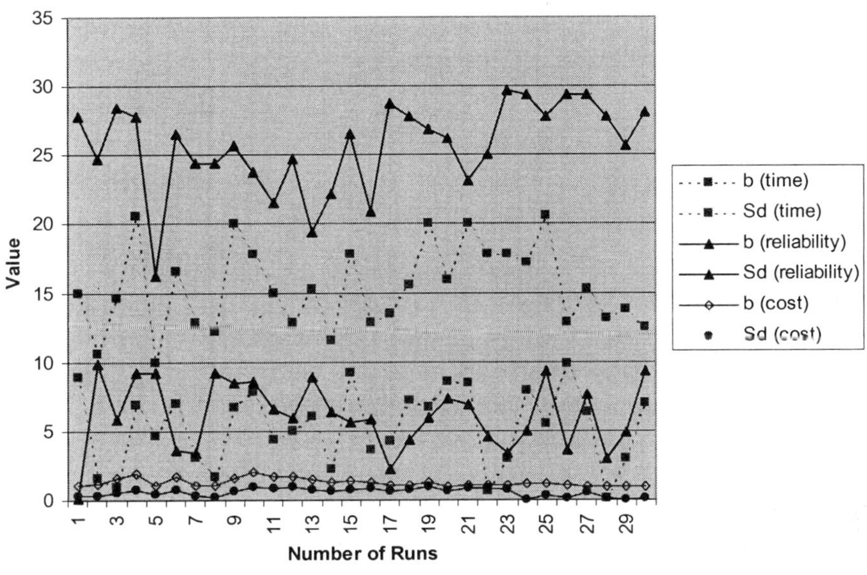

Figure 6. Best Estimated Parameters with 30 GA Runs

From the estimated statistical distributions of the parameter estimates, travelers' implied VOT, VOR, and DORA, and the extent of their heterogeneity could be determined by Monte-Carlo simulations. We performed 2,000 random draws from the normal distributions of $\boldsymbol{\beta}$ ($\beta^T \sim N(b^T, W^T)$, $\beta^V \sim N(b^V, W^V)$, $\beta^C \sim N(b^C, W^C)$), and calculated VOT, VOR, and DORA using Equations 2 to 4. Percentile values, including 25%-ile, 50%-ile (median), and 75%-ile, were then obtained from the 2,000 values of VOT, VOR, and DORA. Travelers' heterogeneity is measured as the inter-quartile difference, i.e., the difference between the 75th and 25th percentile values, because it is unaffected by high upper-tail values occasionally found in the calculation of ratios. We repeated this process for every parameter set $\{b^T, W^T, b^V, W^V, b^C, W^C\}$ identified by the 30 GA runs. The estimates of the median and heterogeneity of VOT, VOR, and DORA are shown in Table 3. In Table 3, we note that the confidence interval represents uncertainty due to statistical error, not heterogeneity. A positive 5th percentile value means the quantity is significantly greater than zero according to a conventional one-sided hypothesis test at a five percent significance level.

Table 3. Estimated Value of Time and Reliability

	Median Estimate	90% Confidence Interval [5%-ile, 95%-ile]
Value of Time ($/hour)		
Median	12.81	[8.66, 16.08]
Heterogeneity (75thc25th)	8.72	[4.16, 16.73]
Value of Reliability ($/hour)		
Median	20.63	[12.81, 28.47]
Heterogeneity (75th–25th)	13.06	[5.62, 23.44]
Degree of Risk Aversion (DORA)		
Median	1.73	[1.26, 2.13]
Heterogeneity (75th–25th)	0.97	[0.41, 1.75]

As shown in Table 3, the median value of time is $12.81, and the median value of reliability is $20.63. Since median time savings in our data peaks at 5.6 minutes in the rush hour and unreliability peaks at three minutes, the average commuter would pay $1.20 to realize time savings and pay $1.03 to avoid this possibility of unanticipated delay. In other words, travelers with the median VOT and VOR would save $2.23 from travel time and its reliability if they use 91X, but they need to pay $3.30 for the toll. So less than half travelers will choose to use the express lanes, and this is confirmed from the loop detector data, as shown in Figure 4. Regarding travelers' heterogeneity towards travel time and its reliability, both measures of heterogeneity in the cases of VOT and VOR are more than 60 percent of their median values, indicating that commuters exhibit a wide distribution of preferences for speed and reliability. By recognizing the heterogeneity in travelers' preference and offering choices that caters to their preferences, road pricing policies can increase transportation efficiency.

Similar results for the median values of VOT and VOR are found in the study of Small et al. (2002). In their study, they estimated VOT and VOR using the combination of RP and SP data. The median value of VOT estimated from RP data is $20.20, and $9.46 from SP data. Our result in this regard falls between these two values. In terms of VOR, the estimated median value from their study using RP data is $19.56, which is very similar to our result. Their estimate of VOR from SP data is not comparable to ours since different measures of (un)reliability are used. Our results validate the analysis from their study and demonstrate the applicability of an approach based on conventional loop data in the study of travelers' behavior.

The median value of DORA is 1.73, i.e., the disutility caused by certain amount of travel time unreliability is 1.73 times more than that caused by travel time of the same amount. Thus, if the commuting alternatives are a 20-minute commute with essentially no possibility of significant delay and a commute that normally takes 10 minutes but has variability of about 6 minutes, the traveler with a DORA equal to 1.73 will be almost indifferent between these two choices. A traveler with a DORA greater than 1.73 is more risk averse and will choose the first alternative. In other words, travelers with DORA greater than 1.0 value more highly a reduction in variability than a comparable reduction in the mean travel time. These travelers are willing to go out of their way to decrease the possibility of a delay, either because they dislike the risk of being delayed or dislike the discomfort normally associated with a delay, such as stop and go traffic. From the operator's point of view, this finding implies that traffic management strategies aimed at reducing travel time variability, such as incident management, deserve serious attention.

5. CONCLUSIONS

It is clear that travel time reliability can have great influence on a traveler's route choice behavior and that it cannot be ignored in any model which purports to predict behavior or provide a basis for evaluation. With respect to the valuation of reliability, direct methods such as revealed preference and/or stated preference surveys have been used extensively in the previous studies. In this research, we proposed an indirect method to study the contribution of travel time reliability in traveler's route choice behavior. We formulated traveler's route choice as a mixed-logit model, with the coefficients in the model representing individual traveler's preferences or tastes to travel time, reliability, and cost. Unlike the traditional approach to estimate these coefficients with RP and/or SP data by simulated maximum likelihood estimation, we adopt a genetic algorithm to identify the coefficients that enable the flows resulting from route choice model to best match the time-dependent traffic volume data obtained from loop detectors. Such an approach eliminates both the cost and biases inherent to RP and SP survey techniques.

We applied the proposed method to newly collected data concerning route choice in the California State Route 91 value-pricing project. Based on travelers' choice of whether or not to pay a congestion-based toll in order to use the express lanes, we are able to estimate how travelers value travel time and travel time reliability. We find that the estimated median value of travel time reliability is substantially greater than that of travel time, and the median value of degree of risk aversion is greater than 1, indicating that travelers value more highly a reduction in variability than in the mean travel time saving for that journey. Moreover, travelers' attitude towards congestion is not homogeneous; in fact, substantial heterogeneity exists in travelers' preference of travel time and reliability. The results of our study yield important insights into commuters' route choice in general and the trade-offs among travel time, reliability, and monetary cost. Our results validate the analysis from some previous studies and demonstrate the applicability of the approach in the study of travelers' behavior.

ACKNOWLEDGEMENTS

The authors thank Professor Ken Small and Dr. Jia Yan of the University of California, Irvine for providing travel time data used in this work. This study was supported, in part, by the California PATH Program; their support is gratefully acknowledged. The views expressed herein are the authors' own.

REFERENCES

Abdel-Aty, M., Kitamura, R., Jovanis, P. "Investigating Effect of Travel Time Variability on Route Choice Using Repeated Measurement Stated Preference Data," *Transportation Research Record,* 1493, 1996, 39–45.

Bates, J., Polak, J., Jones, P., Cook, A. "The Valuation of Reliability for Personal Travel," *Transportation Research Part E*, 37, 2001, 191–229.

Bates, J. "Reliability – The Missing Variable," *Travel Behavior Research – The Leading Edge*, D. Hensher, ed., Pergamon, 2001.

Bhat, C. R. "Quasi-Random Maximum Simulated Likelihood Estimation of the Mixed Multinomial Logit Model," *Transportation Research Part B*, 35, 2001, 677–693.

Bhat, C. R., Castelar, R. "A Unified Mixed Logit Framework for Modeling Revealed and Stated Preferences: Formulation and Application to Congestion Pricing Analysis in the San Francisco Bay Area," *Transportation Research Part B*, 36, No. 7, 2001, 593–616.

Cheu, R., Jin, X., Ng, K., Ng, Y. "Calibration of FRESIM for Singapore Expressway Using Genetic Algorithm," *ASCE Journal of Transportation Engineering*, Vol. 124, No. 6, 1998, 526–535.

Gen, M., Cheng, R. *Genetic Algorithms and Engineering Optimization*, New York: Wiley, 2000.

Jackson, W. B., Jucker, J. V. "An Empirical Study of Travel Time Variability and Travel Choice Behavior," *Transportation Science*, Vol. 16, No. 4, 1981, 460–475.

Kim, K., Rilett, L. R. "Genetic-Algorithm-based Approach for Calibrating Microscopic Simulation Models," IEEE Intelligent Transportation Systems Proceedings, Oakland, CA, 2001, 698–704.

Lam, T. C., Small, K. A. "The Value of Time and Reliability: Measurement from A Value Pricing Experiment," *Transportation Research Part E*, 37, 2001, 231–251.

Lam, W. H. K., Xu, G. "Calibration of Traffic Flow Simulator for Network Reliability Assessment," in *Reliability of Transport Networks*, M. Bell and C. Cassir eds. Research Studies Press Ltd., 2000.

Liu, H., Recker, W., Chen, A. "Uncovering the Contribution of Travel Time Reliability to Dynamic Route Choice Using Real-time Loop Data," submitted to *Transportation Research*, 2002.

McFadden, D., Train, K. "Mixed MNL Models for Discrete Response," *Journal of Applied Econometrics,* 15, 2000, 447–470.

Small, K. A., Winston, C., Yan, J. "Uncovering the Distribution of Motorists' Preference for Travel Time and Reliability: Implications for Road Pricing," submitted to *Economica*, 2002.

Sullivan, E. "Continuation Study to Evaluate the Impacts of the SR91 Value-Priced Express Lanes," final report submitted to the Department of Transportation of the State of California," 2000. See http://gridlock.calpoly.edu/sr91/sr91.htm.

Train, K. *Discrete Choice Methods with Simulation*, Cambridge University Press, 2002.

Chapter 14

TRAFFIC MANAGEMENT SYSTEMS

David Levinson
Department of Civil Engineering, University of Minnesota

Wei Chen
Department of Engineering, University of Minnesota

This study uses regression analysis to evaluate long-run traffic management system performance. Three important traffic management systems in the Twin Cities metro area—Ramp Metering, Variable Message Signs, and Freeway Service Patrols (the Highway Helper Program) were evaluated using multiple regression models to predict link speed and incident rate. We find that ramp meters increase freeway link speed and reduce incident rate. Freeway Service Patrols increase link speed when incidents are present. The results for variable message signs are ambiguous. Regression analysis can be a simple and effective research method for testing the macroscopic association between traffic management and traffic system performance.

1. INTRODUCTION

The Minnesota Department of Transportation (Mn/DOT) Traffic Management Center (TMC) was founded in 1972 to centrally manage the freeway system in the Minneapolis-St. Paul (Twin Cities) metro area. The TMC aims to provide motorists with a faster, safer trip on metro area freeways by optimizing the use of available freeway capacity, efficiently managing incidents and special events, providing traveler information, and providing incentives for ride sharing. The TMC realizes its goal through traffic management systems (TMS), including Ramp Metering, Variable Message Signs (VMS), Freeway Service Patrols (Highway Helpers), High Occupancy Vehicle (HOV) lanes, Loop Detectors, Closed Circuit TV (CCTV) cameras, and Traveler Information.

While the TMC has a long history of operation, the effectiveness of some of the traffic management systems have been recently questioned—do they really help realize the objectives of the TMC, or rather, do they make traffic conditions even worse? This study uses regression analysis to assess the systemwide performance of three important traffic management systems in the Twin Cities metro area: Ramp Metering System, Variable Message Signs, and the Highway Helper Program. The traditional before-and-after study and the regression analysis method are compared, the outline of the regression analysis is presented and its limitations are stated. In the two case studies, link speed and incident rate are employed as response variables respectively.

2. METHODOLOGY

2.1 About the Before-and-After Study

"Before-and-after" studies or "with and without" studies are perhaps the most widely used methods to evaluate system performance. But these methods face difficulties when the object of study is a long existing traffic management system. First, it is usually impossible to isolate the effects of traffic management from the effects of external variations (1). A before-and-after study is persuasive for the evaluation of short-run impacts under the condition that there is no significant variation in external circumstances; however, the evolution of traffic management from initialization to full operation usually covers decades. The external circumstances must have experienced great changes and it is impossible to separate those from other changes also affecting the system. Second, it is quite difficult to separate the effects of one management system from the effects of other systems since almost all of the main freeways are under the combined management of these systems. Third, the traffic management system itself is continuously changing —new facilities are gradually added and some old facilities are gradually removed, accompanying the changes of operation strategies. Even if we can find some freeway segment that has stable before-and-after phases, the limited analysis will not be representative of the whole system.

A famous example of evaluating traffic management system performance using a before-and-after study is the Twin Cities metro area ramp metering shutdown study, described in Chapter 9 (2, 9). During the eight-week ramp meter shutdown, all other traffic management systems were in full operation. Therefore, the effectiveness of the ramp metering system could be evaluated by comparing the system performance before and during shutdown. But such perfect data often cannot be obtained. For example, in order to evaluate the HOV system impacts on traffic flow and safety, Minnesota state legislators suggested opening the HOV lanes on I-394 to general-purpose traffic for a limited period in 2001 for before-and-after data collection. However, this plan was barred by the FHWA due to policy considerations.

A performance evaluation of the traffic management system can provide important information for planning and for the rationalization of operating budget allocations. We explore a simple and effective approach for this task, regression analysis. Compared with a before-and-after study, regression analysis does not try to design the stable external circumstances. Instead, regression isolates the effects of the object of study from the effects of combining factors. It is often quite difficult or even impossible to design or seek the "stable" external circumstances in a dynamic traffic system. For example, when we evaluate the effects of traffic management systems on incident rates, we need to use several years' data to obtain a sufficiently large sample; in this case, it is meaningless to assume unvaried external circumstances. Regression analysis differs from a before-and-after study in that it tries to search out all the potential elements (including traffic management) that affect system performance, record their variation and use these elements as the regression predictor variables to test the association between traffic system performance and traffic management.

2.2 The Response Variable of Regression Model

Performance measurement proceeds by identifying and quantifying some feature of the performance of the traffic system (such as travel time or accident rate) and using this to infer the performance of some part of the traffic management system (1). In regression analysis, the measure of traffic system performance will be employed as the response variable, the traffic management systems will be included in the predictor variables, and their performance will be inferred by their associations with the response variable and by comparison with the coefficients of related predictor variables.

There can be many performance measures of the traffic system (10). However, a measure can be used as the response variable only if it is significantly associated with the operational objectives of the traffic management system; furthermore, it should be straightforward to identify the relevant predictor variables.

Speed and incident rate meet these criteria and will be used as the response variables in the following regression analyses. The reason for using speed instead of travel time is that the regression model will include observations from different road segments, travel time will present no more information than speed, but it will be influenced by the differences in length. Related measures, such as travel time, delays, and travel time reliability, could be derived directly from speed. Some other measures, including environmental impacts and fuel consumption, could also be derived from speed by combining with flow, vehicle type, and gasoline quality.

2.3 The Framework of an Ideal Regression Model

Ideally, we would employ all the relevant elements affecting system performance as its explanatory variables. The relevant elements can be classified into the following four categories:

1. **Infrastructure characteristics** include capacity, geometric structure, pavement quality, and construction activity. Capacity has significant effects on speed, but since detailed information about capacity is difficult to obtain, the number of lanes is used as an indication of capacity. Geometric structure includes the elements of horizontal and vertical curvature, sight distance, and intersection density (e.g. number of intersections per mile). Pavement quality can be good or poor.
2. **Traffic characteristics** include density and the percentage of heavy commercial traffic. Heavy commercial traffic such as trucks have significant impact on freeway capacity and speed.
3. **Traffic management strategies** include Ramp Metering, Variable Message Signs, Highway Helper Program, High Occupancy Vehicle lanes, and some other traffic management strategies such as the Traveler Information Program.
4. **Other factors** include traffic incident impact and weather impact.

Figure 1 shows the framework of the ideal regression model.

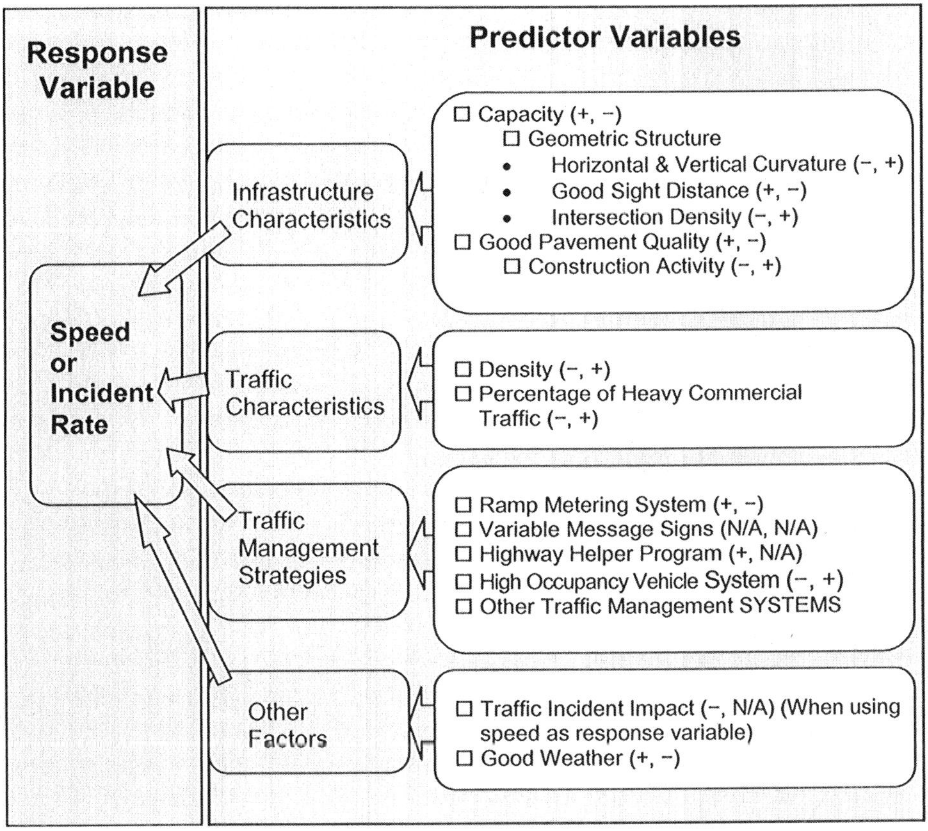

Figure 1. The Framework of an Ideal Regression Model

Note:
1. Hypotheses are given in parentheses – (The expected effect on speed, The expected effect on incident rate);
2. For a numeric predictor variable, if its increase is excepted to be associated with the increase in speed or incident rate, the expected effect is marked as '+'; if its increase is excepted to be associated with the decrease in speed or incident rate, the expected effect is marked as '–';
3. For a dummy predictor variable, if its presence (=1) is excepted to be associated with the increase in speed or incident rate, the expected effect is marked as '+'; if its presence is excepted to be associated with the decrease in speed or incident rate, the expected effect is marked as '–'.

2.4 Limitations of Regression Analysis

When before-and-after is impossible or too costly, regression analysis can be a good substitute. But regression analysis cannot provide all the information we need to know about the traffic management system. For example, regression analysis just tells us the association between ramp metering and system mainline speed, it cannot tell us whether the travel time saving on the mainline caused by ramp metering (if any) could offset ramp delay. Consequently, regression analysis can be a simple and effective research method for testing the macroscopic association or trend between traffic management and traffic system performance; however, to obtain an overall evaluation of each of the traffic management systems, additional research is still necessary.

3. SPEED

3.1 Regression Model

Due to the data limitation we are unable to test all the potential predictor variables described in the ideal regression model. For infrastructure characteristics, we use capacity (number of lanes); for traffic characteristics, we use density; for traffic management strategies, we test Ramp Metering, Variable Message Signs, and the Highway Helper Program; and for other factors, we used traffic incident impact. We also added 22 corridor-specific dummy variables, among these we include segments with and without HOV. Since HOV lanes are rare in the Twin Cities, we could not distinguish between the corridor effects and the presence of HOV lanes (concurrent or separated) when analyzing speed.

Because we are using multi-variate regression, we should use the correlation matrix to detect possible multi-colinearity. We diagnose multi-colinearity if the absolute value of the correlation between two predictor variables is larger than 0.6. From the correlation matrices (Table A1) we find that each correlation is less than 0.6, therefore, multi-colinearity between density and the TMS dummies is not a significant problem.

We pay specific attention to the low correlation between ramp metering and mainline density. It is often believed that a segment controlled by ramp metering will have lower density than a segment without metering. But an obvious linear relationship between ramp metering and mainline density cannot be found from our data. Density is a complex measurement which is associated with many factors (including upstream traffic flows), and ramp metering is just one of them.

Ramp metering affects mainline speed through not only mainline density but also other traffic factors such as drivers' behaviors. When vehicles try to merge from a ramp onto the mainline, mainline drivers usually have to slow down or even change lanes to let them in. That is, entering cars will affect mainline drivers' behaviors even if their merging does not increase mainline density significantly. (To get an intuitive understanding about this, just think that even when the middle lane has the same density as the right lane, the middle lane is typically faster than right lane because the right lane has to sustain the impacts of merging (and exiting) cars). Under ramp metering, cars enter the freeway in a spaced and controlled manner. Even in the case that ramp metering does not significantly decrease mainline density, its reduction of merging disruption will increase mainline speed. Speed and density are both computed from loop detector data, following methods detailed in (12).

Model 1 predicts speed in the incident-free case as:

$$V = f(K, R, M, L_n, D)$$

Where:
V= Hourly average speed (miles/hour);
K = Density (vehicles/mile);
R = Ramp Meter (1,0);
M = VMS (1,0);
L_2, L_3, L_4=*Two-Lane (1,0), Three-Lane (1,0), Four-Lane (1,0);*
D =Corridor dummies

Note: the Highway Helper Program is not included in the incident-free case because when the studied segments are incident-free, the Highway Helper Program should have no effect. Dummy Variables: 1 if present, 0 otherwise

Model 2 predicts speed in the presence of an incident, as:

$$V = f(K, R, M, H, L_n, D, I, I_{U1}, I_{U2}, I_{D1}, I_{D2})$$

Where,
H = Highway Helper Program on Segment (1,0);
I = incident within the studied segment (1,0);
I_{U1} = *incident on the first segment upstream of the studied segment (1,0);*
I_{U2} = *incident on the second segment upstream of the studied segment (1,0);*
I_{D1} = *incident on the first segment downstream of the studied segment (1,0);*
I_{D2} = *incident on the second segment downstream of the studied segment (1,0).*

3.2 Corridor Selection and Study Periods

In total, 22 corridors were selected for this study based on the following three rules:

1. The selected corridors should form a geographically representative sample of the entire system. Based on the geographic characteristics, the freeway corridors within the Twin Cities metro area can be

classified into the following four types: the I-494/I-694 beltline freeway, intercity connector, radial freeway within the I-494/I-694 beltline, and radial freeway outside the beltline (2). The 22 selected corridors covered these four types (refer to Figure 2 and Table A2).

2. The selected corridors should include segments with and without ramp meters, with and without VMS, and with and without highway helpers.
3. The selected corridors should have loop detector data from 1998 to 2000.

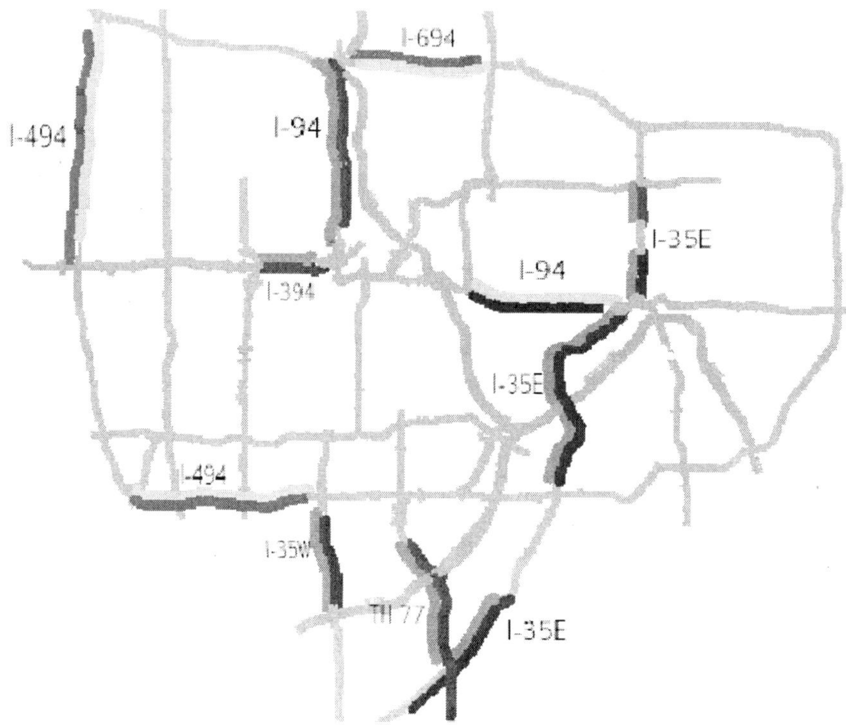

Figure 2. Speed Analysis: Corridor Selection

The study periods range from 1998 to 2000, which includes the periods before ramp meter start-up, ramp meter in full operation, and the eight-week ramp meter shutdown in 2000; before VMS start-up and VMS in full operation; and Highway Helper Program in full operation.

It is noted that no "before" data are included for the Highway Helper Program. The initial patrol routes began in December 1987. Subsequent routes were added after September 1996. We could obtain data before the addition of the subsequent routes. Unfortunately, the loop detector data before 1996 is inadequate.

In addition, the following criteria are applied for data collection:

1. Samples are gathered on Tuesday, Wednesday, and Thursday;
2. Holidays, weekends, Monday, and Friday are avoided;
3. A gap between the "before-after" periods is taken to permit the public to become accustomed to the new improvement before a check on its effect is begun (8). The length of gaps range from 30 to 80 days in 1999. Due to the limited loop detector data, the length of gaps in 1998 range from 10 to 20 days.

3.3 Results

Observations collected in each of the four peak hours: 7 a.m.–8 a.m., 8 a.m.–9 a.m., 4 p.m.–5 p.m., and 5 p.m.–6 p.m. formed four samples. Ordinary Least Squares Regression was conducted on each of the four groups using the statistical software *Stata*. The regression results are summarized in Table 1 and Table 2.

Table 1. Summary of Regression Results of the Incident-free Case: Dependent Variable=Speed

Incident-free	7:00AM—8:00AM		8:00AM—9:00AM		4:00PM—5:00PM		5:00PM—6:00PM	
Number of obs	8988		9030		8937		8888	
R^2	0.4639		0.4694		0.5806		0.6026	
Adjusted R^2	0.4623		0.4678		0.5793		0.6014	
F value	F(27, 8960) = 287.13		F(27, 9002) = 294.99		F(27, 8909) = 456.73		F(27, 8860) = 497.54	
Prob > F	0.0000		0.0000		0.0000		0.0000	
Predictor Variable	Coef.	P-value	Coef.	P-value	Coef.	P-value	Coef.	P-value
Density (K)	*-0.25	0.000	*-0.25	0.000	*-0.26	0.000	*-0.30	0.000
Metering (R)	*4.83	0.000	*2.32	0.000	*3.93	0.000	*4.80	0.000
VMS (M)	*-2.70	0.000	*-2.98	0.000	*-3.12	0.000	*-3.32	0.000

Note: * Indicates that the coefficients are statistically significant at 0.10 level

Table 2. Summary of Regression Results of the Incident Case: Dependent Variable = Speed

Incident	7:00AM—8:00AM		8:00AM—9:00AM		4:00PM—5:00PM		5:00PM—6:00PM	
Number of obs	365		370		387		426	
R^2	0.7315		0.7557		0.7559		0.6900	
Adjusted R^2	0.7057		0.7333		0.7338		0.6639	
F value	F(32, 332) = 28.27		F(31, 338) = 33.72		F(32, 354) = 34.25		F(33, 392) = 26.44	
Prob > F	0.0000		0.0000		0.0000		0.0000	
Predictor Variable	Coef.	P-value	Coef.	P-value	Coef.	P-value	Coef.	P-value
Density	*-0.75	0.000	*-0.58	0.000	*-0.50	0.000	*-0.47	0.000
Highway Helper (H)	*11.44	0.015	*9.25	0.087	8.45	0.308	-1.60	0.911
Ramp Metering (R)	2.94	0.152	-0.31	0.894	*4.10	0.054	*6.54	0.010
VMS (M)	*-2.99	0.029	*-3.24	0.011	*-5.94	0.000	*-3.75	0.010

Note: * Indicates that the coefficients are statistically significant at 0.10 level

The R^2 values suggest that speed is a complex phenomenon of which we only explain about half for the incident-free case and about 70 percent for the incident case. The analysis is based on three years' systemwide data and the number of observations for the incident-free case is large.

Density is an important referent that helps us understand the effects of the traffic management systems on speed. For example, in the incident-free case, comparing the coefficient of the ramp meter dummy (7 a.m–8 a.m.) with the coefficient of density (7 a.m.–8 a.m.) gives us an idea that the effect of one ramp meter on mainline speed is approximately equal to decreasing 60 vehicles per mile on a three-lane freeway segment. The estimate of the coefficient on density is negative and significant for both the incident-free case and incident case, indicating a negative relationship between speed and density, e.g., when the coefficient is estimated to be -0.25 (7 a.m.–8 a.m., incident-free), a density increase of one vehicle/mile/lane will decrease link speed by 0.25 MPH.

For the incident-free case, the estimates for the ramp meter dummy are positive and significant in all four hours, indicating that the operation of ramp metering system increases mainline speed. This result is in accord with previous studies. The 2001 Twin Cities metro area Ramp Meter Study (by Cambridge Systematics) (2) showed that on average, in the absence of metering, freeway speeds decreased by approximately seven miles/hour in the peak period and by 18 miles/hour during the peak hour. This result is based on the eight-week ramp meter shutdown data, while our study is based on three years' data (including data prior to the ramp meter start-up on many facilities, ramp meter in full operation, and the eight-week ramp meter shutdown.

The regression result can be explained as below: if we have two corridor segments with all characteristics the same, except that one has ramp metering and the other does not, we would expect the corridor segment with ramp metering to be 4.8 miles/hour (7 a.m.–8 a.m.,) faster than the corridor segment without ramp metering. It should be noted that the value of thc ramp metering dummy coefficient is a "conservative" estimate, that is, this value should be less than the full effects of ramp metering on mainline speed. As we discussed above, ramp metering affects mainline speed through both mainline density and drivers' behaviors. The effect of metering on mainline density was not explained by the ramp metering dummy. The actual effects of ramp metering might be larger.

For the incident case, two of the four estimates of the ramp meter dummy are insignificant, which indicates that, holding the other terms fixed, corridor segments with ramp metering are not necessarily faster (or slower) than corridor segments without ramp metering.

Unlike Ramp Metering, which has relatively fixed operational hours, VMS is active only when "special events" happen. But it is impossible for us to obtain the detailed starting time and duration of these VMS messages. We defined the VMS dummy as '1' if the studied corridor segment is within the impact area of VMS. The impact area of VMS is defined as the segments that can "see" the VMS messages and the two to three segments downstream of the VMS. Therefore, what we estimate here is actually the association between speed and VMS impact area.

For both the incident-free case and incident case, the estimates for the VMS dummy are negative and significant in all four hours. The negative association between speed and VMS impacting area can be explained as follows:

1. VMS impacts drivers' behaviors. VMS devices installed along the roadside warn of special events such as congestion, incident, roadwork zone, or speed limit to alert travelers of traffic problems ahead. Drivers typically slow down to view the message and to plan alternative routes, and some of them may divert to other roadways.
2. The distribution of the signs contributes to the negative association. Most of the signs in the Twin Cities metro area are located on freeway segments with heavy traffic. These segments are typically more congested and have lower mainline speed.

Then, should we stop using VMS since the VMS impact area is associated with lower mainline speed? Probably not as the speed decrease on one corridor (VMS impacting area) may prevent congestion on some other corridors. Further study is needed to evaluate VMS.

The Highway Helper Program is not included in the incident-free case because when the studied segments are incident-free, the Highway Helper Program is not active. In the incident case, two of the four estimates are positive and significant (7 a.m.–8 a.m., and 8 a.m.–9 a.m.), which indicates that in this case, the corridor segments within Highway Helper patrol areas should be faster than the corridor segments without Highway Helpers. The other two cases are statistically insignificant.

4. INCIDENT RATE

4.1 Data Collection

TMC freeway incident records started from 1991, but we only used the data of fall 2000 for this study. The earlier years' incident data cannot be used for this systemwide analysis because the incident record started at different years for different corridors—some corridors from 1991, while some others even as late as 1998; and based on the record, the number of incidents seemingly increased tremendously in the past 10 years. But this increase was partly caused by the addition of new cameras, the upgrade of equipment, and the improved monitoring methods. In short, more incidents were recorded, but we don't know if more occurred.

We collected the incident data for two periods in fall 2000—37 workdays (from Aug. 22 to Oct. 13) before ramp metering system shutdown (2) and 37 workdays (from Oct. 16 to Dec. 07) during the ramp metering system shutdown. Incident records during these two periods have much higher quality than before, because during these two periods the camera monitoring system covered the whole network and was operated under the same monitoring strategies and equipment conditions. In addition, incident data was counted between 7 a.m. and 7 p.m., which were the operational hours of the traffic management system.

As to incident types, since we want to test the association of incident rate and the traffic management system, we removed the incidents caused by vehicle mechanical malfunctions such as stalls and vehicle fires and the incidents caused by debris on road. Finally three kinds of incidents were included: crash, rollover, and spinout, where crash incidents accounted for more than 97 percent of all incidents.

4.2 Corridor Selection

In total, 26 corridors were selected for this study, which nearly cover the whole Twin Cities metro area freeway network (refer to Figure 3). The unselected corridors were those outside of TMC camera monitoring. The facility status of each corridor was summarized in Table A3.

Figure 3. Incident Analysis: Corridor Selection

4.3 Regression Model

Due to the short incident counting periods (37 workdays before and during ramp metering shutdown respectively) we have to select long corridors to ensure a non-zero number of incidents. When the corridors are long, it is impossible to include some traffic or infrastructure characteristics as predictor variables although these characteristics may be relevant to the response variable. For example, some traffic stream characteristics—such as link speed, flow, or density—should be potential predictor variables of incident regression analysis, but for a long corridor (which has several segments), the speed, flow, or density of the segments vary greatly and none of them could be represented by a single value. Also the geometric characteristics cannot be represented by a uniform format for all the segments of a long corridor. Finally, we included limited predictor variables in the regression model.

The multiple regression model can be represented as follows:

I/mile = f(J/mile, R, M/mile, H,G)

Where
I/mile =Incidents per mile
J/mile = Interchange Density (Junctions/mile)
M/mile = VMS Density
G = Geometrics (presence of separated HOV lanes)

Each corridor has two directions, and each direction will have two observations—Incident Rate before shutdown and Incident Rate during shutdown. Since it is impossible to include detailed traffic or infrastructure characteristics as predictor variables in this model, we use intersection density as a substitute. "Busy" corridors tend to have higher interchange density, and in view of geometric structure, an interchange is more "dangerous" than a straight segment. Therefore, the interchange density of a corridor should be strongly related to its incident rate.

As to VMS, VMS Density is a more reasonable measure than VMS impact area for long corridors. VMS Density is the number of variable message signs per mile that is counted for both directions of each corridor.

4.4 Results

The regression results are summarized in Table 3

Table 3. Regression Results: Dependent Variable = Incident Rate

Independent Variables	Coef.	P-value	T-value
Intersection Density (J/mile)	1.30	*0.013	2.532
Ramp Metering (R)	-1.07	*0.001	-3.300
VMS Density (M/mile)	4.17	*0.035	2.138
Highway Helper (H)	1.45	*0.003	3.085
Concurrent HOV in I-35W	.23	0.788	0.270
Concurrent HOV in I-394	-.94	0.280	-1.087
Barrier-separated HOV in I-394	2.46	*0.008	2.730

Number of observations	98
R-squared	0.3764
Adjusted R-squared	0.3279
F value	7.76
Prob > F	0.0000

Note: * Indicates that the coefficients are statistically significant at 0.10 level.

The R^2 value shows that the regression model only explains about 30 percent of the observations. That is because we included limited predictor variables in this model. Incidents are an irregular and complex phenomena, due to such factors as driver behavior, vehicle conditions, traffic state, and geometric structure or pavement quality, all of which may contribute to their occurrence. Nevertheless, we can still find important associations between incident rate and the TMS components from the regression results.

Intersection Density has a positive and significant relationship with incident rate, which indicates that the more intersections, the higher the incident rate. This result agrees with our expectation. However, it should also be noted that more than half of the surveillance cameras are located at or near the intersections, so 'the more intersections, the higher the incident rate' may be partly due to the fact that 'the more intersections, the more cameras', and the more cameras, the more incidents reported. Still, most major incidents should be reported, even in the absence of cameras.

Ramp Metering has a negative and significant relationship with incident rate, which indicates that ramp metering is effective in reducing incidents. This result is consistent with the Twin Cities Metro Area Ramp Meter Study (2), which showed ramp metering results in annual savings of 1,041 crashes (four crashes per weekday).

The positive and significant relationship between VMS Density and incident rate indicates that corridors with higher VMS Density are typically the corridors with higher incident rate. Unlike ramp metering, where we have observations with and without meters for the same corridor, we can make no claims of causality here, as the presence of VMS did not change on specific corridors.

Highway Helper is positive and significant, which indicates that the corridors under Highway Helper patrol are the corridors with higher incident rate.

5. CONCLUSIONS

This study used regression to evaluate the long-run performance of three traffic management systems—Ramp Metering, Variable Message Signs (VMS), and the Highway Helper Program, in the Twin Cities metro area. Link speed and incident rate were employed as the response variable separately.

To predict speed, a database of about 40,000 observations covering three years' data was established. The long-run and systemwide performance of the traffic management systems were estimated for both the incident-free case and incident case. The key findings are summarized as follows:

- For the incident-free case, ramp metering is effective in increasing mainline speed. For example, from 7 a.m. to 8 a.m., the corridor segment with ramp metering is estimated to be 4.8 mile/hr faster than the corridor segment without ramp metering; and the effect of one ramp meter on mainline speed is approximately equal to decreasing 60 vehicles per mile on a three-lane freeway segment. For the incident case however, corridor segments with ramp metering are not necessarily faster or slower than corridor segments without ramp metering, which indicates the effects of the ramp metering in increasing mainline speed will not always offset the incident influences.
- For both the incident-free case and incident case, the speed of the corridor segment within the VMS impacting area will be lower than the corridor segment outside. The negative relationship should be due to two reasons: 1) VMS messages' impacts on drivers' behaviors; 2) the geographic distribution characteristics of the signs.
- The Highway Helper Program was evaluated only in the incident case. The Highway Helper Program dummy coefficient for 7 a.m.–8 a.m. and 8 a.m.–9 a.m. are positive and significant, which indicates that in this case, the corridor segments within the Highway Helper patrol areas will be faster than the corridor segments out of the areas.

To predict incident rate, incident data was collected for two periods in fall 2000—before ramp metering system shutdown and during ramp metering system shutdown. The key findings are summarized as below:

- Ramp Metering system is associated with a lower incident rate; because we tested the same sections with and without meters, we believe this is a causal effect;
- Both the corridors with higher VMS density and the corridors under Highway Helper patrol are typically the corridors with higher incident rate;

- The operation of Concurrent HOV does not have a significant relationship with incident rate change; however, we can not rule out the possibility that the increase of the incident rate on the general-purpose lanes was offset by the decrease of the incident rate on the HOV lane (or vice versa);
- The operation of Barrier-separated HOV is associated with an increase in the total incident rate of general purpose lanes and HOV lanes. This can be due to two reasons: 1) the high volume and congestion on the general-purpose lanes; 2) the specific geometric design problems of that section.

In future work, improvement could be made through the following aspects:

- For ramp metering evaluation, the current speed regression model provided a "conservative" estimate, which should be less than the full effects of ramp metering on mainline speed. An improved model should be able to estimate the effect of ramp metering on mainline density, which was not explained by the ramp metering dummy. Similarly, density could be modeled non-linearly, because traffic flow observation suggests that density does not affect speed until after a certain threshold.
- Our study found the negative relationship between VMS impact area and mainline speed. But we did not answer the question whether the speed decrease at one corridor (VMS impacting area) prevents more serious congestion in some other corridors. More detailed study should be done to give a comprehensive evaluation of VMS.
- Decreasing data-limitations. A major issue in regression analysis is the quality of database. Regression analysis provides information on relationships between a response variable and predictor variables but only to the degree that such information is contained in the database [6]. For example, the evaluation of VMS is limited by the lack of a detailed activity log. In addition, restricted by the earlier years' incident data quality, we only used the incident data in fall 2000 for incident rate regression analysis. The limited study periods lead to the selection of long corridors when estimating incidents, which prevented us from employing detailed link traffic and infrastructure characteristics as predictor variables.

REFERENCES

1. Banks, J. H., Kelly, G. "Traffic Management Systems Performance Measurement Final Report," California PATH Research Report (UCB-ITS-PRR-97-53), 1997.
2. Cambridge Systematics, Inc. "Twin Cities Metro Area Ramp Meter Study," final report prepared for Minnesota Department of Transportation, 2001 4). Evaluation Methodologies. 7). Benefit/Cost Analysis. 9). Summary of Findings, Conclusions, and Recommendations http://www.dot.state.mn.us/rampmeterstudy/reports.html.
3. Cambridge Systematics, Inc. "Twin Cities HOV Study," final report prepared for Minnesota Department of Transportation, 2002 http://www.dot.state.mn.us/information/hov/.
4. Cook, R. D. *Applied Regression Including Computing and Graphics*, John Wiley & Sons, Inc. 1999.
5. DeGroot, M. H., *Probability and Statistics*, 2nd ed., Addison-Wesley Pub. Co., 1986.
6. Gunst, R. F., Mason, R. L. *Regression Analysis and its Application: A Data-oriented Approach*, New York: M. Dekker, 1980.
7. Hall, F. L. "Traffic Flow Theory: A State of the Art Report," Chapter 2: Traffic Stream Characteristics. Sponsored by the Transportation Research Board's Committee on Theory of Traffic Flow (A3A11), funded by Federal Highway Administration (FHWA) in June 1992. http://www-cta.ornl.gov/cta/research/trb/tft.html
8. Institute of Transportation Engineers (ITE). *Manual of Traffic Engineering Studies*, 3rd ed. Washington, 1964.
9. Levinson, D., Zhang, L., Das, S., Sheikh, A. "Ramp Meters on Trial: Evidence from the Twin Cities Ramp Meters Shut-off," presented at 81st Transportation Research Board Conference, Washington DC, 2002 (TRB-02-2167).
10. Levinson, D. "Perspectives on Efficiency in Transportation," presented at the 81st Transportation Research Board Conference, Washington DC, (TRB-02-2015), 2002.
11. Minnesota Department of Transportation, Freeway Traffic Management Program Status Report, 2001 and 2002.
http://depts.washington.edu/trba3a09/status/jan2001/minnesota.pdf.
http://depts.washington.edu/trba3a09/status/jun2000/minnesota.pdf.
12. Minnesota Department of Transportation Traffic Management Center.
http://www.dot.state.mn.us/tmc/.

APPENDIX

Table A1. Case Study I: The Correlation Matrices of Predictor Variables

1. *Incident-free:*

7:00AM-8:00AM	DENSITY	RM	VMS	ConHOV	BarHOV
DENSITY	1.00	0.19	-0.13	0.08	0.06
RM	0.19	1.00	0.01	-0.03	-0.03
VMS	-0.13	0.01	1.00	-0.05	-0.05
ConHOV	0.08	-0.03	-0.05	1.00	-0.05
BarHOV	0.06	-0.03	-0.05	-0.05	1.00

8:00AM-9:00AM	DENSITY	RM	VMS	ConHOV	BarHOV
DENSITY	1.00	0.19	-0.09	0.15	0.07
RM	0.19	1.00	0.02	-0.03	-0.03
VMS	-0.09	0.02	1.00	-0.04	-0.05
ConHOV	0.15	-0.03	-0.04	1.00	-0.05
BarHOV	0.07	-0.03	-0.05	-0.05	1.00

4:00PM-5:00PM	DENSITY	RM	VMS	ConHOV	BarHOV
DENSITY	1.00	0.09	0.07	0.15	0.08
RM	0.09	1.00	0.01	-0.03	-0.03
VMS	0.07	0.01	1.00	-0.05	-0.04
ConHOV	0.15	-0.03	-0.05	1.00	-0.05
BarHOV	0.08	-0.03	-0.04	-0.05	1.00

5:00PM-6:00PM	DENSITY	RM	VMS	ConHOV	BarHOV
DENSITY	1.00	0.07	0.07	0.12	0.13
RM	0.07	1.00	0.01	-0.02	-0.03
VMS	0.07	0.01	1.00	-0.05	-0.04
ConHOV	0.12	-0.02	-0.05	1.00	-0.05
BarHOV	0.13	-0.03	-0.04	-0.05	1.00

7:00AM-8:00AM	DENSITY	RM	VMS	HHELPER	ConHOV	BarHOV
DENSITY	1.00	-0.11	-0.32	-0.03	0.05	0.02
RM	-0.11	1.00	0.16	0.29	-0.12	-0.08
VMS	-0.32	0.16	1.00	0.25	-0.10	-0.04
HHELPER	-0.03	0.29	0.25	1.00	0.08	0.10
ConHOV	0.05	-0.12	-0.10	0.08	1.00	-0.05
BarHOV	0.02	-0.08	-0.04	0.10	-0.05	1.00

8:00AM-9:00AM	DENSITY	RM	VMS	HHELPER	ConHOV	BarHOV
DENSITY	1.00	0.10	-0.14	0.22	0.01	-0.02
RM	0.10	1.00	0.05	0.28	-0.07	-0.07
VMS	-0.14	0.05	1.00	0.17	-0.14	-0.03
HHELPER	0.22	0.28	0.17	1.00	0.04	0.13
ConHOV	0.01	-0.07	-0.14	0.04	1.00	-0.04
BarHOV	-0.02	-0.07	-0.03	0.13	-0.04	1.00

4:00PM-5:00PM	DENSITY	RM	VMS	HHELPER	ConHOV	BarHOV
DENSITY	1.00	0.02	0.10	0.12	0.03	0.02
RM	0.02	1.00	-0.03	0.32	-0.27	-0.11
VMS	0.10	-0.03	1.00	-0.07	-0.02	-0.17
HHELPER	0.12	0.32	-0.07	1,00	0.05	0.09
ConHOV	0.03	-0.27	-0.02	0.05	1.00	-0.07
BarHOV	0.02	-0.11	-0.17	0.09	-0.07	1.00

Table A2. Case Study I: Corridor Selection

Corridor	Geographic Characteristics	From	To
I-494NB	Beltline freeway	CR 6	I-94
I-494SB	Beltline freeway	Bass Lake	CR 6
I-494WB	Beltline freeway	I-35W	TH 169
I-494EB	Beltline freeway	TH 169	I-35W
I-694WB	Beltline freeway	I-35W	TH 252
I-694EB	Beltline freeway	TH 252	I-35W
I-94WB	Intercity connector	I-35E	TH 280
I-94EB	Intercity connector	TH 280	I-35E
I-94NB	Radial freeway within the I-494/I-694 beltline	Broadway	Humboldt
I-94SB	Radial freeway within the I-494/I-694 beltline	Humboldt	TH 55
I-394WB	Radial freeway within the I-494/I-694 beltline	I-94	TH 100
I-394EB	Radial freeway within the I-494/I-694 beltline	TH 100	I-94
I-35E NB (North of I-94)	Radial freeway within the I-494/I-694 beltline	I-94	TH 36
I-35E SB (North of I-94)	Radial freeway within the I-494/I-694 beltline	TH 36	I-94
I-35E NB (South of I-94)	Radial freeway within the I-494/I-694 beltline	I-494	St. Clair
I-35E SB (South of I-94)	Radial freeway within the I-494/I-694 beltline	5TH Kellogg	I-494
I-35W NB	Radial freeway outside the I-494/I-694 beltline	Mississippi River	86TH
I-35W SB	Radial freeway outside the I-494/I-694 beltline	86TH	113TH ST.
I-35E NB (South of I-494)	Radial freeway outside the I-494/I-694 beltline	CR 11	Diffley RD.
I-35E SB (South of I-494)	Radial freeway outside the I-494/I-694 beltline	Diffley RD.	TH-77
TH-77 NB	Radial freeway outside the I-494/I-694 beltline	127TH	Old Shakopee
TH-77 SB	Radial freeway outside the I-494/I-694 beltline	Old Shakopee	I-35E

Figure A3. Case Study II: Facility Status for the 26 Corridors

Corridor	Direction	Ramp Meter (1, 0)	# of Variable Message Signs	Highway Helper Program (1, 0)	Concurrent HOV in I-35W (1, 0)	Concurrent HOV in I-394 (1, 0)	Barrier-separated HOV in I-394(1, 0)
1	1N	1	1	1	0	0	0
	1S	1	1	1	0	0	0
2	2N	1	1	1	0	0	0
	2S	1	1	1	0	0	0
3	3W	1	1	1	0	0	1
	3E	1	1	1	0	0	1
4	4W	1	1	1	0	1	0
	4E	1	3	1	0	1	0
5	5N	1	1	1	1	0	0
	5S	1	0	1	1	0	0
6	6N	1	1	1	0	0	0
	6S	1	1	1	0	0	0
7	7N	1	1	1	0	0	0
	7S	1	2	1	0	0	0
8	8N	1	2	1	0	0	0
	8S	1	1	1	0	0	0
9	9N	1	0	0	0	0	0
	9S	1	1	0	0	0	0
10	10W	1	1	1	0	0	0
	10E	1	2	1	0	0	0
11	11W	1	1	0	0	0	0
	11E	0	0	0	0	0	0
12	12W	1	1	1	0	0	0
	12E	1	0	1	0	0	0
13	13N	1	1	1	0	0	0
	13S	1	1	1	0	0	0
14	14W	1	3	1	0	0	0
	14E	1	2	1	0	0	0
15	15N	1	1	1	0	0	0
	15S	1	1	1	0	0	0
16	16N	1	1	1	0	0	0
	16S	1	1	1	0	0	0
17	17W	1	1	1	0	0	0
	17E	1	1	1	0	0	0
18	18N	1	1	1	0	0	0
	18S	1	1	1	0	0	0

Table A3. Case Study II Continued

Corridor Direction		Ramp Meter (1, 0)	# of Variable Message Signs	Highway Helper Program (1, 0)	Concurrent HOV in I-35W (1, 0)	Concurrent HOV in I-394 (1, 0)	Barrier-separated HOV in I-394(1, 0)
19	19N	1	1	0	0	0	0
	19S	1	1	0	0	0	0
20	20N	1	1	1	0	0	0
	20S	1	2	1	0	0	0
21	21W	1	1	1	0	0	0
	21E	1	1	1	0	0	0
22	22N	1	0	1	0	0	0
	22S	1	1	1	0	0	0
23	23N	1	1	1	0	0	0
	23S	0	0	1	0	0	0
24	24N	1	1	0	0	0	0
	24S	0	1	0	0	0	0
25	25W	1	2	1	0	0	0
	25E	1	2	1	0	0	0
26	26S	1	1	0	0	0	0

Note:
Ramp Meter=1 if the corridor is under ramp metering control; otherwise, Ramp Meter=0;
Highway Helper Program=1 if the corridor is within highway helper program patrol area; otherwise, Highway Helper Program=0;
HOV=1 if the corridor has HOV lane(s) in operation; otherwise, HOV=0;
For VMS, the number of VMSs per corridor per direction is counted.

Chapter 15

ADVANCED TRAFFIC MANAGEMENT SYSTEM DATA

Robert L. Bertini
Department of Civil and Environmental Engineering, Portland State University

Ahmed El-Geneidy
School of Urban Studies and Planning, Portland State University

With the implementation of Intelligent Transportation Systems (ITS) for system management purposes, there is now the ability to extract archived data that can be used to evaluate the implementation of new operational strategies. In recognition of the need to provide feedback to decision-makers, efforts are underway to provide rigorous documentation of ITS benefits and costs. The objective of this paper is to describe how Advanced Traffic Management System (ATMS) data are being used to contribute toward these evaluations. Case examples are described in the areas of freeway management, incident management, arterial management, and transit management. Building a complete ITS system requires collaboration in time, funding, and institutional arrangements. ITS components that are integrated can result in synergistic effects when considered as an entire system. It is shown that in some cases it is possible to build upon national level statistics describing ITS benefits by using data collected from the systems themselves. It is hoped that further efforts to integrate transportation planning with evaluation methodologies will incorporate the necessary empirical results from a wide variety of studies. In this way, better databases can be developed, and heightened accountability will be more pervasive in the evaluation of ITS improvements.

1. INTRODUCTION

In 1997 in the U.S., automobiles traveled 1.4 trillion vehicle miles (2.3 trillion vehicle kilometers) and households spent an average of 19 percent of their income on transportation—less than housing but more than food

(Northeast-Midwest Institute, 2002). Further, drivers in the 68 largest urban areas in the U.S. experienced an increase in traffic delays due to congestion from 11 hours per year in 1982, to 36 hours per year in 1999 (Schrank and Lomax, 2002). The estimated cost of traffic congestion in these 68 areas totaled $78 billion, representing a cost of 4.5 million extra hours of travel and 6.8 billion gallons (25.7 billion liters) of wasted fuel (Schrank and Lomax, 2002). The average rush-hour trip takes 32 percent more time than the same trip taken during non-rush-hour conditions. Congested travel periods (rush hours) in the nation's major cities have doubled in less than 20 years, increasing from nearly three hours (morning and evening combined) in 1982, to almost six hours in 1999 (Schrank and Lomax, 2002). Congestion is now found during almost half of the daylight hours on workdays (Schrank and Lomax, 2002).

Increasing traffic congestion coupled with improved technology, funding constraints, and increasing environmental consciousness has provided an impetus to develop cost effective systems aimed at improving the efficiency and effectiveness of the transportation system. Intelligent Transportation Systems (ITS) include a wide range of diverse technologies, including information processing, communications, control, and electronics. ITS have evolved with applications, including collision warning systems, ramp meters, advanced signal control systems, transit and emergency vehicle management systems, and others. The goals of ITS deployments include improving traveler safety, traveler mobility and system efficiency; increasing the productivity of transportation providers; and conserving energy while protecting the environment. The strain on the transportation system as a whole is thus eased through the application of modern information technology and communications. Some technologies provide more cost-effective benefits than others, and as technology evolves, the choices to deployers are bound to improve. These technologies are often combined into a single integrated system, providing benefits that exceed the benefits of any single technology (Proper and Maccubbin, 2000).

ITS aims to improve the safety and efficiency of the transportation system. ITS systems themselves offer opportunities for new methods of evaluation and continuing assessment. As an indication of the degree of commitment to ITS in the U.S., during the last decade, federal, state, and local governments have appropriated billions of dollars for ITS programs. In 1998, the Transportation Equity Act for the 21st Century (TEA-21) provided more than $1.2 billion in funding to support ITS through 2003. Of that, $603 million was targeted toward research and development. Another $679 million was intended for deployment of ITS projects (Sundeen, 2002). Further, the Intelligent Transportation Society of America (ITS America) estimates that more than $209 billion will be spent on ITS programs by 2011.

There has been recognition of the need to demonstrate the benefits of ITS, providing a necessary feedback loop to decision-makers. In order to facilitate evaluations of ITS investments, the USDOT through its ITS Joint Program Office (established in 1994) continues to collect information regarding the impacts of ITS projects on the operation of the surface transportation network. The results of most ITS related projects and model deployments have been perceived as promising and efforts continue toward defining the magnitude of their benefits (Proper and Maccubbin, 2000). The objective of this paper is to describe how advanced traffic management system (ATMS) data are being used to evaluate the benefits of ITS investments.

2. EVALUATION PERSPECTIVES

Transportation improvements have frequently been deployed in order to make the system more efficient by reducing travel time, the number of stops, and delay. In the past, data collection experiments would be designed for limited time periods to collect data at the precise points of interest. This process was often manual and costly, with many people required to collect a small amount of data. Bias was then introduced by temporally extrapolating these data collected from one or two days over an entire year. The data that were used to estimate the benefits of the improvement had limited temporal coverage but were collected from the precise spatial points of interest.

Many ITS deployments include surveillance systems that are used in the operation of the system. For example, ramp metering systems usually include inductive loop detectors on the freeway and on-ramps in order to detect the presence and traffic state of vehicles. This information is often used to set the ramp meter timing, but from an evaluation standpoint, it is not possible to "choose" the loop detector locations, and it is impossible to move the detectors. Despite the fact that the detectors may have been located specifically to operate the metering system, it is recognized that the surveillance system can also be used for incident detection and verification. It has also been shown (Bertini, Leal, and Lovell, 2001; Nee, Ishimaru, and Hallenbeck, 2001; Ishimaru, Hallenbeck, and Nee 2001; Ishimaru and Hallenbeck, 1999) that these systems can be used to extract relevant performance characteristics for the transportation network and then tracked over time. In contrast to past evaluation efforts where an experiment could be designed and data could be sampled from "ideal" locations for short periods, ITS deployments have provided opportunities to sample data from "non-ideal" locations (established for traffic management purposes) over very long periods. The bias that results originates from the need to extrapolate over space, rather than over time, since data can be collected indefinitely.

3. ITS BENEFITS OVERVIEW

Since December of 1994, the USDOT's Joint Program Office (JPO) for ITS has collected information describing the impact of ITS projects on the operation of the surface transportation system. Data collected as part of these efforts are available in the ITS Benefits Database on the JPO Web site (www.its.dot.gov). The JPO also collects information on ITS costs, and maintains this information in the ITS Unit Costs Database. The database is a central site for estimates of ITS costs data that the JPO can use for policy analyses and benefit-cost analyses. In addition, the database can be viewed and downloaded as a cost-estimating tool for those implementing ITS projects and programs at state and local levels.

The development and deployment of ITS technologies offer a wide variety of opportunities for local, regional, and state agencies to improve the capacity, reliability, and efficiency of their transportation systems. Due to many factors, the quantification of ITS benefits and costs has been difficult using traditional transportation planning and analysis methods because traditional transportation planning models lack necessary sensitivity to many benefits derived from ITS technologies, and because information on the impacts and costs of many ITS technologies is not yet well-understood.

The Federal Highway Administration (FHWA) and others have recognized this potential barrier to integrating ITS into the transportation planning process. In 1997, FHWA and its partners began development of the ITS Deployment Analysis System (IDAS), which is a tool designed to help planners better address these issues (Cambridge Systematics, 2002). Cambridge Systematics, Inc. led the development team and the software is now available for use. According to product documentation, IDAS is designed to assist public agencies and consultants in integrating ITS in the transportation planning process. IDAS offers the capability for a systematic assessment of ITS with one analysis tool and is used for determining the benefits and costs of various ITS deployments. IDAS provides users with the following capabilities:

- Comparison and screening of ITS alternatives;
- Estimation of impacts and traveler responses to ITS;
- Estimation of life-cycle costs;
- Inventory of ITS equipment, and identification of cost-sharing opportunities;
- Sensitivity and risk analysis;
- ITS deployment and operations/maintenance scheduling; and,
- Documentation for transition into design and implementation.

As with any model, IDAS is not without limitation. IDAS operates as a post-processor for travel demand model output, and incorporates benefit and cost information from many disparate studies, with data coming from different locations and from different timeframes. Thus it should be emphasized that IDAS is only a tool and should be used with care. More research is needed to quantify actual ITS deployment benefits, and the results of such research should be incorporated into future ITS evaluation activities.

4. ITS COMPONENTS

ITS deployments themselves typically include surveillance systems that enable a more comprehensive understanding of how the existing transportation system operates and facilitates proactive strategies for managing it more efficiently. ITS deployments have benefited from advances in computer processing and miniaturization, communications technology, and enhanced institutional arrangements. Ten ITS systems will be introduced with some examples of how archived data have been used to provide evidence for the effectiveness of these systems. The ITS benefits and unit costs database has classified the benefits of implementing ITS into the following 10 program areas (USDOT, 2002a). Note that each program area includes different ITS applications and that there is some potential overlap:

- Freeway management
- Incident management
- Transit management
- Arterial management
- Emergency management
- Electronic payment
- Traveler information
- Crash prevention and safety
- Operations and maintenance
- Road weather management.

The ITS benefits and unit cost database also describes seven categories of benefits to be used for ITS deployment evaluations:

- Safety improvements
- Delay savings
- Throughput
- Customer satisfaction
- Cost savings
- Environmental
- Other.

In line with the scope of this chapter we concentrate on the benefits by program area and use some real examples used in the evaluation process. The examples are derived from past and ongoing efforts to evaluate specific systems using archived ATMS data.

5. FREEWAY MANAGEMENT SYSTEMS

Three primary ITS functions make up freeway management systems: monitoring and surveillance, control of freeway operations, and the display or provision of information to motorists via dynamic message signs, highway advisory radio, in-vehicle navigation or information systems, or specialized information transmitted only to specific set of vehicles. Evaluations of freeway management system improvements such as ramp metering systems have demonstrated improvements in safety, reduction in travel time and delay, increased flows, and flow improvements (USDOT, 2002b).

Despite early efforts to deploy metering and management systems, actual traffic monitoring over a widespread area and real-time response is easier now due to advances in technology and greater system coverage. Typical traffic operations centers (TOCs) collect and process surveillance and monitoring data, most often from inductive loop detectors, and supplemented this with closed circuit television (CCTV) cameras that are also directly controlled from the TOC. The ability to collect data and reflect on it in real time has made a difference.

5.1 Interstate 5 Evaluations in Portland, Oregon

Presently, projects are underway by the authors to evaluate the performance of ramp metering and incident management in the Interstate 5 corridor in Portland, Oregon. The Oregon Department of Transportation (ODOT) has deployed a systemwide ramp metering program throughout the Portland metropolitan area. As part of the system itself, approximately 400 inductive loop detectors have been installed. Loops are included on each metered on ramp and in the freeway mainline lanes just upstream of each metered ramp. However, there are no detectors on off-ramps and there are few detectors at intermediate points (between interchanges) on the freeways. These detectors report speed, count, and occupancy every 20 seconds, but ODOT only archives data aggregated over 15-minute periods. Through special arrangement for the evaluation projects, the raw data are being archived. Thus far, the loop detector data has been validated with vehicle count data manually extracted from the video surveillance system. Figure 1 shows two sample validation curves, which include cumulative vehicle arrivals (plotted on oblique axes in order to magnify the details). The curves extracted from the loop detectors are aligned with the curves extracted from the surveillance video, indicating that the detectors are functioning reliably.

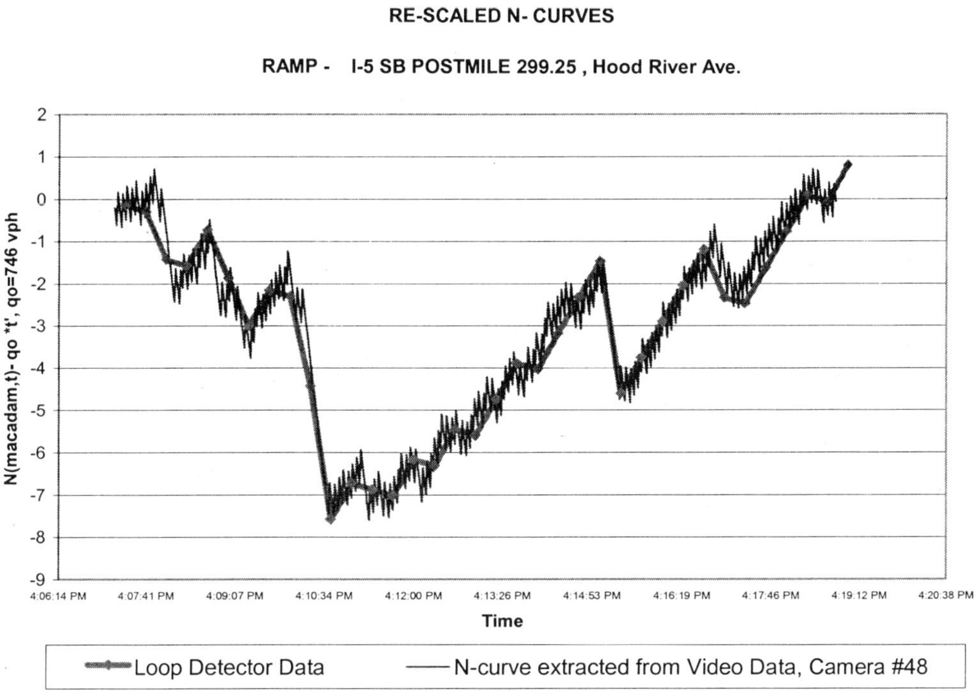

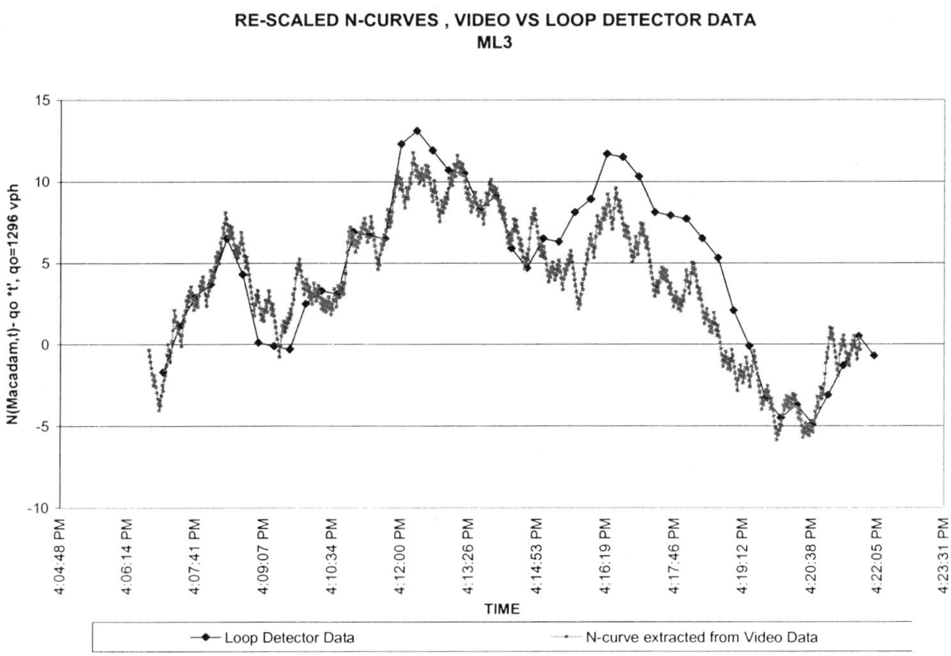

Figure 1. Validation of Loop Detector Data

The ramp metering evaluation will not include a true "before" and "after" component since ODOT is not able to shut down the meters. The project will include a comparison of actual ramp and freeway corridor performance using actual detailed counts and speeds extracted from the raw loop detector data. Using simulation tools, attempts will be made to evaluate different metering strategies and to create hypothetical performance characteristics "without" metering. It is recognized that relying on the fixed loop detector locations, with potentially large spacing, some bias will result in the analysis due to assumptions made about speeds over long freeway sections. As an example, Figure 3 shows a map of a section of Interstate 5 describing corridor speeds measured by loop detectors. When computing corridor performance, each detector is assigned to an influence area bounded by the midpoints between detectors. If the head or tail of a queue is present in the section, speed/travel time computation errors will be introduced which will in turn affect the calculation of performance measures such as vehicle miles (kilometers) traveled, delay, vehicle hours traveled, etc. Using a probe vehicle (at approximately the same time), Figure 2 shows the speed profile experienced by an actual vehicle traversing the section. Experiments are underway to examine the benefits of fusing the loop detector data with probe vehicle information (incident response vehicles and express buses are equipped with automatic vehicle location systems).

The incident management evaluation underway relies on the automatic vehicle location (AVL) system data provided by the incident response vehicles themselves, as well as an archived incident database that includes input from the incident responders, TOC dispatchers, and other emergency vehicle personnel.

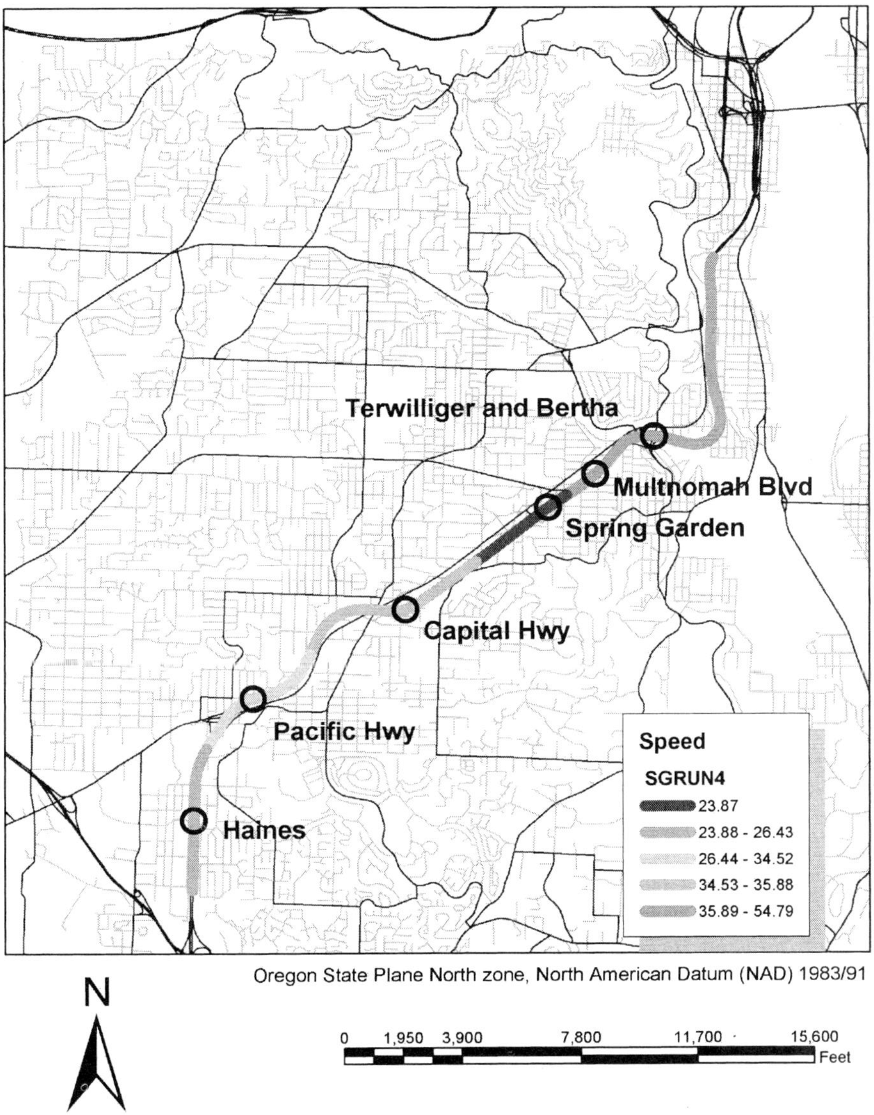

Figure 2. Speeds Extracted from Loop Detectors

5.2 Minnesota Ramp Metering System Evaluation

Recent public opposition threatened to abandon ramp control as a traffic management option in the Twin Cities of Minneapolis and St. Paul. In response to this, the Minnesota DOT was asked to produce tangible independent evidence of the effectiveness of ramp metering. A data collection procedure started with the ramp meters in operation, and continued with the meters shut down. A comparative study was conducted to compare before and after shutdown data (Cambridge Systematics, Inc., 2001; Levinson et al., 2002). In order to identify the temporal and spatial extents of congestion, occupancy contour plots were used (Bertini, Leal, and Lovell, 2002). Figure 4 shows two plots of occupancy with and without ramp meters along a 16-mile section of Minnesota Trunk Highway 169 (TH-169). Note the increase in occupancy (corresponding to increased travel times across the loop detectors) when the ramp meters were turned off compared to the occupancies measured with ramps turned on during another day. The before analysis indicated congestion somewhere between stations 17 and 18 while less congestion between stations 22 and 23 was reported in the after plot. Tables 1 and 2 summarize performance characteristics for a portion of TH-169. As shown, the speed dropped by nearly 18 percent after the shut down of the ramp metering system. Table 2 shows that the vehicle miles traveled (VMT) decreased by approximately 9.4 percent after the metering system was shut down.

The analysis performed by Cambridge Systematics, Inc. (2001) indicated that ramp metering is a cost-effective investment for the Twin Cities area, finding that after the meters were turned off, there was an average nine percent traffic volume reduction on freeways and no significant traffic volume change on parallel arterials included in the study. During peak traffic conditions, freeway mainline throughput declined by 14 percent in the un-metered condition. It was also estimated that the ramp metering contributed to an annual savings of more than 1,000 crashes or approximately four crashes per day. From an environmental perspective, ramp metering results in a net annual savings of 1,160 tons (1,052 metric tons) of emissions.

In parallel to the above study, a microsimulation analysis (Hourdakis and Michalopoulos, 2002) computed nearly the same benefits gained from applying ramp metering technology. The main result of the simulation process was that it has developed a prototype validated by empirical analysis under the relatively unique circumstances of a shutdown. See Chapter 9 of this book by Zhang and Levinson for another evaluation of the Twin Cities ramp metering shut-off.

Table 1. Minnesota TH-169 Average Speed

Stations	Before Shutdown Speed (mph)		After Shut Down Speed (mph)		Percentage Decrease Speed (mph)	
	Cumulative	Average	Cumulative	Average	Cumulative	Average
16	190,000	65	130,000	48	32	26
17	170,000	57	140,000	47	18	18
18	210,000	75	185,000	65	12	14
19	185,000	66	145,000	53	22	20
20	180,000	63	160,000	56	11	11
21	180,000	62	150,000	52	17	16
22	190,000	67	160,000	55	16	20
Average Speed Reduction from Station 16 to 22 =						18%

Table 2. Minnesota TH-169 Vehicle Miles Traveled

Station	Miles	VMT Veh-miles Before	VMT Veh-miles After	VMT Veh-miles Before - After	% Difference VMT Before - After
15	0.098	4637	4183	453	9.8
16	0.17	11478	10355	1122	9.8
17	0.26	13387	12027	1359	10.2
18	0.37	18667	16760	1907	10.2
19	0.50	24065	21699	2366	9.8
20	0.45	22381	20312	2069	9.2
21	0.42	19436	17770	1665	8.6
22	0.45	20214	18560	1653	8.2
Total		34268	21670	12597	9.4

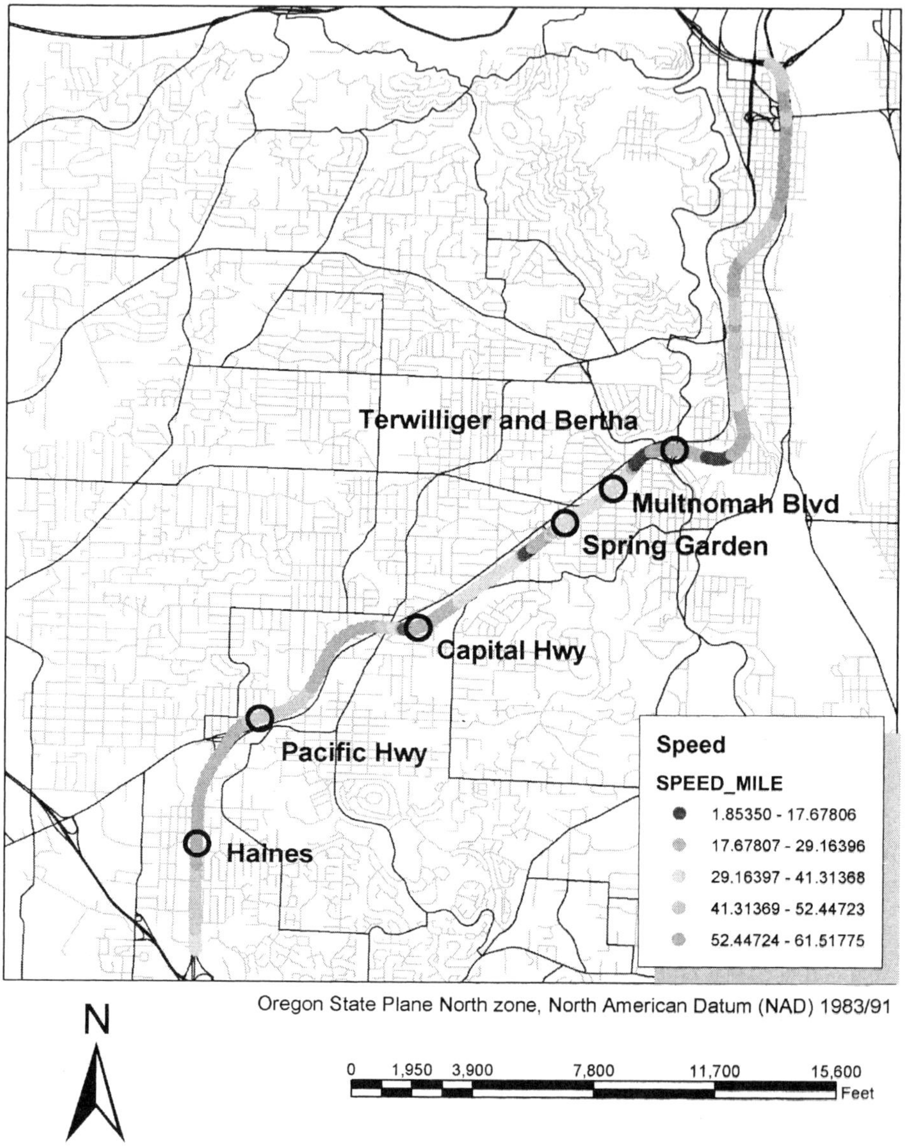

Figure 3. Speeds From Probe Vehicle

5.3 Incident Management Systems

Incidents are defined as crashes, breakdowns, and other random events that occur on our highway system. Congestion caused by incidents are serious problems that face any transportation agency. Incidents are known to cause more than 50 percent of urban congestion and lead to economic losses, air pollution, and human pain and suffering. Many urban areas have developed quick response incident management systems, recognizing that transporting victims to trauma centers within the "golden hour" can save lives. Further, through coordination among highway operations, law enforcement, and emergency personnel, secondary crashes can be prevented and responder safety can be enhanced (El-Geneidy and Bertini, 2003). So incident management systems are coordinated, preplanned, and/or real-time use of human resources to reduce the duration of incidents (Zografos, Androutsopoulos, and Vasilakis, 2001). Incident management systems contain components such as incident detection, incident verification, response to the incidents, clearance of the incidents, and traffic management at the incident locations. In many locations, incident data are archived on a regular basis to identify locations of high incident frequency. These locations can be used in planning the responders' routes on the highway and for identification of reasons for incident causation in an effort to improve the existing roadway characteristics to avoid future incidents at the same location. Numerous studies have been conducted to evaluate the implementation of incident management programs. Most of these studies came to the same findings that incident management programs have a substantial effect on delay time. (Chapter 11 of this book by Parthasarathi, Levinson, and Gillen also examines driver's willingness to pay for freeway service patrols).

5.4 Bay Area Freeway Service Patrol Evaluation

Incident management programs have been very popular additions to the transportation system. In many ways, the Bay Area Freeway Service Patrol Evaluation (Skabardonis et al., 1995) set the standard for comprehensive evaluations of incident management systems since it was a true before-and-after analysis. The study collected 276 hours of field data on one nine-mile (14.5 kilometer) freeway section, for 24 weekdays before and 22 weekdays after the freeway service patrol (FSP) was implemented. Field data included incident observations, probe vehicle travel times and speeds, flows, and occupancies extracted from archived loop detector data. The loop detectors were spaced at approximately 1/3 mile (0.5 kilometer) increments on the freeway mainline (and on-ramps) and the probe vehicles traveled at seven-minute headways during peak periods. Based on estimated savings in incident delay and fuel consumption, the study found that the FSP was cost effective for that particular freeway segment. It may have been tempting to try to extrapolate the results of the analysis to other freeway sections in the Bay Area or in other area. However, the researchers emphasized that the results would only be applicable "to sites with traffic and incident characteristics similar to the ones in the study area" (Skabardonis et al., 1995).

5.5 Los Angeles Freeway Service Patrol Evaluation

The Los Angeles Freeway Service Patrol Evaluation (Skabardonis et al., 1998), a true "before-and-after" analysis, measured the effectiveness of the FSP on a 7.8-mile (12.6 kilometer) section of the I-10 freeway in Los Angeles. An evaluation methodology was developed to estimate incident delays based on field data from loop detectors and probe vehicles, and to derive estimates of savings in performance measures in the absence of data for "before" FSP conditions. The methodology required the application of response time (and thus incident duration) savings due to the presence of the FSP on the freeway. Field data were collected in the corridor for 32 weekdays, for a total of six hours each day. This 192-hour database includes detailed descriptions for 1,560 incidents, probe vehicle travel time runs at 5.7-minute headways, and archived flow, occupancy and speed data from 240 loop detectors. This study found that the FSP program was also effective for the corridor studied.

5.6 Oregon Region 2 Incident Response Evaluation

In Oregon, an evaluation of the rural Region 2 Incident Response (IR) program (Bertini et al., 2001) involved a statistical analysis of archived incident data, estimation of reductions in fuel consumption and delay, calculation of program costs, and development of a decision-making tool for design/expansion of the incident management program on future corridors. The methodology consisted of a quantitative analysis of archived incident data during two distinct phases since the IR program's inception. The study focused on a 51-mile (82 kilometer) corridor on Oregon Highway 18 and a 41-mile (66 kilometer) corridor on Interstate 5 in Lane County. As shown in Figure 5, Phase 1 covered the period between February 1995–March 1997 and Phase 2 covered the period from March 1997–December 2000. Figure 5 also shows the total amount of IR resources deployed. As shown, during Phase 1 on Highway 18, IR personnel invested approximately 36 hours per month, while during Phase 2 (continuing today), there is one full-time IR staff member deployed (173 hours per month). Figure 5 also indicates that the staffing level has increased over time on Interstate 5. It was not possible to conduct a true "before-and-after" study, since it is the IR staff themselves who are the roving data collectors. Thus, the numbers of reported incidents (rather than the actual number of incidents) has increased because the IR personnel are physically monitoring the status of the roadways. Figure 6 is a tree that displays the number of incidents observed during the two phases. This illustrates that potential bias that can be introduced when using a data collection system that relies on the incident response personnel themselves.

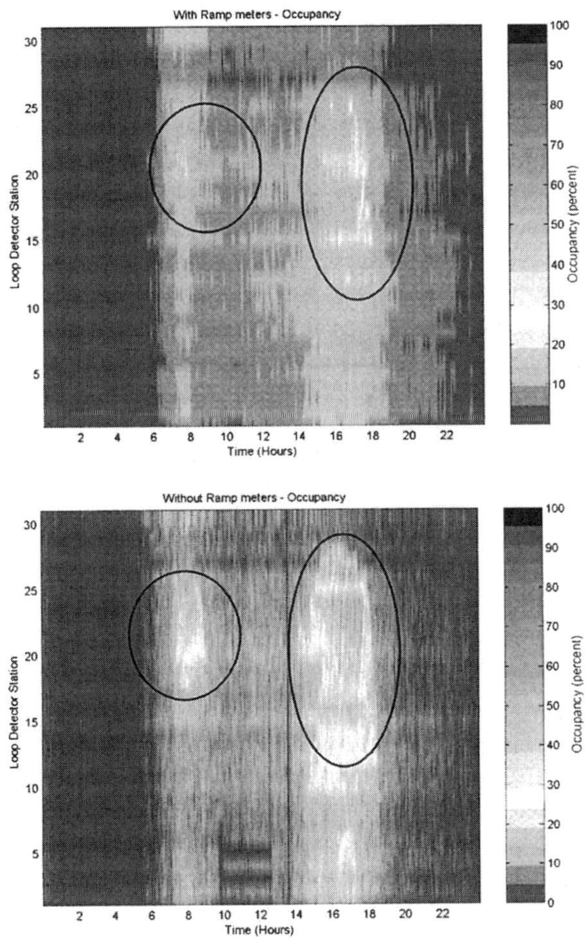

Figure 4. Before and After Occupancy (Percent) Plots from Minnesota

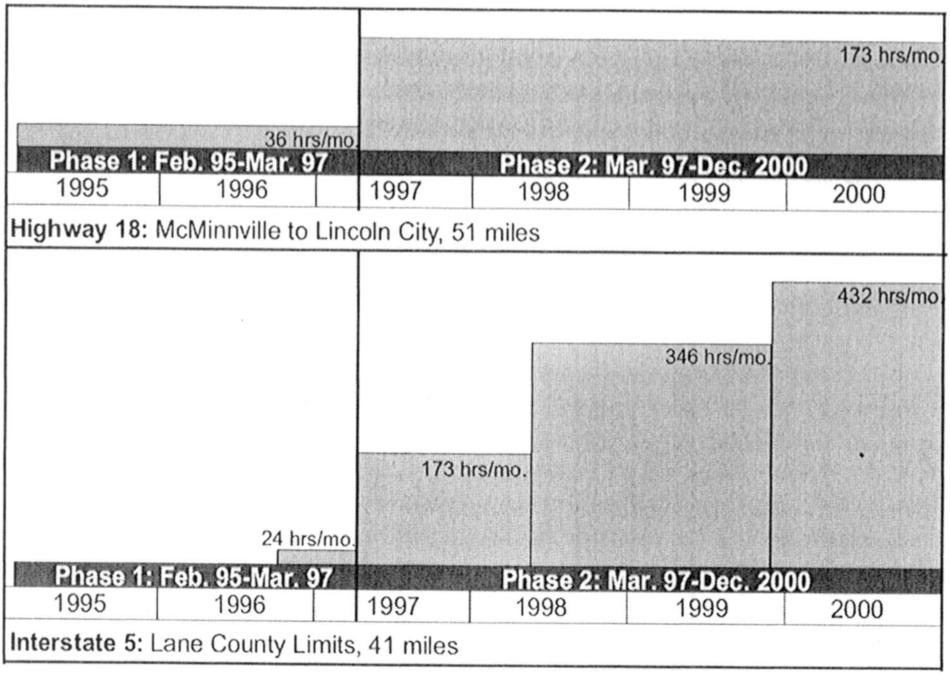

Figure 5. Incident Response Phases

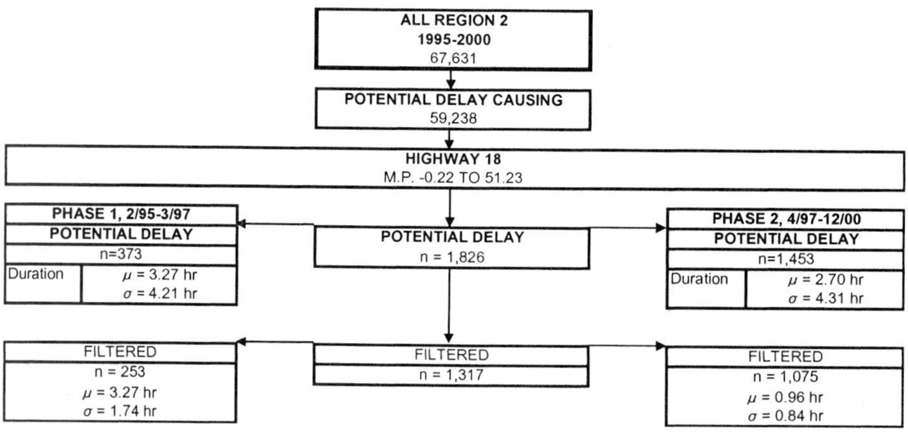

Figure 6. Incident Response Data Collection

5.7 Transit Management Systems

Transit management systems are concerned with increasing operational efficiency of all transit modes and increasing ridership by making the transit system more reliable. (McQueen and McQueen, 1999) The emergence of the global positioning systems (GPS) and the increase in its accuracy has helped this field substantially. Several transit agencies have equipped their vehicles with GPS to create automatic vehicle location (AVL). AVL technology has been widely implemented in North America and Europe. In the year 2000 about 35 bus systems had AVL technology implemented in the U.S., in both light-rail and bus systems (APTA, 2001).

The Tri-County Metropolitan Transportation District of Oregon (TriMet) operates 97 bus routes and a 38-mile light rail line within the tri-county Portland metropolitan region. TriMet's bus lines carry approximately 200,000 trips per day, serving a total population of 1.3 million persons within an area of 590 square miles (1,530 square kilometers). TriMet is considered as one of the leading ITS deployers in the U.S. TriMet has implemented a Bus Dispatch System (BDS) as a part of its overall operation and monitoring control system. (Strathman et al., 2002; Strathman et al., 2000; Strathman et al., 1999) The main components of the BDS include:

- Automatic vehicle location (AVL) based upon differential global positioning system (GPS) technology, supplemented by dead reckoning sensors;
- Voice and data communication system using radio and cellular digital packed data (CDPD) networks;
- On-board computer and control head displaying schedule adherence information to operators, detection, and reporting of schedule and route adherence to dispatchers;
- Automatic passenger counters (APCs) on front and rear doors of most vehicles (Kimpel, 2001); and
- Computer-aided dispatch (CAD) center (Strathman et al., 2001).

The implementation of the BDS in Portland, Oregon has resulted in substantial savings to the existing system and increased the service reliability in the region for both bus and light-rail (Strathman, et al., 2002). The total annual benefits derived from implementing the TriMet BDS system is estimated at $5.4 million dollars, and the present value imposing a 12-year expected life on the BDS is $47.8 million.

5.8 Arterial Management Systems

An arterial management system is used to manage traffic by employing various detection and control devices along arterial roadways. This includes surveillance and traffic signal control, and sometimes includes audio or visual information on arterial roadway conditions. Detectors collect basic traffic condition data (typically flow and speed information) and adaptive control systems can be used to coordinate traffic signal control across a metropolitan area by adjusting the lengths of signal phases and cycles. Without centralized control, vehicles would be delayed at intersections irrespective of actual traffic conditions as the vehicle progressed through the route. This caused undue vehicular delay to all vehicles including transit vehicles. Using knowledge of real-time traffic characteristics and coordination, arterial management systems have contributed to reductions in red light violations of 20–75 percent and reductions in fuel consumption by 2–13 percent in the studied areas (USDOT, 2002a). It was shown that St. Paul, Minnesota, traffic signal preemption systems reduced crashes for emergency vehicles by 71 percent in seven years (USDOT, 2002a). An arterial management system can be also monitored by the existing vehicles running on the system. For example several transit agencies have equipped their vehicles with GPS which reports the location of the vehicle back to a dispatch center every few seconds.

As an example, using some of TriMet archived data, a fusing process was developed as shown in Figure 7. This figure displays time-space diagrams for both TriMet buses and "ground truth" probe vehicles that were traveling on Powell Boulevard at the same time on the same day. The bus AVL data was extracted from archived data for Route 9 beginning at Front Avenue on the west side to the intersection of Powell Boulevard and SE 39th Ave. The probe vehicle data were collected with GPS installed on the vehicle. The bus AVL data were archived through BDS described above. A comparison between travel time for both the bus and the vehicle is shown in Table 3. The integration between these two systems can also be compared using vector analysis in Geographic Information Systems (GIS). Figure 8 shows an interpolated surface comparing a bus speed "surface" with a "surface" constructed from probe vehicle speeds. The surface was created using 20 runs collected by the GPS installed on the probe vehicles. The surface was interpolated using a krigging method in the ArcGIS software. Another vector surface was created for 20 bus trips using the same method and during the same period of time. Both the probe vehicles and buses had the same origin and destination. Looking in depth at the comparison, the bus has behaved in the same way as the probe vehicle yet the percentage of drop in speed at some locations were not similar. These differences are due to the variations in speed between the two modes during free flow travel time. Statistical relations between the probe vehicle and bus performance can be developed for reporting arterial performance to travelers and to quantify improvements to arterial management systems.

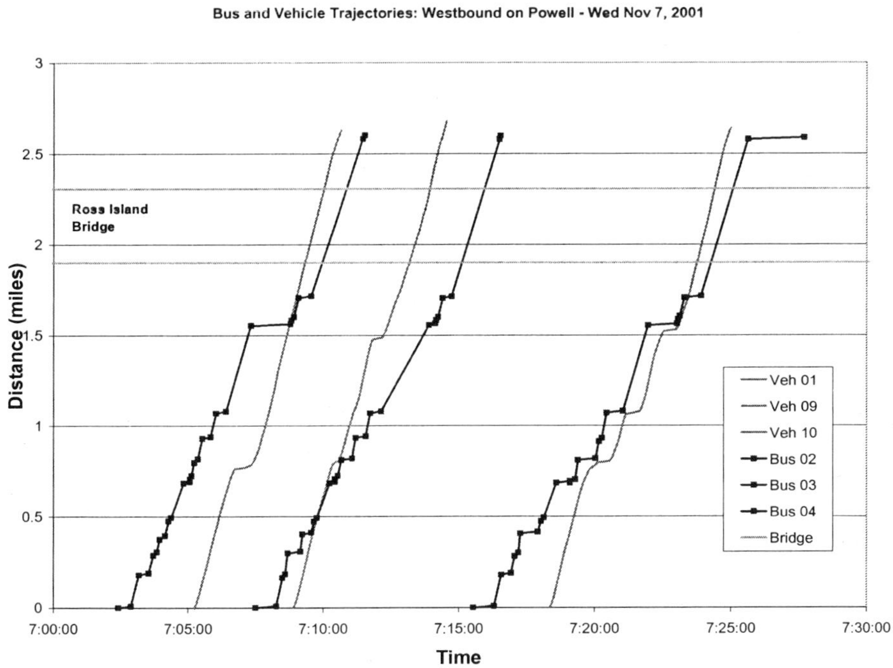

Figure 7. Time Space Diagram Fusing AVL Data

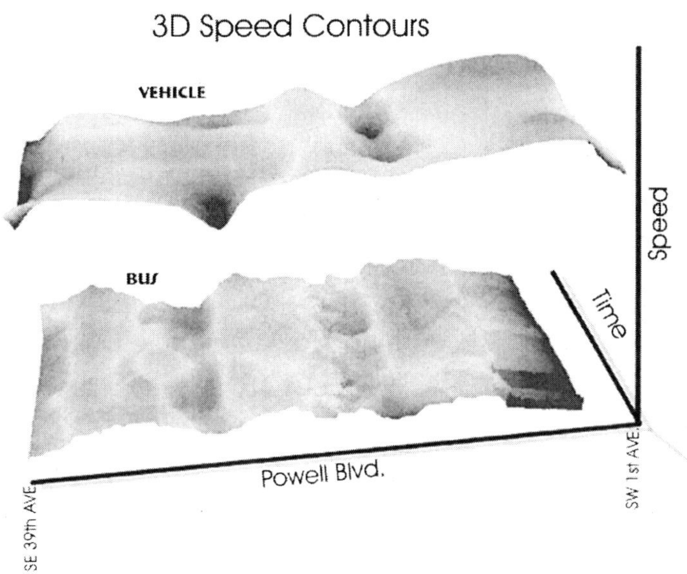

Figure 8. Interpolated 3D Surfaces Comparing Probe Vehicle and Bus Speeds

5.9 Emergency Management Systems

Emergency management systems are used by fire departments, police departments, ambulance services, and freeway service patrols. These systems respond to emergencies and direct the various departments to the incident location through the shortest path in order to clear the incident or save a life. These systems include traffic signal priority to give the right of way to the departments' vehicle. The emergency management systems use the AVL technology in order to locate the nearest vehicle and direct it to the incident. This system is managed by a transportation management center. The delivery of emergency service to the communities is an important responsibility that should be met when any person is facing an emergency.

A study of the Minnesota Highway Helper Program found that the program reduced the duration of a stall by eight minutes. Based upon representative numbers, annual benefits through reduced delay totaled $1.4 million for a program that cost $600,000 to operate. While in another pilot study looking at the Courtesy Patrol Program in Denver, Colorado, the estimates concluded a reduction cost in traffic delay by $0.8–$1.0 million for the morning period and by $0.90–$0.95 million in the evening. The study assumed a time value of $10 per hour. Program costs varied between the tow truck operators between $29 to $38 per truck-hour, which results in a benefit-to-cost ratio of 10.5:1 to 16.9:1 (USDOT, 2002a).

Table 3. Travel Time Comparison Between Bus and Probe Vehicle

Vehicle		Bus	
Departure Time	Travel Time	Departure Time	Actual Travel Time
7:05:15	0:42	7:00:22	0:58
7:08:54	0:46	7:02:52	0:53
7:18:21	0:38	7:08:16	0:49
7:32:48	0:35	7:16:18	0:49
7:38:06	0:43	7:23:04	0:50
7:56:15	0:35	7:30:24	1:02
7:59:45	0:41	7:35:06	0:54
8:22:12	0:32	7:49:10	0:47
8:44:03	0:42	7:54:22	1:07
8:49:30	0:34	8:05:20	1:05
9:01:03	0:48	8:21:00	0:44
9:07:54	0:32	8:23:04	0:49
9:18:30	0:37	8:48:14	0:55
9:22:03	0:33	9:10:24	0:49
9:35:00	0:34	9:20:24	0:45
9:36:21	0:33	9:35:06	0:46
9:49:42	0:39	9:52:06	0:46
9:50:30	0:31		
Mean	0:38		0:52
Variance	0.007		0.014
SD	0.085		0.119

5.10 Electronic Payment

Electronic payment systems are present on many of the highways in the U.S. Several DOTs are turning to toll collection in order to finance new roads and maintain existing highways. The congestion caused upstream of toll booths began to be a problem so the idea of electronic payments has emerged as an important response. Typically, drivers subscribe to an electronic payment system and are given radio frequency (RF) transponders that communicate with the toll collection system. Vehicles passing through the toll facility entrance and/or exit are not required to stop as their payment is automatically deducted from their accounts (Klein, 2001). Electronic payment is also used for collecting transit fares and commercial vehicle operating fees where the transponder can be used in various ways and it is linked to a bank account or credit card line. A typical manual toll lane might process 350 vehicles per hour while applying electronic payment on all lanes will result in about 1,200 vehicles per hour (ITE, 2000). If the toll plaza was eliminated the rate could be 2,000 vehicles per hour per lane. This application will save on both toll booth construction and administration fees.

5.11 Traveler Information

Traveler information systems are used to inform travelers regarding road conditions via broadcast media. The system collects data regarding the current status of the transportation network and broadcasts it to travelers via communication channels and media (McQueen et al., 1999) The objective is to provide travelers with current information so they can avoid congested routes. This kind of system tries to avoid the externalities caused by additional vehicles in the congested system. The communication system can be one-way or two-way where the vehicle will be equipped with GPS to identify the vehicle location and a traveler information center would direct the vehicle to an uncongested route. This system is known as a vehicle-motorist service information system (Hulse, Dingus, and Barfield, 1997). Several DOTs have started to apply similar systems and have begun to broadcast one-way communication to travelers via the radio and via the Internet. In Seattle, Washington, as shown in Figure 9, a Web-based traveler information system is available on the Internet (Washington Department of Transportation, 2002). The system is updated every minute. This kind of information system can also be implemented for transit. Several transit agencies have implemented Internet-based trip planners to transit riders. These trip planners save time and increase reliability to transit services.

5.12 Crash Prevention and Safety

In 1990, there were an estimated 16 million U.S. vehicle crashes. Forty-five thousand fatalities occurred during these crashes, along with 5.4 million nonfatal injuries and 28 million damaged vehicles. The average cost per crash is approximately $8,600. Crashes are mainly caused by human errors, including errors in recognition, decision, and performance. An ITS-based crash prevention and safety system will include an advisory crash avoidance system to alert the driver with a warning when the vehicle detects a crash is about to occur. This system can include an advisory system to indicate the optimum headway and the best speed (Dingus, et al., 1997). Vehicles can also be equipped with an in-vehicle safety and warning system where warnings of immediate hazards and road conditions affecting the roadway ahead of the driver are reported to the driver.

5.13 Operations and Maintenance

Operations and maintenance systems are created during the process of implementation of any ITS application to measure the success or the decline of the system. Operations and management systems are encouraged by the USDOT. The USDOT is responsible for monitoring 75 metropolitan areas in the U.S. that have deployed ITS and received federal funding for ITS investments. In addition, archived surveillance and performance data can be used later for generating various performance measures (Bertini and El-Geneidy, 2003; Bertini, Leal, and Lovell, 2002) and feeding performance data back into the planning process. Performance measures can lead to a better understanding of the existing system and the archived data can be used by various stakeholders in ways we cannot yet imagine. Collection of every single type of data needed for advanced traffic control for the entire traffic system is unrealistically costly and inefficient. Processing of disorderly and incomplete information reported from the field is usually complex and time consuming. (Klein, Yi, and Teng, 2002).

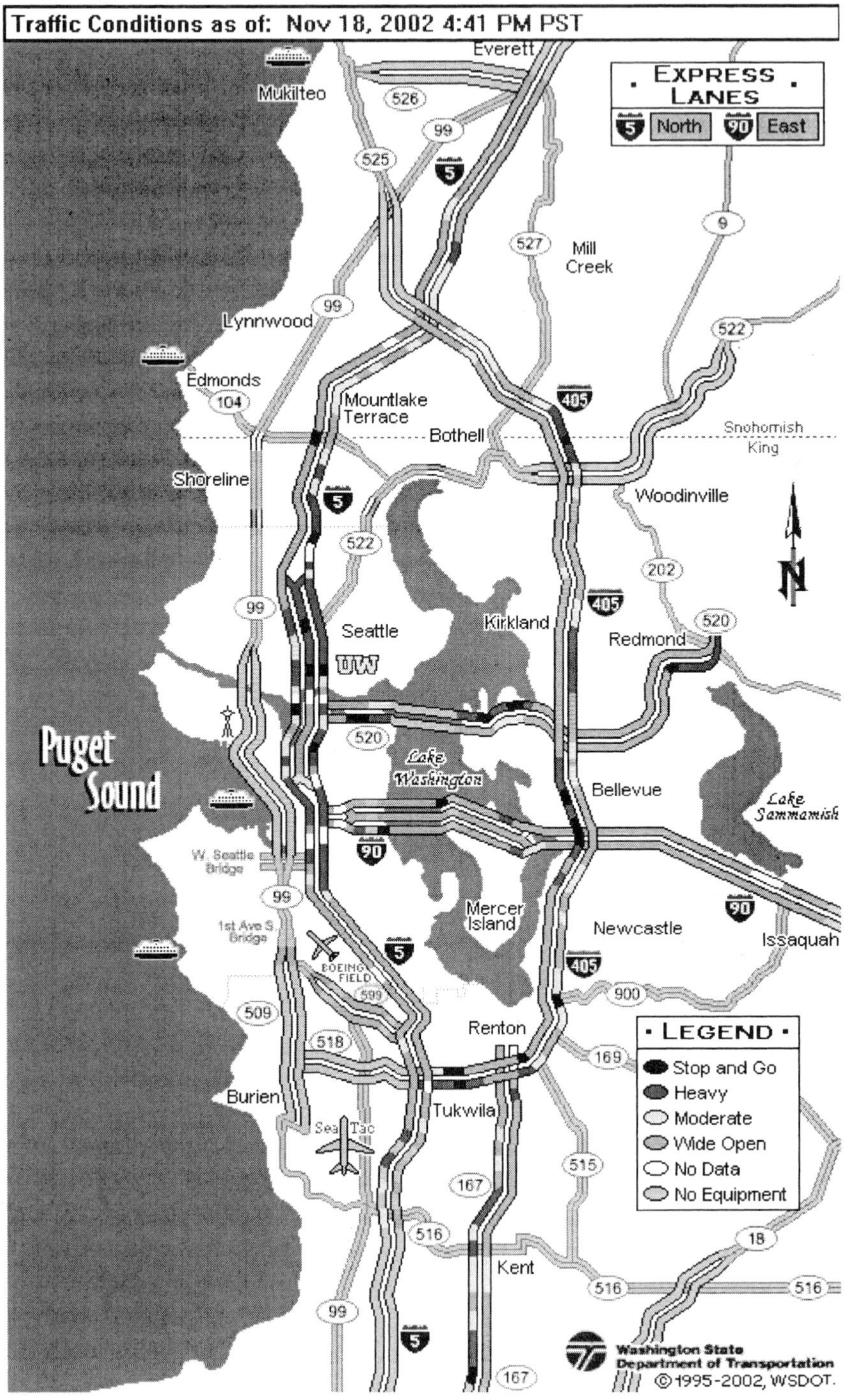

Figure 9. Seattle Online Freeway Condition Map

5.14 Road Weather Management

Weather impacts on transportation are pervasive. The weather can cause many incidents especially in the cold regions of the country. A study trying to quantify the benefits of an anti-icing program in seven different states in the United States was conducted in order to encourage the use of anti-icing/road weather information system technologies. Thc strategy of anti-icing involves the use of chemical freeze point depressants to prevent a bond from forming between pavement and snow or ice. NCHRP Project 20-7, Task 117 was initiated to address these needs and quantify the benefits (Boselly, 2001). The study concluded that the anti-icing program can reduce costs of providing a defined level of service by 10–20 percent, while the snow and ice control costs per lane mile can be reduced up to 50 percent.

6. CONCLUSIONS

After considering the 10 different ITS component systems it is clear that each system cannot be deployed to stand alone in the overall transportation system. Building a complete ITS system requires collaboration in time, funding, and institutional arrangements. ITS components that are integrated can result in synergistic effects when considered as an entire system. It is shown that in some cases it is possible to build upon national level statistics describing ITS benefits by using data collected from the systems themselves. Thus far, the quantification of ITS benefits has not been statistically sophisticated. Often, benefits are expressed as being "certain," when this is far from the truth. For example, the measurement of any reduction in mean travel time as a result of an ITS deployment involves bias; thus any benefit should be expressed along with its associated variance. In addition, there is no guarantee that travel time reduction due to the installation of ramp metering in one city will result in similar benefits in another city—particularly if the nature of system integration and institutional cooperation is widely different. It is hoped that further efforts to integrate transportation planning with evaluation tools such as IDAS and microsimulation will incorporate the necessary empirical results from a wide variety of studies. In this way, better databases can be developed, and heightened accountability will be more pervasive in the evaluation of ITS improvements.

ACKNOWLEDGEMENTS

The authors are indebted to numerous individuals for the provision of data and assistance in preparing this paper. Oregon Department of Transportation (ODOT) video and loop detector data were provided by Jack Marchant and Dennis Mitchell of ODOT Region 1. TriMet data were generously provided by Steve Callas of TriMet and Tom Kimpel and Prof. James Strathman of Portland State University. Sutti Tantiyanugulchai assisted with providing the Powell Blvd. data. Prof. David Levinson, University of Minnesota, kindly provided data from the ramp meter shutdown study and Shazia Malik of Portland State University assisted with processing the Minnesota data and gathering important background information.

REFERENCES

American Public Transit Association. *APTA Vehicle Data Book*, Washington, DC, 2001.

Bertini, R., Tantiyanugulchai, S., Anderson, E., Lindgren, R., Leal, M. "Evaluation of Region 2 Incident Response Program Using Archived Data," Portland State University, Transportation Research Group, Research Report, 2001.

Bertini, R. L., El-Geneidy, A. M. "Using Archived Data to Generate Transit Performance Measures," Washington DC, Transportation Research Board, Annual Meeting.

Bertini, R. L., Leal, M., Lovell, D. J. "Generating Performance Measures from Portland's Archived Advanced Traffic Management System Data," Washington DC, Transportation Research Board, Annual Meeting, 2002.

Boselly, E. "Benefit/Cost Study of RWIS and Anti-icing Technologies" (20-7(117)), Washington DC, National Cooperative Highway Research Program, Transportation Research Board, National Research Council, 2001.

Bureau of Transportation Statistics. *Omnibus Travel Survey, 2000.*

Cambridge Systematics, Inc. "Twin Cities Ramp Meter Evaluation Technical Report," Minneapolis, MN, Minnesota Department of Transportation, 2001.

Cambridge Systematics, Inc. "Intelligent Transportation Systems Deployment Analysis System," Software Documentation, 2002. Retrieved November 19, 2002, from http://idas.camsys.com.

Dingus, T. A., Jahns, S. K., Horowitz, A. D., Knipling, R. "Human Factors Design Issues in Crash Avoidance Systems," *Human Factors in Intelligent Transportation Systems,* W. Barfield and T. Dingus eds. Mahwah, NJ: Lawrence Erlbaum Association, Inc., 1997.

El-Geneidy, A. M., Bertini, R. L. "Integrating Geographic Information Systems and Intelligent Transportation Systems to Improve Incident Management and Life Safety," the 8th International Conference on Computers in Urban Planning and Urban Management Conference, Sendai, Japan, 2003.

Evanco, W. M. "A Data Fusion Framework for Meta-evaluation of Intelligent Transportation System Effectiveness" (Report 0495 18B40A), MITRE working note, Center for Information Systems, 1996. Retrieved November 19, 2002, from http://plan2op.fhwa.dot.gov/pdfs/Pdf1/Edl04454.pdf

Hourdakis, J., Michalopoulos P. G. "Evaluation of Ramp Control Effectiveness in Two Twin Cities Freeways," Washington DC, Transportation Research Board, Annual Meeting, 2002

Hulse, M. C., Dingus, T. A., Barfield, W. "Description and Application of Advanced Traveler Information Systems," *Human Factors in Intelligent Transportation Systems*, W. Barfield and T. Dingus eds. Mahwah, NJ: Lawrence Erlbaum Association, Inc, 1997.

Institute of Transportation Engineers. *Intelligent Transportation Primer*, Washington, DC, Institute of Transportation Engineers, 2000.

Ishimaru, J., Hallenbeck, M. E. "FLOW Evaluation Design Technical Report," Washington State Transportation Center (TRAC), 1999.

Ishimaru, J., Hallenbeck, M. E., Nee, J. "Central Puget Sound Freeway Network Usage and Performance," Washington State Transportation Center (TRAC), 2001, 1999 update.

Klein, L. A. *Sensor Technologies and Data Requirements for ITS,* Norwood, MA: Artech House (Intelligent transportation systems library), 2001.

Klein, L., Yi, P., Teng, H. "Decision Support System for Advanced Traffic Management through Data Fusion and Mining," Washington, DC, Transportation Research Board, Annual Meeting, 2002.

Levinson, D., Zhang, L., Das, S., Sheikh, A. "Ramp Meters on Trial: Evidence from the Twin Cities Ramp Meters Shut-off," Washington DC, Transportation Research Board, Annual Meeting, 2002.

McQueen, B., McQueen, J. *Intelligent Transportation Systems Architecture,* Norwood, MA: Artech House (Intelligent transportation systems library), 1999.

Nee, J., Ishimaru, J., Hallenbeck, M. E. "HOV Lane Performance Monitoring: 2000 Report," Washington State Transportation Center (TRAC), 2001.

Northeast-Midwest Institute. "Roads and Highways," 2002. Retrieved November, 18, 2002 from http://www.nemw.org/roadshighways.htm.

Peng, Z., Beimborn, E., Neluheni M. "A Framework for the Evaluation of the Benefits of Intelligent Transportation Systems" (Report). Milwaukee, WI, Center for Urban Transportation Studies, University of Wisconsin Milwaukee, 2000 Retrieved November 19, 2002, from http://www.uwm.edu/Dept/CUTS/its/itsb121.pdf.

Proper, A. T., Maccubbin, R. "ITS Benefits: Data Needs Update 2000," 2000. Prepared in connection with the 12th July ITS Benefits Data Needs Workshop, Mitretek Systems.

Schrank, D., Lomax, T. "The 2002 Urban Mobility Report," Texas Transportation Institute, Texas A&M University System, 2002. Retrieved November 18, 2002 from http://mobility.tamu.edu.

Skabardonis, A., Noeimi, H., Petty, K., Rydzewski, D., Varaiya, P., Al-Deek, H. "Freeway Service Patrol Evaluation," University of California at Berkeley, California, PATH Research Report, UCB-ITS-PRR-95-5, 1995.

Skabardonis, A., Petty, K., Varaiya, P. P., Bertini, R. L. "The Los Angeles Freeway Service Patrol Evaluation," University of California at Berkeley, California PATH Research Report, UCB-ITS-PRR-98-31, 1998.

Strathman, J. G., Kimpel, T. J., Dueker, K. J., Gerhart, R. L., Turner, K., Griffin, D., Callas, S. "Bus Transit Operation Control: Review and an Experiment Involving TriMet's Automated Bus Dispatching System" (Paper 01-0438), Washington, DC, Transportation Research Board, Annual Meeting, 2002.

Strathman, J. G., Dueker, K. J., Kimpel, T., Gerhart, R., Turner, K., Taylor, P., Callas, S., Griffin, D., Hopper, J. "Automated Bus Dispatching, Operations Control, and Service Reliability," *Transportation Research Record,* 1666, 1999, 28–36.

Strathman, J. G., Kimpel, T. J., Dueker, K. J., Gerhart, R. L., Turner, K., Taylor, G., Griffin, D. "Service Reliability Impacts of Computer-aided Dispatching and Automatic Vehicle Location Technology: A TriMet Case Study," *Transportation Quarterly*, Vol. 54, No. 3, 2000, 85–102.

Sundeen, M. "The Expanding Role of Intelligent Transportation Systems," National Conference of State Legislatures, 2002. Retrieved November 18, 2002, from http://www.ncsl.org/programs/esnr/ITStranrev02.htm.

United States Department of Transportation (USDOT). "ITS Benefits and Unit Cost Database, 2002a." Retrieved November 18, 2002, from http://www.benefitcost.its.dot.gov/its/benecost.nsf/ByLink/deskReference

United States Department of Transportation (USDOT). "Measuring ITS Deployment and Integration" (Electronic Document Number (4372)), U.S. Department of Transportation, Joint Program Office for Intelligent Transportation Systems, 2002b. Retrieved November 18, 2002.

Washington State Department of Transportation. "Puget Sound Traffic Conditions," 2002. Retrieved November 18, 2002, from http://www.wsdot.wa.gov/PugetSoundTraffic/.

Zografos, K. G., Androutsopoulos, K. N., Vasilakis, G. M. "A Real-time Decision Support System for Roadway Network Incident Response Logistics," *Transportation Research Part C,* Vol. 10, 2002, 1–18.

Chapter 16

ITS IN EUROPE

An Economic Evaluation

Reinaldo C. Garcia
Department of Energy, Transportation, and Environment:
German Institute for Economic Research

This chapter provides an economics analysis of Intelligent Transport Systems (ITS) in Europe. Descriptions of ITS applications covering all modes of transport (road, rail, air, navigation) are provided, including the European Global Navigation Satellite project, the Galileo project. The chapter concludes discussing the future of ITS technologies in Europe, regarding its integration across organizations and modes.

1. INTRODUCTION

Public authorities and private organizations seek new solutions to the challenges faced on today's transport network, as mobility management presents an increasingly difficult task. With major infrastructure investment reaching its limits, Intelligent Transport Systems (ITS) are a viable solution to make the movement of people and goods more efficient and economical for all transport modes. By integrating information, communication, and control devices, ITS technologies enable authorities, operators, and travelers to be better informed and to take coordinated decisions.

Intelligent Transport Systems are vital for the development of a European transport policy requiring better use of its existing transport infrastructure. ITS applications cover all modes of transport providing a vast range of services:

- in the management of road, rail, air, waterborne, and urban traffic including: advanced information for users, traffic control, incident management, and vehicle safety and control systems;
- in the management of public transport, freight movements, and other fleet applications;

- in the electronic payment and the enforcement of regulations;
- in the planning of policy-making activities.

Intelligent Transport Systems are a key enabler for the integration of different transport modes to provide door-to-door transport services. ITS has the capability to enable travelers and freight distributors to avoid delay, increasing the productivity of their transport operations. Moreover, ITS alternatives may have lower acquisition and life cycle costs compared to traditional transportation improvements (Federal Highway Administration, 2001.)

The potential of Intelligent Transport Systems encouraged the European Union (EU) to make them an integral part of its common Transport Policy establishing a coordinated European ITS infrastructure. ITS applications are claimed to provide an essential contribution for sustainable European development, improving the safety, and decreasing the environmental costs of the transport sector. Particularly, ITS technologies such as satellite navigation and positioning systems, and advanced traffic and management systems are designed to improve overall transport efficiency and safety.

This chapter presents a discussion of the implementation of Intelligent Transport Systems in Europe. Section 2 describes the implementation of ITS in urban road traffic management. Section 3 presents the ITS technologies in the rail transport sector discussing issues of interoperability among the different European countries. Section 4 describes ITS applications for the air transport sector, including an ITS pilot project. Section 5 examines the ITS technologies for the shipping industry, not only for maritime but also for inland navigation systems. Section 6 presents the European Global Navigation Satellite project, the *Galileo* project, and its central role as an ITS technology for all transport sectors. The chapter concludes with an analysis and major expectations regarding ITS technologies for the European transport sector.

2. ITS TECHNOLOGIES IN THE EUROPEAN ROAD TRANSPORT SECTOR

In urban areas where more capacity is needed, it is becoming impossible, for a number of reasons, to build enough new roads or new lanes to meet transport demand. By applying the latest technological advances to transport systems, ITS can help meet increasing demand for road transport by improving quality, safety, and effective capacity of the existing infrastructure.

Intelligent Transport Systems in the road transport sector represent a wide collection of applications, from advanced signal control systems to ramp meters and collision systems. Some ITS technologies provide more cost-effective benefits than others, and as the technology evolves, the choices facing deployers change. Several technologies can be combined in a single integrated system, providing synergistic benefits that exceed the benefits of any single technology. As current research in the United States suggests, it is important to know which ITS technologies provide the greatest benefits to meet the growing transportation demands of the expanding economy (USDOT, 2000.)

Recent research shows that implementing ITS systems through pricing transport services has a strong potential impact on policy goals, including road pricing, infrastructure tolling and road usage by heavy goods vehicle (DIW and FAV, 2002; Clement, 2002.) Suggested priorities for the European Union (EU) road pricing policy focus on the introduction of electronic license plates and on the compatibility of electronic payment systems. Electronic road pricing clearly has a European dimension, originating from the need to guarantee interoperability among the different countries. It is crucial to apply similar electronic road pricing systems all over Europe, avoiding cross border stops. Due to the different degrees of implementation of electronic road pricing, the EU requested the convergence of different systems, as major European cities are bracing themselves for a broad introduction of road pricing.

London became one of the largest cities in the world to apply road pricing when in February 2003, London introduced a toll of £5 ($7.80) per day for most drivers entering an inner zone of about 26 km^2 (10 mi^2). Its charge was adopted following a Road Charging Options for London (Rocol) study estimating that a £5 a day charge would lead to a 10 percent reduction in traffic congestion. Nevertheless, London is not the first city in the world to do so, as Singapore introduced a paper-based road-pricing scheme in the 1970s that went electronic in 1998. Afterwards, cities like Oslo, Bergen, and Trondheim in Norway, and many parts of the United States have also implemented different forms of electronic road pricing.

London's scheme, which has faced legal challenges and huge controversy, hopes to raise a net of £160 million a year, which will pay for improvements in public transport (Financial Times, 2002.) London's system relies on cameras scanning the license plates of cars entering the tolling zone. London authorities will not be limited simply to a flat rate charge for motorists. Charges can be altered according to the time of entry to the zone, reducing peak-hour congestion, as well as to the engine-type, encouraging greener vehicles. At first, London's scheme will be kept relatively simple, exempting some types of vehicles and discounts for those living inside the zone. Government officials are also working on a national lorry (truck) charge, which could be more complex than London's road pricing scheme.

Road pricing for vehicles weighing 12 metric tons or more using the German federal motorway will be introduced by January 2003 (Figure 1.) The German Federal Ministry of Transport, Housing and Construction will impose a distance-related road charge applying two possible Global Positioning Systems (GPS): Toll Collect or Ages systems. Toll Collect applies on an onboard electronic unit making it possible to calculate the distance driven on motorways by tracing the GPS-signals of the vehicle. Toll Collect is being proposed by a consortium involving Telekom, Daimler Chrysler, and Cofiroute. Ages is similar to the Toll Collect system but requires a pre-paid smart card inserted into a special reader in the vehicle GPS-receiver. Ages is being proposed by a consortium involving Vodafone, Aral, and Shell. The introduction of each system has an estimated production cost of $400 per unit.

A recent study evaluated the collected revenues implementing three similar scenarios for the German toll collect system (DIW and FAV, 2002.) The scenarios apply charges of 0.08/km, 0.13/km, and 0.20/km assuming an increase of two percent per year of the kilometer growth rate for the first scenario and, decreases of three to four percent for the other scenarios. Under these scenarios, the collected estimated revenues vary from $2 billion to $6 billion per year by 2005. Even though the forecasted estimates must be treated with caution, they show the potential to collect huge revenues when applying a toll collection system. An intense debate exists about how to apply the collected revenues. According to German federal law, collected road pricing revenues through tolling of Heavy Goods Vehicles (HGV) cannot exceed the corresponding infrastructure costs. Nevertheless, there are few constraints to using the collected revenues for other transport modes including rail, aviation, or shipping. Other European countries are experiencing similar political debates concerning road pricing policies.

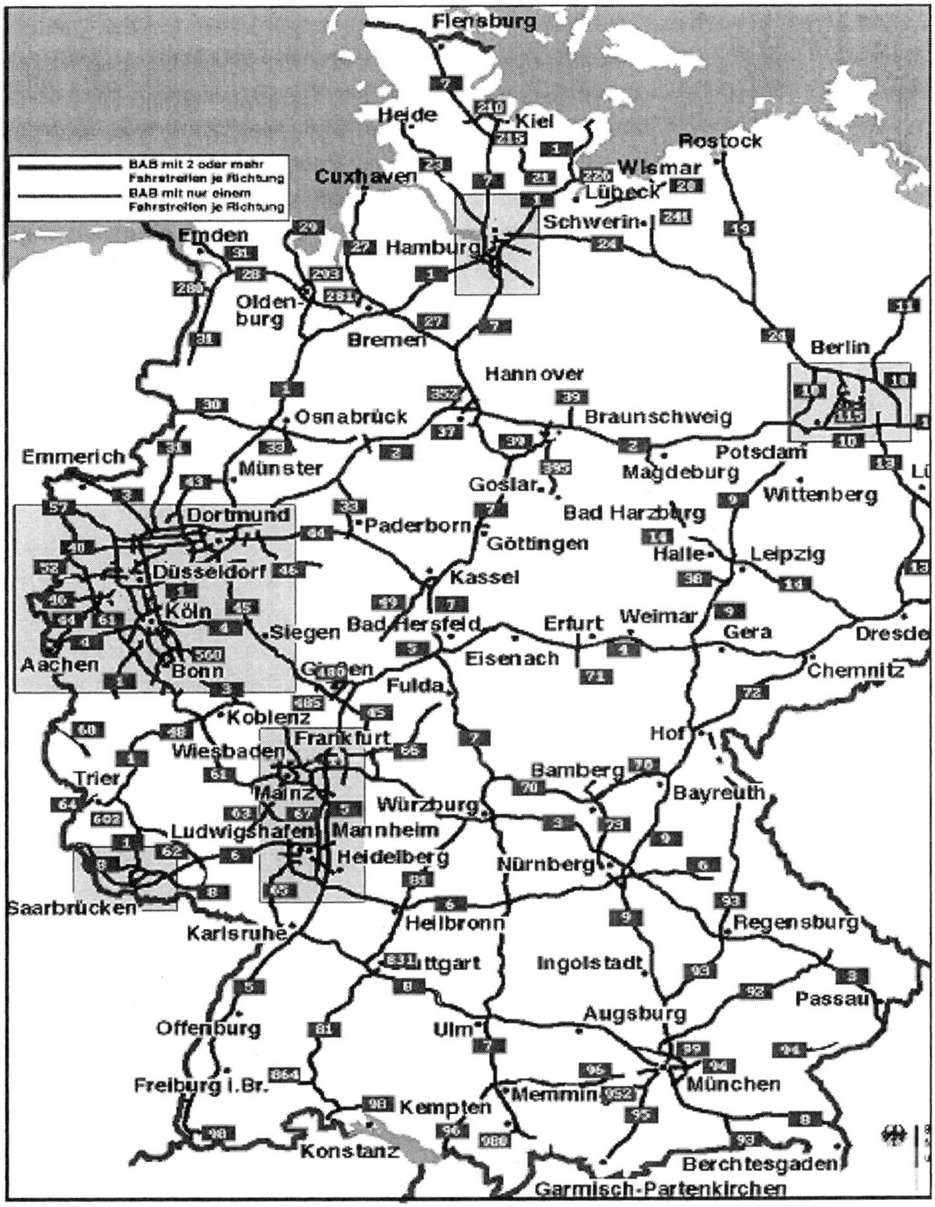

Figure 1. Federal Motorways – Germany, 2001 (Source: German Federal Ministry of Transport, Housing and Construction.)

The new Dutch government halted implementation of a 2002 national road charging scheme. The pricing scheme would have gone beyond tolls on individual roads and cities. The Dutch government would replace transportation taxes Dutch drivers currently pay with a system charging drivers based on how much they drive. Presently, Dutch drivers pay a 25 percent sales tax on new cars, and a vehicle tax based on the price and weight of the car and the type of fuel used. With the technology known as MobilMiles, all these taxes would be replaced by a system that uses GPS and other wireless technologies to charge drivers on a pay-as-you-go basis. Drivers would be charged a flat price per kilometer but later fees would depend on road categories and time of day. The implemented pricing scheme would rise to $6 billion per year. The main obstacle for the Dutch road pricing implementation was the possible reaction of the drivers to the proposed system.

Tolls can be controversial as the higher they are, the more likely they are to deter motorists. A recent project, applying road pricing in two test sites located in Norway and England, estimated a 10 percent reduction in peak period traffic in Trondheim, Norway, and a 15–20 percent decrease in daily car travel in Bristol, England (Hayes, 2002.) While the reduction in auto use in Trondheim was due mainly to drivers changing their time of travel, the reductions in Bristol were attributed to drivers switching to public transport. One can say that acceptance of congestion prices will depend on the magnitude of the tolls and the availability of alternatives for those who would be "tolled off."

Recent European projects are testing other ITS management measures, including bus priority at traffic lights and the use of automatic vehicle location technology (Rochez, 2001; Rochez, 2000; Mike, 2001.) Guidelines formulate the operation of fully integrated traffic management systems, combining traffic control, public transport management, and driver information. Optimizing the timing of traffic signals showed a 25 percent decrease in peak-hour delay in the city of York, England. Intelligent Transport Systems also support transit agencies that aim to increase their safety and the operational efficiency. Automated vehicle location and driver information systems were tested in European cities including London, England; Gothenburg, Sweden; Turin, Italy; and Piraeus, Greece (Rochez, 2000). Bus location data obtained from automated vehicle location systems provided bus headway information and detection, complementing bus loop detector data. Bus headway data applied a selective priority approach where buses having the greatest headway (i.e., running late) were selected for full priority, while other buses with lower headway received lower priority. The detector bus priority system costs €15,000 per junction and €150 per bus for London. The cost savings resulted from a reduction of passenger waiting times in the bus stops, and analyses are being made to better evaluate the monetary benefits for the users. Further savings in the transport sector can be obtained extending ITS applications to intermodalism (Rochez, 2000.)

Intermodal transport systems require the exchange of information between operators and their customers. ITS can enable more effective planning, helping travelers and distributors to avoid delays and congestion, increasing the productivity of transport operations (European Commission, 2001.) Cooperative information systems with Internet-based communication interfaces provide services including booking and shipment status information. These new ITS systems can improve not only the quality of road transport but rail transport as well.

3. ITS TECHNOLOGIES IN THE EUROPEAN RAIL SECTOR

Recent years have seen a continuous decrease in the share of rail for European freight transport. Even in long-distance transport, owing to better road infrastructure and vehicle efficiency and interoperability, rail freight transport has not achieved comparable results to the road transport sector. The quality of road services was improved by new infrastructure like fast motorways, reliable vehicles, freight tracking, and flexible management. Even though the rail achievements have not been as significant, recent European experience suggests that under appropriate policies, the rail system can compete with the road sector.

The deployment of harmonized systems for communication and train control and the creation of trans-European traffic management facilities are vital for the integration of the European rail network, as they will create a rational European network, increasing the quality of the rail services and their flexibility for the benefit of passengers and freight customers (improving travelling time and reducing costs.) Intense European funding has been devoted to formulating the telecommunication systems of the rail networks. ITS technologies applied to train-ground information exchange, and to systems for fleet and infrastructure management significantly reduce the costs and improve the quality of freight transport. Concepts and strategies for intelligent freight trains include train identification, electronic braking, and train integrity checking. Additional technologies provide information, automation, and cargo monitoring functions. A rail traffic management system aims to improve real-time rail dispatching and route planning, flow at rail nodes, and the customer and operating staff satisfaction (Barbu, 1999.) Furthermore, the pan-European traffic management system will improve the reliability of international trains reaching their destinations in a timely manner, implementing a profitable ITS application in the short term.

European projects involving international rail networks must deal with all countries involved, as each country owns its own rail system (Leboeuf, 2000.) A pilot project implemented an ITS technology for the corridor Tauro-Giao-Gothard-Rotterdam involving Italy, Switzerland, Germany, and Holland (Figure 2.) The implemented technology improved interoperability of the trans-European rail network and optimized the rail operations on a Europe-wide scale. The analysis compared the existing situation with a scenario where ITS was implemented and operated in the described rail corridor. The analysis assumed that the system was owned by a consortium of infrastructure

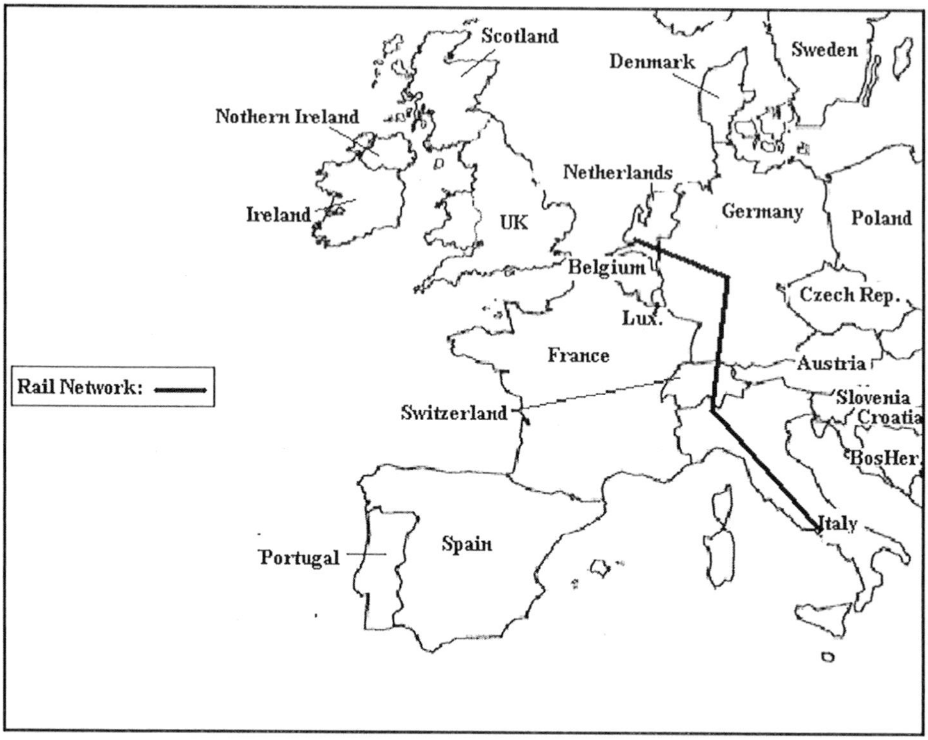

Figure 2. Rail Network: Rotterdam, Gothard, Giao and Tauro Route Representation

entities. The infrastructure managers operating the system would receive financial benefits through fares paid by trains using the corridor. Under these scenarios, the implemented ITS system would earn a rate of return of 10 percent over 30 years. Further integration among the communications of the different European countries is necessary to apply any new ITS system.

The European communications policy for train control developed an integrated system based on Global System Mobile (GSM) communications to support rail traffic management applications. Recent research has specified the architecture of the European Rail Traffic Management System (ERTMS), applicable to international railway corridors (Mertens, 1999.) Intelligent tools supporting train-ground information exchange, and fleet and infrastructure management systems significantly improved the costs and the quality of rail freight transport.

The new European standard for railway communications technology (GSM-R) supports a diversity of uses ranging from operational to safety-related control systems. It makes a significant contribution to the overall interoperability of the European railway networks. GSM-R has the potential to provide new value-added services to the customer, and to support rail maintenance and operations, enabling the rail sector to compete more effectively. ITS applications are reviving the rail sector and increasing its competitiveness. High-speed rail on distances of up to 1,000 km is becoming competitive on downtown-to-downtown journeys. ITS technologies have enabled rail to compete with air transport, compelling the air transport sector to improve its efficiency.

4. ITS TECHNOLOGIES IN THE EUROPEAN AIR TRANSPORT SECTOR

European Air Traffic Management (ATM) is characterized by a set of problems causing safety, capacity, and economic shortfalls in the air traffic sector. The predicted future growth in air traffic may be hindered by problems such as the increase in congestion on the ground and in the air, and the increase in noise levels at the airports and surrounding sites. The high density of air traffic in the core area and the complex airspace structure create delays with an already unacceptable associated cost. Moreover, European air traffic demand will double within the next 10 years, and nothing changing, this situation will cause safety and congestion problems (Suarez, 2000.)

Air traffic growth requires a more efficient use of existing capacity in the air transport system. The increased traffic at airports, coupled with constraints on constructing new runways, calls for more efficient use of existing ground infrastructure. Intelligent Transport Systems such as the Airport Surface Movement Guidance and Control System (A-SMGCS) have been developed to enable the integrated management of ground movements at and around airports (Monzel, 2000.) Moreover, new ITS tools will also allow the daily operational plan of the air traffic sector, including enroute air traffic, to be a dynamic process. ITS tools such as the Traffic Load Analyzer or Medium Term Conflict Detection will be fed with more precise data updated in real time (Suarez, 2000.) There will be a shift of tasks and new roles will emerge around flight planning, reducing the traffic complexity in the air sector and the workload of the air traffic controller. To achieve an improved European ATM system in the medium term, between 2005 and 2010, critical functions and operational services were identified in the areas of free-flight operations, terminal area sequencing, airport operations control, and gate-to-gate aircraft flight management.

Exchanging available data to ensure the effective distribution of information and decision-making will ensure a more efficient use of the available capacity. A recent study allocated most importance to system functionalities increasing peak hour capacity at airports, minimizing the delay of flights and reducing controller workload (Monzel, 2000.) A simulator was designed and implemented for an automated A-SMGCS. Project demonstrations were completed at several airports: Cologne/Bonn, Germany; Paris/Orly, France; Braunschweig, Germany; and Bergamo, Italy. Before installing the full system at the Cologne/Bonn airport, the three other airports served as test sites for technology-specific trials.

A pilot guiding system using switchable signs was set up in Orly. Whenever a controller confirmed the taxiing route suggested by the system, the data were directly transmitted to display panels located along the route. This method reduced radio communication and taxi time. The demonstration system was fully installed at the Cologne/Bonn airport. Potential conflict situations between aircraft, or aircraft and vehicles could be displayed, and early avoidance actions taken.

ITS applications are being applied to decrease the noise levels at airports and their surroundings, and to change the approach and take-off procedures of commercial aircraft. Improved flight procedures have been developed and validated at the airports of Amsterdam (Schiphol), Madrid (Barrajas), and Napoli (Capodichino) (Stephane, 2001.) Definitions of new approach and take-off procedures, and implementation of supporting tools for air traffic controllers and pilots are being developed. Procedures for noise abatement include increased final altitude approach with advanced ITS applications of continuous descent approach, and delayed flaps or gear extension. A cost-benefit analysis is difficult to make as trials are still evaluating the proposed procedures. The planned Instrument Landing System (ILS) has an estimated annual cost of €13.5 million per airport, including maintenance and operating costs. Benefits can be achieved not only by noise reduction but also by an increase in airport capacity.

Recent projects are examining ITS contributions to increase safety among airline pilots (Roessingh, 2001.) Advanced glass cockpits in modern commercial aircraft shifted the pilot's role, which is now reflected in crew training procedures. To deal with the pilot's increasingly supervisory tasks in the new working environment, adequate training schemes allow a high degree of automated functions according to standardized operational rules. A set of real-life incident scenarios and an assessment of simulations by performing tests with British Airways pilots are addressing human factors related to flight operations safety (Roessingh, 2001.)

A well-functioning air traffic system must be seen as an integral block for future sustainable growth in the European Union and neighboring countries. The three main areas of market, environment, and regulation are addressed providing a harmonized, deregulated, and liberalized air transport market. Growing demand in air transport will require more focus on enhanced efficiency in using existing infrastructure and aircraft, reduction of environmental impacts such as noise and emissions, and securing and improving air transport safety standards. Similar issues have to be addressed for the navigation transport sector when applying ITS technologies.

5. ITS TECHNOLOGIES IN THE EUROPEAN NAVIGATION TRANSPORT SECTOR

The exact positional data between ships and European shores dates back to 1951 when the first radar station was set up in Liverpool, England. Since then, Europe decided to identify the needs for information services aiming to enhance the cooperation between ships and shore to the benefit of navigation safety, protection of the environment, and the efficiency of navigation traffic.

In the 1980s, basic definitions such as Vessel Traffic Systems (VTS) external and internal functions were established. Conceptual tools such as the model of the ship navigation decision process and the involvement of VTS were designed and tested. By the 1990s, a number of Vessel Traffic Systems had already been implemented throughout Europe, becoming clear that its implementation had technical and legal limitations. The technical limitations resulted from the restricted range of radar and the lack of exchange of digitized information between ships and shore. The legal and administrative limitations arose due to the national jurisdictions operating VTS cover only territorial waters, and because the impact of vessel traffic management on the economy of transport, a matter for private industry, is not equally perceived throughout Europe as a possible theme for cooperation between private and public entities.

European Vessel Traffic Management and Information Systems (VTMIS) have focused on traffic management, with an emphasis on safe navigation. Measures to improve shipping safety require justification and careful evaluation regarding effectiveness and efficiency. Effective shore-based management, monitoring, and control of shipping imply that VTMIS must be located in the most suitable areas capturing and collecting traffic data. A Vessel Traffic Service has been specified and put in a mobile shelter. The mobile shelter measures traffic in different places simply by connecting a VTS system with an analysis tool evaluating traffic flow and density (Doussin, 2001.) The project defines a communication standard operated between a weather forecasting and a fishing monitoring system. The demonstration shows that different technology systems are able to communicate with the Evaluation and Traffic Flow (EPTO) tool using standardized messages. Tracks are visualized on the VTS displays and on the EPTO screen with traffic statistics being computed. Environmental data are sent to EPTO by the weather forecast system concurrently.

Studies to make intermodal transport more attractive show information exchange to be needed between operators and customers. This requires the development of standardized solutions for electronic data interchange (EDI) and methods for information transfer. A framework has been developed for the optimal control of cargo inflows and infrastructure (Froese, 2000; Heijden, 2000.) The framework of the Vessel Traffic Management and

Information Systems provides pan-European methods to exchange information between existing systems. Particularly, the functions of the River Information Systems (RIS) concept were detailed including voyage, terminal, and lock planning services.

Policies have been drawn to improve the safety on inland rivers and to increase the commercial benefits of the skipper reducing his workload (Broeke, 2000; Heijden, 2000.) Specifications have been defined to manage the information flows between a vessel and the shore, or another vessel. An architecture was then developed for information flows aboard a vessel, providing the skipper with the applications needed to exploit River Information Systems. A traffic simulation program was used to analyze the efficiency and safety of vessel traffic flows applying VTMIS. Simplified models of navigators and maneuvering of inland navigation vessels were implemented. Safety considerations for the simulations were based on an accident database for the river Waal in the Netherlands, and an analysis of the way elements of a RIS technology could have prevented accidents was also made.

The simulation program provided interesting results regarding the number of interactions. Interactions are encounters where one of the vessels has to make a small maneuver to ensure safe overtaking and passing distances. A failure to implement the right maneuver would lead to a collision. Even though estimated total accident costs must be treated with caution, in the analyzed scenario they were estimated to be over \$2 million (Froese, 2000.) The estimated costs did not consider some effects such as damage done to the environment by collisions between vessels carrying hazardous materials. For example, assuming that all licensed vessels would be fitted with VTMIS applications, the simulations estimated a reduction of 20 percent in the costs for this case studied.

Terminal optimization requires the introduction of new ITS technologies focusing on transshipment techniques and on the consequences for interoperability of other transport equipment. Freight transshipment at nodal points adds costs and transport time to the door-to-door movement of freight, representing one of the main bottlenecks in intermodal transport. The efficiency of the transfer between ships and land transport modes is vital to integrate shipping transport into European transport networks. A pilot plan for automated handling of freight produced prototypes of new wagons for efficient handling of intermodal transport units (Pedersen, 2000.) The cost estimates consisted of the cost allocation for the ITS terminal and for the ITS ship. Moreover, the cost estimates for the ITS implementation included infrastructure, personnel, and overhead and financial costs. This case scenario assumed a terminal with an annual capacity of 876,000 TEU (Twenty-foot Equivalent Units, a standard container size), equivalent to three daily arrivals and departures of a 400 TEU vessel 365 days per year. The total annual cost for the ITS implementation in the terminal was estimated at \$16 million. The introduction of the ITS system to a container terminal raised the annual productivity per employee by 400 percent, from 1,000 TEU to 5,000 TEU per employee.

The ITS terminal concept just described has the potential for lower investment requirements and higher efficiency than other port-ship transshipment systems. ITS technologies supporting all different modes of transport can have a significant impact in the competitiveness of the European economy. The Galileo European project can be considered one such ITS technology where all modes of transport can benefit from Galileo's implementation.

6. GALILEO ITS TECHNOLOGY

The European transport program has developed the Galileo system for the integration of information, communication, and navigation technologies in the transport sector. Galileo is a core element of a future Global Navigation Satellite System providing positioning, navigation, and precision timing services worldwide. It is being developed by Europe, with Russian participation, and it will replace the current European navigation systems when operational in 2008. Galileo will have an open access service free of user charges, offering a modern Global Positioning System (GPS). Galileo will also have a controlled access service offering guarantee and liability. The European Union identified the need for Galileo due to the high integrity and guarantee levels required for many transport applications, and to avoid reliance on U.S.-controlled GPS satellites.

Markets for commercial applications applying Galileo technologies already exist in all modes of transport. The forecast market for value-added applications in road segment is expected to rise from \$5 billion to \$40 billion between 2002 and 2020 (Campagne, 2000.) In aviation, rail, and maritime segments, the market is forecast to be \$900 million, \$680 million, and \$50 million by 2020, respectively (Campagne, 2000.) The forecasts have been used to assess the potential recoverable costs as a percentage of benefits for end users with Galileo's implementation. Benefits for end users are defined as the reduction of costs, or increase of profits, by applying satellite navigation systems. The future benefits were assessed performing interviews with end users, organizations, and experts.

The European annual benefits due to satellite navigation applications are estimated at \$15 billion in 2008, increasing to \$53 billion in 2017. The potential recoverable costs are equal to the increase of turnover by European industry from the sales of open access service receivers and controlled access application equipment. The potential recoverable costs were estimated at \$1.5 billion in 2008, increasing to \$7.6 billion in 2017 (Campagne, 2000.) The Galileo investors can retrieve their investment by a general levy on the worldwide sales of receivers and equipments. Key Galileo economics variables still to be examined include the potential payment structure, the risk factors, and the financing mechanism.

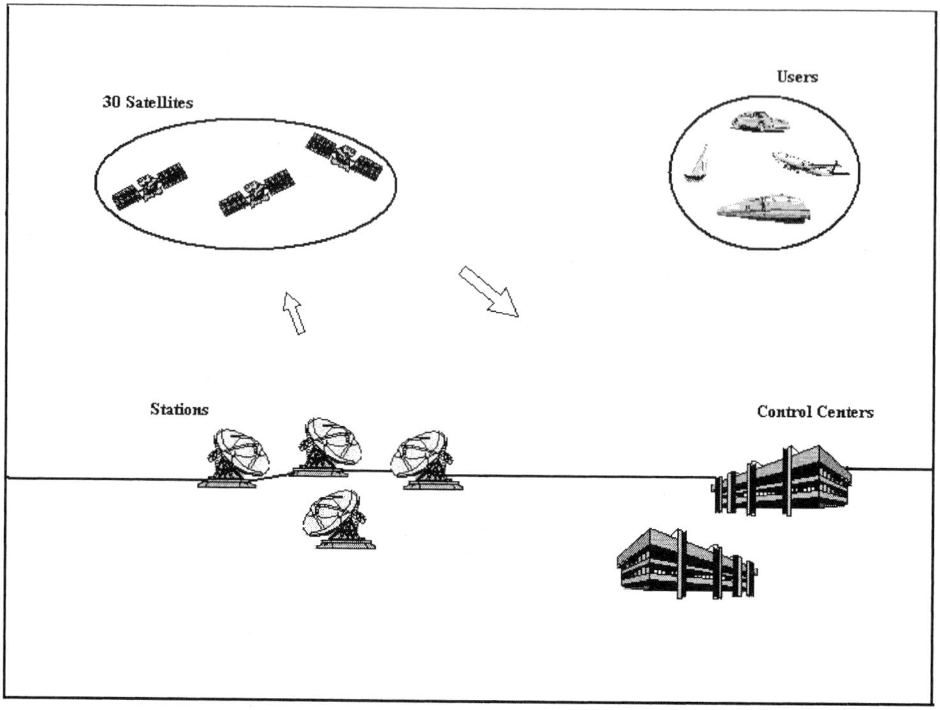

Figure 3. Galileo Program: 30 Satellites, Users, Control Centers, Link-up Stations

Financial mechanisms analyzed the joint ventures, and shared and private concessions involved when implementing the Galileo system. Joint ventures seem to be suitable for the design phase as risk factors are difficult to allocate. Shared concessions seem to be suitable for the building phase because the need for cash flow increases and no market revenues are generated. Private concessions are substantial for the operation phase when there is a decrease in risks and an increase in cash flow. The identification of the market, the analysis of the potential benefits, and the possibility to recover costs help in deciding among the different options for public-private partnerships.

The services offered by the integration of satellite navigation systems into transport have a great potential to support transport efficiency, a priority for the European Union. This leads to an important market for commercial applications in all transport modes where the number of potential users is extremely important, where a large demand already exists, and where the development of positioning systems based on Galileo seems promising. The identification of the market, the analysis of the potential benefits, and the possibility to recover the costs from those value-added services will contribute to the feasibility of a self-financing Global Positioning System in the medium term, and to assess the different options for a public-private partnership. In that context, the European ITS projects are providing appropriate information to take these relevant decisions.

7. CONCLUSIONS

Rapidly growing traffic in transport will have serious impacts on safety, reliability, efficiency, and the environment over the next decades. ITS research and technology development have been analyzed to make improvements on all of these fronts, for all modes of transport. Intelligent Transport Systems are also a key enabler to integrate different transport modes providing door-to-door transport services.

To integrate and to improve the efficiency of the different European modes of transport, a coordinated European policy for ITS implementation has been established. Identification processes, mainly based on pilot fields and intense research, have examined a broad range of possible ITS applications. The ITS market structure has also been defined in terms of a market user's unit in each transport sector, which can be furnished with ITS commercial applications and value-added services.

Recent projects estimated the ITS market in monetary terms using current market prices, and a technology-driven approach for assessing value added services. Studies involving cost-benefit analysis describe the potential economic benefits of ITS applications. Private entities are being encouraged to participate in ITS developments, reducing and spreading the financial risks and investment needed by the public sector.

The emphasis in ITS development is to apply technologies that integrate the operation and management of transport and logistic systems, across organizations and modes. ITS will enable the long-term vision of a European transport system where door-to-door seamless travel, for people and goods, will be possible. New ITS technologies under development will also make it possible to deploy new transport concepts in the future. The European transport program has definitely contributed to the development, assessment and demonstration of ITS applications, laying the groundwork for a large deployment of ITS in the future.

REFERENCES

Barbu, G. "Intelfret: Intelligent Freight Train," work funded by the 4th Framework RTD Program of the European Commission, Final Report, Foundation European Rail Research Institute, Utrecht, Netherlands, 1999.

Broeke, I. A. A. "Indris: Efficient River Information Services," work funded by the 4th Framework RTD Program of the European Commission, Interim Report, AVV, Rotterdam, Netherlands, 2000.

Campagne, P. "Vast: Value-added Services for Transport," work funded by the 4th Framework RTD Program of the European Commission, Interim Report, France Development Conseil, Vincennes, France, 2000.

Clement, L. "Eurotoll: European Projects for Toll Effects and Pricing Strategies," work funded by the 5th Framework RTD Program of the European Commission, Interim Report, Lyon, France, 2002.

DIW & FAV. "Desire: Design for Interurban Road Pricing Schemes in Europe—German Case Study," work funded by the 4th Framework RTD Program of the European Commission, Interim Report, Berlin, Germany, 2002.

Doussin, M. H. "Movit: A Mobile VTMIS Using Innovative Technology," work funded by the 4th Framework RTD Program of the European Commission, Interim Report, INGENIA DECAN, Marseilles, France, 2001.

European Commission. "Intelligent Transport Systems: Results from the TransporResearch Program," Brussels, Belgium, 2001.

Federal Highway Administration. "Intelligent Transport Systems Benefits: 2001 Update," U.S. Department of Transportation, Washington DC, 2001.

Financial Times. "London Takes its Toll," 22/Aug., London, England, 2002.

Froese, J. "Incarnation: Efficient Inland Navigation Information System," work funded by the 4th Framework RTD Program of the European Commission, Final Report, ISSUS, Hamburg, Germany, 2000.

Hayes, S. "Concert-P: Cooperation for the Evaluation of City Road Pricing Tools," work funded by the 5th Framework RTD Program of the European Commission, Interim Report, Barcelona Tecnologia, Barcelona, Spain, 2002.

Heijden, W. F. M. "Rinac: River-based Information, Navigation and Communication," work Funded by the 4th Framework RTD Program of the European Commission, Final Report, TNO-FEL, The Hague, Netherlands, 2000.

Leboeuf, M. "Optirails: Optimization of Traffic through the European Rail Traffic Management System (ERTMS/ETML)," work funded by the 4th Framework RTD Program of the European Commission, Final Report, SYSTRA, Paris, France, 2000.

Mertens, P. "ERTMS EUROSIG: Development of the Complete ERTMS Concept," work funded by the 4th Framework RTD Program of the European Commission, Final Report, Alsthom Transport S.A., Paris, France, 1999.

Mike, S. "Music: Management of Traffic Control Using Traffic Flow Control," work funded by the 4th Framework RTD Program of the European Commission, Interim Report, University of York, York, United Kingdom, 2001.

Monzel, F. G. "Defamm: Demonstration Facilities for Airport Movement Management," work Funded by the 4th Framework RTD Program of the European Commission, Interim Report, Airways Navigation Systems GmbH, Stuttgart, Germany, 2000.

Pedersen, J. T. "IPSI: Improved Port/ship Interface," work funded by the 4th Framework RTD Program of the European Commission, Final Report, Kvaernerships Equipment AS, Lier, Norway, 2000.

Rochez, C. "Income: Integration of Traffic Control and Other Measures," work funded by the 4th Framework RTD Program of the European Commission, Final Report, STRATEC Brussels, Belgium, 2000.

Rochez, C. "Direct: Data Integration Requirement of European Cities for Transport," work funded by the 4th Framework RTD Program of the European Commission, Final Report, STRATEC Brussels, Belgium, 2001.

Roessingh, J. J. "Ecottris: European Collaboration on Transition Training Research for Improved Safety," work funded by the 4th Framework RTD Program of the European Commission, Interim Report, NLR, Amsterdam, Netherlands, 2001.

Stephane, P. "Sourdine: Study of Optimization Procedures for Decreasing the Impact of Noise around Airports," work funded by the 5th Framework RTD Program of the European Commission, Final Report, ISR, Massy Cedex, France, 2001.

Suarez, N. "Torch: Technical, Economical and Operational Assessment of an ATM Concept," work funded by the 4th Framework RTD Program of the European Commission, Interim Report, Madrid, Spain, 2000.

USDOT. "The Change Face of Transportation," U.S. Dept. of Transportation, Bureau of Transportation Statistics (BTS00-007), 2000.

Chapter 17

MAINSTREAMING INTELLIGENT TRANSPORTATION SYSTEMS

Findings from a Survey of California Leaders

Elizabeth Deakin

Department of City and Regional Planning/UC Transportation Research Center

This paper investigates factors affecting ITS implementation as a "mainstream" transportation planning activity. It draws upon interviews with 51 leaders from a cross-section of jurisdictions and agencies in California. The interviews revealed that the vast majority of elected officials and senior staff are familiar with ITS. However, they are irritated by ITS literature, which they view as heavily promotional and full of jargon. Many believe that ITS is being implemented fairly quickly overall and that ITS elements that are not proceeding well suffer from institutional problems or market weaknesses. Respondents do not see a problem in fitting ITS projects into mainstream transportation planning processes, but complain of a lack of good information on ITS benefits and costs. Many are concerned that ITS evaluations have been less than arm's-length, and focus too heavily on system benefits rather than traveler benefits. Many believe that the private sector should be left to implement certain ITS applications, but they also think that earmarked funds for ITS applications would speed implementation of other measures. Respondents suggested that the state DOT should lead by example, implementing ready-to-go technologies on its own facilities and within its own agency. Stronger partnerships with local government and other state agencies, developing mutually beneficial, multipurpose applications, were also recommended. Finally, respondents urged that future ITS work should pay more attention to legal and institutional issues and provide a clearer sense of "next steps." The findings should be of use to state and local organizations with an interest in encouraging ITS implementation.

1. INTRODUCTION

Intelligent Transportation Systems (ITS) are the subject of considerable research and development across the U.S. and in other developed countries. Millions of dollars have been invested in technologies to improve traffic operations, increase safety and security, improve transit reliability, lower public and private costs of fare and toll collection, and produce a variety of other social, economic, and environmental improvements in transportation systems and services. (1)

The California Department of Transportation (Caltrans) has been a leader in investing in ITS. For the past 17 years, Caltrans has sponsored both research and demonstration projects ranging from adaptive traffic control and mobile surveillance to real-time traveler information systems. (2) Like the federal government and many other states, Caltrans is now interested in commercializing ITS advances, where appropriate, and in "mainstreaming" ITS as part of the transportation planning process—that is, planning and implementing ITS not as a separate R&D program but as a regularly considered, important alternative in planning, designing, and managing transportation systems.

To date, however, ITS implementation has not been as routine as Caltrans would like. ISTEA and TEA-21 gave metropolitan planning organizations (MPOs) significant responsibilities for project development and selection across the country; California law, some of it predating ISTEA, gave even greater decision authority to the MPOs and to county transportation agencies. (3) In addition, significant responsibility for state projects has been delegated to Caltrans' district offices. Hence, project development and programming require collaboration among multiple offices and levels of government. Inclusion of ITS technologies and approaches depends, in turn, on staff and decision-makers amongst all of the involved organizations understanding what ITS can contribute and believing that it is worthwhile.

Several of the MPOs in California have been active in promoting various ITS technologies, and several California cities likewise have been early implementers. (See, e.g., 4, 5, 6, 7) Overall, however, ITS implementation has been spotty, and slower than the Caltrans ITS sponsors would have liked. In addition, ITS elements have been added to certain projects only to be dropped when funding ran short, or have been given relatively low priority for implementation.

This paper investigates some of the factors affecting ITS implementation by exploring the perspectives on these new technologies with California decision-makers in state, regional, and local agencies, as well as with key opinion leaders in the private and nonprofit sectors. The paper summarizes the methodology used to conduct the research, presents the findings, and distills out the key points and suggestions for future directions. Better understanding the issues ITS raises among these decision-makers is a first step toward developing a more robust California strategy for mainstreaming ITS. The findings also should be of use to other state and local organizations with an interest in ITS implementation, revealing barriers to ITS as well as opportunities for enhancing ITS acceptance.

2. RESEARCH METHODOLOGY

The research project began with a detailed literature review of ITS technologies and functions, their benefits and costs, and implementation experiences to date. Background papers were prepared for a number of key technologies and applications, and were reviewed by an advisory committee established by Caltrans. (The background papers are posted at www.uctc.net/mainstream.) Two meetings of the advisory committee, one held at the start of the project and a second held after the background summaries were prepared, were organized to discuss ITS implementation issue and review and expand a set of hypotheses on possible reasons for ITS's mixed reception (Table 1.).

Interviews were then scheduled with decision-makers, senior staff, and opinion leaders throughout the state. In the interviews, the respondents were asked to discuss their familiarity with ITS in its various forms, what they think about ITS's usefulness in addressing transportation problems, and the pros and cons of ITS applications as they see them. They also were asked for their perspectives on the implementation of ITS technologies, and whether they had particular interest in or problems with them. Respondents were asked for suggestions on what would make implementation more likely or have it occur at a faster rate than at present. Finally, respondents were asked whether they were aware of any examples of ITS implementation that they thought to be particularly noteworthy, either as successes or as failures. Respondents were also given the opportunity to raise additional topics and issues if they so chose.

The objectives of the interviews were as follows:

- To assess respondents' knowledge of ITS as well as their sources of information;
- To obtain respondents' views on near-term applications as well as longer-term possibilities;
- To explore respondents' views on ITS benefits and costs;
- To discuss implementation, including whether respondents felt it was faster or slower than expected;
- To explore possible reasons for slow implementation, including understanding of the opportunities, fit with the planning and funding processes, level of support, concerns about particular proposals, or other factors that the respondents may have identified; and
- To identify cases that respondents see as particular successes or particular failures. TRB 2003 Annual Meeting CD-ROM Original paper submittal—not revised by author.

Table 1. Possible Reasons for Slow Implementation of Intelligent Transportation Systems (Hypotheses)

Information	**Fit with Existing Planning and Funding Processes**	**Impacts**
Many of the public officials and staff members responsible for transportation plans and programs are only vaguely familiar with ITS technologies.	Commonly available planning and evaluation tools do not address ITS very well if at all, so analysts don't know how to incorporate ITS options into their evaluations.	Some ITS technology suggest central control over facilities and services that currently are controlled separately, raising political and institutional issues that have not been addressed.
ITS research and development has been carried out by technology specialists who are not usually involved in policy development, and do not know how to effectively communicate their findings to decision-makers.	Current planning regulations, e.g., for air quality plans or CEQA mitigation, do not address ITS or are unclear about how it figures in.	Insufficient attention has been paid to consumer conveniences, environmental benefits, and neighborhood enhancements that ITS could provide, e.g., multi-purpose transportation and parking cards, emissions monitoring devices, neighborhood permit parking cards.
There is relatively little information on the costs and benefits of the various ITS options.	Few regional or local agencies have developed staff positions with specific ITS responsibilities.	Concerns persist that ITS technologies for autos and highways enhance auto use and in so doing have adverse impacts on transit use, lead to more emissions and energy use, further support sprawl, and harm the central city and older suburbs.
Planners and analysts need training on ITS, but it is not readily available either in university curricula or in continuing education and training courses.	Prior commitments represented by long-range plans and multi-year programs crowd out ITS options.	
The image of ITS that many public officials have is fully automated guideways and vehicles, options that are seen as too far in the future to be worth analyzing as part of ongoing planning efforts.	It's not clear what funds a region or locality could or should use for ITS projects.	
Public awareness of near-term ITS options is low.		

Each interview was conducted in accordance with a protocol that included a set of open-ended questions in the form of an interview guide.[1] Respondents were all senior state, regional, and local officials (elected officials, elected and appointed board members, senior agency staff) and leaders of other key interest groups including environmental groups, automobile clubs, and business leaders. All were from the State of California. The respondents were identified through the author's own knowledge as well as through publicly available sources such as the Internet and government directories. The intent was to obtain a reasonably representative cross-section of information and opinion, rather than to poll a fully random sample of officials and interest group representatives.

For public officials, potential respondents were identified by first selecting their political jurisdiction or agency and then identifying the persons holding particular titles (council member, supervisor, board member, department head, etc.) The initial sample of local governments was selected based on size of jurisdiction (50,000–250,000; 250,000 and higher) and location of jurisdiction (region of state, urban, suburban, rural), to obtain a sample that reflects the state's composition and diversity.

Regional agencies were selected to include both the large urban areas and the smaller ones. Their managers then were selected for a possible interview based on their title and position. A similar process was used for state agencies, where staff members from transportation, energy, and air quality agencies were selected for possible interviews.

Interest groups interested in ITS issues were identified by reviewing the literature and seeing what groups had participated in ITS forums or published articles or reports on ITS. From this list, a set of organizations was identified. Web sites and other published sources were used to identify individuals for possible interviews.

In total, 12 elected officials, 25 planning and engineering staff members from local (city and county) jurisdictions, 10 regional agency staff, 10 state staff members, and 10 members of interest groups were identified for possible interviews. All of these individuals were asked by letter, fax, and/or phone to participate in the interviews. Of the 67 persons contacted, 51 agreed to an interview. Nine were elected officials, 10 were planning staff, 10 were engineering staff, 7 were regional agency staff, 6 were state agency staff, and 10 were representatives of environmental, business, and auto or trucking interest groups. The other 16 persons initially contacted either did not respond to three separate requests (11, including three elected officials, three regional agency staff members, two state agency staff members, two local engineers, and one county planner), or refused to be interviewed (five, including two state agency staff members and two local engineers who stated that they were too busy to be interviewed, and one planner who stated that he was not interested in the topic.) Table 2 summarizes the sample statistics.

Interviews were conducted both in person, 24, and by telephone, 27. All interviews took place at the time and location or manner preferred by the subject. No interviews were taped, although the author took detailed notes including direct quotations during the interviews. Because there was some potential risk that in the course of an interview a respondent might make statements about individuals, projects, or agencies that if revealed could be embarrassing, respondents were promised confidentiality and were promised that their identity would not be revealed.

The interviews ranged in length from 35 to 90 minutes, with most interviews taking about one hour.

Table 2. Interview Sample

	Elected Officials	Local Gov't Planners	Local Gov't Engineers	Regional Agency Staff	State Agency Staff	Interest Groups	Total
Initial Sample	12	12	13	10	10	10	67
Interviewed	9	10	9	7	6	10	51
Not Interviewed		3	2	4	3	4	16
Too Busy			2		2		4
No Interest	3	1	2	3	2		11
No Response	3	1	2	3	2		11
Response Rate	75%	83%	69%	70%	60%	100%	76%

3. FINDINGS INFORMATION ABOUT INTELLIGENT TRANSPORTATION SYSTEMS

The interviews began with a discussion of the respondent's understanding of Intelligent Transportation Systems. Contrary to initial hypotheses that many would be only vaguely familiar with ITS, all the respondents said that they were either reasonably familiar with these new programs and technologies ("as familiar as I am with standard transportation programs and technologies," as one elected official put it) or were very familiar with them. The programs and technologies that came to mind first when thinking of ITS differed by the agency and title of the respondent. Elected officials mentioned automated highways, smart cards for tolls and transit payments, and advanced traffic management systems. Planners mentioned advanced traffic signal equipment, bus rapid transit, toll tags, and smart cards. Engineers and regional agency staff were more comprehensive, typically listing seven or eight categories of ITS using nomenclature and abbreviations from the ITS National Architecture. (8)

All of the local engineers and state and regional agency staff had learned of ITS as part of their professional programs; some had also studied ITS as part of their graduate education. (Education in ITS was reported primarily by individuals under 40, although four middle-aged respondents said they had first learned of these technologies in the 1970s and saw the current programs as "the latest round" of work on new technologies.) In contrast, local planners had most commonly learned about ITS from their engineering or regional agency counterparts, by participating in project reviews for local and regional agencies, where proposals for ITS occasionally came up, or through publications, especially Transportation Research Board papers.

Elected officials, in contrast, said they had learned about ITS mostly from news media (news articles, professional press) and to a lesser extent, from presentations or memos from staff. They all felt that if they wanted more information they would be able to get it from either their own staff or regional agency staff. One pointed out that the elected officials who serve on transportation agency boards get briefings and information packets that get them up to speed on transportation options, although he also said that these packets tend to lack details on markets and costs.

Based on their knowledge of the options, almost all of the respondents listed private sector freight operations, using logistics, global positioning systems, and telecommunications for real-time dispatching and tracking as the most important short-term application of ITS. Advanced traffic signal systems timing and intersection controls were the second most commonly mentioned as important short-term application of new technologies. The majority also listed automated toll collection, smart cards for transit, consumer route-finding systems (on the Internet, built into some vehicles, or for handheld computers), and GPS and other systems for tracking buses and adjusting schedules.

State and regional staffers and local engineers also mentioned traffic operations centers, ramp metering, weigh in motion, and automated commercial vehicle safety checks, and but no one else did.

For long-term applications, most respondents believed there would be substantial improvements in the technologies that they mentioned for short-term application. For example, 35 of the respondents felt that advanced signal systems would become ubiquitous and would be better integrated with transit operations. Another 31 of the respondents expressed the hope that eventually multi-purpose smart cards would be available. Several expressed frustration at how long it was taking for smart cards to be implemented in the U.S., noting that they were ahead of the U.S. in several countries overseas. As one elected official put it, "It's a shame that we are getting different technologies for tolls and for transit. Of course, it took 10 years to get either of them going here, which itself is shameful. It probably would have taken twice as long if they had tried to make the same thing work for tolls and transit. Eventually, though, I think the public is going to demand that they have a single smart card that can pay for parking, tolls, and transit. Why not?"

Fifteen of the respondents mentioned fully automated guideways and vehicles as the options that they believed ITS experts expected to see in the future, though several also noted that federal funding for these programs had been cut. Most of the respondents were skeptical about these strategies, commenting that they did not personally think these options would be around for a very long time, except perhaps in limited applications like airport transit systems. Four questioned whether automated guideways would really work, saying that they had not heard a clear explanation of how the added traffic carried on such facilities would be accommodated getting on or off locally owned streets and arterials.

Asked how informed they thought the public was concerning ITS, respondents were divided. Most elected officials thought the public had pretty good awareness of available and upcoming options, including toll tags, smart cards, GPS route-finding systems, traffic advisories available on computer, commercial vehicle operations management, and so forth. Planners and interest groups representatives also agreed that many members of the public were interested in technology and wanted to try such things as smart cards. State and regional officials, in contrast, felt that citizens were not very knowledgeable about ITS. Pressed for examples, several mentioned a lack of public interest in traffic management systems as their reason for believing the public is ill-informed about ITS.

A number of the respondents, and in particular elected officials, interest group representatives, and planners, commented on the quality of the information available on ITS. They characterized most of the available information as “too technical” and “way too long”. Many also thought the literature was too promotional. As one planner put it, “they list a large number of benefits but it is hard to find cost information, or any sense of ‘compared to what’?” Twenty of the respondents specifically commented on the lack of believable, dispassionate evaluation of the ITS options.

While most of the respondents felt that they had a reasonably good understanding of ITS, most also complained about the use of jargon to describe the options. As one elected official put it, “The technical people continually use initials to describe their work. They don’t seem to understand that when they do this with a general audience, it is anesthetizing. They should be instructed to speak and write in plain English. These are not difficult concepts, and they shoot themselves in the foot by continually using these abbreviations.” A regional agency official commented, “The term ‘architecture’ is proving to be a mistake. We are finding that people outside the group discussing it think we are talking about building things, structures. It should have been called guidelines or framework, not as glorious sounding, but more informative.” An interest group representative said, “It’s alphabet soup. It doesn’t communicate.”

Ten of the respondents, including six elected officials, felt that there was particularly poor information about public investment strategies for ITS—either what needed to be done in the public sector or what it would cost.

4. FIT WITH PLANNING AND FUNDING PROCESSES

Initial hypotheses suggested that a poor fit with existing planning and funding processes might explain slow ITS implementation. The interviews provided mixed support for these hypotheses. About half the respondents challenged the basic premise of slow implementation, arguing that many ITS applications have taken off in the market and are well on their way to being the norm, or were already widely implemented in California or elsewhere. The others felt that implementation was hampered mostly by a lack of clear priorities for ITS investment and by a lack of funding dedicated to ITS.

Respondents who argued that ITS was, in fact, being implemented quickly pointed to the widespread use of information technologies in freight applications, consumer adoption of GPS devices and computer-based route information, automated toll collection, advanced traffic signal systems, transit smart cards, transit priority systems, and transit monitoring systems. They agreed, however, that institutional conflicts had gotten in the way in some cases. "California has put a lot of money into technology and system development, but we haven't been particularly skilled at handing the institutional issues. We were slow to get automated toll collection, way behind New York and the New England states. Labor issues and contracting problems seem to get in our way. We have spent years on an integrated fare collection system in the Bay Area but have not really faced up to the underlying problem, which is how to allocate costs and revenues, and that is a problem because underlying that is insufficient revenues for transit." Respondents who argued that ITS was not being implemented very quickly commented primarily on traffic operations centers and traffic management systems. Most of these respondents were state and local officials with responsibility for highways, and auto and trucking interest group representatives. Their diagnoses of the problem were not, however, identical.

State officials felt that the problem was largely that metropolitan regions did not give these ITS projects priority. With few exceptions, they felt that MPOs, both the elected officials on the board and staff members, lacked interest in the ITS options and were more comfortable with and interested in traditional capital projects. Two exceptions specifically noted were the Bay Area, where MTC had designated staff and funding for ITS, and the San Joaquin Valley, where an inter-jurisdictional traffic management center had been put together.

Local government officials, in contrast, thought the problem depended on the application. For traffic signal systems, they felt the issue was simply one of funding. Five of the respondents pointed to the state's Fuel Efficient Traffic Signal Timing Program (FETSIM) of the 1980s as a good example of what can be done if a program is established and funded. Under the FETSIM program, almost all of the signal systems in the state were timed with modern methods, and traffic engineers and their consultants were trained in state of the art signal timing and learned about advanced signal equipment. Many used that knowledge even after the program ended. (9) These respondents felt that a new signal program would be welcomed. For ramp meters and traffic operations centers, the locals saw the problem as institutional and political rather than technical or financial. "Sure, we know how to do it, we can show that it would help. We already have a lot of ramp meters working. Where we don't have them are in places where the locals don't trust the state not to divert too much traffic to local streets. And a lot of times they have bad experiences to point to that make them not trust the state. That's also why some locals are not so enthusiastic about a joint traffic operations center. It's a question of control, and trust."

Asked whether a lack of planning and evaluation tools was a barrier, the respondents who had an opinion unanimously disagreed. (Twelve of the respondents did not feel sufficiently knowledgeable about available methods to comment on this topic.) The respondents felt that there were plenty of methods that could be used to evaluate ITS options, and what was missing was not planning tools but basic information on costs and benefits. "If we had information that our policy board would accept, we could put it into our evaluations," said one regional agency official in a comment typical of those made on this topic. "We don't really need any more analysis methods, and we certainly don't need any requirements to use them."

Ten of the respondents commented that rather than invest in new analysis tools, they would prefer demonstration projects. Said one, "Elected officials are more easily convinced by a project that works than by a technical report or a modeling run. Show them what can be done and they are willing to listen and give it a try if it makes sense." Others added that case studies that had carefully documented benefits, costs, public reaction, etc. were very helpful, especially when written for a non-technical audience.

At the same time, many of the respondents noted that there was not enough transportation funding to go around, and even projects with considerable popular support and strong technical merit had to wait for funding. Prior commitments represented by long-range plans and multi-year programs took precedence, and crowd out ITS options. Local officials and interest group members added that projects like traffic calming and sidewalk installation and repair had plenty of public support but couldn't compete with large regional projects; it took federal legislation to make funding available for these measures, and even then they have a hard time competing unless the MPO has set aside funds for them. In this context, 15 of the respondents advocated earmarking funds for ITS, but a larger number (28) commented that giving ITS special precedence seemed unfair, especially after so many years of heavy funding. "ITS has gotten a lot of research and development money over the last 10 or 15 years," one respondent said. "It's time to start showing what all that money was good for. If these are good ideas, they should be able to compete on their own, and not need further special treatment."

Several respondents argued that Caltrans should be spending the money under its control for ITS if it believes these are high-priority investments. "Lead by example," one respondent put it. Another put it, "Caltrans has been funding the research. If it has produced good products, Caltrans should get on with it and implement them." Variable message signs, weather advisories, automated tolls, mainline flow metering as well as ramp metering, freeway patrol services tied to detector and camera data, telecommuting, and teleconferencing for employees were some of the measures that respondents mentioned as item that Caltrans could implement on its own.

Twenty-six of the respondents felt that it was not so much funding availability per se that was limiting ITS implementation, but rather the lack of a clear picture of what would be gotten for the money. Several respondents used traveler information systems as an example. "We already have (radio traffic advisories)," one respondent argued. "They tell you what has been reported, whether it is one person who phoned in or several, they check the information with the CHP and Caltrans and tell you what they have to say … That is pretty good. People already can get a cheap add-on for their (hand-held computer) that will give them alternate routes, if they don't know them already, and believe me, commuters figure out every alternate route in the first two weeks on the job. If we are going to keep spending public money on traveler information, somebody is going to have to make it clear what the government is going to give you that we don't already have from the private sector." Another respondent, voicing similar sentiments, added, "It is not just that we could make it better. You have to show that the added expenditures make sense at the margin, that it will be enough better that I should be willing to pay for it." Several expressed concerns that evaluations were being performed by ITS advocates; as one put it, " People who spend their days promoting new systems are not the right people to be evaluating them"

Speaking of funding and priorities, 20 of the 51 respondents suggested that at least some ITS technologies should now be left to the private sector to further develop and market. One respondent put it this way: " There are a lot of projects that have positive benefit-cost ratios. The issue is how these beneficial projects stack up against each other. And when we are looking at a field where the private sector is already active, providing us with a range of products, free to pretty expensive, I want to see some evidence that a public expenditure will produce a worthwhile added benefit. Another respondent said, "I don't want to just fund some ITS project just because there is a 'not invented here' attitude among the ITS staff. If the public sector has done a lot of work but now the private sector has moved in and taken off with an idea, great. Declare it a victory and move on to something else."

5. IMPACTS OF ITS

A third set of hypotheses considered ITS impacts as potential barriers to implementation. The interview respondents largely supported these hypotheses.

Most respondents agreed that the ITS technologies that suggest central control over facilities and services that currently are managed by separately raise political and institutional issues that have not been addressed adequately. As noted earlier, several respondents felt that disinterest in automated guideways and slow implementation of traffic operations centers and ramp meters partially reflected this concern. Along the same lines, most respondents felt that there was lingering concern that ITS programs for highways could encourage more auto use and in so doing have adverse impacts on transit use, lead to more emissions and energy use, further support sprawl, and harm the central city and older suburbs. To some extent, transit ITS projects such as Bus Rapid Transit are dispelling this concern, providing an example of how ITS can help transit, inner cities, and older suburbs.

However, most respondents felt that the biggest issues concerning ITS impacts had to do with user-side benefits and costs. All of the elected officials, all of the planners, all of the interest group representatives, all of the regional agency officials, and about half of the local engineers and state agency representatives thought that far too little attention had been paid to the consumer conveniences, environmental benefits, and neighborhood enhancements that ITS could provide.

"Why aren't we giving the consumer multi-purpose transportation and parking cards? Why aren't we even trying a demonstration project that allows a toll tag to pay for parking in major facilities?," asked one respondent. "I can only conclude that the interest in toll tags is mostly to make the facility operate better, not really to help the consumer out.... If we cared about the consumer we would get moving."

Coordination with other state programs also could be improved, as several respondents noted. One suggested linking traffic and environmental data: "...we could add remote sensing equipment (emissions monitoring devices) and combine that with vehicle identification, speed and flow measurements, and so on, and greatly improve our air programs. But there is a lot of turf here and hardly any of the ITS (work) builds this sort of environmental linkages."

Several local respondents suggested ways that ITS technologies could be more useful to local governments:

"We should have a demonstration program for a single transportation pass that pays for transit and parking and maybe taxis, too."

"It would be great if we had smart cards that also could serve as neighborhood permit parking cards so that we could read them electronically just by driving by the vehicles. We could enforce these programs more easily."

"There should be some way to use all this new technology to automate origin destination surveys."

" I can't get a straight answer on how many commute trips never use the freeway system at all, and for those that do, how many miles they spend on freeways versus arterials versus local streets. Couldn't all these detectorized freeways produce that information?"

"Couldn't we use these new technologies to catch speeders and other bad drivers? Couldn't part of the ITS research program be to figure out how to do that institutionally if it is legal issues that are in the way?"

These respondents suggested that ITS projects would be implemented faster "if it were a two-way street—the state should be interested in what would help us out, not just ask us to help them manage their freeways better."

6. OTHER ISSUES

Respondents were asked whether there were other issues that they would like to raise. Two issues were suggested by a number of respondents.

First, over half of the respondents commented that there was a need for more work on the institutional and legal aspects of ITS proposals. "There is a lot of good technical work but we are continually getting hung up on institutional conflicts," as one respondent put it. "Legal issues, like how to develop an enforceable agreement on ramp metering and arterial signal timing that protects local interests, could use attention," another added.

Second, 20 respondents suggested the need for both state and local strategies for ITS. One elected official's comments summarize the overall sense of frustration with existing programs and the need for direction: "I don't get any sense of priorities from the materials I see," said the official. "Some sense of the relative importance of the various strategies is needed."

7. SUMMARY AND CONCLUSIONS

Open-ended interviews of 51 leaders from a cross-section of jurisdictions and agencies have been used to explore implementation issues associated with Intelligent Transportation Systems. The interviews reveal several important points and offer direction for future work.

First, contrary to our initial expectations, the vast majority of elected officials and senior staff feel reasonably familiar with ITS. However, they are irritated by ITS literature, which they view as heavily promotional and/or technical, and full of jargon.

Second, and also contrary to expectations, there is considerable sentiment that ITS is being implemented fairly quickly, and that the ITS elements that are not proceeding quickly suffer from institutional problems or lack markets.

Third, respondents do not see a problem in fitting ITS projects into the planning process; rather, they see a lack of good information on benefits and costs of various options. Further, in the most common view, benefits of various ITS proposals not only must be weighed against costs, but the proposals also must be weighed against alternative projects and other currently available approaches to the same issue.

Fourth, respondents are concerned that ITS evaluations have been less than arm's-length and that there are too few demonstration projects and case examples carried out by dispassionate evaluators. They are distrustful of technology and program evaluations carried out by their own proponents.

Fifth, respondents characterize available ITS literature and evaluations as focused on why the system would operate better, not why travelers would want this. They feel there is not enough user (customer) orientation in ITS programs.

Sixth, many believe that government should recognize that the private sector has assumed the leadership in some ITS applications and that government efforts should move on to focus on topics where the value added by government involvement will be greatest.

Seventh, many respondents would support special programs for ITS applications, providing funding for planning and implementation, training staff and consultants, and building longer-term capacity for using ITS technologies. Some, however, feel that ITS has already had heavy support and should compete on its own.

Eighth, many believe that government, and the state DOT in particular, should lead by example, implementing ready-to-go technologies on its own facilities and within its own agency. Many more demonstration projects also would be useful, in the respondents' view.

Ninth, many argue for stronger partnerships with local government and other state agencies, looking for ways that ITS technologies could be mutually beneficial and multi-purpose.

Finally, respondents urged that future ITS work should pay more attention to legal and institutional issues and to implementation strategies, to provide a clearer sense of priorities and "next steps."

The identification of these issues is a first step toward developing a more robust strategy for mainstreaming ITS. The findings should be of use not only to California but also to other state and local organizations with an interest in ITS implementation, as they reveal barriers to ITS as well as opportunities for enhancing ITS acceptance.

ACKNOWLEDGMENTS

This paper was prepared with funding from the California Department of Transportation (Caltrans) as part of the Mainstreaming ITS study being carried out at the University of California, Berkeley. Additional information on the Mainstreaming ITS study can be found at www.uctc.net/mainstream. The author benefited from comments received on a draft of the paper from the project advisory board. All opinions expressed are those of the author and not necessarily those of Caltrans or the advisory board members. The author is solely responsible for the contents of the paper and any errors or omissions.

NOTES

1 The full protocol and the sampling methodology appears on the project Web site, www.uctc.net/mainstream.

REFERENCES

1. http://www.itsa.org/whatits.html
2. http://www.path.berkeley.edu
3. Deakin, E. "Transportation in California: The Coming Challenges," *California's Future in the Balance, Policy Issues Annual*, Pat Brown Institute, Cal State University Los Angeles, and Institute of Governmental Studies, University of California, Berkeley, 2001.
4. Dahms, L. D. "Partners Join Forces to 'JUMP Start' San Francisco Bay Area Traffic," *ITE Journal*, Vol. 62, No. 12, December 1992, 22–24. TRB 2003 Annual Meeting CD-ROM Original paper submittal – not revised by author.
5. Yee, B. M., Jack L. F. "San Francisco Red Light Camera Enforcement Program," Institute of Transportation Engineers Meeting (67th: 1997: Boston, Mass.). Compendium of technical papers [CD-ROM].
6. Giuliano, G., Randolph W. H., Jacqueline M. G. Los Angeles Smart Traveler Field Operational Test Evaluation, "Partners for Advanced Transit and Highways," University of California, Berkeley, Institute of Transportation Studies Report No UCB-ITS-PRR-95, 41, various pagings, 1995.
7. Sullivan, E. C. "Impacts of Implementing the California Route 91 Variable Toll Express Lanes," Institute of Transportation Engineers, 67th Meeting, Boston, MA. Compendium of technical papers [CD-ROM], 12 p.
8. United States Federal Highway Administration, Intelligent Transportation System Architecture and Standards, Federal Register, Vol. 66, No. 5, FHWA docket no. FHWA-99-5899, 23 CFR parts 655 and 940, Jan. 8, 2001, 1,335–1,454.
9. Deakin, E., Alexander, S., Adolf, D. M. "The Fuel Efficient Traffic Signal Management Program: Final Report to the California Energy Commission," Berkeley: Institute of Transportation Studies, University of California, vii, 49 pp, 1984.

Chapter 18

INFORMATION SYSTEMS TO IMPROVE SURFACE TRANSPORTATION

Directions for Intelligent Transportation Systems Assessment and Development

Thomas A. Horan
School of Information Science, Claremont Graduate University

This chapter draws upon evaluation findings from previous chapters and related studies to outline ITS research and assessment directions. After reviewing several types of system benefits possible from ITS, the author summarizes evaluation developments. The general theme of these developments is that there is considerable benefit data supporting near-term mobility improvements, substantially less information about other benefit areas (e.g., safety, environment), and some indication of differential benefits to various user groups. The balance of the chapter considers three directions for ITS assessments. First, there is a need to assess the role of ITS as a contributing force to the efficient performance of the transportation system. Second, there is a need to consider the role if ITS in satisfying stakeholder demand for transportation information and services. Third, there is a need to assess ITS within the context of information and communications revolution, which is substantially impacting the manner by which society conducts business and social affairs. The chapter concludes by noting that the new transportation professional will need to address the complexity of transportation systems.

1. INTRODUCTION

During the late 1980s, momentum gathered for a "smart highways" program in what was soon to become the landmark Intermodal Surface Transportation Efficiency Act (ISTEA) legislation. In 1990, *Mobility 2000* was organized to provide estimates on how such intelligent-vehicle highway technologies could improve mobility over the course of the upcoming decade (1990–2000). Congress commissioned the U.S. General Accounting Office (GAO) to conduct a review of emerging intelligent vehicle-highway systems (GAO, 1991). New Jersey Senator Frank Lautenberg (1991) moved to the forefront of the policy issue by introducing the "Intelligent Vehicle Highway Act of 1991 (S. 999)". In his introduction of this act, he noted the worsening congestion problems and the promise that new technologies held in offering solutions to these vexing transportation problems. The senator's bill was subsequently integrated into the overall transportation legislation and provided the legislative authorization and context for the ensuing federal ITS program.

Now a decade later, the chapters in this volume provide a sobering reminder of the difficulty of integrating new technologies into an already mature transportation system. The chapters also encourage new thinking about how technologies can be designed and deployed to produce demonstrable social benefits. This chapter considers future directions for ITS deployment in light of what has been learned about ITS system elements, with special attention to the changing transportation and societal context in which ITS operates. The chapter opens with a consideration of the main impact areas for ITS, and then explores three emerging themes in greater detail: the move toward ITS as a performance information system, the opportunity to create a more interactive transportation system with ITS, and the consideration of ITS within the broader information and communication technology (ICT) milieu. The chapter closes with a discussion of future benefit-cost evaluations and the need for broader assessments of ITS. Throughout the chapter, this author draws upon prior work in the ITS evaluations (at the GAO and elsewhere) as a reference point for discussing ITS developments.

2. DECONSTRUCTING ITS SYSTEM BENEFITS

Several evaluation guidelines were developed at the outset of the ITS program (see USDOT, 1993, 1994). The two-fold theme of these recommendations was that the success of ITS could be marked by: (1) how well it produced demonstrable benefits across a range of impact areas and (2) the extent to which this performance would garner support from public and private stakeholders (Horan, 1994). This two-fold theme typically manifested itself in the identification of key benefit areas and the specific ITS user-oriented systems (or "market packages" in the terminology of the National System Architecture) that could be deployed. The following list (also summarized in Table 1) is a representative list of central ITS benefit areas with candidate systems for delivering these benefits.

- *Mobility and Access:* Core traffic management and transit operations systems are heavily oriented toward enhancing mobility. Some traveler information systems and "new mobility" systems place a greater priority on access, as do broadband telecommunications systems that allow for trip substitution.

- *Safety and Security*: Surveillance and control systems can play an important role in security and extreme event management. E-911 and emergency management systems provide integrated delivery systems for mobile emergencies. In-vehicle devices are often touted as able to achieve safety improvements.
- *Economy:* Mobility and access are critical for economic performance of regions. The most direct contributors to economic efficiency are new freight and goods movement systems, and well as electronic tolling systems that both ease congestion and provide mechanisms for new revenue sources.
- *Environment:* More efficient traffic management and transit and goods management systems can aid the environment by reducing emissions from congestion. GIS systems have the potential to play an important role in enhancing cross-agency consideration of environmental impacts. Broadband telecommunication systems can help reduce unnecessary trips to work and shopping.
- *Social/Equity:* An ongoing concern of transportation policy is that the benefits from new systems be spread across income and spatial dimensions. Technology systems that play important roles in this regard include universal pass systems (for transit dependent users), just-in-time transit and paratransit systems (for disabled and reverse work commutes), and driver aid systems (for older drivers).

Table 1. ITS Systems Related to Transportation System Plan Goals

Benefits	ITS Technology Systems	Sample Markets
Mobility and Access	Transportation management technologies for integrated system performance	Commuters
	Broadband networks for telework and virtual work	Teleworkers
	Multi-and intermodal transportation and information systems	Commercial drivers Bus riders
	Performance (data) systems on information flows by mode	Transportation managers
Safety and Security	Surveillance and control technologies for emergency management	Transportation managers
	Wireless emergency management systems	Rural travelers
	In-vehicle safety systems	Elderly drivers
Economy	Goods movement systems	Commercial drivers
	ETC toll technologies	Commuters
	Traffic management systems	Transportation managers
Environment	Broadband systems for trip reduction	Multimodal travelers
	GIS system for environmental modeling	Transportation planners
Social/Equity	Universal transit passes	Bus riders
	Just-in-time transit and paratransit	Transit dependent
	Interactive and visual technology systems	Travelers
	Providing innovative services to all citizens, including transit dependent	Citizens

As noted in the table, these systems provide benefits to a variety of transportation users and stakeholders. Users include driving commuters, transit users, commercial (truck) drivers, and rural and elderly travelers. Stakeholders include transportation managers, transit operators, emergency service providers, and environmental and metropolitan planners (see Lappin, 1996). Indeed, as ITS progresses, the full range of users can and should be as broad as the transportation system in total. However, these users can have widely varying expectations for ITS and can differ substantially in the range of benefits received from these systems.

2.1 Findings from Previous Chapters

With the possible exception of security, these benefit areas and users have been recognized since the outset of the program. However, they have not been equally pursued throughout the decade-long life of the federal program. Rather, the bulk of the assessments have addressed the mobility problems for commuters, with some consideration for improving access to goods and services.

Such program priorities were apparent even in the early days of the ITS program. For example, the aforementioned GAO report noted that most of the ITS evaluations (including the few benefit-cost evaluations) addressed short-term mobility improvements. As a consequence the GAO report made three recommendations: (1) that the federal (ISTEA) legislation contain a provision for evaluations of ITS projects, with specific reference to impacts on congestion, safety, the economy, energy, and the environment, (2) that (ISTEA) legislation include a robust field operational test program for experimenting with a range of technological solutions and in accordance with a strategic research vision, and (3) that (ISTEA) legislation closely monitor appropriate levels of public funding, with specific regard to expected private sources.

While the ensuing legislation (ISTEA and the Transportation Equity Act for the 21st Century, or TEA-21) contained legislative requirements that were consistent with these recommendations, the general concern about the range of benefit data remains. The picture that emerges from the chapters in this volume is one where there have been important lessons learned relative to the first two recommendations, though the benefit-cost side of ITS remains illusive. Some of these findings are discussed below.

2.1.1 Beyond Mobility

In general, the pattern of findings reported in this volume as well as in the broader ITS evaluation literature suggests the achievement of modest to moderate near-term mobility improvements from generally off-the-shelf ITS technologies. For example, Skabardonis (Chapter 8) updated the findings from ATSAC and FETSIM, two widely cited sources of mobility benefits. He found, for example, that signal timing optimization of coordinated signal systems produced an average 7 percent drop in travel time, 13.8 percent reduction in delays, 12.5 percent reduction in stops, and 7.8 percent decline in fuel use for a typical weekday. Similarly, the chapter by Levinson and Zhang (Chapter 9) documented operational improvements available through aggressive implementation of ramp metering in the Twin Cities. While demonstrating a positive productivity benefit from ramp metering, they also demarked differential benefits to two classes of commuters (short distance and long distance), noting that the benefits to short-distance commuters were often negative when weighed against the additional queueing time.

In addition to the research by Levinson and colleagues, the politically mandated (by the Minnesota legislature) evaluation of ramp metering in the Twin Cities represented one of the most visible benefit-cost assessments of ITS-related systems in the U.S. The study found a 22 percent decrease in freeway travel times with meters, which more than offset ramp delay reduction during the no-ramp meter test period (Cambridge Systematics, 2001). There was, however, a decrease in fuel consumption without ramp metering (an estimated 5.5 million gallons), thus revealing a trade-off inherent in this system. On the issue of stakeholder acceptance, the research data showed a number of changes in attitudes among area travelers that occurred when meters were shut down during the test period. These included the belief by survey respondents that congestion had worsened. However, there was a decided minority (around 20 percent) that supported the continued shutdown of the meters.

The evaluation also calculated a benefit-cost ratio for the ramp metering system. Accounting for the cost of the entire congestion management system (including changeable message signs, traveler information, and other components), the estimated benefit-cost ratio for ramp metering was 5:1. While the generalization of these findings may be open to question (the Twin Cities is generally viewed as having the most integrated ramp metering system in the U.S.), the evaluation did demonstrate that benefit-cost assessments can be performed on deployed systems, and these systems can produce favorable results. Taken together with the Levinson and Zhang chapter, the data also suggest that these benefits can vary substantially across user groups.

Unfortunately, demonstrable mobility findings were not as easily measured in the case of transit applications. Giuliano and O'Brien (Chapter 7) report that, for the half dozen transit (APTS) projects they reviewed in detail, technical implementation (when it did occur) did not always translate into project success. A major limiting factor in this case was that full-scale technical implementation (e.g., smart card technology) relied on institutional integration. Appropriately, they noted that an integrated socio-technical approach is needed to understand the context in which the technology is being deployed, as inter-agency coordination can be critical to successful transit system deployment (especially for easy-pass systems).

Despite the oft-cited problems with achieving systemwide impacts via transit improvements, transit related evaluations do suggest that small-scale improvements can be made. Sullivan (Chapter 6) notes the favorable views by local users to a transit information system deployed in San Luis Obispo. (The fact that the ITS implementation was linked to a service cutback significantly affected the overall opinions about the transit service being provided). Lehtonen and Kulmala (2002) report on a similar scale deployment in Helsinki, Finland, where transit line improvements were made in connection with a system improvements (signal-priority treatment as well as transit information) and this indeed produced both system improvements and favorable perceptions. Garcia (Chapter 16) provides an interesting extension into the intermodal and international arena, reporting that ITS-related systems are usefully being deployed in rail, air, and vessel systems throughout Europe.

Similar to a decade ago, performance outside of traditional mobility improvements has been harder to document. For example, none of the chapters provides tests explicitly aimed at safety enhancement, though gains have long been predicted for this area. This author and others have noted the rise of mobile Emergency Management Systems (EMS) as an emergent form of safety-related ITS system (Horan, 2003; Comcare Alliance, 2001). While early safety-related ITS systems tended to hone in on collision avoidance technologies, it is worth noting that wireless 911 has become a "travelers' safety net", particularly in rural areas. These systems can assist with notifications of adverse weather situations as well as in the notification and dispatch of emergency service personnel. While there has been much discussion on the in-vehicle safety hazards of cell phone technology, there has yet to be a focus on these mayday safety benefits and how they may offset driver risk from using cell phones. This is especially surprising in light of several state-level attempts to restrict in-automobile use of cell phones (Cohen and Graham, 2003).

Similarly, there has been a paucity of innovation in terms of environmentally aimed systems. At the outset of the ITS program, there was considerable interest in considering environmentally enhancing aspects of ITS. A national conference on the subject highlighted a number of ways that information from the transportation system could enhance environmental gain (Hennesey and Horan, 1995). Several demonstrations examined the multi-modal dimensions of ITS (Public Technology Institute, 1999). Indeed, one of the unmet challenges for ITS is ensuring that the benefits ITS yield (in terms of reduced congestion) are not undone by increases in ITS-induced VMT or modal switching.

In the area of economic impacts, while much as been learned about the total costs of ITS deployment, there remain significant uncertainties both in terms of the public return for these investments as well as private sector participation and success in the ITS arena. It has been estimated that the costs for ITS infrastructure in large metropolitan areas is approximately $469 million, resulting in a nationwide cost of approximately $35.2 billion for the nation's largest 75 regions (Cheslow and Staples, 2001). An extensive database maintained by DOT contains these cost estimates as well as other benefit-related findings and data (DOT, 2002). However, little is known about the extent to which the forecasted "80/20" split between private and public investment in ITS is being met, including the level of consumer telematics purchasing needed to realize full benefit of systemwide ITS deployment.

In terms of the public investment, the next step would be to connect these costs to regional benefits from ITS, and preliminary steps have been taken in this manner (Turnbull, 2001). However, these analyses inevitably lead to a decomposition of benefits by various stakeholders. One principle reason for this is the marginal benefit can vary substantially among users. For example, given that the principle benefit of many systems is saving time, the value of the system becomes quite dependent on the value of time held by users—a value that can vary considerably. Thus, the perceived benefits of ITS can vary across a range of demographic, social, and economic circumstances. It is this more relative stakeholder analysis that forms the second major dimension of benefit-cost evaluations.

2.1.2 Stakeholder-oriented Benefits

At the outset of the ITS program there was an understandable pressure to produce system-level quantifiable information on impacts. Yet, as the various operational tests proceeded, it became clear that such benefits vary substantially across users of the system.

This can be seen in the chapters in this volume. For example, the research on consumer choice by Liu, Recker, and Chen (Chapter 13) makes an important point about ITS impacts, a point that was substantially understated at the outset of the ITS program: namely that consumers value travel time reliability as much as they do travel time savings. Such findings confirm both what had been found in traveler information field demonstrations (such as in Washington, DC) as well as demonstrated in experimental settings (Evans, et al., 2002). As alluded to above, related research also suggests substantial variability in the value of time (Mokhtarian, 2003). This variability means, for example, that while certain travelers (e.g., commuters) may highly value travel time savings, others do not (Richardson, 2003). These more precise travel time value estimates are needed in order to customize systems to deliver travel time savings to those customers who will most value this benefit.

The evaluation of Freeway Service Patrols by Levinson, Gillen, and Parthasarathi (Chapter 11) gets at this notion of consumer value by examining willingness to pay for mobility servicc; they found that interest in paying for freeway service patrols varied as a function of a number of consumer factors such as length of commute, length of expected waiting period, and ownership of a cell phone. The implications of these findings are two-fold. First, it is a reminder that the marketplace often serves as the best evaluator for services and products. That is, should the service be valuable (and efficient), there will be a demand for the service and that meeting this demand will create a self-regulating market where consumers can provide their own evaluation of the value of the service in terms of the price they are willing to pay.

The second implication pertains to the differential willingness to pay for ITS services depending on the benefit achieved relative to the situation of stakeholder (e.g., long versus short commute). It is worth mentioning that their chapter focused on mobility (in terms of shortened wait time), while experience in the private markets suggests even higher perceived benefits in terms of safety (though this is implicit in their measure). For example, in a market research study conducted by this author, southern California commuters expressed a much stronger interest in paying for the safety aspects of ITS than for the mobility aspects. (Wells and Horan, 1998). The market behavior of consumers has confirmed these research findings, as deployment of telematics services (e.g., Onstar) has a strong safety element.

But of course, the traveling consumer is not the only stakeholder in the process. Deakin (2003) has found that local transportation managers are an important stakeholder in the ITS deployment process, yet often lack appropriate information about the benefits of ITS relative to the deployment costs involved. The National System Architecture provides a valuable high level gameplan for ITS deployment, but there is a wide consensus that the terminology and methods used to devise a regional ITS architecture do not jibe well with the parallel processes used by transportation planners to determine transportation project priorities. In part, this needs to be corrected with better information that local planners use to assess ITS impacts. However, in part it is also a conceptual issue as in some cases evaluating ITS relative to capital improvements is comparing "apples and oranges". That is, ITS is becoming less of a separate infrastructure system (such as would allow for an "apples to apples" comparison) and more of an underlying information system for the entire surface transportation system. This leads to the overarching challenge of determining the integrated value of ITS-infused systems.

2.1.3 The Challenge of Determining Systemwide Impacts

The ITS field has grappled with the nature and style of evaluations that would best capture the expected impacts of information technologies on the transportation system. Brand (Chapter 3) summarizes the phases by which ITS can qualitatively influence the nature of travel and transportation. Similarly, during the evaluation phase of the National System Architecture, it became apparent that it would be difficult to separate out the impact of an *integrated* ITS effort vis-à-vis a baseline case of *independent* ITS deployments though the synergy of integration was conceptually apparent (USDOT, 1996).

Among candidate systems, the implementation of electronic toll collection (ETC) continues to provide the clearest example of ITS-infused system value. As presented by Burris (Chapter 10), ETC can produce demonstrable benefits relative to costs with benefit-cost ratios approaching 35:1 for high-volume applications. However, in many ways ETC is an exception to the ITS rule. What makes ETC unique is that there is a clear inefficiency in the system (stopping and paying for tolls) that is improved directly as a result of a technology system (ETC) that heretofore did not exist. As Lee (Chapter 4) suggests, the more typical systemwide case is one where the "before" instance already includes considerable electronic or ITS-related systems (e.g., mobile reporting of incidents, ongoing freeway surveillance systems). As a consequence, it is much harder to tease-out the marginal contribution of new or integrated ITS to the system. In this manner, the paradox faced by the transportation industry is similar to the "productivity paradox" that has confronted IT managers in the private sector (see Brynjolfsson and Hitt, 1998 and Lewis, Chapter 2). To quote Nobel Laureate Robert Solow (in 1987) "computers appear everywhere except for in the productivity statistics." A variation of this observation surely applies to the visible impact of ITS in the transportation system, which is still in an early phase of deployment.

3. ASSESSMENT DIRECTIONS

Given the findings reported in this volume and related developments in the ITS field, there are several important areas for further exploration. Sussman (1999) has noted that ITS can be considered a complex large integration system ("CLIOS") and a key ingredient to assessing such a system is to understand the context in which it operates. This section considers three contextual factors: (1) the drive to develop a performance approach to transportation systems, (2) the drive to better connect with customers of the transportation system, and (3) the need to consider ITS within the technology-infused society that we live in. Table 2 provides a summary of these evaluation directions, which are discussed below.

3.1 Performance-based ITS

While the nomenclature of "ITS" (and the funding program under this nomenclature) was probably needed to solidify early support for testing and deploying these technologies, it belies the fact that at its best ITS is an embedded information network in service of the entire surface transportation system—that is, it is not a separate infrastructure element. It provides the information system to support a full range of desired transportation benefits and, idcally, will become indistinguishable from the overall package of effective surface transportation upgrades that over time integrates technology into a range of information, management, and pricing functions.

Perhaps the most important challenge for the ITS field is to undertake this transformation into a justifiable case for investment as part of overall transportation system improvements. At the national level, there has been interest in recasting the ITS program to focus more squarely on its role in bringing IT to improve the management and security of the transportation system (Johnson 2002). The idea has been to use ITS to demonstrably impact transportation system performance through real-time systems management, seamless traveler information systems, and development of performance indicators for use in both planning and operational management.

In terms of new concerns for security, the information systems embedded in surface transportation provide a crucial platform for managing the system during extreme events and provide surveillance and control systems for necessary homeland security activities. This would include the use of wireless emergency management services, biometric-related border crossing services, and cargo tracking and surveillance systems. The next generation of ITS needs to be assessed in terms of how it can perform "critical infrastructure" functions for the surface transportation system. While the benefits of such a system during extreme events may only be available through simulation, benefit-cost analysis can assist in comparing competing approaches. Such analyses can be particularly helpful in identifying the cost implications for the local agencies that will be required to maintain such systems.

A recent NSF study on civil infrastructure has identified the linkages across infrastructures and how IT can enhance performance data for not just transportation, but all civil infrastructures including water, electricity, energy, and telecommunications (see Zimmerman, 2002). The underlying theme of these analyses is that IT has come to play an integral role in monitoring how an infrastructure is performing and providing feedback to infrastructure planners and designers as to areas for infrastructure improvement.

The monitoring of environmental performance has traditionally been given a secondary priority, especially in light of the extensive systems available for monitoring the mobility aspect of transportation systems (TRB, 2002). A bold research initiative may be needed to fully explore the range of environmental performance data available from new technologies and how that might be integrated into transportation plans and programs (Deakin, 2002). The dimensions of this initiative have been documented in a National Academy of Sciences (2002) report calling for the establishment of a Surface Transportation Cooperative Environmental Research Program.

While these topics focus on development of performance-based information systems, an important consideration is their development for use by a broad range of interests. Often performance information systems are devised for professional system managers. While system managers continue to be an important client for these systems, it is equally important to make the information readily available to planners, local agencies, and, significantly, the actual users of the transportation system. In terms of public policy, there is also a need to ensure that a wide range of users benefit from ITS performance improvements, including non-traditional users such as transit dependent riders and elderly travelers.

Table 2. ITS Evaluation and Research Directions

Theme	Specific Research Questions	Impacts
Enhanced Transportation Performance	How can ITS be deployed to assess transportation system performance, including its use of TS data in transportation planning? How can ITS best ensure security on the transportation system? What are the information requirements and needs to assess a full range of environmental performance impacts and opportunities? What are innovative uses of ITS to improve performance in non-traditional transportation users, such as transit dependent rider and elderly travelers	Ensures that ITS is deployed in a manner that monitors and contributes to full range of benefit areas across a full range of users.
Interactive Transportation System	What customer-based information systems are needed to facilitate efficient and intermodal transportation choices? How can ICT be used to enhance inter-agency collaboration in the design, use, and safety of new or existing transportation systems? How can GIS and visual information systems be used to engage wider range of community participation in transportation decision-making?	Ensures that ITS contributes to the use and participation of a wide range of user groups in the transportation system (e.g., commuters, rural and elderly travelers, transit dependent riders).
Broader ICT Context	Under what scenarios does telecommunications access lead to transportation substitution, including work (e.g., video-conferencing) and non-work (e.g., telemedicine) applications? What are the implications of ICT impacts for understanding and forecasting land use changes, including technology influences on spatial location of industry and workforce? What influence is the wireless infrastructure having on traveler and system safety and information usage?	Ensures that ITS leverages related ICT developments to enhance service in a cost-efficient manner.

In terms of methodology, examining these new information system approaches to IT requires a rethinking the traditional benefit-cost approach. That is, these studies can take more of a systems development approach, including requirements analysis, development of prototype systems, simulations, field-testing, user feedback and impacts, and systems refinement and technology transfer. For example, for both security and environmental indicators, there appears to be a full development effort needed, from developing a framework on indicators that can be tracked, to piloting the system, to implementing these measures into an operational as well as planning process. Unfortunately, this will only complicate future benefit-cost assessments for the value that will be contributed will be information to inform transportation system management and decision-making.

3.2 Interactive ITS

The stakeholder vector of ITS evaluation also warrants further attention. In the decade since ITS began, the rise of the Internet has enhanced possibilities for how users can interact with the transportation system. Indeed, broader technological forces that have facilitated the rise of customer-driven services (air reservation systems, customized on-line computer ordering) are raising consumer expectations about the expected level of interaction with e-government type services (Horan and Reany, 2002).

Perhaps the most important step is devising means to directly and effectively communicate *with transportation service users* about service options and conditions. Early ATIS systems can be viewed as preliminary attempts to communicate with travelers. A number of barriers to the widespread use have been noted, including concerns over credibility (and timeliness of information) and continued reliance on free (and less specific) sources such as radio. However, as irregular non-work travel rises compared with routine commutes, there is an opportunity to customize traveler information around distinct and identifiable market segments: (1) information seeking commuters, (2) flexible (in terms of time) travelers and commuters, (3) human service travelers (including transit dependent and elderly), (4) recreational travelers (especially as relates to seamless regional intermodal services), and (5) commercial and just-in-time freight deliveries (Horan, 2002). In this sense planning and performance is recast as delivering quality services to these major user segments and organizing an ITS system to play a critical role in delivery of such services in a socially equitable manner.

Whereas the performance-related recommendations took as their point of departure the robust design of an information system, this direction is firmly grounded in the *communications* element of ITS and the use of interactive systems to facilitate decision-making. The guiding philosophy of this research area should be to "give the information away"; that is, facilitating the developing and use of distributed, user-oriented traveler and transportation information.

Given this orientation, the general methodology has a strong user acceptance and technology transfer orientation. New systems should not only be developed, but also tested on real-world applications, and then a process of diffusion and adoption support should be created and supported. For example, research could be conducted to the extent to which transportation corridor managers are utilizing Internet technology to distribute traffic and travel information to travelers along the transportation corridors (an example of this would be the U.S. 50 corridor reconstruction project outside of Sacramento; see Rees, 2002).

By linking ITS technologies with related Internet communication opportunities, the transportation profession could enhance access and participation in transportation decision-making and service use. Information technologies are slowly contributing to making planning less of a bureaucratically removed enterprise and instead something that is more a technology-enabled interactive experience, where technology plays a vital role in communicating problems and choices.

The advent of geographic information systems and related visual technologies has provided a new means by which land use and transportation planners can engage the public in land use and transportation decision-making (O'Looney, 2002). For example, a particular GIS program, Community-Viz, provides a promising platform for meaningful interaction with the community about land use alternatives (Orton Foundation, 2001). While the transportation community is generally aware of the power of visualization in communicating plans, it has yet to harness the power of the Internet to communicate with significant stakeholders in the design, management, operations, and use process. It is important to note that the potential value of using interactive technology cuts across modal lines—for example, a recent initiative by the Robert Woods Johnson Foundation (2002) is exploring how better use of technology may aid in the understanding and design of pedestrian systems.

In California, efforts have been made to develop GIS software to assist planners in making intermodal and related investment decisions (Caltrans Division of Planning, 2002). For example, Caltrans has developed the California Transportation Investment System (CTIS) and the Intermodal Transportation Management System (ITMS), both of which are based on a GIS platform. The sustainability movement has also developed benchmarks that can be used to measure community-wide indicators, which cut across domains such as transportation, housing, and environment (California Energy Commission, 2001)

A relatively under-utilized aspect of these systems is the provision of data to assist with service planning. Performance and user (satisfaction) data could be actively treated as input into the transportation planning process. There has been limited experimentation asking performance questions and then using that information in an interactive way to plan future systems. There has been limited use of interactive technologies, such as remote control voting technology in outreach meetings and use of Web sites to provide community forums on service and facility improvements. An aggressive effort could be made to assess the best use of these technologies and then work with local planning and community groups to aggressively test and evaluate alternative approaches to bringing interactivity to the local level. This may be especially challenging in low-income communities with less computer access, though local public facilities (e.g., schools, libraries) could become partners in providing online access in neighborhoods.

3.3 Broadened Nature of Information Systems

A common criticism of the ITS program—and one that underlies the recommendations here—is that it has focused too narrowly on near-term operational issues while neglecting broader trends and opportunities. To borrow an expression used by former Transportation Research Board Executive Director Thomas Deen, "we stare at ants while buffalo roar by".

At the very minimum, there is a need to understand the broader influence technology may be having on the business and social networks that are creating the demand on the transportation system. It is clear to even the most casual observer that information and communication technologies (ICT) have profoundly affected our economy, society, and systems, including infrastructure systems. As Manuel Castells (2001) noted in his recent treatise on the subject "The Internet Galaxy is a new communications environment. Because communications is the essence of human activity, all domains of social life are being modified by the pervasive uses of the Internet.... A new social form, the network society, is being constituted around the planet, albeit in a diversity of shapes, and with considerable differences in its consequences for people's lives, depending on history, culture, and institutions. As with previous instances of structural change, this transformation offers as many opportunities as it raises challenges."

Given widespread popular interest in our wired world, it is not surprising that the influence of information and communication technologies (ICT) has been a subject of considerable interest to planners, policy-makers, and academics (see Graham and Marvin, 1999). In the transportation literature, this has often focused on specific traveler behavior impacts, such as telecommuting impacts on trip substitution and traveler information impacts on time and mode of travel (see Mokhtarian, 2000). In the regional planning and economics literature, there has been a burgeoning field of inquiry on the spatial impacts of ICT on business and residential location choice (see, for example, Wheeler, et al., 2000). The environmental literature has looked across ICT uses (e-commerce, travel, etc) to grapple with net gains and net loses on environmental quality (see Levitt, 2002).

If nothing else, these works have erased any naive assumptions about first-order ICT impacts on regional transportation system performance. ICT both encourages certain forms of decentralization and encourages other forms of agglomeration. ICT facilitates both trip substitution of certain kinds and longer home-to-work distances. Indeed, as the above Castells quotation notes, there are invariably both "opportunities" and "challenges" to these new technological systems. Further, the influence of these systems needs to be understood within the context of specific and local social, economic, and cultural transactions. It is these transactions that will drive ICT (and ITS) impact on the transportation system.

For the new evaluation generation, an overriding research need is to determine the potentially positive contributions that ICT—either in the ITS program or more broadly—could make to the achievement of the transportation goals and to craft a set of tests, systems, and market conditions that facilitate desirable and effective forms of technology use relative to these goals. Such an evaluation agenda should not be *a priori* constrained by a set of programmatic systems (e.g. ATMS, ATIS)—it should include yet transcend these technological demarcations. Moreover, as ITS becomes mainstreamed into the transportation practice (from both a funding and functional perspective), it will make less sense to tease out the specific contribution of ITS and, conversely, will be more instructive to consider a range of information and communication technologies that can impact the transportation system.

While there are several research endeavors that have been undertaken to understand the general societal influences of ITS, numerous issues remain. For example, there needs to be closer analysis of the conditions whereby telecommunications access leads to transportation substitution, including work (e.g., video-conferencing) and non-work (e.g., telemedicine) applications. There also needs to be a better understanding of ICT impacts on understanding and forecasting land use changes, including technology influences on spatial location of industry and its workforce. Wireless systems present an emergent competing infrastructure and research is needed to better understand how the wireless infrastructure influences traveler and system safety and information use.

A common thread throughout these possible endeavors is the need to treat ICT as an influence occurring "outside" of the traditional ITS purview. *That is, the questions suggest we examine ICT impacts as they are occurring in the marketplace and seek to understand how these broad impacts are becoming manifest on the transportation system.* In terms of methodology, the underlying approach is to look for naturally occurring developments (typically in a longitudinal fashion) and tease out their transportation influences. For example, the rise of wireless systems can be analyzed over several years to understand how they are impacting transportation safety communications, and then these trends could be examined spatially to determine where significant coverage or EMS gaps exist. While these questions suggest independent studies, it is worth considering them as part of ongoing efforts to learn about ICT developments and impacts and feed that information into the transportation planning and management process.

4. TOWARD AGILE SYSTEMS

The field of transportation is changing from a capital-based facilities approach to a systems-based operational approach. Sussman summarized this change in his article "The New Transportation Faculty" (Sussman, 1999), where he outlined changes occurring throughout the transportation profession. In this and subsequent work, Sussman (2002) underscores the importance of viewing ITS as a part of the general shift toward treating surface transportation in a holistic manner that relies on technology, pricing, and numerous other system elements to create a highly adaptive system.

A new 10-year ITS Program Plan has been developed. In this plan, the importance of the consumer is explicitly recognized. The relevant section states that the ITS program should focus on: "Providing effective, end-to-end, seamless, multi-modal transportation services for people wherever they live, work, and play regardless of age or disability. Opening employment and recreation opportunities and helping make travel time more productive, by flexibly enabling more travel choices for more people (ISTA, 2001)". The challenge is to deliver a system that will indeed produce this easy and seamless experience. The following are two interrelated development threads for achieving this challenge in a manner that enhances the agility of the surface transportation system.

4.1 Personalized Transportation Services

When thinking about the possibilities for a technologically infused transportation system, it is instructive to consider the influence of American's Sabre airline reservations system. Even the prescient Robert Crandall (former chairman and CEO of American Airlines) could not have foreseen the extent to which consumers would take control over their travel choice. The Sabre system was originally designed for the travel agent. But, of course, the Internet changed all that, making the travel agent one of the many functions to be "disintermediated". In the spirit of these times, the Sabre system gave birth to Travelocity, which has since become emblematic of the interactive services possible in transportation. Among those other e-commerce enterprises that continue to shine despite the dot-com implosion, a fundamental principle is the dedication to a consumer focus, alternatively termed mass customization (e.g., Dell), mass personalization (e.g., Amazon), or, more generally, customer relationship management (CRM).

For the surface transportation professionals generally and the ITS program specifically, the corresponding challenge is to devise and execute an information system that can satisfy the individual traveler and affect overall system choice and performance. The lesson from CRM approaches (and the longer history of customer-centric management models) is that information systems can allow for both highly tailored relationships with customers while generating overall system efficiencies through a large number of customers. In this vein, the ATIS, ATMS, and AVI systems need to become an integrated means by which travelers can develop customized traveler plans—plans that can ostensibly benefit from archival and predicative information on system performance. This begs the development of a more flexible transportation management network that can respond to personalized information and choice.

4.2 Adaptive Network Management

It is clear that managing complex systems like the surface transportation system requires a set of principles and knowledge at the interface of several fields: transportation, engineering, economics, planning, social science, and information systems. Yet we are only now beginning to understand how these systems perform. The PeMS system being tested in California (Skabardonis, 1999) is an example of the next generation of archival-predictive model that holds promise for using traffic data combined with management control. It suggests a new level of operations management that needs to be integrated with policy, financing, and engineering approaches to transportation management

As noted above, a new reservation information system has played a key role in evolving a dynamic air travel reservation market. A similar level of information appears to be missing from the surface transportation system. While ITS has increasingly allowed information to be available to consumers, it has not achieved the level of user acceptance and use that air travel systems have. However, there is abundant reason to believe that information about choice enhances system efficiency. In surface transportation, choice has been constrained due to a number of policy, market, and technological circumstances. However, there are an increasing number of modal options being pursued in metropolitan areas—transit, light rail, car sharing, and e-commuting. A role of the ITS system should be to provide the information needed to choose between these modal options, and this should include priced travel options, as well as alternative-time travel options.

At the heart of dynamic transportation systems lies real or near real-time knowledge of how these systems are performing. ITS can help improve system performance by providing the information tools for managers to continuously measure actual performance in real time. But having the information is not enough. The key step would be to use information on system performance to build awareness and use among the traveling public. In this manner the user enters into a dynamic dance with the information system and the infrastructure, making the entire system more responsive and agile.

5. CONCLUSION

During the first decade of ITS testing and evaluation, the dominant paradigm was one of government-supported testing, demonstration, and limited deployment of ITS elements. Most deployments and subsequent findings credit ITS with playing a cost-effective role in achieving near-term transportation improvements. Yet ITS is seldom viewed as a core strategic element to future transportation systems. What is needed is a strategic approach that integrates supply, demand, and the power of information technology to manage the system both tactically and strategically. In the next generation, ITS must move toward a self-evaluating information system where the benefits of information are realized through a dynamic information market. In the future, is it not inconceivable to think that surface transportation information will become as important to travelers as, say, package location information is to couriers like Federal Express. In short, it is appropriate for our age to consider information about the infrastructure as important as the infrastructure itself.

ACKNOWLEDGEMENTS

The observations contained in this report are distilled from a number of research studies undertaken by the author over the last decade. The author gratefully acknowledges the support of several sponsors, including the California PATH program, the Mineta Transportation Institute, the California Department of Transportation, the State and Local Policy Program/University of Minnesota, the ITS Institute/University of Minnesota, Minnesota Department of Transportation, and the U.S. Department of Transportation. Earlier versions of selected findings contained in this chapter are referenced, as appropriate, to supporting reports and publications.

REFERENCES

Amin, M. "National Infrastructures as Complex Interactive Networks," *Automation, Control and Complexity, New Developments and Directions*, T. Samad and J. Weyrauch, eds., New York: J. W. Wiley, 2000.

Brynjolfsson, E., Hitt, L. "Beyond the Productivity Paradox: Computers Are The Catalyst For Bigger Changes," *Communications of the ACM*, Vol. 41, No. 8 (August 1998), 49–55.

Caltrans. California Transportation Plan Symposium and Futures Conference, Sacramento, Los Angeles, 2000, 2001.

Castells, M. *The Internet Galaxy*, London: Oxford University Press, 2001.

Center for Transportation Analysis, Workshop on Implications of the New Digital Economy on Transportation: Developing Research and Data Needs. Sponsored by Oak Ridge National Laboratory, Oak Ridge, TN and Transportation Research Board, Washington, DC. May 8, 2001.

Cheslow, M., Staples, B. "Working Paper: National Costs of the Metropolitan ITS Infrastructure – Update to the FHWA 1995 Report – Revised," Mitretek Report, EDL report #11923, August 2000.

Deakin, E. "Mainstreaming Intelligent Transportation Systems: Findings from a Survey of California Leaders," in *Assessing the Benefits and Costs of Intelligent Transportation Systems*, D. Gillen and D. Levinson eds., Norwell, MA: Kluwer Academic Publishers, 2004.

Deakin, E. "Sustainable Development & Sustainable Transportation: Strategies for Economic Prosperity, Environmental Quality, and Equity," California Futures White Paper, 2001.

Deakin, E. "Transportation Technologies: Implications for Planning," California Futures White Paper, 2001.

Evans, G., Wener, R., Phillips, D. "The Morning Rush Hour: Predictability and Commuter Stress, *Environment and Behavior*, Vol. 34, No. 4, July 2002, 521–530.

Gifford, J. L., Horan, T. A., Sperling, D., eds. *Transportation, Information Technology and Public Policy*, Fairfax, VA: George Mason University, The Institute of Public Policy; Davis, California: University of California, Davis, The Institute of Transportation Studies, 1995.

Golob T. F., Regan, A. C. "Impacts of Highway Congestion on Freight Operations: Perceptions of Trucking Industry Managers," *Transportation Research Part A - Policy and Practice*, 2001.

Giglierano, J., Malu, R. "Effect of Online Shopping on Vehicular Traffic," MTI Report 01-20.

Guiliano, G. "Information Technology, Work Patterns and Intra-metropolitan Location: A Case Study," *Urban Studies*, Vol. 35, 7, 1,077–1,095.

Helling, P., Moktarian, P. "Worker Telecommunication and Mobility in Transition: Consequences for Planning," *Journal of Planning Literature*, forthcoming.

Horan, T. "Toward Consumer-Driven Transportation Systems," *TR News*, No. 218, January–February, 2002, 31–37.

Horan, T., Reany, W. "Network Management Approaches: Cross-Industry Comparisons and Implications for ITS Development," report prepared for California PATH Program, August, 2001.

Horan, T., Serrano, K., McMurran, G. "GIS for Livable Communities: Examination of Community Perceptions of Assets, Liabilities, and Transportation Improvements," report prepared for Mineta Transportation Institute, September 2001.

Intelligent Transportation Systems of America. "Ten Year Program Plan (Draft)," 2001.

ICIS. "Information Technology and Infrastructure Workshop," available at http://www.nyu.edu/icis/itworkshop. Accessed August 2001.

Lappin, J. *A Practical Guide to Consumer Research for ITS Field Tests and Deployment Programs*, Cambridge, MA: Volpe National Transportation Systems Center, September 1996.

Lautenberg, F. Press Release on Intelligent Transportation Systems, Washington, DC, 1991.

Lehtonen, M., Kulmala, R. "The Benefits of Public Transit Signal Priorities and Real Time Passenger Information," paper presented at the Annual Meeting of the Transportation Research Board, 2002.

Levitt, J. ed. *Internet in the Conservation Age*, Washington, DC: Island Press, 2002.

Mobility 2000. *Mobility 2000 Presents Intelligent Vehicles and Highway Systems*, Dallas, Texas: Texas Transportation Institute, July 1990.

Mokhtarian, P. "Telecommunications and Travel," Millennium white paper prepared for the Transportation Research Board, 2000, included in the *Regional Futures Compendium of the Capital Region Institute (Valley Vision),* Sacramento, California.

Mohktarian, P. A. "Synthetic Approach to Estimating the Impacts of Telecommuting on Travel," *Urban Studies,* 35(2), 1998, 215–241.

National Academy of Sciences, "Surface Transportation Environmental Research: A Long-Term Strategy – Special Report 268," Washington, DC, 2002.

O'Looney, *GIS and Transportation*, Redlands: CA: ESRI Press, 2002.

Orton Family Foundation, Community–Viz Overview, 2002.

Public Technology Institute. *Roads Less Traveled: Intelligent Transportation Systems for Sustainable Communities*, 1999.

Rees, L. "California Department of Transportation's Context Sensitive Solutions Policy: Evaluating the Continuous Community Involvement Requirement in District 3," Sacramento County, U.S. Highway 50 Corridor, master's chapter prepared for University of Southern California, November 26, 2002.

Robert Woods Johnson Foundation, Pedestrian Transportation and Health Initiative, 2002.

Skabardonis, A. "Freeway Performance Measurement (PeMS) Project," presentation at TRB Freeway Operations Committee Meeting, 78th TRB Annual Meeting, Washington, DC, 1999.

Transportation Research Board. "Surface Transportation Environmental Research: A Long-Term Strategy, Special Report 268," Washington, DC: Transportation Research Board, 2002.

U.S. Department of Transportation. "Benefit-Cost Database," available at: http://www.benefit cost.its.dot.gov. Accessed December 15, 2002.

Wachs, M. "Mobility for California's Aging Population," CPRC Brief, No. 6, May 2001, California Policy Research Center, University of California Strategic Planning on Aging.

Wells, K., Horan, T. "Acceptance of ATIS Technologies: Findings from Southern California," *Transportation Research Record*, 1999.

Wheeler, P. ed. *Fractal Cities*, London: Routledge, 1999.

Zimmerman, R., Cusker, M. "Bringing IT to Infrastructure," white chapter prepared for ICIS/NSF Workshop on IT and Infrastructure, Arlington Virginia, June 25–27, 2001.

GLOSSARY

AAA – Automobile Association Of America
ACAS – Advanced Collision Avoidance Systems (Acas)
ACM – Automated Coin Machine
AHS – Automated Highway System
AHS – Automated Highway System
AI – Artificial Intelligence
APC – Automatic Passenger Counters
APTS – Advanced Public Transportation System
ARTS – Advanced Rural Transportation Systems (Arts)
ATIS – Advanced Traveler Information Systems
ATMIS – Advanced Traffic Control and Information Systems
ATMS – Advanced Traffic Management Systems
ATSAC – Automatic Traffic Surveillance and Control
AVC – Average Variable Cost
AVCSS – Advanced Vehicle Control and Safety Systems
AVI – Automatic Vehicle Identification
AVL – Automatic Vehicle Location
AVM – Advanced Vehicle Monitoring
AVMC – Advanced Vehicle Monitoring and Communications
BAS – Broad Area Surveys
BCA – Benefit/Cost Analysis
BDS – Bus Dispatch System
CAD – Computer-Aided Dispatching
CADS – Computer-Aided Dispatch And Scheduling
Caltrans – California Department of Transportation
CCTV – Closed Circuit Television
CDPD – Cellular Digital Packet Data
CIC – Critical Intersection Control
CMEM – Comprehensive Modal Emissions Model
CO – Carbon Monoxide
CVO – Commercial Vehicle Operations
DOT – Department of Transportation
ERGS – Electronic Route Guidance System
ETC – Electronic Toll Collection
FETSIM – Fuel Efficient Traffic Signal Management
FHWA – Federal Highway Administration
FSP – Freeway Service Patrol
GIS – Geographic Information Systems
GPS – Global Positioning System
HC – Hydrocarbon

HOT – High Occupancy/Toll
HOV – High Occupancy Vehicle
IDAS – ITS Deployment Analysis System
INFORM – Information for Motorists
IR – Incident Response
ISP – Information Service Providers
ISTEA – Intermodal Surface Transportation Efficiency Act of 1991
IT – Information Technology
ITS – Intelligent Transportation Systems
ITS – Intelligent Transportation Systems
ITSA – Intelligent Transportation Society Of America
JPO – USODT's Joint Program Office
LORAN – Long Range Navigation
LOS – Level of Service
MDT – Mobile Data Terminals
MnDOT – Minnesota Department of Transportation
MOEs – Measures of Effectiveness
MVM – Million Vehicle Miles
NESCAUM – Northeast States for Coordinated Air Use Management
NOx – Oxides of Nitrogen
O3 – Ozone
ODOT – Oregon Department of Transportation
ORT – Open Road Tolling
PAS – Private Assistance Services
PATH – Partners for Advanced Transit and Highways
PM10 – Particulate Matter
RF – Radio Frequency
SOx – Sulfur Oxides
TATS – Traveler Advisory Telephone System
TDM – Traffic Demand Management
TEA-21 – Transportation Equity Act for the 21st Century
TMC– Traffic Management Center
TOC – Traffic Operations Centers
USDOT – United States Department of Transportation
VES – Video Enforcement System
VHT – Vehicle Hours of Travel
VKT – Vehicle Kilometers Traveled
VMS – Variable Message Sign
VMT – Vehicle Miles Traveled
VOC – Volatile Organic Compounds
VPLPH – Vehicles Per Lane Per Hour

Transportation Research, Economics and Policy

1. I. Salomon, P. Bovy and J-P Orfeuil (eds). *A Billion Trips a Day.* Tradition and Transition in European Travel Patterns. 1993 — ISBN 0-7923-2297-5
2. P. Nijkamp and E. Blaas: *Impact Assessment and Evaluation in Transportation Planning*. 1994 — ISBN 0-7923-2648-2
3. B. Johansson and L.–G. Mattson (eds): *Road Pricing:* Theory, Empirical Assessment, and Policy. 1995 — ISBN 0-7923-3134-6
4. Y. Hayashi and J. Roy: *Transport, Land-Use and the Environment.* 1996. — ISBN 0-7923-3728-X
5. T.F. Golob, R. Kitamura and L. Long: *Panels for Transportation Planning*. Methods And Applications. 1997 — ISBN 0-7923-9966-8
6. T.H. Oum and C. Yu: *Winning Airlines:* Productivity and Cost Competitiveness of the World's Major Airlines 1997 — ISBN 0-7923-8010-X
7. I. Savage *The Economics of Railroad Safety.* 1998 — ISBN 0-7923-8219-6
8. I. Pitt and J. R. Norsworthy *Economics of the U.S. Commercial Airline Industry:* Productivity, Technology and Deregulation. 1999 — ISBN 0-7923-8505-5
9. J F. McDonald, E.L. d'Ouville, and L N. Liu *Economics of Urban Highway Congestion and Pricing.* 1999 — ISBN 0-7923-8631-0
10. D. Gillen and D. Levinson (eds.) *Assessing the Benefits and Costs of ITS:* Making the Business Case for ITS Investments *2004* — ISBN 1-4020-7677-0

Kluwer Academic Publishers – Boston/Dordrecht/New York/London